Brother Will

Brother Will

A Biography of

WILLIAM C. MARTIN

James E. Kirby

ABINGDON PRESS / Nashville

BROTHER WILL: A BIOGRAPHY OF WILLIAM C. MARTIN

This book is printed on acid-free paper.

Library of Congress Cataloging-in-Publication Data

Kirby, James E.
    Brother Will: a biography of William C. Martin / James E. Kirby.
      p.   cm.
    Includes bibliographical references.
    ISBN 0-687-09467-4
    1. Martin, William C. (William Clyde), b. 1893. 2. Methodist
Episcopal Church, South—Biography. 3. United Methodist Church
(U.S.)—Biography. I. Title
BX8495.M327 K57   2000
287'.6'092—dc21   99-040481
[B]   CIP

00 01 02 03 04 05 06 07 08 09 — 10 9 8 7 6 5 4 3 2 1

MANUFACTURED IN THE UNITED STATES OF AMERICA

For

Patty,

David,

and Patrick

Contents

⸻

Foreword

◆━━◆

As the sixth person entrusted with the title "Bishop in Residence" at Perkins School of Theology, it is a special honor to write a few lines about the book telling the story of the first person to occupy this office, William Clyde Martin. So many unique distinctions will be discovered in the remarkable life of this unusual person, including his 1938 election as a bishop by the Methodist Episcopal Church, South, in the last General Conference held by that denomination.

This story will reveal a very special relationship with Southern Methodist University that covers not only most of Will Martin's life but the larger portion of the history of this university as well. Until the research for this book revealed the information, the repeated invitation for Will Martin to join the faculty at SMU and the encouragement that he gave to those invitations were unknown. As a student in the first decade of the life of SMU, then as a Dallas pastor, and as a longtime member of the Board of Trustees, William C. Martin played a decisive role in many of the decisions that shaped what Perkins and SMU have become. The lasting legacy of his witness will continue to be found in the archives lodged in Bridwell Library.

In 1980 in Little Rock, Arkansas, I was one of five bishops elected by the South Central Jurisdictional Conference. The high point of that experience for the five new bishops was a day of orientation, following the adjournment of the conference, when Bishop William C. Martin was the primary resource person. He was then in his eighty-seventh year, and all of us recognized that his counsel and encouragement were treasures that were literally beyond description.

Only a couple of years later, when the biography of Bishop G. Bromley Oxnam was published, the College of Bishops of the South Central Jurisdiction proposed that a biography of William C. Martin, covering the same period of history as Oxnam's life, would provide a complementary insight into the dramatic events of the twentieth century.

Bishop Martin's letters and papers, and a daily diary he had kept for sixty-four years were in Bridwell Library at SMU. The time seemed right for this work to begin. The College of Bishops of the South Central Jurisdiction, with the assistance of Earl Carter, executive secretary of the jurisdiction, developed a plan that included limited financial support from each annual conference in the jurisdiction. Working with Neil Alexander from The United Methodist Publishing House, the College of Bishops received a commitment from the Publishing House, and the search for an author began. From many suggestions, attention focused upon Dr. James E. Kirby, at that time serving as dean of Perkins School of Theology. Not only were the records and papers of Bishop Martin easily accessible to Dean Kirby, but he also possessed a wealth of personal information. His father had served in the cabinet with Bishop Martin in the Northwest Texas Annual Conference. Furthermore, Dean Kirby was an accomplished author and a renowned church historian, having spent a lifetime in teaching and research with a special interest in United Methodist history.

The project consumed a major portion of Dean Kirby's attention across a number of years. During this time he spoke to many groups—local churches, historical associations, and the South Central Jurisdiction Conference of 1996—describing his research for this book.

Dean Kirby has included me among those with whom he has shared exciting discoveries of his research, and portions of his writing as it took shape. It was especially exciting for me when the diary confirmed the relationship of William C. Martin with my father. In the early years of their ministry, he and my father rode the train together from Houston to Cameron, Texas, to attend the Texas Annual Conference where they were both ordained elder. In that same year, when I was only two years old, the Martin diary reveals details of a revival meeting Martin held for my father. The memory became a legend in my family.

So many happenings of historical importance were part of the inspiring life of William C. Martin that this book will be a treasure for all who want to understand Methodism in America in the twentieth century. The United Methodist Church will continue to be indebted to Dean Kirby, to Bridwell Library, to The United Methodist Publishing House, and to all who made any contribution toward bringing this book to completion. Most of all, we are eternally indebted to God for setting apart such a clear and strong witness to the gospel in the midst of the challenging changes of the twentieth century.

John Wesley Hardt
Bishop in Residence
Perkins School of Theology
Southern Methodist University

Introduction

————⊲◁◁⦚♪⦚▷▷⊳————

What is it that makes a man worth remembering? The inscription on the plain red granite marker standing under the trees on the low rise in the cemetery in Little Rock reads, "William C. Martin, a Bishop in the Methodist Church." There have been many bishops in the Methodist Church, a fair number of whom I have known personally and a few of them I have known well. In scholarly work I have studied and written about even more of them. What I like about Martin's memorial is the eloquence of what it does not say about the man.

I certainly never expected to be writing about him. My father was one of his district superintendents in the Northwest Texas Conference and I often heard the stories of "Bishop Martin"—none of those folks would have presumed to call him "Will"—and his work with them in the cabinet. He was strong, fair, and predictable, and he demonstrated that he cared, as a pastor might care, for the people who served with him. He remembered our birthdays and graduations with a letter and sent me a wedding present. He knew how to make appointments, too, although he didn't always get them right. When he stayed in our home, my mother knew he wanted his fried eggs to be hard, a piece of information learned from seeing them come back into the kitchen until they reached the proper firmness. And she knew that when "Miss Sally" came to be with him at the conference, after she received her orchid down front and acknowledged the ovation of the delegates, she would line the cabinet spouses up with her on the back row of the church, and after the Ministers' Wives Luncheon she would be gone.

If you heard him once, you would remember how he sounded as he called at the opening of the conference session, "Now my brethren, let us be in order." His voice was deep and resonant. When he preached, he enveloped the pulpit, covering its sides with his massive hands. There was no escaping the fact that he was a "big" man—a presence. His piercing black eyes seemed to see everything in the room at once, but there was nothing unkind about them. He was always business, even to the point of wearing his usual black suit when walking on a beach.

As if it were this morning, I remember the way his hands felt as they covered my head—all of it—when he transferred to me authority first as a deacon and then an elder to "preach the Word and administer the Sacraments in the Church of God." A friend of mine, who was also ordained under those hands, asked me recently if I remembered what it was like. Who could forget? He held us with gentle strength and the sound of his voice repeating from memory the ancient formula of the rite of ordination leaves no doubt in my mind almost half a century later that if power and authority could be given through the laying on of hands, it had been done to us by Bishop Martin. He made us report the number of pastoral calls we made, too, and I was never very comfortable with that. I would have been even more uncomfortable had I known at the time how many he made in the years he was a pastor.

When the College of Bishops of the South Central Jurisdiction proposed this biography and asked me to write about him, I had no real idea of the depth of the man or how fascinated with him I would become as I learned more of his story. Much of that account is contained between the covers of diaries that he faithfully kept from 1914 until near the close of his long life. I can affirm it to be a unique and somewhat daunting experience to read through a man's life one day at a time and to realize what he chose to remember and decided to forget. There is a certain impersonal quality to the diaries, just as there was to Will Martin, and there are also glimpses into the very depths of his being.

In addition to the diaries, the Martin papers fill almost thirty-five boxes in the archives of the Bridwell Library and contain literally thousands of letters that he wrote and that were written to him. Many of his replies are typed on the letters that he received. He had his secretary slip them in as carbons, so that question and answer were often contained on the front and back of the same page. The archives contain items that are related to the church and Martin's work in it. There are no letters to or from Sally in those boxes, and none from his father or Sally's mother. His daughter, Catherine Makoul, believes he destroyed them all after they moved to Little Rock in retirement. It is a great loss, for his relation to Sally is one of the most interesting aspects of his life.

But even with the gaps, the story is clear enough to follow the growth and maturation of William Clyde Martin from his birth in Randolph, a small town just north of Memphis, until his death. He suffered the loss of his mother when he was only eighteen months old and his childhood years were spent in the care of her father, J. W. Ballard. Until he joined the army, he was called "Clyde," and the Ballards still refer to him that way. The two persons, whom Martin described as the most influential persons in his early life, his father, Jack Martin, and his grandfather, were hardly the types one would choose to bring up a motherless child. As a matter of fact, Jack Martin had little to do with the first four years of his son's life. Martin later said that his maternal grandfather was both "father and mother" to him. Strangely, he doesn't mention his grandmother.

J. W. Ballard, who sometimes had problems with liquor, was a hard man with plenty of faults, yet Martin loved him dearly. At one time he was said to have been active in the church, but fell away and had no use for it when Martin was a boy. Clyde worried about the safety of his immortal soul for a good portion of his early life. The Tennessee Ballards were hardworking, poor, farming folks who would have been glad for Clyde to join them for the rest of his life on the land he had inherited from his mother. They certainly held no great ambitions for him beyond that. His father, living in the company of men in the lumber camps of Arkansas and east Texas, had numerous encounters with the law, "offending the peace and dignity of the State of Arkansas," and when Clyde was a teenager Jack was involved in a complex series of events surrounding a murder. He was tried and convicted of manslaughter, but he eventually was pardoned by the governor and never went to jail.

From the time Martin began first grade until he graduated from high school, he lived with relatives or boarded with strangers, but he was seldom in the same place more than a year. Despite this lack of stability, his good mind absorbed a better education than anyone might have predicted. Even the earliest years of his diary are written in clear, precise English prose, and the words are spelled correctly. He had facility with languages, majored in Latin and Greek in college, and became fluent enough in French to serve as an interpreter for his military unit in France. Years later he was still able to converse with his great granddaughter in the language.

His early life was spent almost entirely without the influence of women, and to an outside observer he seems never to have learned to understand them. He just never got the hang of it. The ones he saw in the lumber camps were hardly role models for young boys, and he, on his own, rejected them. When Martin was eight years old his father married a widow who had two children about Martin's age. Martin lived with them off and on, and years later, in 1918, he married Sallie Beene (she later changed the spelling to Sally), his stepsister. Among all the women he ever knew, he certainly never knew what to make of the strong-willed, emotional, and outspoken Sally, though he loved her dearly.

Martin was bright and curious, and he loved to read. From the years spent with his Ballard kin along the banks of the Mississippi, he learned to appreciate the out-of-doors. As a boy he spent days hunting and fishing. He was one of those rare individuals who was fearless. He never saw a cave he didn't want to explore or a mountain he didn't want to climb. While waiting for trains or when restless he walked the streets of major cities at all hours of the day and night. When he entered the army in World War I, his family feared most that he might expose himself to needless danger as, in fact, he did on one occasion.

When he was a teenager he decided it was time for him to be religious. It was not some blinding revelation but a conscious decision taken by an intentional young man. Accordingly, he presented himself at the altar of the Methodist summer revival and joined the church. He was, however, troubled that he felt neither the joy nor assurance of his salvation, which he had expected.

After graduating from Prescott High School, where he played on its first football team, he entered the University of Arkansas in Fayetteville. He went to study law, perhaps even to set his father's record straight, but that was soon changed. He decided he was called to preach and began preparing to enter the ministry of the Methodist Episcopal Church, South. Once set on that course, he never wavered from it nor questioned the validity of his call. The first step was to transfer to Hendrix College in Conway, Arkansas, a Methodist institution.

Martin graduated in December 1917, and was called immediately into military service where he served with the 13th Evacuation Hospital of the Army Medical Corps. After the armistice he took advantage of a Y.M.C.A.-sponsored program that allowed AEF personnel who were college graduates to attend universities in Europe. Martin was accepted in the Free Church College of the University of Aberdeen in Scotland. It was a life-changing experience. When he got home, he completed his theological education in the new School of Theology at Southern Methodist University in Dallas and began his long association with Methodists in the State of Texas.

Circumstances seemed to smile on Will Martin—he was often in the right time at the right place. A vacancy in a large congregation in Houston just at the time he graduated, coupled with an episcopal decision to ask SMU's theology dean to suggest a student to serve as an interim pastor until the annual conference met, sent him to Grace Methodist Church, the third largest congregation in the city affiliated with the Methodist Episcopal Church, South. He did so well in six months the church was ready to keep him, and despite the fact that he and the congregation were told by the bishop he could not stay, "it happened" that at the last minute he was sent back and remained four more years. Martin was a conscientious and hardworking pastor who improved himself, and took advantage of the abundance of his energy to do the work of more than one man. Because he did well he was rewarded with more responsibility, and about the time most of his contemporaries were ready for a middle-sized appointment in a county-seat town, he was the governor's pastor at First Methodist in Little Rock.

From there he moved on to Dallas, to one of the great pulpits in the Methodist Episcopal Church, South. He served seven years, a feat almost unheard of in those days. Through all those years he remained steadfast, if not straitlaced on traditional issues—he was opposed to smoking, drinking, dancing, and card playing. He would not allow his children to attend the movies on Sunday, nor could they drink root beer until the chairman of his Board of Stewards in Little Rock provided him with a little education on the subject. He thought divorced persons should not remarry and would not officiate at such unions. He was an "old time," devout Methodist in every sense of the word. But he kept open and he grew through the years, too. Like a lot of people, in and out of the church, he was troubled at times about the meaning of the miracles in the New Testament, and he sometimes suffered his own dark night of the soul.

From Dallas, he was thrust into the episcopacy to spend the remaining twenty-six years of his ministry in four episcopal areas. He soon found a place in the wider arena of the ecumenical movement, perhaps the most significant religious movement of the twentieth century, and gained national and international prominence. Before his service was complete, he served as second president of the National Council of Churches, represented the Council of Bishops of the Methodist Church at the organization of the World Council of Churches in 1948, and became a member of its Central Committee. He received almost every honor the Methodists could bestow on him and led some of its most significant programs. The Tennessee farm boy was the guest of John D. Rockefeller, Jr., at a dinner honoring the Japanese crown prince. He visited American troops serving in Korea and called at the White House on more than one occasion. Somehow through it all, he never lost a child-like trust and outlook on life. He was known even to ask a waitress "Is the food good here?" when he entered a restaurant.

Like any man in authority, he did not always manage to make everyone happy, and there were some who opposed him. He fought many battles during the Cold War with persons who saw the National Council of Churches as a Communist front organization and wanted to get the Methodists out of it. He defended a young preacher who was criticized for preaching a dramatic sermon the Sunday following the Kennedy assassination. And he sat on a committee that decided to let black students live in a dormitory on the SMU campus years before the Supreme Court of the United States struck down the "separate but equal" practices of the schools. He led the clergy in his own city in affirming the need and the moral efficacy of peaceful integration. And he continued to care for people, too. His papers contain literally hundreds of telegrams and letters to persons who worked with and served under him remembering special occasions or the "home going of a loved one." He had a way with words and compassion, too.

His life with Sally is a story all its own, filled with infinite complexity and variety. Small in size, but with a strong will and a temper to match her red hair, Sally Martin could and did speak her mind. She struggled throughout their marriage to establish a place for herself in a life almost entirely dedicated to work. William C. Martin was married to the church. Moreover, he lived out of his head, and she out of her emotions. He, like his father, was almost never tired, while Sally's energy was always low and she was frequently sick and exhausted. He was rational to a fault and so dedicated to discipline and acceptance of duty as the "sublimest" way of life that he sometimes found it hard to open the place in his life for Sally that she needed and demanded. One of the most memorable and revealing entries in his diaries reads, "Dave Lacy took me to the station and S to the hospital." There is no doubt that Sally sometimes used her poor health to protect herself from things she did not want to do, and she used it on occasion to try to manipulate her husband, too.

A lovely woman with exquisite taste, Sally was both exasperating and fun, and she sometimes believed it her duty to put Martin in his place as well as to support him in his career. For a significant portion of her life as the bishop's wife he was gone and she was alone. She was as competitive as he and loved nothing better than to beat him at table games; he kept a record of the number of fish they each caught if they were together. He loved her with all his heart, but it sometimes was not enough. And there were the three children, too. Daughter Mary Catherine once told me that the only thing that kept her father from being pompous was that he had "a neurotic wife and three god-awful children." They kept him honest, but there is no doubt he sometimes had trouble understanding a strong-willed wife and middle-child daughter.

Will Martin was happiest when he was in the church. His life was his work, and even when on vacation, he found it hard to relax and let it go. He loved Colorado and its mountains and found them renewing, but even when there he spent mornings buried in a library. He was an avid reader of everything but fiction. Most of that reading, however, like his life, was focused on the church and doing its work more effectively. When he became too interested in something that was outside of it, like the years he read about Abraham Lincoln and studied astronomy, he gave it up. It was not the best use of his time, he said.

In his personal life, he was always aware that, like his father, he had a volatile temper and was constantly on guard lest it get the better of him. He fought a constant battle to control his weight, too. He sometimes lost, but he never abandoned the field even in defeat. Self-discipline was the hallmark of his life. There is so much to admire about him, but I doubt that he ever really can be known. Few people during his lifetime knew him well. Lynn Landrum, the "fly in the ointment" journalist who made Martin's life miserable in Dallas was one of them; Paul Quillian, who died too young, was another. Martin shared much of himself in his long and intimate correspondence with Albea Godbold and a unique picture of him is available there. The group of laypersons who organized and enjoyed the Supper Club for thirty years knew him, too.

I am grateful to many people who took time to talk to me about Bishop Martin, and I am especially grateful to the members of his family who were willing to trust me with intimate recollections of him and Sally, and gave me hours of their time to talk and read what I have written. Walter Vernon, who at one time wanted to write this biography, recorded several hours of interviews with Sally and Will Martin in which they tell their own story. They are stored in the archives. More people in Dallas than I can easily name here shared their stories with me in formal and informal settings.

The Perkins School of Theology has assisted me with grants of time and money to conduct this study. I am grateful for that, and I am especially indebted to the Bridwell Library, which has been a home away from home for me. The staff has been unfailing in their willingness to help and have allowed me privileges in the use of their materials, which have made my study easier. Page Thomas, the Methodist librarian, who surely must cringe to hear the sound of my voice, has, nevertheless, with grace and patience generously looked for one more item in the cave of the archives or tried to answer my last question. Bishop John Wesley Hardt, whose father was a contemporary of Martin's, has encouraged me to keep at the work and read carefully what I have written as has Bishop Monk Bryan, Martin's student assistant at First Methodist in Dallas. The College of Bishops of the South Central Jurisdiction authorized the project and has supported it. I thank them, too.

1

Clyde

—⟨⟩—

The car carrying the newly appointed pastor of the First Methodist Church, South, in Little Rock, the Rev. Dr. William C. Martin, and his entire family was headed north to Memphis. Because their destination was unusual, it was an exciting summer excursion. They were going as a family for the first time to meet the members of their grandmother Martin's family, the Ballards of Randolph, Tennessee, with whom William C. had lived after his mother's death. It was the only time they ever made the trip together. Wife, Sally, oldest son, Donald, daughter, Mary Katherine, and John Lee, the youngest, were excited by the prospect. Sally did not know her husband's relatives well, since Donald or John and William C. would usually visit them without her, and even their trips were infrequent.

When they reached Memphis, before driving the last thirty miles to their final destination, they stopped to eat lunch and made a purchase at the farmer's market. For the balance of the trip they shared the car with a full stalk of bananas. It was a treat for Ballard kinfolk who did not have the means to enjoy such luxuries, and William C. Martin's way of expressing his love for the people who had provided the only stable and consistent influence in his early childhood. His mother's brother, Uncle Perry Ballard, killed a pig and got up at two o'clock in the morning to begin cooking the barbecue; fifty-five relatives turned out to welcome the Arkansas Martins at dinner. When they were safely home again, Martin mused in his diary, "Strange that I should have come out of the past into the present in so short a time."

To the Tennessee Ballards, then and now, and everyone else who knew him before he was drafted into the army during World War I, he was "Clyde" Martin. It was the federal government of the United States following its "standard operating procedure" of using first name, middle initial that changed him to William C. Years later Sally said he never liked Clyde anyway, and she was probably right since he never used it after returning from France. The power of the government notwithstanding, friends from high school and college days and kinfolk spoke of him as Clyde throughout his life. A sure way to identify early acquaintances or members of his mother's family in his correspondence is to see the salutation, "Dear Clyde."

The Ballards lived in and around Randolph, about thirty miles north of Memphis, when William Clyde was born to John Harmon Martin and Leila Catherine Ballard Martin. Sally said she never heard Martin's father called anything but "Jack," but she knew him after he came to Arkansas and in middle Tennessee he was called by his proper name of John. Although his wife's name is spelled "Leila" on her tombstone in the Randolph cemetery, Jack Martin, whose spelling left a great deal to be desired, wrote to her as "Lelia." Randolph, of which nothing today remains except for the cemetery, a Methodist church, and a group of houses in an area known to the locals informally as "Ballardtown," was the first town established in Tipton County, Tennessee. Leila was born there and so was her father, James William Ballard. "J. W.," as he was known to everyone, and as is inscribed on his tombstone, was born August 28, 1846. Until recently family members assumed his given names to be James Wesley since he had a son by that name, but it was, in fact, not J. W. but his father who was James Wesley Ballard. He, too, was known as "J. W.," and legend says he was buried standing up. Clyde saved a photograph of his grandfather and wrote his name on the bottom, "James William Ballard."

Tipton County had been settled in 1821 by General Jacob Tipton, Orville Shelby, Jesse Benton, an old, dedicated enemy of Andrew Jackson, and a few others. General Tipton named it for his father. The legacy of the founders is seen in names of towns and places like Benton's Trace, Tipton, and Shelby County. Randolph, Mason, and Covington were the three principal towns in Tipton County; Covington remains the county seat despite one abortive effort to move it to Randolph. Randolph, named for Virginian John Randolph, in its early years was a thriving Mississippi River town. Situated under one of the Chickasaw Bluffs on a small inland stream below the mouth of the Big Hatchie, it benefited and prospered from the river traffic. Goods were received and forwarded from Randolph to the towns of Tipton, Haywood, Fayette, Madison, and Hardeman. In time it became the shipping point for all the western counties except Shelby and Fayette, and carried on a lucrative trade with many of the newly established counties in the east. Early in its history it vied successfully with Memphis for economic power in the region. Phelan's *History of Tennessee* reports that 40,000 bales of cotton were shipped from Randolph in 1836. A plan, promoted by Governor Cannon, to build a canal to connect the Tennessee River with the Hatchie River, which was navigable as far up as Bolivar, could have routed the whole trade and traffic from north Alabama and the Tennessee Valley through Randolph and relegated Memphis to the future of an insignificant river town. But the dream never became more than that, and when the railroad came to Memphis Randolph's economic future was determined. Merchants doing business under the bluff at Randolph moved to seek new opportunities in Memphis. By the end of the century, when Clyde was born, what was left of Randolph had given up all its lofty aspirations and settled into life as a sleepy and none too prosperous village on the bluffs above the Mississippi.

Its early history was marked by a series of disasters. During the Civil War a group of marauders made headquarters in some of the caves below Randolph, and on one occasion they fired on a Union gunboat as it was going downriver. When the boat reached Memphis, the captain went directly to the district military commander, a general named William T. Sherman, and complained. Sherman decided to teach the citizens of Randolph a lesson about keeping better company and sent a detachment of his troops from Memphis north with orders to burn everything in the town except for one building, which was to serve as a stark reminder of the cost of rebellion. That experience was minor in its consequences compared with the activity of Mother Nature when the Mississippi changed its course, leaving the town high and dry.

The seven living sons and daughters of James William Ballard were a family of poor, hardworking, farming folk who lived up from Ballard's Slough on the high ground around Randolph. The slough connects the Big Hatchie with the Mississippi; Mike Ballard, a distant cousin of Clyde's and the family historian, can take you to the place on that body of water where he launches his boat for some good fishing. It is also a place of tragic memory, for J. W.'s oldest child, James Wesley, drowned there when he was eleven. He was in a boat with his sisters when he became entangled in the trees and was knocked into the water. J. W. Ballard owned land near the river, a parcel of which was given to his daughter Leila "in recognition of her love and affection" just after the first of the year, 1894. Always called the "bottom field" because of its location next to the Mississippi, it was willed to Clyde at Leila's death, and he and his family, in turn, owned that 150 acres for the better part of nine decades. The Ballards and the Martins valued land, and they would have been happy for Clyde to have settled in the area around Randolph to farm as his kin had done before him.

Clyde's father, Jack, hailed from Dover in Stewart County, Tennessee. Clyde's paternal grandfather, James Marion Martin, was next to the oldest of nine children born to John and Matilda Martin. Grandfather Martin was born in Stewart County November 27, 1831, married Mary Elizabeth Fowler (b. Jan. 18, 1838) on February 24, 1859, and settled on land he already owned around Leatherwood Creek. County abstracts show that James Marion Martin bought thirty-nine acres from William E. Stavely in 1865, and we know he continued to acquire more land through the years since in 1871 he sold one hundred acres located, as the deed

records, next to his two-hundred-acre tract. That land was ultimately sold by his heirs, one of whom was Jack Martin, in 1896.
Other members of the Martin clan lived on Standing Rock Creek,
located in the vicinity but still a fair distance from Leatherwood
Creek by horse and buggy.

James Marion Martin is reported in family lore to have
returned from his Civil War service an invalid, but the historical
record confirms that story to be fiction rather than fact. He did,
indeed, serve in the Civil War. Along with his brothers Andrew
and William Francis, J. M. Martin enlisted for the duration of one
year in the Army of the Confederate States at Fort Donelson, Tennessee, on November 28, 1861. Just over two months later, on
February 16, 1862, all three brothers were taken prisoner when
the Union army captured Fort Donelson. From there they were
transported to Fort Douglas, Illinois, and imprisoned. James Marion was exchanged in Vicksburg, Mississippi, in early September
1862, and re-enlisted for the duration of the war in Jackson, Mississippi, eighteen days later. Once again he saw only brief service
since during the retreat from Tippah Ford, Mississippi, on
December 4, 1862, James Marion Martin deserted. It is possible,
of course, that it was more than a simple case of desertion since
the brothers had by then served their original enlistment period of
a year. They may have decided, as hosts of others did, that they
had done their duty and were needed more at home to take care
of their families than in the service of their country. He was never
prosecuted. There is no record, however, of his being injured or
disabled while in the army.

He and his wife, Mary Elizabeth Fowler Martin, also had nine
children, four boys and five girls. The couple died less than two
months apart in 1892, the year before Clyde was born so he never
knew them. John Harmon, their oldest son, was born January 14,
1860, in Dover and grew up there. He had little formal education—at best no more than a few years of elementary schooling.
The few remaining letters that he wrote make this abundantly
clear. Family lore, again related to the tale of James Marion Martin's alleged disability, says that John had to begin work at age fifteen in order to support the family. Such stories are not

uncommon. His earliest work was in the iron mines near his home, but by the time he and Leila Catherine Ballard married in 1891, he was working in the lumber camps of Arkansas and east Texas.

Leila Catherine Ballard, Clyde's mother, was the third child and second daughter of James William Ballard and Susan Johnson Ballard. One of nine children, she was born in Randolph, Tennessee, September 28, 1872, and received a minimal education in the schools there. The gift of the bottom field from her father would seem to indicate that she was a favorite child. J. W., as everyone who knew him could attest, was a man of strong opinions. Two of Leila's sisters, Mary Alice and Lavina, "Vinie," were disinherited because they married against their father's will. On the surface, at least, it seems that J. W. approved of John and Leila's union.

John Martin's motivation for entering the timber business in east Texas and the circumstances of his meeting and courting Leila Ballard are unknown, but just prior to their marriage part of it was done by correspondence, some of which survives. On November 23, 1890, he wrote with deep feeling, unsteady spelling, and no punctuation:

> dear miss I will answer your kind letter I was truly glad to hear from you and hear that you was well you said that you would like to see me and that you could see more pleasure with me in one day that you could with any body else in forty years if that is so you shall see lots of pleasure soon fore if we both live we will spend a few days together soon if it is your good will you said not to expect to find you ritch that is not what makes me remember you so well it is your good kind heart I am as pore as any body and not good looking by any meanes but that aint going to keep me from coming just the same I have thought a thousand times to day how well I would like to be there to spend this day with you

And then in gallant, literary fashion he concluded with lines of verse, copied from some unknown source: "may happiness ever be thy lot where ever thou shalt be and joy and pleasure light the spot that may be home to thee."

The proposed visit obviously went well and this affair of the heart progressed rapidly. Jack, as he was now called, wrote Leila again on January 6, 1891, from Grant in east Texas.

> dear love and friend we have got back to Texas all safe . . . Lelia I have studied lots about you since I left there Lelia I thought when I left there I would ask you to wait on me until the first of July but if the time will suit you I will come after you the first of March Let me know in your first letter if the time suits you fore my life will not be happy to me any more until I am with you so I will close fore this time please don't let any one see this letter.

Less than two weeks later he had the answer he wanted and wrote on January 19 to say: "I received your kind letter to day it was great pleasure to me to read it and know that you was so willing to come with me. I am sorry that I did not bring you with me while I was there."

He promised to come for her by the end of the month unless something happened "that I don't know anything about." He was concerned, however, about what J. W. and Susan Ballard might say.

> But what about your Pa and Ma will you ask them if it is agreeble fore us to mary or do you want me to write to them I would like fore it to be satisfactiory with all.

We don't know what Leila might have said to her parents, but in two weeks the marriage was arranged.

"Miss Lelia C Ballard with pleasure I will answer your kind letter that I received yesterday," Jack Martin wrote on February 1, 1891:

> I was truly glad to hear from you I hope that all you wrote was true you said I was all the one you ever loved I can say the same about you and tell the truth that being the case I think that we can live a hapy life Lelia you said that you would look fore me the 25th of February if it is agreeable with the old folkes you can look fore me the 24 which will be on Tuesday and we will mary on the 25.

And that is what they did. Leila had just turned eighteen in September, Jack was thirty-one. He was to follow the lumber business for the rest of his life, and after the wedding, Jack took his bride to live in the Lindsey Springs lumber camp near Lufkin in east Texas. Perhaps because she became pregnant or because life was too difficult for her there, she soon returned to Randolph.

Although Jack Martin had very little formal schooling he was always good at math. He could work problems in his head with speed and accuracy that would baffle most folks, and he had the reputation among co-workers of being able correctly to estimate the yield of a stand of timber within a few board feet. He was sharp-eyed and an expert marksman. Physically he was a big, lanky, strong man with coal black hair and piercing black eyes, rawboned and taller than his son, Clyde, who when a man was just over six feet tall and near two hundred pounds. In addition to his quick, good mind, Jack was a man of boundless energy and immense physical strength. If he was ever tired, he rarely admitted it, and he thought people who got that way were lazy. His ability to work circles around any other man and his vast store of energy were both traits Clyde inherited. He was accustomed to the hard life of a lumber camp and had more than his share of encounters with the law.

William Clyde, born July 28, 1893, the first of two children born to Jack and Leila Martin, was also the first grandson of J. W. Ballard. Why they named him Clyde is a mystery, but it is fairly certain he was named William for his grandfather. On the Martin side, Jack Martin had a brother whose name was also William and with whom Clyde and his father lived for a time while Jack was in the lumber business in Arkansas. Leila and Jack's second child, Richard Kirkland Martin, was born eighteen months after Clyde, but he lived only a few weeks. Leila survived his birth, but just over a month later she died of an infection, "blood poisoning" they called it, on February 19, 1895. She and her infant son are buried together in the old cemetery in Randolph. Although Clyde was only eighteen months old at the time of his mother's death and scarcely knew her, she had a lasting influence on his life. In addition to willing him the bottom field, which he owned for the better part of a century, just before she died, she asked Jack to promise he would see that her son had a college education. The story told in the family recounts that when Clyde was just beginning to crawl his mother placed three items on the floor in front of him, food, a toy, and a book, and waited to see which he would select. Without hesitation Clyde crawled to the book. Although Jack was hesitant to promise to see him through college, since he had no way of knowing he could keep such a vow, he agreed with Leila to do his best to help him, and did, in fact, see Clyde graduate from Hendrix College and the theology school of Southern Methodist University; and it was Jack who lent him money to attend seminary.

Clyde never knew either of his paternal grandparents for both James Marion and Mary Elizabeth Fowler Martin died a year before he was born. They are buried in the Leatherwood Cemetery behind the Leatherwood-Asbury United Methodist Church in Stewart County, Tennessee. Grandpa J. W. Ballard and his children were all the family that he knew in his early years. He lived with them in Randolph until he was four, and he quickly became the apple of Grandpa Ballard's eye. Clyde's early life was spent almost entirely in the company of men, first with the Ballards and later when living in the lumber camps with his father. That experience exposed him to such brutality and debauchery that he reacted by turning entirely away from that style of life. In a sense, Clyde was largely on his own during early childhood, and the lack of stability which has destroyed other persons in similar circumstances only seems to have made him stronger and more self-reliant. He grew into a fearless adult. There were no significant female figures during the formative years of his childhood. He had no memory of his mother, Susan Johnson Ballard; his maternal grandmother died in 1895, and he had no memory of her either. J. W.'s second wife, Francis Ellena Berlin, is almost never mentioned, even though she lived until 1925 and Clyde was sometimes in touch with her. The women he saw in the lumber camps tended to be inappropriate role models for a small boy. These experiences left their mark, and both his wife and daughter sometimes expressed their frustration at his seeming inability to be sensitive to their needs.

"Grandpa was both father and mother to me," Clyde wrote in his journal. "He took me when I was only a few months old and cared for me day and night. I loved him with my whole heart. No child ever loved more intensely. He had many faults and grievous ones. Yet he had a great loving heart."

J. W. Ballard certainly had his faults. He was not a religious man, even though at one time he was said to have been converted and was a loyal member of the church; his first wife was a "shouting" Methodist. But J. W. had "backslid," and Clyde thought "it seemed beyond human or even divine power to renew his faith," even though he tried. Ballard had problems with drink, and Martin once remarked to his daughter that if the Ballards as a group had spent as much money on books through the years as they had on whiskey, they would have been living in a different world. Moreover, Clyde described his grandfather as having "an unforgiving spirit," a person who never was able to forget or forgive any injury, no matter how slight. He said, "It was this sin more than anything else that caused his spiritual ruin." J. W. disowned two of his daughters because they married men of whom he did not approve. When Grandpa died in May 1915, Clyde had surrendered to the call to preach, was consumed by ambivalent feelings, and reflected them in his diary. "My love and sympathy for him were not as great as they had at one time been. I had to a certain degree separated us." He continued, "It will always be one of the regrets of my life that I was not able to do more for him." And in a way already revealing the approach he would take to his life's work in ministry he prayed, "God grant that I may, in a manner, atone for my weakness here by doing double service in the days that are to come."

Despite his sense of failure and frustration in the attempt to reform and convert his grandfather, when in old age William C. Martin wrote in a small notebook the names of the most influential people in his life, James William Ballard and John Harmon Martin headed the list. The one thing they had in common is that both men had been the object of his pastoral concern for the salvation of their souls until the very day they died. With a sense of very personal failure, Martin felt guilty for not having done enough to influence either of them to follow a Christian life, and he was always anxious about their fate in the hereafter.

It is hard to imagine a more disrupted and unsettled childhood than Clyde Martin's, even though as an adult he remembered with appreciation the Ballards as "big-hearted, loving people . . . with many hardships connected with their lives." With the exception of the four years he lived with them, before he entered high school he rarely lived in any one place longer than a few years. He was not infrequently boarded with persons who were not even family. When viewed from a distance and with any objectivity, it is little short of amazing that he emerged from childhood with a strong sense of self-worth, a well-formed identity, a good education, and on a career path from which he never wavered. That he did is testimony to his disciplined determination and a single-minded commitment to achieve the goals he set for himself. The man, as is often the case, was formed in the child.

After Leila died, Grandpa and his new wife, whom Clyde's daughter says she never heard him mention, with his young uncles Perry, Dick, and Ed, were his primary family. Uncle Perry, close to Martin's own age, was always his favorite—more like a brother and good friend than an uncle. The Ballard men took care of him, loved him, and even taught him to read before he was four. In October 1897, he left Randolph for the first time to live with his father at Uncle Will Martin's place near Friendship, Arkansas. Jack had taken a job with the Ozan Lumber Company, which had a camp near there. Clyde's stay, however, turned out to be little more than a brief visit and he was soon back in west Tennessee with the Ballards—"Grandpa met me in Memphis," he remembered.

The next year he lived in Friendship with Uncle Will's family and then boarded with the John Gorham family, John Gorham and his brother, Jack. When the Gorham family house burned, an event Clyde remembered well, he returned to Uncle Will's and alternated living with the two families until the fall of 1899 when he was six and began school in Pleasant Grove, Arkansas. He remembered Mr. Hendrix was his teacher there. Later that year he moved to the Southern Pines Lumber Co. camp at Lindsey Springs with Papa, where they lived with the Williams family. The census of 1900 may reflect their "official" residence for it lists Clyde and his father living once again with Uncle Will and Aunt Anna Martin in Red Land Township, Hempstead County, Arkansas. The next year (1901), however, we know they were living in a boarding house in the lumber camp, and that Jack suffered a broken leg in an accident. The family story is that he was taken to the doctor in town on a railroad handcar. By whatever means he reached town, it proved to be a momentous event in the lives of Clyde and Jack Martin, for while recovering Jack renewed his acquaintance and friendship with the widow Nancy "Nannie" Jacob Wingfield Beene, who was living in Blevins, Arkansas. They said she first saw him when he was riding into town on the handcar. He married her on December 17, 1901. Nannie Beene's first husband, Henry Lee Beene, had died of tuberculosis in 1897 at the age of thirty-one, leaving her with two children, Brice, age four, and Sallie Katherine who was two. Nannie was twenty-eight when she and Jack married. She never made any bones about her conviction that the Beenes died early because they had bad genes and were weak; Sallie and Brice both remembered hearing their mother say in their presence that it was a shame they were doomed to an early death because of their Beene ancestors. There was reason for her concern about her children's future, though it proved to be unwarranted. Nannie's father, Jacob (Jake) Wingfield, had died at the age of twenty-five just before she was born. Heredity notwithstanding, Brice and Sallie both lived far into their nineties. Nannie herself took to bed in her early fifties and was cared for by Brice and his wife, "Jack," for the remainder of her life.

Sallie Beene's paternal grandfather, Lemuel Dee Beene, was born in Alabama, met and married Lucy Ann Elizabeth Harris in Mississippi, then bought land and moved to Arkansas. A successful and respected farmer, he served a term in the Arkansas legislature and was active in the political affairs of Hempstead County, Arkansas, until his death in 1897. Lucy's family was originally from North Carolina.

After his father's marriage to Nannie Beene, Clyde went back again to live with the Ballards; Brice and Sallie lived with Nannie's mother, Grandma Smith, while Nannie followed Jack to the lumber camps in east Texas. Grandma Martha E. Smith's first husband was Jacob F. "Jake" Wingfield, for whom Nannie was named. She and Jake married October 21, 1869. Nannie also had a sister, Maud. After Jake died in 1872, Martha Long Wingfield married John Smith and two children were born of their union, Anna and Stella. Aunt Stell, as she was known, and her husband, Martin Nelson, were special favorites of the William C. Martins. Stell was only eight years older than Nannie's daughter, Sallie. Anna died in her early thirties of tuberculosis. Grandma Smith's father, William Richard Long, had served six months in the Indian Wars in 1836 as a member of the Tennessee Volunteers and drew a pension for his service.

Once settled in their new home, Jack and Nannie had their children join them, and Clyde spent part of both 1902 and 1903 with them in Diboll, Texas. The Temple-Inland Lumber Company had established the town of Diboll. It was and is a company town, likely the most remote and smallest location for a Fortune 500 company in America today. With a million acres of land in twenty-one counties, Temple-Inland Lumber remains the largest landowner in the state of Texas. Diboll began when T. L. L. Temple started a sawmill there in 1894 and named the place after a local family. He came to stay. Arthur Temple, one of his descendants, moved to Diboll when he became president of the company in 1951 and still lives there. When Clyde lived in Diboll just after the turn of the century, employees of Temple-Inland Lumber rented company owned housing and shopped in the company store using script stamped with T. L. L. Temple's name for money. Although life in the lumber camps was hard and raw, Clyde often reflected on the days in Diboll with fond nostalgia and more than once went back to visit the Lindsey Springs campsite.

Sallie remembered Clyde was "a rather little bad boy" with too much imagination, who sometimes "showed off" and was punished at school, lost things, and loved to climb trees even when he got stuck and needed help to come down. He was big for his age and Sallie said he was always pitting his strength against somebody—even once against a horse that was moving away with the carriage. Instead of taking the horse by the bridle to make it stop, he grasped the back of the carriage and tried to hold it. Sallie laughed at him when he did it. He liked to read, spent time alone in his room, and was a good student. To their credit, the family recognized his ability and went to considerable trouble to keep him in the best schools available. He doesn't say what he remembered about Sallie in those early years, but their picture shows her holding gently to his arm.

Clyde was living with the family in Diboll on April 18, 1903, when a child, John Harmon Martin, was born to the Martin-Beene union. Living for only a few weeks, he died July 8 and was buried in Ryan's Chapel cemetery near the Lindsey Springs camp. The chapel is located on FM 2497, which runs west out of Diboll. "Alas how changed that lovely flower which bloomed and cheered our hearts," it says on his tombstone. The Martin children later calculated that had he lived he would have been their "double half step-uncle once removed." During the summer Clyde went back to Tennessee where he spent his time working on the farm, tramping through the woods, fishing with his uncles, and hunting. The Ballards taught him about the woods and the river and conveyed to him a sense of curiosity, wonder, and appreciation for nature, which he never lost. Throughout his life he loved the out-of-doors, especially the mountains, but gave up hunting after he decided it was not an appropriate form of recreation for a preacher. He later took it up again with Donald and John Lee, his sons, hunting rabbits in the Trinity River bottom in Dallas.

In the fall of 1904, and for the next two years, Clyde was sent to school in Blevins, where he lived with Grandma Smith, but for some undisclosed reason in 1906–1907 he was again in Randolph with the Ballards. He recalled Miss Lizzie Melton was his teacher there. Finally, in 1908, at the age of fifteen, he experienced a substantial period of time in one place. For three years he lived and boarded with the Thomas family while he attended the last years of elementary school in Pleasant Grove, Arkansas. Mr. Harris taught him. But he remembered that in those days "I was, and had been for some time, traveling under full steam the road that leads to physical, moral and spiritual ruin." He failed to say exactly what he was doing or thinking, but in the spring of 1910 he determined on his own to reform.

In the fall of 1910, perhaps sensing his son was having problems, Jack Martin sent him to live with Aunt Alice and Uncle Fletcher Smith so he could attend high school in Prescott. It is likely Clyde's permanent residence was with John Harmon and his wife, Nannie Martin, in Hempstead County, Arkansas, for the census in 1910 lists him there. Later he moved in Prescott to live with the D. E. Cummins, who became a second family to him. Their son Bryce, he said, "was like a brother to me." David Cummins was one of the dearest friends he ever had. They were, he said, like "David and Jonathan." Moving to Prescott "broke me away from my old companions and environments and placed my thoughts on something worth while."

There was a traumatic event in Clyde Martin's life about this time about which he does not comment and which his children discovered only later in their lives. Few but his closest acquaintances ever knew of it. Nobody claimed Jack Martin was a candidate for sainthood, for he had numerous encounters with the law for a variety of offenses like Sabbath breaking, playing cards, and shooting craps. These, in the official language of the court, offended "against the peace and dignity of the State of Arkansas," and he compiled an impressive record of arrests and convictions. It is interesting, and somewhat surprising, that Jack Martin apparently did not drink. He was, however, not unfamiliar with violence. At one time he, along with his brother-in-law, card-playing buddy Fletcher Smith, was accused of assault and battery, but was not convicted.

June 28, 1909, Jack Martin was involved in a capital offense committed in the Hackadam Lumber Camp, operated by the Ozan Lumber Company. In an altercation, a Syrian "peddler" named Ollie Katter was murdered. Jack Daniels was charged with the murder by J. C. Pinnix, prosecuting attorney for the Ninth Judicial Circuit of Arkansas, and Jack Martin was charged with "aiding and abetting" Daniels in the act. A warrant was issued for their arrest by Justice of the Peace W. E. Walston, and both were taken into custody by the sheriff of Pike County. Released July 3, 1909, on bond of $1,000, they were ordered to appear for trial in Pike County Circuit Court on the first day of its September term. In September, Jack Martin and three others were indicted by the grand jury for the crime. Some of the persons were his card-playing friends. The original indictment named Jack Daniels, Jim Clark, J. J. Cox, and Jack Martin, but Daniels and Clark were never tried. Martin and Cox, who remained free on bond in the interim, were tried two years after the offense. While out on bond, Jack Martin continued his usual and favorite forms of recreation and was indicted a number of additional times for "gaming," and "Sabbath breaking." Surely if these had been considered grave offenses, his bond would have been revoked, and he would have served time in jail while awaiting trial, but he remained free. By September 26, 1911, when he and Cox appeared in court, the original charge against Jack Martin had been reduced to second degree murder. They were tried together in Murfreesboro, Pike County, Arkansas.

The overwhelming impression gained from reading the transcript of the Cox-Martin trial is that few of the persons involved appear to be telling the truth. Only with some effort can the bare outline of the facts be ascertained from it. Mr. Cox, the operator of the commissary at the lumber camp, had words with Joe Hassan, the companion of Mr. Katter, who was waiting by his wagon for Katter to finish some business with the manager of the boarding house, Mrs. Kirkpatrick. During the argument, Hassan thought himself threatened by Cox, who was armed at the time with a shotgun. Cox said he had the gun only because he was on his way to hunt birds to feed the cats who lived at the store. A fight started between the two men, which was witnessed by most of the people in the camp. When Katter heard the commotion, he ran quickly out of the boarding house to aid his friend and joined the fight. Hassan appeared not to be greatly in need of help when Katter arrived, having managed successfully to disarm Cox and strike him with the shotgun. At the trial Joe Hassan testified that he and Ollie Katter had used only their hands to beat Cox, but a number of witnesses said each had a stout piece of lumber which he used liberally on Cox, who was during a good portion of the altercation flat of his back on the ground. At one point, however, in desperation and, he testified, fearful for his life, he managed to reach into the pocket of his trousers where he had concealed a two-shot derringer. Without actually removing the pistol he fired upward through his clothes. The shot struck Katter in the chest, and he staggered away from the fight and fell dead after taking only about thirty steps. Cox admitted firing the fatal shot and claimed self-defense.

Jack Martin, who, like most of the people in camp, had heard the noise and seen the fight from a distance, ran to the sleeping shack to get his rifle. He said he needed it because he was not sure what was going to happen. Witnesses said that at the moment Katter backed away from the fight Jack Martin was standing on the porch of the shack with his weapon in his hand, and they saw Martin shoot him. Those who knew Jack Martin also knew him to be sharp-eyed and a crack shot. The jury must have heard similar stories, for after a short period of deliberation it brought in a verdict on Cox of "Not guilty by reason of self-defense," and found Jack Martin guilty of manslaughter. He was sentenced to two years at hard labor, but he was released on $4,000 bond and the payment of court costs of $678.65.

Reading the testimony raises the obvious question why the medical examination of the body of Ollie Katter, conducted by Dr. Purtle after the shooting, did not conclusively show whether Katter's fatal wound was caused by a rifle bullet or one from the derringer. Dr. Purtle, an eyewitness to the shooting and friend of

Jack Martin, was not forthcoming in his testimony and the facts he presented raise considerable doubt about both his competence as a doctor and his commitment to conduct a thorough examination. The prosecutor, in fact, asked him with obvious frustration at one point during his testimony if he had been to medical school. He said he had.

The trial concluded on September 29. Four days later Lula Thornton, a resident of Hackadam Camp, came forward to testify that Hettie Daniels, wife of the original defendant, Jack Daniels, and Leila Pickett told her they did not actually know who killed Ollie Katter, but after Mrs. Kirkpatrick, the boarding house operator, said it was Jack Daniels they urged her to accuse Jack Martin because he had money and could get off. Jack Daniels was a poor man who would not. She admitted she never told Jack Martin what she knew and had lied in her testimony. Two others, P. A. Thornton and Bertha Lyons, also testified they had heard Mrs. Pickett say she had changed her statement and accused Martin to help Jack Daniels. Based on this new evidence, Jack Martin filed an appeal for a new trial, but his appeal was denied on October 19 by the Ninth Judicial Circuit.

He then appealed to the Arkansas Supreme Court in a brief filed and recorded on January 8, 1912. The Court heard the motion a week later and its "Proceedings" on January 15 report a decision upholding the finding of the lower court. Martin was ordered to prison.

As it happened, however, Jack Martin never served a day in jail for whatever his part in the crime had been. Following the ruling by the Arkansas Supreme Court, Cox wrote Governor George W. Donaghey to say he could not sit idly by and see an innocent man punished. He restated the testimony he had given in 1909 at the preliminary hearing and again in the trial that he had fired the shot that killed Ollie Katter. He also alleged that several people in the lumber camp were prejudiced against Martin and perjured themselves on the witness stand. In addition to Cox's letter, a petition was circulated which was eventually signed by almost 2,000 citizens of Pike County and all the members of the jury that handed down Martin's guilty verdict. On February 3, 1912, Governor Donaghey pardoned Jack Martin.

Few people who knew William C. Martin, including some who knew him well, ever heard of his father's criminal record. Indeed, his own children did not know of it until their cousin William told them of the incident and they asked Uncle Brice Beene about it. He told them what had happened. Donald, after moving to Little Rock, looked up the trial records. Martin did not record anything about it in his diaries, nor did he speak of it in later years. It is not difficult to imagine the concern and humiliation he must have felt to see his father put through such an ordeal. In one sense, it was a clear travesty of justice, but in another it was a side of Jack Martin that could not be denied, even by one who loved him as much as his son did. That he determined to put it entirely out of his life and never speak of it to anyone is understandable. Martin's children believe that their Uncle Brice went to see his stepfather while he was in jail during the trial, but they have no idea whether their father went with him. It seems apparent that Martin erased whatever record of the event which might have existed. While living in retirement in Little Rock, he went through his papers and apparently destroyed all the letters from his father. None of them are present in the Martin archives and only two or three were among Donald's papers. During the time he was sorting his papers Martin makes a diary entry reporting a disagreement he had with Sally about what should be done with them. What remains is the clear testimony of the influence exerted on his life by his father, and his concern for the well-being of Papa's soul. Both were clearly evident at the time, too. It is probably no coincidence that Clyde's original intention upon going to college was to study law.

Leaving Randolph for Arkansas in the summer of 1915, three years after his father's pardon, having finally settled Grandpa Ballard's affairs and marked his grave with a suitable monument, Clyde wrote in his journal: "Oh may God prepare my heart to carry the message of salvation to my father and to other lost men and women." After going with his father to visit a logging camp Clyde observed in the journal, "Oh how I love him! Grant Oh God that his thoughts may be turned from material wealth to heavenly riches." He resolved again the following summer "to make a strong effort to get Papa to join the church. I have been praying to this end for some time and I am trusting that God will answer my prayers." Those prayers continued unanswered throughout the remainder of Jack Martin's life.

———

While Jack was awaiting trial, Clyde entered high school. He said that the move to high school in Prescott "placed my thoughts on something worth while. I came out of school the following Spring with my ideals in life greatly raised." Working at home during the summer of 1910, he was plowing one day "when the thought came to me that I ought to be religious." Deliberate and intentional then as always he would be, he devised a plan of action to gain the prize—"I finally resolved to seek salvation in the revival that would be held that Summer." The first revival was held by the Baptists, but in those days everybody in town went to all of them. Even though he attended regularly there was no surrender, "because I wanted to be converted in a Methodist Church." The Methodist meeting was led by Brother Hill, the pastor, who was, as judged by Clyde's seventeen years of life experiences, "in many respects a poor preacher." Although the dry and unemotional sermons during the revival moved him not a whit, he had made up his mind and when the call was made at the end of the service he went down to the altar to surrender his life. He found himself the only penitent. Although he held out to the very end of the meeting, at the closing service Clyde presented himself for membership, and was baptized and received into the Methodist church at Harmony—"but my heart was still heavy."

During the next year in Prescott, he attended church and Sunday school regularly, read his Bible and prayed at night, but in spite of this discipline did not believe himself to have grown spiritually. When summer came, bringing with it the next season of revivals, fear overcame Clyde since he was sure he would never be able to do what was expected of him. It was, in fact, many years before revival meetings did not have an adverse effect on his sense of well-being. The typical entry in his dairy reported that he suffered "a feeling of depression" at those times. However, on this particular occasion he was spared when the pastor who was to hold the meeting was abruptly dismissed for "imprudent" conduct, and the revival was canceled.

Back in Prescott the Methodists had a new pastor, Brother B. A. Few, who took real interest in Clyde. After Christmas Clyde was elected president of the newly organized Epworth League, and he said he began to take the sacrament of Holy Communion for the first time. The summer revival in Blevins in 1912 went off on schedule. The new pastor, J. H. Bradford, "a man I always loved," called on Clyde, who was helping with the singing, to pray at one of the services. "I was dumbfounded . . . but I started and some way I got through with it." Feeling entirely unworthy and hypocritical, "I determined to do it no longer. I resolved to make no more pretensions to religion." But when Nannie asked him why he wasn't going to church the next evening and learned the reason, "she began to talk to me and pray with me and my heart was softened."

Adam Guthrie organized the first football team in Prescott High School history in the fall of 1911. He had just returned from playing at the University of Arkansas under Coach Hugo Bezdek and knew what needed to be done. The team wasn't much—they lost to Hope and were tied in a rematch, but the players themselves had potential for greatness. The football field in Prescott bears the name of the left halfback, David Cummins, Clyde's dear friend, who was killed in World War I while serving with the Navy. Left end Arthur Hamilton became a general in the air force—the mascot, John C. Munn, achieved the rank of brigadier general in the United States Marines. Lagneia McMillan, right halfback, coached football in South Carolina, Bud Hale played professional football on the West Coast, and center, Clyde Martin, became a Methodist bishop. Not a bad beginning.

Football certainly wasn't Clyde's entire life. Dixie Dees taught him English and Expression in his junior and senior years. "I will never know how much I owe to her influence but the chances are that I should never have gone to college had I not met her," he wrote after he enrolled at Hendrix. Perhaps it was Dees who taught him to spell correctly and gave him the command of English grammar which marked his writing and speaking throughout life. From the first one begun in 1914, Martin's journals are precise and lucid. Dees married well, too. Grady Gammage, who taught with her in Prescott from 1910 to 1912, went on to become president of Northern Arizona State Teachers College, and of Arizona State Teachers College, Tempe, which is now Arizona State University. An impressive building on the campus honors his service.

Clyde graduated from Prescott High with eleven others on May 23, 1913. As president of the student body and of his class, he gave the farewell address at the graduation ceremonies and announced his intention to attend the University of Arkansas to become a lawyer. Perhaps in recognition of this ambition, just prior to the end of his senior year he served as judge in a mock trial sponsored by the Zenith Society. The experience undoubtedly brought back unpleasant memories of his father's brushes with the law, and one cannot help thinking that Jack Martin's convoluted legal tangles must have influenced Clyde's decision to study law in college.

The senior play, *The Melting Pot,* was performed and Professor O. L. Dunaway, superintendent of schools, addressed the class at commencement; diplomas were presented by local attorney, the Honorable G. R. Haynie. A big picnic closed the festivities. Although Prescott won the baseball game, the newspaper account noted it "was a poor one from start to finish."

Despite his decision to devote his life to the law, religion had only begun its work with Clyde Martin. Once enrolled in the University of Arkansas at Fayetteville, he played varsity football and enjoyed the preaching of M. N. Waldrip, from whom he also bought books. We are diminished in our knowledge of this period since during the thirties Clyde decided to destroy the diary that covered his "Razorback" year. But before he burned it, he wrote a three page summary that tells of his call and surrender to preach. "Sometime in the latter part of February or the early part of March [1914], I yielded to what I considered a call to the ministry." In ways far deeper and profound than ever he could have imagined at the time, he continued, "I have never doubted for a moment the genuineness of that call. The finger that points me to the ministry has not, for a single instant, been hidden." This summary also tells us that it was his decision to enter the ministry that caused him to begin the practice of keeping a diary. He kept it faithfully until 1980, when at age eighty-seven he allowed it to lapse.

The year at the University of Arkansas was an eventful one that he greatly enjoyed. He would always remember the university fondly. In addition to football and classwork, Clyde took advantage of the cultural events the university provided. He saw the Ben Greet Players productions of *A Midsummer Night's Dream, As You Like It,* and *The Tempest.* Lasting friendships were formed, too. He met freshman Jerry Wallace from Russellville, later Canon Wallace of the Episcopal Church, with whom he stayed in touch throughout his life, and R. O. Rainwater, J. A. Winn, W. K. Newton, Vance L. Sailor, Boyd Best, Maurice Alcorn, W. H. Courson and W. W. McConnell. Whenever he was at the Mount Sequoyah Assembly or in the vicinity of Fayetteville he seldom failed to take time to walk over the campus. Those journeys renewed the memories of a formative and enjoyable year in his life.

The year was over almost before he knew it, and in the company of good friends Clyde left Fayetteville on the train the night of June 4, 1914, for home. The day after he arrived he began work on the farm. Although before coming home he had made up his mind not to apply for license to preach, he was advised by his pastor, Brother J. H. Bradford, and by the presiding elder, Brother W. M. Hayes, to obtain a local preacher's license at the July meeting of the District Conference in Okolona. The Quarterly Conference of Friendship Methodist Church recommended him for the license on June 20. Clyde was troubled about taking the step because he did not feel ready and was unsure about his worthiness. After reading John Wesley's sermons "Justification by Faith" and "Witness of the Spirit," he was even more convinced that in spite of the certainty of his call "there was a great blessing in the Christian religion that I had never experienced." Without the assurance of God's pardon he "resolved to seek it." The night before the licensing committee meeting at the District Conference, Brother T. O. Owen of Hope preached to the conference on the "witness of the spirit." Shaken badly because "I knew I did not have it," Clyde prayed alone past midnight. The next morning, July 16, outside the committee room, he spoke at length with D. D. Warlick, an older preacher in whom he had confidence, and asked whether to go on. "He told me to go right ahead that I was all right and had just been expecting too much. . . . I took his advice, passed the examination and was given local preacher's license."

Once licensed, Clyde began to assist in revival meetings in Bingen, Friendship, and Pisgah. In Doyle, he preached his first sermon. The sermon was based on John 12:32: "And I, when I am lifted up from the earth, will draw all men to myself" (RSV). In all he "tried to preach" seven times, "but the sermons were of but little value." A thousand people pledged themselves to pray for him—maybe just enough to help him get by.

Clyde's original intention was to transfer at the end of his first year from the University of Arkansas to Vanderbilt University in Nashville. This plan was thwarted by the fight in Vanderbilt's Board of Trustees over a proposed gift of a million dollars and control of the university. The Methodists lost the battle for control and withdrew their support. The immediate result of this division was the creation of Emory University in Atlanta and Southern Methodist University in Dallas.

The Methodist connection of a school mattered to Clyde. In the fall of 1914, influenced, he said, by Woolford Baker and loyalty to the Little Rock Annual Conference of the Methodist Episcopal Church, South, he enrolled in Henderson-Brown College in Arkadelphia. "I fully realize that in going there I will sacrifice some things that I would have gotten at Hendrix but I feel that my patriotism to my conference demands that I make the sacrifice." We know that the presence of a red-headed, high-spirited coed named Sallie Beene, about which he is silent, was at least as influential in his choice as denominational loyalty and "patriotism." It proved to be a mistake. "Here my spiritual growth was hindered by jealousy." Sallie's presence was the obvious cause of his malady. She admitted later she had been "a little fickle" in those days, and remembered "a lot of crushes" and many dates. And she also said years later, "I think deep down inside all along that I knew someday I was going to marry him." She did little in those days, however, to ease his pain or enhance his spiritual growth.

Clyde, always a serious student, enrolled for courses in French, English, Bible, chemistry, mathematics, and Greek, and played football until he decided he had to give it up "on account of my work." At a Y.M.C.A. conference at Hendrix College in Conway, he saw his old friend from the University of Arkansas, Jerry Wallace, and in November, 1914, he attended the sessions of the Little Rock Annual Conference of the Methodist Episcopal Church, South, and was admitted on trial with thirteen others. The Henderson-Brown experience lasted only one semester, for in early December he left school "hoping to rid myself of my evil passion [jealousy] by service," and returned to Randolph. His plan was to find a church in which he could preach, but a talk with church officials in Memphis offered no encouragement. Nor was he successful in arranging a place to work as a supply (part-time) preacher. In the end he had to content himself with preaching about half the time in several small churches near Randolph. In the meantime, Grandpa Ballard had become ill and needed care. Things were not good at home either. Papa had lost his job with the lumber company and Sallie had been taken out of school.

The time in Randolph weighed heavily on Clyde. He began the Course of Study, a four-year curriculum required of Methodist clergy to qualify for ordination. It consisted of a set of readings for four years determined by the bishops and required the writing of papers on designated topics. In addition to the required books for the Course of Study, he read William Taylor's *Holy Living and Holy Dying* but found it failed to provide the inspiration for him that it had John Wesley. He was more impressed with the *Memoirs of Carvasso*, an English Methodist class leader in the late eighteenth and early nineteenth century. "Oh for the spiritual power and zeal that this man possessed."

The first written assignment in the Course of Study was a sermon on repentance, and he found it "a hard matter to hold my mind to the task." Several philosophies of life were written to the diary, one of which he was certain was comprehensive enough to "meet the needs of everybody." Probably to their chagrin he spoke often with Uncle Perry, who was twenty-five, and Uncle Ed, who was twenty-three, about their religious commitment—they were known from time to time, like their father, to take a drink—and resolved to speak every day with at least one person about the state of his or her soul. Letters were written frequently to Nannie and Sallie, and in between there was time to break a young horse to ride and wander in the woods. Walking remained his favorite pastime throughout life. The land inherited from his mother was mostly covered in timber, and its harvest provided some needed income. The sale netted $1,000, sufficient to repay the $250 he owed Grandpa Ballard for taxes he had paid on Clyde's land from the time of his mother's death until 1915. An additional $250 went to repay stepbrother Brice for a loan that had covered a portion of Clyde's college expenses.

Despite the fact that a number of places to preach were eventually arranged, Clyde was not happy with either his preaching or the "half saved" state of his soul, and he decided that the "blessing" being sought should have come at conversion. "My preaching was good enough from an intellectual point of view but it was sadly lacking in spirituality," he said. Like Jacob wrestling the angel, determined not to let go without being blessed, Clyde resolved not to preach again until he had received "the blessing." And so, with the single-minded determination he had shown in deciding to become religious, he set out to acquire the assurance of God's pardon in his life; the decision was duly entered in his journal entry April 23, 1915. Thinking of Grandpa Ballard's condition as much as his own, he wrote: "I am conscious that the pathway of some of my close relatives lies along the very brink of death and that they must soon, very soon, topple over it unprepared yet with this knowledge I lose no sleep over their condition. What better proof do I need that my heart is not right with God's?" Disconcerting conversations with folks like Sister Irvine of Randolph and Brother Sol Forbess, who recounted outpourings of the spirit and the power which accompanied it at their conversions, further convinced him that he must seek a positive assurance that God's spirit was in his heart.

He began his quest by reading the Bible, early British Methodist Adam Clark's *Commentary on the New Testament,* William Arthur's *Tongue of Fire* (required for the first year of the Course of Study), Telford's *Life of John Wesley,* the *Methodist Hymnal,* and Tillett's *Personal Salvation.* He spoke with the pastor in Randolph, Brother Dallas, who told him about his religious experience, and read of John Wesley's search for it among the Moravians. The account of the gift of the spirit to the early church recounted in the first two chapters of Acts was carefully studied. Clyde interrogated himself mercilessly—"Have I ever been truly justified or are all my sins yet unforgiven?" He prayed for certainty in his relation to God. By April 27 he was worse and noted that "dark fears are beginning to clutch at my heart." Again he decided not to preach, "because I had nothing to preach." Uncle Perry was afraid he was about to give up the ministry entirely and had him come for a visit to his house to urge him to stay the course. "His sympathy for me caused me to take a long cry."

Clyde's uncertainty was as much about the nature of God as it was about his unsettled condition. Why would God withhold a blessing so earnestly sought and sincerely desired? Perhaps God was testing him. He remembered the experience of the children of Israel and the early disciples who also were tested. "Perhaps," he said, "God is withholding this blessing from me to try my faith"; the thought strengthened his resolve to wait for it.

On April 29 he read John Wesley's sermon "The Almost Christian" and decided it described his condition exactly. Wesley said in the sermon, which is the second of the forty-four "standard" sermons that are at the heart of Methodist doctrine, that "the *almost Christian* does nothing which the gospel forbids" (John Wesley, *Sermons on Several Occasions* [London: Epworth Press, 1954], 12). There is a real and sincere desire to serve God as well as to abstain from evil. The fearful aspect of the "almost Christian" state, according to Wesley, is that it is possible to remain in that condition forever. Clyde's determination to "seek the blessing unceasingly" was reaffirmed. Coming home from Randolph on May 1, he read of Peter Böhler, the Moravian, in John Wesley's *Journal*. It was Böhler who told Wesley in answer to his question "What shall I preach?" to "Preach faith till you have it; and then, because you have it, you will preach faith." Clyde decided to follow Böhler's advice, as had Wesley, and preach again. This decision was strengthened by a conversation with the presiding elder, Brother W. A. Freeman, who told him he needed time for his faith to mature. That made sense to Clyde. "I now see that I have been too hasty, too ready to take into my own hands matters that can be properly attended to by God alone."

His quest for the assurance of God's favor was interrupted when Grandpa Ballard became seriously ill on April 30 and it was determined he needed to go into Memphis for an examination. An appointment was made and Clyde went with Uncle Perry to take him on Monday, May 10, 1915. After seeing the doctor, they were told J. W. should be hospitalized and undergo surgery for the removal of his prostate gland. The operation a week later was judged a success, and the doctor expressed confidence that his recovery would be speedy and complete. But on May 28 J. W. underwent a second operation, which Clyde watched. "It was brutal. For near forty minutes the surgeon was working constantly. Before he had been at work ten minutes my hopes died within me. I knew that it was beyond human endurance to stand such an operation as that one." Grandpa Ballard died the next day. Clyde was named executor of his estate.

"Without being given time to mourn my grandfather's death, I was hastened into the duty of disposing of his estate." It required the next few weeks, and in that time Clyde's preoccupation with "secular" matters, which he did not find easy, caused him to lose ground in his spiritual quest. However, it was obvious by this time that he needed to go back to school and he resolved then and there to complete both college and seminary. Having decided what he should do, he wrote Bishop Warren Candler in Atlanta and resolved to enroll in Emory University in the fall.

Clyde preached his last sermons in Elm Grove and Hopewell in

July, and he and Grandma Ellena Ballard took the steamboat down the Mississippi to Memphis, where he helped her get situated with her nephew, C. K. Berlin, with whom she was to live. Afterward Clyde took a few days "to learn some things about the religious organizations of this city." He visited with the pastor of the First Methodist Church, Dr. T. E. Sharp, and inquired about the advisability of obtaining a clergy pass from the railroad. Dr. Sharp advised against it because, he said, "preachers ought to be men and entirely free from the ministerial whine." But he did encourage him to return to college to finish his degree and also to attend seminary afterward.

In spare time he read *Oliver Twist* in the Cassitt Library and visited a rescue mission in the evening. It was the first one Clyde had ever seen. Hearing the men who were there quote long passages of scripture from memory, he resolved to learn to do the same. Nearly everyone who heard him preach throughout his life remembered he always quoted his text, no matter how long, from memory. He talked with Clarence Croswell who was captain of the football team at Henderson-Brown, too. Although he said he did not learn as much in Memphis as he had hoped, he felt his time had been well spent. On July 20, he took the train and set out for Prescott to visit his family.

Once at home Clyde fell quickly into helping with the usual chores, such as canning, and assisted Brother Hayes, the presiding elder, in some of the smaller churches. He preached in the protracted meeting, but "the sermons were without power because of my failure to prepare myself for them." However, the meeting soon closed because of the beginning of the cantaloupe harvest. That gave time for some work on the Course of Study, study of Purves's *The Apostolic Age* and Johnson's *Ideal Ministry,* "a great book," plus some needed review of Latin in preparation for the college course. Even though he managed to finish the work on Angus-Green's *The Cyclopedic Handbook of the Bible,* Grandpa's death had put him far behind in the syllabus. Continuing to preach, he was disappointed because "not a single person responded to my propositions," but there were lessons to be learned in the failure. "I am more and more convinced of the futility of trying to persuade men to give up their sins unless there is divine power in the words of the speaker."

———◦◦◦◦◦———

September 1, 1915, Clyde made "what I consider one of the most important decisions of my life." Rather than follow his earlier plan and enroll in Emory, he decided to enter Hendrix College in Conway, Arkansas. Emory he knew had a greater endowment, larger faculty, and better reputation, but Hendrix had the advantages of being nearer home, was less expensive, more influential in the Arkansas Conference, and provided the opportunity to meet and know persons with whom he would be associated during his ministry. "This last consideration I believe to be sufficient to outweigh all the advantages of Emory." Leaving home on September 6 he spent the night with the Cummins family in Prescott and was in Conway the morning of September 7 to make arrangements for school. Although he arrived too late to secure a room in the dormitory, he was successful in finding one just off the campus in a house where two other Hendrix men, C. D. Meux and Reuben Hays, were living. Both were serious students and it proved to be a good place to live, and the beginning of a long friendship with Meux. Academically, Clyde learned that his work at the University of Arkansas and at Henderson-Brown would enable him to be classified as a sophomore, and he signed up for courses in mathematics, chemistry, Latin, and Bible. All except the Bible course were considered among the hardest subjects in the school.

Satisfied with the arrangements at Hendrix, he made a quick trip to Tennessee to see "my people." As always, he was invited to preach in Randolph and did so on Sunday morning from a text in Genesis. He discovered that despite a protracted meeting, the church "was in a more inharmonious condition when the meeting closed than it was when it opened. . . . Oh God, have mercy on that church." Although he does not say why the division existed, he resolved on the spot to go back the next summer and hold a meeting of his own.

The real reason for the trip, however, was to see about purchasing a farm for Aunt Vinie, his mother's sister. Aunt Alice was reasonably well off since her husband, Henry Hathcock, died leaving her a house, but Aunt Vinie had nothing. J. W. Ballard disinherited Alice and Lavinia, who was known as Vinie, because they married against his will. The bulk of his estate, property worth $2,000 plus $1,000 in life insurance, had gone to Grandpa's second wife, Ellena Berlin Ballard. Clyde had inherited the bottom field from his mother when she died, and he felt remorse that he should have been favored. "Those of us who had been given a share of the land felt that it was our duty to buy her a home." Clyde further resolved "When I am able I am going to pay to Aunt Alice or her heirs the same amount that I paid aunt Vina. I shall not feel that the land is justly mine until this has been done." He made good on his commitment in 1944 when he sent checks for $125 to each of her four children.

The course work at Hendrix proved demanding and Clyde admitted, "I have never before been compelled to study as hard as I am studying now." He played tennis for exercise four days a week despite the fact that it cut into his study time, and joined the Y.M.C.A. and the Franklin Literary Society. By October he was contemplating the possibility of going on for a master's degree in an "eastern university," but was still open to attending a theological school. His lack of funds was a serious problem and it was certain that he would need to find a way to earn some money during the summer. He weighed carefully the amount of time he could spend in extracurricular activities, too. "I don't want to go through college without getting my share of such things as give culture and intellectual and spiritual broadening to one's life nor do I want to allow such things to so predominate in my college career as to interfere seriously with my regular college work."

His most significant decision, however, was a resolution "never to be married." "I am firmly convinced . . . that my usefulness as a worker in God's kingdom would be greatly lessened by matrimony." He added, "Nothing should be allowed to hinder one from the work that God has planned for Him to do. May this always be my attitude toward His work." The Martin resolve concerning marriage was short-lived, but his attitude toward

God's work never changed and eventually proved detrimental to his marriage.

Bishop Henry Clay Morrison presided in November over the sessions of the North Arkansas Conference which were held in the new Conway Methodist Church; Jerry Wallace came down from Russellville for a visit and told Martin of his plan to become an Episcopal priest. The Christmas holidays were spent in Blevins; he and Sallie made the trip home together from Little Rock after buying gifts for the kinfolk there. Sallie gave him money for Christmas. In free time he read Eleanor Porter's *Pollyanna*, Huxley's *Science and Culture*, Arnold's *Sweetness and Light*, and reread *Silas Marner*. Just after January 1, 1916, Clyde returned to school with a stopover in Little Rock where he heard Brother Forney Hutchinson, pastor of First Church, preach on Sunday morning. It was the start of long years of pleasant association. Bishop Winchester of the Episcopal Church preached in the evening service at the Y.M.C.A.

The college grind quickly overtook him when he got back to Conway and he realized he was "inclined to be peevish and irritable." But a thought came that helped to put things in perspective: "I cannot allow my desire to make good grades interfere with my being a courteous, patient, gentleman." And neither grades nor high ecclesiastical office ever moved him from that resolution, although he once confessed to daughter, Catherine, that he knew he had to hold his temper in check. Clyde Martin was unfailingly "a courteous, patient, gentleman."

After learning about the Rhodes scholarship, he considered applying for it, but realized a successful application would require a strong record of leadership as well as high academic marks. Obtaining those offices, he feared, might compromise his convictions. And, then, there was the consideration whether three years at Oxford would be better than three in seminary in Atlanta. He need not have worried for he later discovered he was too old to be eligible. Final exams came and Clyde finished the semester with a 92 average. Latin, mathematics, and history ("Development of Modern Europe") filled out the second semester, but when at leisure he read Jack London's *Call of the Wild* and Charles Dickens's *David Copperfield*. "I think I like it better than any novel I have ever read," he wrote, "and my admiration for Dickens which has always been great has been doubled and trebled." This was the beginning of a lifelong love affair with Dickens, too.

The study of modern European history heightened his awareness of the events sweeping that continent. War had been declared on his twenty-first birthday but he took no notice of it in his diary and, like most Americans, probably failed to grasp the implications for their future. But this war, which was to engulf a large portion of the world, soon would make itself felt in Conway, Arkansas, too. To get a better grasp of the situation he read Albert Bushnell Hart's *The War in Europe*. "I think I cannot afford to ignore this the greatest and most far reaching in its effects of all the movements of the human race." In just over two years he and many other Americans would be in France.

A great and protracted revival was held on the Hendrix campus. Brother Burk Culpepper of Memphis came to do the preaching. He was a modern, up-to-date preacher who used expressions like "he's a cutter" and a "crackerjack" in his descriptions of persons. Martin did not find the innovation to his liking. "What has come over our people," Clyde fumed, "that they demand and enjoy such ranting?" But he changed his mind after attending every service, morning and night, for two weeks and decided it would be better to forget the first sermon. Besides, "with God's help" Clyde was able to lead two students to Christ "and helped with many others." The climax of the meeting came at a "men only" service in which Culpepper was supposed to preach on "civic righteousness," but he never got past the testimony meeting. "Some of the most wicked and hard hearted men of the town gave over to the appeals of the preacher and their friends. Strong men broke down and wept. . . . It was one of the greatest services I ever attended." The results were impressive, too. Sunday, March 19, 229 people joined the church, half of them under the age of fifteen. In the evening Clyde attended the Baptist church where "thirty-five or forty" people were baptized—"by immersion, of course." That mode of baptism was not to his liking, and he noted, "I could not help but think how senseless is such a custom."

There were practical results from the meeting for Clyde, too.

He now resolved to keep two notebooks to help in his "sermon building"—one with stories that might be "helpful in making plain a truth," and the other "good, clean, laughable anecdotes as come under my notice." More important, he came to a new awareness of the meaning of conversion. "Conversion seems to be nothing," he wrote, "more nor less than a calm, deliberate but determined resolution to trust God for all things and to obey as nearly as possible the commands of His Son, Jesus Christ." It was a breakthrough.

The Home Mission Board, through the offices of Dr. Anderson, near the end of the spring term offered to employ Clyde for the summer as a missionary for the northern ends of Conway, Pope, and Johnson counties. Despite some trepidation about how the folks at home, who needed his help, might regard his being away for the entire summer, he decided to accept. It was his calling and he needed the money. In the meantime, he determined to spend all his leisure time in prayer, undertook a project to improve his vocabulary, and still found time to read *The Mill on the Floss* and *Don Quixote*. In May "the final sprint in the race of the college year" was upon him. An examination on Cicero was taken for entrance credit, and reading completed of the Gospels of Mark and Luke in the Latin translation of the Bible, the *Vulgate*. Bad news came from Tennessee in a letter from a cousin who informed him that "two of my uncles who had resolved to leave the accursed stuff alone, had been tampering with whiskey again. . . . The power of sin is indeed great." Clyde's last examination was taken on June 8 and plans completed to spend ten days at home. "While at home, it is my purpose to make a strong effort to get Papa to join the church." A veiled reference about another important matter is left hanging to be discussed "after its outcome is known" as was an earlier statement about a life changing resolution that had been made. Since both came close to his trip home, it is not difficult to imagine each had something to do with Sallie, as they did.

The opportunity never presented itself to speak to Papa about his church membership, but Clyde was able to do some good work with prospective students on behalf of Hendrix. He and Sallie drove together to Nacogdoches, Texas, to visit Uncle Will and

Aunt Anna Martin, and the secret is revealed about the life-changing event. "As a result of calm meditation . . . I came to the conclusion that married life was the right and only right life for me," and he decided to propose to Sallie. She accepted and plans were made for a wedding after graduation. "I really love Sallie and I am quite sure she loves me." And that marked the beginning of a great story of its own.

They found Uncle Will in poor condition, suffering from paralysis, and without consulting either Nannie or Papa, Clyde decided that he and Sallie would stay until Aunt Anna could dispose of some property and then they would all return together. "Uncle Will is one of the best men I have ever known, big hearted and generous. I love him and am going to try to do for him what I am sure he would do for me if circumstances were reversed." The little party left Nacogdoches in the afternoon, reached Texarkana at eleven o'clock that night, and arrived home the next day. Imagine the shock their arrival produced. Mamma felt she should have been consulted before the decision was reached to move Uncle Will and Aunt Anna into her home and "the slightest bit of friction was experienced on Mama's part," but her feelings were never known outside the family. Clyde left the next day for Conway and a summer doing the Lord's work.

A pleasant surprise was waiting for him when he stopped to see friends in Prescott. He learned he had won the William A. Owen scholarship medal for his poem "Do You Know," and third place in the mathematics contest. Brother Anderson was not in town when he arrived so Clyde had three days of leisure and time to prepare for the summer's work. When they were finished, he set out with a suitcase full of clothes, 100 small song books, 200 Bibles plus his *Discipline,* and a copy of Tillett's *Personal Salvation.* The air was full of "war talk" because of the events with Pancho Villa in Mexico, and patriotic sentiment was rampant, but Clyde judged "the need must be much more urgent than it is at present before I shall feel constrained to offer myself as a soldier."

In the meantime, he had volunteered for the Lord's army. He rode the mail hack seventeen miles to Appleton, located at the foot of Oak Mountain in the Boston range, and found himself "farther from a railroad than I had ever been before." He spent the first few days attending the holiness revival five times and hoeing in Brother Carter's, the preacher, cotton patch. On Saturday night Clyde began his own revival in Mt. Zion preaching on "The Influence of the Holy Spirit." The people were generous and hospitable, the material for sermons and his voice held up, and although the revival ended without a single conversion, "I did not allow myself to become discouraged."

From Mt. Zion he moved on to Appleton, where folks told him there was no hope of a revival. For a time it looked as if they were right, but on Friday night a young man, Harrison Hicks, became the first person ever converted under the ministry and preaching of W. Clyde Martin. The meeting was protracted for another week and five more persons came forward, and then ten and fourteen more until a total of fifty-two persons were converted and thirty-eight added to the membership of the church—mostly persons between the age of fourteen and twenty-five. Nathan Carter, the preacher's son, was one of them. Seeing the joy on the faces of those who came in response to his altar calls, Clyde suddenly realized "I had been cheated out of a blessing at the time I was converted due to the coldness of the church and of the preacher. Never have I felt that thrill of joy that came into the hearts of the people who were converted in this meeting."

When they finally decided to close out the meeting, it had run for twenty-one days. Clyde had preached thirty-six times, more than in all his previous life together. The next week evangelist Martin rested, caught up on long overdue correspondence, and bought a tent with $60 of his own money. The next preaching place was Zion's Hill, a community about twelve miles south of Appleton. At first the folks were lukewarm about a revival and "the prospects for a good meeting were gloomy." But he and Brother Carter stretched the tent in a good location and opened for business anyway. He roomed at Brother Beeson's who lived near the tent. The citizens of Zion's Hill were hospitable, and attendance at night was good, but not much interest was shown in the meeting until the end of the week when the first people came to the altar. In all, eighteen were converted in a meeting that ran for sixteen days, and ten joined the church. There was some excitement when a Campbellite preacher known for breaking up the meetings of other denominations came, but he sat through the service without saying a word. And there would have been more excitement had the young men who were fond of shooting pistols around the tent decided to cause trouble but they, too, cooperated by staying away.

The Methodists, who shared a meeting room with the Campbellites when they would agree to have them, were anxious to build a building and persuaded Clyde to stay a few days longer to help them raise money. In two days he had $300 in pledges and had been in touch with the Conference Board of Church Extension to enlist its support. The church would be built.

He moved to Cleveland, a village of about 200 people, on August 19. The sight of nearby Oak Mountain raised his spirits. Being in the mountains always had that effect. The town was full of churches and the occasion provided the first opportunity for Clyde to experience the "Advents." Brother Carter had come on ahead to pitch the tent and open the meeting. He had preached for two days when Clyde arrived. Attendance was good and order "fairly respectable." The meeting dragged on for fourteen nights without success and Clyde was ready to strike the tent and move on when at the eleven o'clock service on Thursday "the Holy Spirit seemed to get hold upon the entire congregation," and continued until Sunday when the revival ended. That afternoon twenty-four persons were baptized—by immersion. Clyde admitted that his voice by that time had almost completely failed.

A return visit to Zion's Hill to see about the progress toward building the new church also provided time to stay with the Beesons again, to hunt squirrels, and to give his voice a rest. Ever serious and introspective, he resolved after the last trip not to hunt again because "there is something about it that savors of idleness of a kind that a preacher should not be guilty of." There were ways to enjoy the mountains and forests without a gun. It was decided that actual construction on the building would begin October 1. Brother D. L. Jordan was to be in charge.

As he left on the mail hack to return to school seventy-five days after he began the work "with dire misgivings as to what my success would be," Clyde had reason to be encouraged. He had helped in four revivals, preached ninety-three times, visited in a hundred homes, sold 300 Bibles, and earned $125 from the Mission Board for his services. He went from Atkins to Russellville for a brief visit with Jerry Wallace, who was home from the Episcopal seminary in Sewanee. Among other things they discussed were questions of ecclesiastical authority, and Clyde learned that Episcopalians considered Methodist bishops "not validly consecrated and our church is therefore an outlaw church." Later he reflected in his diary that "Jerry Wallace is the most brilliant young man that I have ever been associated with but I can't understand his reasons for taking the stand that he has in regard [to] church affairs."

Tuesday night he was once again in Conway to begin his junior year at Hendrix. His roommate from the preceding year, C. D. Meux, had already arrived. The courses that semester included Latin ("Roman Comedy"), beginning Greek, "Forms of Discourse and Literary Criticism," and philosophy. Three short courses of six weeks each in psychology, logic, and ethics brought the total to eighteen credit hours. The question of declaring a major was also before him. English was his preference, but since there would be some difficulty in getting the required number of hours he opted for Latin with a minor in Greek. The total enrollment of Hendrix College in the fall of 1916 was 260, all but 30 of whom were men.

In addition to his academic work, Clyde took on a full load of extracurricular activities. He was a member of the publishing board for the campus paper, the *Bull Dog,* associate editor of the literary magazine, the *Mirror,* assistant business manager of the yearbook, the *Troubadour,* chairman of the Y.M.C.A. Bible Study Committee, and assistant teacher of the college Sunday school class. This was also the year that he began the practice of keeping a notebook in which he recorded all of his reading. Another resolution from the past was set aside this year, too. Clyde admitted that on account of the "general backwardness of Arkansas" he had thought he would join an annual conference "in a more progressive state farther west," but the summer convinced him "to cast my lot with Arkansas." Despite these best-laid plans, he would serve only three years of his long ministry in the state, but live there in retirement.

As usual there were plenty of lectures, plays, and athletic contests. He experimented with sleeping and eating less, preached for his friend B. F. Musser at Capitol View Church in Little Rock, and toured the state capitol while he was there. "Musser is a great fellow," Martin said, "a product of the Howard County hills." On November 17 he accepted the invitation of the *Bull Dog* to return to Henderson-Brown to cover the football game with Hendrix for half of his expenses. "Everything was exactly as it was when I had seen it last. Even the cat and dog were sleeping in the same corners by the fire." His reception, about which he had some concern because of the abruptness of his departure, was warm, but Hendrix lost the game.

A highlight of the term was the Y.M.C.A.'s presentation of Leavitt's painting *The Last Supper*. The artist himself brought the painting, which was twenty-two feet long with life-size figures of the disciples, and lectured twice each day—a grand experience. There was the annual meeting of the Little Rock Conference in Malvern just before Thanksgiving. Sallie came for a day, too. "She was enjoying the very best health and was buoyant in spirit," and when she left he was filled with loneliness. Clyde and Brother Canfield, whom he knew on the Prescott Circuit, were entertained during conference, as was the custom of the time, in the home of Dr. Hodges. He had to forgo hearing Bishop McCoy preach on Sunday in order to return to Little Rock to preach twice for Musser, but he noted that the list of appointments indicated that "Hendrix men were standing head and shoulders above their brethren." He wrote up the conference for the *Bull Dog*.

After conference it was the same, unbroken routine of college work until the Christmas holidays. On the way home he stopped in Little Rock for a brief time with Musser and some Christmas shopping and reached Prescott at nine o'clock in the evening. The next day was spent "shaking hands" with old friends and meeting the new preacher, Brother Parker, and then going out to Blevins to be rejoined with his home folks. In the evening there was a Christmas tree program at the church—"so far as I know no whiskey was on the ground," a marked improvement over what might have been expected in years past. After preaching in Blevins he spent the night with Grandma Smith and her daughter, Anna, who had just been diagnosed with tuberculosis. Most of the time, however, was spent with Sallie, "among the happiest hours of my life."

He did find time to take the train to Hot Springs for a few days with his roommate, and his family, too. Meux met him at the station. Together they paid a visit to Brother Waldrip, who had just arrived and was unpacking the books of his impressive library, toured the city, drank the water, went to a movie and spent the night with the Meux family. Later they visited the bath houses, including the Fordyce, "a veritable model of sanitation and purification," and ate in the stately Arlington Hotel, which became a favorite retreat for him and Sallie. Before leaving, Clyde and Meux made another visit to Waldrip to buy books. Two volumes of (Elbert) Hubbard, *Philistine*, Frank Crane, *Footnotes on Life*, a volume of Tagore's *Poems*, and a volume of *Methods* for church work went back to Conway. Clyde judged his visit to Hot Springs "satisfactory in almost every respect," but regretted he didn't take a bath or go up into the tower because of the fog. That was an oversight he was to remedy on almost every future visit for the rest of his life.

The volume *The Poets of the Future*, containing his poem "Do You Know?" and 139 others written by college students all across America was waiting when he returned. Martin's poem reads in part:

> Do you know where the blue-birds winter,
>   How the chimney-sweep fastens her nest,
> Why the whippoorwill's note is so mournful,
>   Where the plump, purple grapes are the best?

Can you tell where the blue-bells are thickest?
  Where the lazy trout basks in the sun,
Where the yellow plums ripen the quickest,
  How the blacksnake devises to Run?

Do you know what the tall pines whisper,
  When the South Wind rustles their leaves,
How the squirrel hides food for the winter,
  How honey is made by the bees?

.   .   .   .

You may have read books by the hundred,
  You may solve every problem with ease,
Yet I will not say you are learned,
  Unless you can answer these.

His red, leather-bound copy in the archives is inscribed "Given to Sallie Beene as a Christmas present by W. C. Martin, 1916."

In three weeks the end of the semester and exams were on them. However, prompted by reading an editorial, Martin decided to chew his food thoroughly. The author claimed this simple practice would enable one to thrive on less than half as much food and enjoy better health. Self-improvement was always at the top of his agenda. The exams were passed with "good" grades and his spring courses were "more nearly what I wanted than anything I have had thus far." They were Greek ("Kenephon's Anabasis"), Latin ("Private Life of the Romans"), in which letters of such writers as Pliny and Juvenal were read, "Eighteenth Century Prose Writers, Ruskin, Carlyle, Macaulay and Arnold," and another English course on style and criticism to be jointly offered by Professors Greene and Simmons.

He unwisely took it on himself, though at the suggestion of another student, to speak to classmates who were playing cards of "the disreputable kind." His efforts were not appreciated even though they left off cards. "This incident has brought to my attention again the fact that one cannot deal with sin without becoming involved in unpleasant conditions." But duty demanded action and there was the consolation that "a man's character will take care of his reputation."

Selling ads for the *Troubadour*, the college yearbook, was a new experience for him, and it afforded an opportunity to meet members of the business community in Little Rock. That was like "another world" when compared with the campus and its life. His trip included a visit to the state legislature, which was in session, something Clyde had always wanted to do. Like most citizens who have the experience, the conduct of the members of that body failed to live up to his expectations. Anyone could see that conversations went on unabated during the business, feet were on desks, and all were smoking. After thirty minutes and no progress he moved from the Senate to the House of Representatives. There things were worse because of the larger numbers. One member was in the midst of a bombastic speech concerning insurance. "For ten minutes he talked without saying anything, which was of no matter because nobody would have heard it if he had. . . . I left feeling very much disappointed and a trifle disgusted."

World affairs were discouraging, too. Germany repudiated her submarine policy and announced her intention to sink all vessels found in certain waters. A few days later she eased the tension somewhat by proposing to come to terms without a declaration of war. The gathering threat of war had caused Clyde to consider what role he would take if it should be declared. In these early days he had no clear answer to guide him.

The Y.M.C.A.'s annual revival was of greater immediate concern and it was held February 11-18. Brother Wheeler came to do the preaching at the two daily services. He failed, however, to connect with his audience because Clyde thought he failed to recognize the conditions at Hendrix.

Selling ads in Little Rock provided the opportunity to drive out to Fort Logan H. Roots to see several of his Prescott classmates who had just returned from service on the U.S.-Mexican border with the National Guard. Never again, was the general sentiment. He also got a glimpse of barracks life—swearing, playing cards, and smoking. "The horrors of war," he concluded, "are not on the battle field but in the barracks." He was later to come to a more realistic assessment.

Life continued apace at Hendrix into spring. There was a mass meeting to protest the poor quality of the food. Clyde was named to the committee appointed to see President Reynolds about it. Mrs. Hubell, who had been in charge, resigned and Mrs. Hulen who had managed the women's dormitory took over. This necessitated the women taking their meals with the men and some improvement in the fare. The trustees had dinner with them, too—"strong men of influence and wisdom."

Getting away from the campus during the spring, Clyde walked twelve miles to a mountain where he spent a cold night alone but watched a glorious sunrise. He walked the twelve miles back in five hours, arriving home "very much exhausted but with the feeling that I had spent the night and day profitably as well as pleasantly." Perhaps the outing helped to prepare him for the disappointment that was on the horizon. Clyde had been active in the work of the Y.M.C.A. and had decided that he was the logical person to become its president during his senior year. But the nominating committee brought another name and Clyde was faced with a struggle to carry on what he knew to be right. "In this incident I see a foretaste of the struggles that will come from disappointments that will come in later life, perhaps in the matter of appointments. Oh God, fortify me against that day."

The European War continued slowly to press in upon him. A number of American ships had been sunk and a special session of Congress had met on April 2 and was advised by President Wilson that a declaration of war was required. The resolution was passed by both houses three days later, and America was finally at war with Germany. A draft was proposed that required all males between the ages of nineteen and twenty-five, who were not engaged in essential work, to serve. Clyde was included. "My plan now is to make no effort to evade it if I am included in the call." The bill passed with amended age limits of twenty-one to thirty-one; an officer training site was ordered for Fort Logan H. Roots in Little Rock, and Hendrix students and professors began to apply. Most were accepted. On the spur of the moment Clyde obtained and prepared an application, but at the last minute decided to wait. He was glad he did.

2

Europe

—⚬⫷⫸⚬—

"For some time I have been considering the question of what my duty is in the present crisis."
—Diary, May 1, 1917

Clyde's obvious choices were limited—volunteer for some branch of the service with the possibility of a commission or wait and be drafted. Other less certain options were to seek employment in the Y.M.C.A. doing religious work or take a chance that his ministerial status might exempt him from the draft entirely. Either would defer him from military service. A ministerial classification was not entirely out of the question since a few local draft boards had deferred Hendrix ministerial students, judging their courses there equivalent to those of a seminary. A talk with the authorities at the draft board in Little Rock added no additional information.

Just as he was considering his next step, Sallie wrote to say that she and Brice had the measles and Mamma and Papa were likely to have them, too. He was needed immediately at home to help with the crop. Since the semester was not yet over, Clyde had to make arrangements to finish his work, but his professors were understanding and he was able to leave the same day. The next morning he was home and working in the field. There was corn to be planted and cantaloupes to be hoed. The work was hard but a refreshing change.

Clyde discovered Sallie and Brice were under the weather but not seriously ill. However, Grandma Smith's daughter, Anna, was near death with tuberculosis. She died in a few days. Only thirty-two years old, she had been sick for many years. "I have never known a person who was more patient with suffering or more cheerful under adverse circumstances," Clyde reported in his diary.

A newspaper article soon announced that the Hendrix faculty had decided to dismiss school three weeks early because of the war. No examinations would be given and daily grades would be recorded for the semester. This meant Clyde would miss only three weeks of school rather than six. He could return to school in early June, complete his courses, and go directly from there to his summer's preaching assignment in the Fayetteville District.

A letter from his roommate, Meux, brought additional news of Clyde's election as editor-in-chief of the student newspaper, the *Bull Dog.* Another informed him that W. R. Schisler, who had been elected president of the Y.M.C.A., would not be returning to school and Clyde had been elected in his place. A busy semester was in the offing, and Clyde began to think immediately of resigning the Y.M.C.A. presidency to serve in his original office as chair of the religious service committee because he thought it more important. The best news from Meux was of winning the Mirror Prize for the best literary article of the year. Although the honor was significant, "The five dollars will be very acceptable."

But for now there were sick folks to care for and chores that began shortly after five o'clock in the morning and continued until sunset. His original plan to study two hours a day was quickly abandoned. There was also a lot of work to be done around the house, a yard to clean up, a room to paper, dead trees to take down. The days passed quickly with little reading except for the Arkansas *Gazette* and a daily passage from the Bible. One Sunday afternoon was spent on Jack London's *Sea Wolf,* which he judged inferior to *Call of the Wild,* but was not a complete waste of time since it called attention to Browning's "Caliban," which he read with interest and pleasure. Frank Musser dropped by for a brief visit on his way to preach the graduation sermon at Nashville and Blevins high schools. He was thinking about the military chaplaincy, he said.

A storm that damaged Papa's timber necessitated a trip to the logging camp at Graysonia where he was working, and afforded another opportunity to be with him at his work. "I found it to be a typical log camp with all the inconveniences and unpleasantness incident to camp life. . . . The food is poor, the beds hard but the worst part [is] that the men with whom he is constantly associated are, for the most part, devoid of any sense of moral purity. . . . Papa seems no nearer a Christian life than when I was with him last."

Without a doubt, the best part of the experience at home was being with Sallie. "She approaches more nearly every day an ideal girl."

On June 5, 1917, Clyde registered for the draft in McCaskill along with about sixty others, and returned to Conway to complete the semester at Hendrix. A night with Musser in Little Rock provided some time to visit Hendrix men in the Officer's Training Camp at Fort Roots, and to see more of army life firsthand. Information was also obtained at the naval recruiting office about the hospital corps. There Clyde learned it was possible to enlist as a second apprentice and spend six months in training at the Great Lakes Naval Station. This now seemed to him the best way to go. A chance meeting with Jerry Wallace, now serving in St. Mark's Mission in Pulaski Heights in Little Rock, prompted a second night's stay.

Clyde arrived back in Conway on June 7 in time to help get the campus ready for the one hundred or so preachers who attended the summer Pastor's School. Paul Kern of Southern Methodist University and Harry Ward of Boston University School of Theology were the featured speakers. Kern told Clyde that the faculty at SMU (the university opened in 1915) was now fully capable of doing the work being offered, and from Kern's lectures Clyde concluded the school in Dallas "is more modern in its teaching and more radical in some of its views" than Emory as it was represented to him by Dr. Sledd. Pacifist Harry Ward's views on war and peace caused Clyde to change his mind about joining the navy and to resolve again to look for something in the war effort of a religious nature.

Brother Davidson, the presiding elder, who was to direct his summer work, was present at the pastor's school and together they planned a schedule. Brother J. F. Carter, a younger minister with whom Clyde was also to work, was there, too. The thought of being in the heart of the Ozarks again was invigorating, but what to do in the future remained uncertain. Whether to remain in school, and be drafted, or accept an appointment to a church at the annual conference, which would provide an exemption, now were the obvious questions. For a brief time, Clyde was also giving some consideration to serving on the mission field. This would, of course, involve Sallie, and he needed to discuss it with her. Before he could do it, however, a conversation with C. N. Weems, missionary to Korea who was living in Conway while on furlough, shined the white light of reality on that idea. Funds to support missionaries were limited and it was very difficult to get accepted by the church. Specialists were more in demand than "all 'round men." However, Clyde persisted in exploring the idea further and wrote W. W. Pinson, secretary of the Foreign Mission Board of the Methodist Episcopal Church, South, for advice. He was not encouraging.

Except for his English course, which required Clyde to take an examination after the opening of school in the fall, the incompletes were shortly removed. At last he was within twenty hours of graduating and able to finish in one semester. But the immediate business at hand was the revival meeting in Highfill which was about to begin.

Leaving Conway by train for Highfill the night of July 10, Clyde missed the connection in Rogers and had to lay over a day and a night before there was another train, but the Methodist preacher Brother Yancy proved to be both a native of Tipton County, Tennessee, and a willing host during the interim. The train to Highfill, twenty miles to the west, finally came at eight o'clock the next morning. Once there, the pastor, Brother Chancellor, was waiting for him at the station. A good man, he nevertheless lacked the ability to express himself adequately in public address and had few social graces. Clyde took notice. "These two failings almost inevitably unfit a man for preaching the gospel in our age or in any other for that matter." The work to be done in the revival he knew would fall heavily on him.

Poles were cut for the revival tent but it failed to arrive and services were begun in the church building. "I felt that somebody had failed to keep his promise with me and that bore on my mind rather heavily." That proved to be an omen of things yet to come. The crowds dwindled to a handful after two weeks and on July 15 the meeting closed. All together eleven were converted and two joined the church. This marked the first time that Clyde had been entirely on his own to conduct a revival and his awareness of God's presence made it a success despite poor attendance and few conversions. He was paid $36.50 for the two weeks' work.

The schedule next called for him to open in Goshen but allowed time for a morning in Fayetteville. There he paid a visit to the pastor, Brother Boggs, and had a look around the university. "I went to Gray Hall, the dormitory in which I had roomed and found my old room. . . . I shall always have a peculiar tenderness toward that room in which I spent nine of the most eventful months of my life. . . . It was there that I fought the struggle with my call to the ministry and dedicated my service to God." There he also began to keep a journal. By chance, Professor Winfrey of Hendrix was teaching in the summer session at Fayetteville, and Clyde was able to make arrangements for the French course he needed in the fall.

The mail car left at one o'clock in the afternoon for the two hour trip to Goshen. Since the meeting was not scheduled to begin until Wednesday night, the pastor was not in town but at his home four miles away. There was no alternative but to make the trip on foot. The parsonage, where Brother Ditterline was living with George, his fifteen-year-old son, was a small cabin on top of the mountain, half a mile off the road. Flies swarmed in the house like bees, beds were unmade, the floors unswept; food was littered on the kitchen floor "and everything had a musty, mouldy odor." "I have recently taken a special pride in my ability to adjust myself to any condition" Clyde wrote, "and here was a chance to put that talent to the test." But the scenery and view from the top of the mountain were "dazzling."

A bare handful of people showed up the first night of the revival. The next day the tent, with a seating capacity of 500, was stretched and ready, but heavy rain reduced the crowd to a remnant on Friday night. Monday there was time enough to go back to Fayetteville for a conversation with the officials at the draft board there. The selective service act provided that students enrolled in divinity school on May 18, 1917, were exempt, along with all ordained ministers. While Clyde was clearly not eligible under either of these provisions, a slim possibility remained that so many ministerial students were at Hendrix it might be considered a divinity school. But that was too much of a stretch for Clyde to be comfortable, and he left Fayetteville for Goshen having decided "I wouldn't lift a finger for the difference between being drafted and not being drafted. I was willing to leave it entirely with the Lord."

His serial number, 618, made it likely that he would be called in the second draft. Brice had gone in the first draft along with a number of neighbors, Sallie reported. She wanted assurance that Clyde would not be taken. Had she known what he was doing, she might have been even more concerned that he might "be taken" in another way. Lake Clark, one of three daughters in a home where Clyde was entertained during the revival in Goshen, had been attracted to him and asked him to "correspond" with her after the meeting was over. Being "somewhat attracted to her," and unable to think of a way to tell her diplomatically about his relation to Sallie, Clyde agreed, but learned a lesson. "This incident has taught me . . . that I must not become so intimate with any young woman that she would be justified in thinking that I could ever become more to her than a mere friend." This resolve, however, did not keep him from deciding "to correspond with her until I see a suitable place to leave it off."

In addition to the time he spent with Lake, Clyde had managed to read James Stalker's *Life of St. Paul* and William Henry Fitchett's *Wesley and His Century,* noting the parallels between the two individuals. Both Paul and Wesley sought peace of mind in their early lives, struggled trying to attain it through their own efforts, failed, and were finally forced to fall back on the grace of Christ for what they desired—a story with which Clyde obviously identified. Once again he confirmed his conviction that "without the co-operation of the Holy Spirit a preacher is unable to touch a human soul," and judged his own sermons as "too little dependent upon the Spirit's power."

The revival in Goshen lasted a day less than three weeks, a week longer than planned. There were fifteen conversions and eleven joined the church. Clyde was paid "liberally" for his services but failed to say exactly how much. On the trip back to Fayetteville he decided "the country between Fayetteville and Rogers is the prettiest I have ever seen."

Pea Ridge, the site of a battle during the Civil War, was next. For once the Methodists were the leading church in the town of 400, but Clyde soon discovered that the pastor was given to harsh criticism of his flock. There wasn't much enthusiasm in any of the services, but those during the day were best. Most of the people attending were already church members and the "unsaved seemed unconcerned." The weather was bad, too. But in the home where he was staying, he talked often with Mrs. Anderson, "a remarkable character" who claimed to have received the "baptism of the Holy Spirit." The song leader, Brother Ezra Ricketts, took him in his car across the state line into Missouri, his first visit to the state, and Brother Putman, a merchant, took him and the Presbyterian preacher to see the Elkhorn Tavern on the battlefield. Pea Ridge also turned out to be the home of a Hendrix classmate, A. W. Martin, who later became a Methodist preacher and member of the faculty of the Perkins School of Theology at Southern Methodist University.

The meeting lasted two weeks and ended with twenty conversions and "four reclamations." Twenty people joined the Methodist church and three the Baptist. The most notable and memorable event was the conversion of the blacksmith, A. L. Warren.

Clyde had expected to go directly to Robinson, but, at Brother Carter's direction, he rode the train to Elm Springs for the night. The next day he made the ten-mile drive with Carter in a buggy to Robinson. It turned out to be a town with a store, a post office (in the store), two churches, and a school. The big tent was up by quitting time the day they arrived, but the evening congregation was small even counting the dogs, one of whom was so noisy that prayer had to be suspended while he was put out. The meeting finally produced twelve conversions, but the services never really got moving. The people were cold and refused to do any personal work to promote the revival. But Clyde had a nagging sense that the lack of success was partly due to his neglect of duty. He had spent afternoons in visits to local sights, including a cave that he explored with Carter. There was no way Clyde Martin could resist a cave. But on reflection he decided that such adventures did not promote the cause, and he determined to say in the words of Mr. Wesley, "leisure and I have parted." The meeting closed on Sunday, September 2. They paid him more for his services than his guilty conscience would allow him to take.

And then he was off, "with some of the same anxiety that must have been in Saint Paul's heart as he looked toward Rome," to hold the long anticipated meeting in Randolph, Tennessee. After spending a day in Memphis, he arrived in Tipton to find nobody to meet him, but he managed to get to Randolph just as the preaching service began. The large crowd included "most of my people," none of whom was having any active part in church affairs. Uncles Dick and Ed had given over to drink again, and Uncle Perry was holding a grudge against a man he suspected of burning his barn. All three had automobiles "which had been at least a small factor in their downfall."

In the now usual pattern, the tent failed to arrive, but the pastor, Brother Wadsworth, had made good preparation. Clyde preached "straight ahead" until Sunday without visible results, but then things began to change. Uncle Dick was reclaimed on Sunday evening, Uncle Ed had come earlier, but Uncle Perry and his wife didn't come down until the middle of the second week. "I had prayed for his conversion with more fervor, it seemed to me, than I had ever prayed for anything." Throughout the time Clyde was warmly received in the homes in Randolph. "I worked at it harder, enjoyed it more and felt that it was the most profitable [meeting] I had ever been in." While there he also completed the sale of his timber for $200 and leased the land for six years.

After the meeting closed in Randolph, Clyde went back to school having held five meetings in eleven weeks, preached 130 sermons, witnessed 90 conversions and reclamations, and handed out $15 worth of Bibles. All totaled, he had received $250 for his work. Despite being a week late, he had no problem in getting registered for the hours he needed for graduation and set to work. He was enrolled in "Anthology of Latin Verse," French philosophy, English composition, and English history. In addition he had to take an examination on two books of the Vulgate and write a thesis. His election as editor of the *Bull Dog* was nullified by a change in the constitution of the Joint Session of the Literary Societies, but he was actually relieved not to have the responsibility. Roommate Meux, whom he had not expected, returned to school, an event "for which I was devoutly thankful." The total enrollment at Hendrix declined to 230; only about 100 former students returned.

His work as president of the Y.M.C.A. demanded a great deal of time, but his heavy load of courses limited what he could do. The probability of being drafted occupied him too. Learning more about the war work of the Y.M.C.A., Clyde applied for a position. He was aware when he did, however, that being subject to the draft made his chance of being accepted unlikely. The same was true of his being granted an exemption because of his ministerial student status at Hendrix. A trip to Little Rock to preach for Frank Musser in early November broke the monotony and enabled him to visit Camp Pike for another look at military life. Musser had been accepted for Y.M.C.A. service and expected to leave for Russia in two weeks. His invitation to Clyde to fill in for the rest of the conference year at the Capitol View Church was tempting but impossible to accept.

The special event of the semester, not counting the fire that destroyed the college heating plant, was the showing of *Birth of a*

Nation, "the most elaborate and expensive motion picture ever made." Faculty and students bought $3,700 worth of Liberty Bonds in the Second Liberty Loan Campaign, and the practice was adopted in the dining room of having two meatless and one wheatless meal each day to help the war effort.

A telephone call from home on November 2, 1917, brought Clyde the news that the expected draft call had come. He was ordered to report for a physical examination on November 6, 1917. In response, he requested permission to report in Faulkner County, where Conway was located, for the physical. When the transfer was approved, he filed affidavits claiming exemption from service on the grounds of being a ministerial student. Since the board in Faulkner County had already granted exemptions to two Hendrix ministerial students, he was optimistic that his request would be approved, too. It was, but final approval had to be granted by the district board. The reason for making the application is given in a diary entry: "I felt some hesitancy in asking for exemption and if it had been a question between going in or staying out, I think I would not have made any claim but I had been considering for some time . . . going into Y.M.C.A. War Work and had made application . . . for an appointment."

His application was approved by the Y.M.C.A. War Work Council. "This [is] not equivalent to an appointment but is a long step toward one." He would enter the Y.M.C.A. college for four weeks training in January 1918. In the meantime, however, a new draft law was passed that revoked all exemptions. Various representatives from the military came on campus to speak; the Governor himself came and spoke on war conditions, and Clyde read Arthur Guy Empey's *Over the Top.* "The book contains some of the most horrible and gruesome scenes imaginable described in such a straight forward, matter-of-fact way that it seems that the writer is relating something that he has imagined or dreamed rather than something he has actually seen."

Sallie came to Conway so they would spend Thanksgiving Day

together. It was her first visit to Hendrix. They had not seen each other for six months, but the opportunity for a "long talk" that he hoped to have with her never materialized. Certainly he told her what he was planning for the future.

The next day, November 30, Clyde, W. H. Bryant, and Stanford Hayden went to Little Rock to inquire about a hospital unit that was being raised to higher strength. One hundred and two enlisted men were needed by December 15, and all three signed up on the spot. Since the new draft law had revoked all exemptions, "I felt confident that I would be called in the next draft . . . so it was a question with me to choose between the hospital work and the infantry and since the former is much more in line with my life calling I decided to join." He passed the physical without difficulty and was sworn in with the other two men. Eventually the unit would contain nine men from Hendrix. They expected to be called to active duty between the first and tenth of January 1918. "I am of the opinion that I shall have a better chance for religious work as a regularly enlisted man than as a Y. secretary for the reason that a great many men will consider an able-bodied young man in Y. service as a slacker which attitude would completely block a man's chances for doing good."

The first page of the diary for 1918 contains a summary of the reasons that led Clyde to volunteer for military service. "I felt sure that sooner or later I should be definitely attached to some part of the fighting force," he wrote. A visit with a chaplain at Fort Roots had convinced him there was no place for which he was qualified in the Chaplain's Corps. No openings appeared in the second best alternative, the Y.M.C.A., and the consideration of how soldiers might view "an able bodied Y. man" put the whole idea of Y. service in a negative light. His preaching commitments for the summer of 1917 and the longer term of enlistment it required thwarted the possibility of entering the Navy Hospital Corps. Finally, his conscience would not allow him to accept appointment to full-time work in a local church in order to avoid the draft. So he enlisted in the branch of service most compatible with his commitment to ministry, the Army Medical Corps. "Thus, gradually my mind was made up and I shall never have it to say that I enlisted without due consideration."

Clyde's trip home for the Christmas holidays was delayed three days by a case of roseola. Once on the way he stopped in Little Rock for a talk with Dr. Snodgrass, the man who organized the hospital unit in which he had enlisted. The doctor confirmed that he expected the unit would be called just after the first of January; the initial period of training would be at Fort Roots in Little Rock. After a visit with Meux, who was now serving the 28th Street Church, Clyde took the train to Prescott, finally arriving at home on Monday, Christmas Eve. He told Mamma about enlisting and she was disappointed that he had not tried for the exemption or taken a church at conference. For some reason he did not tell Papa until later. "This may be my last Christmas at home, yet I am not going to allow that possibility to interfere with the enjoyment of it for myself nor for the others. In fact I have succeeded in making the matter of coming back or not coming back a question of secondary importance. The question that faces me is this, 'Will I do my full duty?' "

Clyde also expressed anxiety about the temptations he might expect in the army. "Will I be able to hold my own against the forces of evil, is a question that is constantly recurring." The ones that concerned him most were not the blatant abuses, but the subtle manifestations that might lead to irreverence or failing to continue to seek to influence persons for God. That he might lack time for Bible study and prayer was on his mind, too, but, finally, "I have this confidence in God, namely, that by some means or other he will keep me from wandering completely away from him."

To spend time with Papa, Clyde had to work, since "it is his nature to work." Working together provided the opportunity for talk about a variety of topics, including the Christian life and its practical benefits. "A man who for almost sixty years has given almost no thought to spiritual matters is naturally rather callous toward doctrinal questions," so Clyde stressed the practical implications of Christian living. They also talked about the reasons that led him to join the hospital corps since Papa, like Nannie Jacob, thought it was a mistake to volunteer. But Jack Martin soon understood that his son "was not rushing into the service from any fool hardy notion or any love of adventure." It is clear that he knew his son well enough to be suspicious. In fact, Sally remembered they were afraid his sense of adventure would lead him to do something foolish and dangerous just for the experience. They were not entirely wrong. All of his life Clyde Martin was an almost totally fearless individual. On Sunday following Christmas, when Papa left for the lumber camp, they shared a sad and "speechless on my part" farewell.

While at home there were trips to Belton to see friends, Sunday services to attend in McCaskill with Brice and Sallie, and a night in Blevins with Grandma Smith, "one of the finest and most consecrated old ladies I have ever known." The time spent with Sallie was the best. They talked for hours. "The more I see of her the better pleased I am with her as a life companion." He liked her religious development and found it similar to his own, but most of all "her strongest point is her practical good sense. Tho not highly educated so far as books go, she is able to make the most of any situation." He added, "I congratulate myself that I have in her a real jewel, a pearl of great price."

He left for Conway a day later than he had planned. "If I had allowed myself to do it, I could have become grief-stricken almost over the fact that I was looking for what might be the last time on the scenes of the old home but for the sake of the others I suppressed these emotions and went away feeling that I would be permitted to go back again." Mamma went with him as far as Prescott. There he learned that Bryce and David Cummins were both already in service. Looking back over the holidays Clyde said, "I feel no pang or regret except that they are gone." New Years Day came and went without a single resolution. He finally got to Conway late at night and went home to a "cold and desolate" room.

He did not have long to wait. On Sunday, January 5, 1918, he received word that he had been ordered to Camp Greenleaf, Fort Oglethorpe, Georgia, for training. As always, he was introspective. "These are momentous hours, the real magnitude of which I shall not know until I have seen farther on. I realize that I am about to change worlds. A clean break in my life is about to occur."

Sunday, January 6, 1918, two Hendrix members of the hospital unit received orders to report for active duty. Their orders included Clyde's name with an incorrect address, which explained why he had not also received notification. He had to begin his military career by tracking down his orders. With scarcely enough time to pack his belongings before taking the train, he had a brief conversation with Dr. Reynolds, president of Hendrix, shook hands with a few friends, and was gone. Stanford Hayden rode with him as far as Little Rock, and they agreed not to leave Little Rock before Thursday night and to meet in Lytle, Georgia.

Clyde reached Adona, Arkansas, the address to which his orders had been sent, by nine o'clock Monday morning and found them waiting at the post office there. Somebody else's had been sent to his address in Belton. The postmaster said he intended to return them on the next train, so it was fortunate Clyde did not delay leaving Conway. Because of his agreement with Stanford not to leave Little Rock before Thursday, he still had four days in which to complete some work on his courses. Finding a room in Little Rock, he managed to read five to eight hours a day, wrote letters to Sallie and Papa, and consulted a dentist and a lawyer. In the event of his death, he directed his Tennessee property should go to Papa for use during his lifetime, and then to Sallie to "be used by her until her death or marriage and in either event it will go to Mamma to be used by her until her death, if she be living, and if she be dead or at the time of her death it is to go unconditionally to Hendrix College." The obligation he had assumed to his Aunts Vinie and Alice were to be covered by $1,000 of government insurance, the benefits of which they would share equally in case of his death.

When Hayden failed to appear by Thursday as agreed, Clyde and Bill Bryant left Little Rock on the ten o'clock train. In Memphis Bill left for Chattanooga, but Fay Russell turned up on the train coming from Little Rock. Snow delayed their arrival in Nashville, but Clyde passed the time listening to an "entirely unedifying and unenlightening" argument between a Church of God preacher and some "traveling men and a sailor" about miracles. He drew two lessons from the experience: (1) "Zeal without judgment and moderation may be harmful to the cause it seeks to advance and (2) matters pertaining to the Bible and religion have not ceased to be interesting as topics of conversation." At 4:00 A.M. they boarded the sleeper for Chattanooga but were still in Nashville at 9:00. The train finally was off at 11:00 and Clyde ate lunch in the dining car "for the novelty of it—just knowing how other people live was worth more than the price." The price of his meal was a steep $1.20. Reading Davidson's Old Testament theology book was dull, but the Cumberland Mountains were lovely. The Tennessee River was frozen solid when they crossed.

Bill Bryant was waiting when they arrived in Chattanooga and together they took a room for the night. When Hayden failed to appear the next morning Clyde took the opportunity to attend services at the First Methodist Church while waiting for him. Sunday afternoon was spent looking around the city and meeting with A. N. Chambliss, an attorney in the Hamilton Building, to prepare a will. He took the necessary information from Clyde and agreed to mail the document when it was ready. He did not charge for his services. It was, he said, his contribution to the war effort. Early Monday morning Clyde had his picture made in a cap and gown for the Hendrix College yearbook, the *Troubadour*. Then Bryant, Russell, Porter Weaver, and Clyde reported to camp to begin their military service.

The largest medical training facility in the United States, Camp Greenleaf was located at the north end of Chickamauga Park, opposite Fort Oglethorpe, ten miles out of Chattanooga. Combined, the camp and the fort contained 30,000 men. After the usual delays the Hendrix men were assigned to Headquarters Company, Battalion 14, a unit consisting of 120 enlisted men, an acting captain, four lieutenants, and a major. Instead of being quartered in permanent barracks as they had expected, they were assigned to six-man tents without floors. Sleeping gear consisted of a steel cot, a bag of straw, and three wool blankets to protect against the cold. They were next taken to be sworn in but after a two-hour wait the officers discovered it had already been done. Long waits, Private William C. Martin discovered on his first day, were "to be a part of army service." He never got used to it and disliked that aspect of the military almost more than anything else.

After a restless night because of the cold, the day officially began at 6:00 A.M. Following breakfast at 6:30, there was a ditch to be dug, but "work was what I wanted and I felt good when I was put to doing something." William C.'s first military responsibility and leadership opportunity came in the afternoon when he was put in charge of the incinerator. Such are the benefits of a college education. The day ended with lights out at 9:30 P.M. and the onset of another cold night.

A routine was quickly established, but the bulk of the days were spent gathering wood, stretching tents, and burning rubbish. Most of the men in the company had been assigned from Fort Slocum, New York, and Camp Meade, Maryland. They ranged in age from eighteen to thirty-five, in occupation from "monkey trainers to dentists," and came from many different states. Most were profane and told vulgar stories, too. "For a time these words grated on my nerves terribly but already I am growing accustomed to hearing them and it will soon be a task for me to keep from using them myself." But he recognized these troops to be "at heart real men" and enjoyed working with them. The fact that Martin was a preacher became known the first day, but nothing more was said about it. William C. soon discovered there was a Y.M.C.A. hut less than a quarter of a mile from the tents which offered reading and writing materials, a movie projector, and some athletic equipment. There was a good staff and lectures every evening on a variety of topics ranging from sex to "being happy." It was obvious now, he said, that "the Y.M.C.A. is the means that God has put into my hands here for keeping close to Him."

After a week in camp all of the Hendrix men who had enlisted together except Martin and Porter Weaver, who were to remain together for the duration, were assigned to other parts of the country and shipped out. Weaver was from Mountain Home, Arkansas.

Drill was twice a day, at 8:30 A.M. and 2:00 P.M. It consisted of fitness exercises, hikes, litter drills, and sanitary drill. Classes were held in the morning from 9:30 until 11:25, and two hours in the afternoon. Lectures were given on subjects such as anatomy, first aid, prevention of disease, care of hospitals and clinics. They learned the proper use of the gas mask and were exposed to chlorine and tear gas in the "gas house," making more vivid the horrors of war. Always there were fatigue duties, too. Wednesday, Thursday, and Friday, Clyde was assigned to kitchen police— peeling potatoes, washing pots and pans, carrying wood and water, serving food. Cold and exposure finally got the best of him, and he answered sick call three days in a row. In spite of it all, William C. still managed to take the examination in Old Testament theology, leaving only the one in English history between him and a college degree. In short order, he was appointed private first class and passed the examination to become a corporal. Three weeks to the day after arriving at Camp Greenleaf, he became Corporal William C. Martin. Rank had its privileges. At meals he could move to the front of the mess line, was exempt from fatigue duties, which afforded more spare time, and received a 20 percent increase in pay from $30 to $36 a month. The increase almost covered the monthly premium on the $10,000 military life insurance policy he purchased.

February 10, the unit was divided into three parts, Headquarters, 13th Evacuation Hospital, and 14th Evacuation Hospital, and assigned to permanent quarters. They had been in tents for four weeks. The 13th Evacuation Hospital was formally recognized on February 13 and moved into Barracks 13. "If 13 is an unlucky number there is small chance that we will ever get across the ocean." Although they walked half a mile through the mud carrying their gear to their new quarters, it was a good experience for Corporal Martin. "As I pulled thru the mud this morning with a fifty pound burden on my shoulders, I was enjoying deeply the assurance that no condition could stand between me and my Savior so long as I kept my heart clean." Martin shared a front room in the building with Corporals Stark, Young, and Morrison Allen. All three were from New York. Bill Stark was from White Plains, Allen from New York City, and Charles Young from Brooklyn. Clyde was well satisfied with the arrangement, glad to be out of the cold.

His greatest pleasure came from watching and relating to the men, but he stayed involved with the Y.M.C.A. and resolved to do more religious work on his own. Somehow he found time to write two articles on camp life, which were published in the Blevins newspaper.

Corporal Martin was in his new quarters only a short time before he was ordered to take charge of a squad of twelve men and moved to another barracks. Weaver was one of the twelve. "I am finding in him a staunch and dependable friend." Shortly after receiving this new assignment, Martin was rewarded with his first twenty-four hour pass and managed for the first time to tour the city of Chattanooga. By chance he met Stanford Hayden at the Y.M.C.A. and spent most of the time with him and his three friends. They did little touring, mostly moving from one picture show and drugstore to another. Seeing Hayden was worth it, but not much else was enjoyable to William C. "By the experience of the afternoon I was shown how limited is the range of some men in the matter of finding amusement." He was back in camp on Sunday morning in time to hear "a great sermon by a great preacher," Bishop Theodore Henderson of the Methodist Episcopal Church; that same day he learned there was another ministerial student, McKindley Payn, in the company. He regretted having to miss the bishop's second sermon but needed the time to prepare for the sergeants' examination, which he passed. February 25, William C. Martin's warrant for promotion came through. He had been in the army just six weeks, but now the men called him "Sarge," and a few of them named him "Bill."

About the middle of March they were moved again as the unit was brought up to full strength in anticipation of assignment overseas. Sgt. Martin was put in charge of the second platoon and a barracks housing 42 men. All of the 125 draftees now assigned to the 13th were from Toledo, Ohio, and with few exceptions all had been rejected in the first draft. "They had all kinds of physical defects. Flat feet, web toes, six toes, tuberculosis, venereal diseases and so on through the entire category of ordinary diseases." The range of their nationalities was broad, too, and "roll call was a great tussle every morning for the first few days." The youngest man in the group, Abraham Margules, was a Russian Jew who had been in the country only six years. He was from Brooklyn. Those unfit for duty were replaced.

Despite the heavy demands, Martin found time when not on duty to climb Lookout Mountain, and in May to make a trip to Atlanta to attend the General Conference of the Methodist Episcopal Church, South, and visit R. T. Ross, a friend studying at Emory School of Theology. Ross took him to see the theological buildings and the chapel, "one of the most magnificent rooms I have ever been inside." There he saw chairs made for Asbury and stood in John Wesley's pulpit. "I almost felt that I was treading on holy ground."

After a good night's sleep "between real sheets" and a "tasty" breakfast he toured the rest of the campus—seven buildings on fifty-three acres. Of the 210 students enrolled, 150 were in the school of medicine. At the site of the General Conference he and Ross met Dr. Reynolds and Professor Greene, who were delegates. Bishop Eugene R. Hendrix, for whom the Arkansas college is named, preached at the morning worship hour, but Martin had to admit he "was somewhat disappointed in the sermon." The opportunity to see his friend B. F. Musser was a highlight of the trip. Together they toured Fort McPherson, where Musser was chaplain of a motor repair company. Martin left Atlanta on the night train, "feeling that the day had been very profitable . . . in that it had redirected my attention to the great work of the M.E. Church, South and had strengthened me by the association with men whose ideals are in harmony with my own." He was disappointed only in not getting to see Bishop Warren Candler. "To go to Atlanta without seeing him was almost like going to Mecca and failing to visit the shrine of Mohammed." Had he known what Martin said, Candler would doubtless have liked the analogy, and agreed with Martin's assessment of the serious nature of this lost opportunity. He was a man with a very large ego.

The new recruits were soon trained and brought into good physical condition. "I enjoyed the work greatly," Martin said, "and the experience of being in charge of a body of men was of considerable value." He added, "I am not in favor of universal military training if it results, as it most probably would, in the maintenance of a large standing army . . . but I do believe that we should have some system that would give to our young men (and young women as well) the benefits that I see coming every day to the men who are here." His own training was enhanced by practical, hands-on experience in sixteen days of duty at Newell's Sanitarium in Chattanooga. He witnessed a number of operations and was given instruction in the care of wounds. "I enjoyed the work a great deal and from it I saw that hospital work would not be irksome to me." While in the city, he heard William Jennings Bryan lecture at the Christian Church and shook hands with him. Spring came and its beauty reminded him once again "that war was entirely out of place in the quiet beauty of a new spring."

Martin was also working on his French, which he had studied in college, with the help of phonographic records. In addition, the Y.M.C.A. provided language instruction. By the time the unit reached France, he was proficient enough to act as its interpreter, and half a century later could still carry on a conversation with his great-granddaughter in the language.

Sherwood Eddy's book *With Our Soldiers in France* provided some helpful information about life at the front. A more moving picture was given in the letters of Alfred Eugene Casalis, a French theological student who was killed at the age of nineteen. Still his most rewarding and satisfying experience remained the comradeship with the men, something he had not expected. "There is something exhilarating in the association with real men on an equal footing." He learned about discipline, too. "I have considered a number of problems regarding discipline which has been a part of my work and altho a majority of army officers seem to have decided otherwise, I am firmly convinced that the best sort of discipline is that born of deep-seated respect and devotion rather than of fear." He added, "I have had no difficulty in dealing with the men and my orders have been obeyed." It is no exaggeration to say that this same philosophy directed his association with those placed under his charge through his entire life.

On May 30, 1918, the 13th and 14th Evacuation Hospitals were ordered to Camp Gordon, twelve miles from Atlanta. Camp Gordon was a National Army Training Camp, hurriedly built to house 150,000 troops. Its base hospital had 43 wards with a capacity of 4,000 patients. The 13th Evac was housed in vacant wards for two nights and then, once again, went into tents. Martin bunked with Sergeants Stark, Ross Colbert from Claypool, Indiana, and Morrison Allen. Stark was the only married man among them. All three had been promoted at the same time. The majority of men were assigned to work in the wards, but Martin had little, sometimes nothing, to do.

He did finally hear the patron saint of southern Methodism when Bishop Candler preached at Wesley Church and, as an added bonus, attended a Sunday school class taught by the bishop's brother, Asa, the mayor of Atlanta. But his mind was more on other, more personal matters. The hospital had received orders to France but was unable to embark until its war strength had been raised from 179 to 237 men, and currently none were available. All hope of getting a furlough before embarkation had vanished. But, as always, the army worked according to its own logic and to Martin's great surprise he and eight other men were granted a week's leave. In ten days he was on his way home to get married.

One of the great decisions of my life has been made. When I was home Christmas, Sallie and I discussed the question of marriage and at that time she said that she thought it best not to marry until I had returned from the war. I told her that I considered it a question for the woman to decide since she had greater responsibilities in the matter and that I would not urge the question at all. Nothing more was said about it until about a week ago when she wrote that she believed she had rather have a husband than a sweetheart in the army. At first I thought she was merely in fun but in a second letter she made it plain that she was in earnest about it and after considering the matter carefully and after consulting Sgt. Stark who married a few days before he enlisted and Uncle Noth Thompson, I wrote her that if she had considered the matter carefully and was still of the same opinion, that we would be married when I came home and that I would bring her back to Atlanta to stay with me as long as I was there.

Whether he knew it or not, Sallie became ill after W. C., as she now called him, left for the army. In time she admitted her illness was caused by a combination of loneliness and grief. She missed him. Marriage, even with the uncertainties created by the war, was preferable to being alone and she decided to go ahead. The required permission of the colonel was asked and granted. A hurried trip to Fort McPherson to see Musser brought the startling news that he, too, was to marry the following Wednesday, but he agreed, if he could make the arrangements, to officiate at the ceremony in Blevins.

The furlough came through on Tuesday, June 24, 1918. That morning, before leaving, William C. found and negotiated the rent on a room for Sallie. Sgt. Stark's wife went with him and she said, "the girl would like the room." As luck would have it, he missed his connection in Memphis and had to lay over for an entire day in the city. He went to the wharf and took a steamboat ride to see the fleet anchored on the Arkansas side of the river and assessed the prospects for a crop. Most of the rest of the time he spent at the house of Charlie Berlin, Grandma Ballard's nephew. When he finally reached Prescott in the afternoon he was surprised to find Papa waiting for him at the station. "On the way home we talked about almost everything except the main object of my visit which was not mentioned." The comment offers an interesting, though confusing, insight into their relation to one another and to Jack Martin's feelings about the marriage of his son and stepdaughter.

Sallie met the train in Blevins and "was looking unusually well." She had made all the arrangements for the wedding. Everyone "seemed willing to the agreement except Brice and I think he was embarrassed more than unwilling." It is not difficult to imagine how small-town Arkansas folks might have been prone to talk about the marriage of a stepbrother and sister on the spur of the moment in the midst of a war, but we will never know the real cause of Brice's distress. Through the years he and William C. Martin were closer than brothers often are.

There was always work to be done at home. "I was glad of the opportunity to swing a plow once more." He rode horseback to Blevins and spent a night with Grandma Smith. Tom Smith took him in his car to Washington to purchase the marriage license. He and Sallie went to church together in McCaskill on Sunday morning, and they asked him to preach at the evening service. He agreed and spoke to a large congregation. "Monday morning was a period of seriousness with me which came near being despondency. In the afternoon I was to take one of the most important steps of my life and one which would mean more than almost any other such occurrence for determining the usefulness of my life. That hour, however, was too late for decision. That had been made during calmer and more composed days and I was altogether willing to abide by it."

Chaplain Musser came in on time with his bride and at three in the afternoon, July 1, 1918, William Clyde Martin and Sallie Katherine Beene were married. Neither Papa nor Mamma nor Brice attended the wedding. Brice, in fact, stayed away from home during most of the time W. C. was there, "whether from dissatisfaction or from embarrassment I do not know."

Immediately after the close of the ceremony, the newlyweds were rushed to the station in Prescott for the trip to Memphis. They honeymooned there, staying at the Peabody Hotel. Time was too short for a trip to introduce Sallie to the kinfolk in Randolph, but they saw the wharf, and watched airplanes land at the airport. The next day they met by chance a friend from Henderson-Brown at the hotel and she joined them for a trip to the zoo and a movie. They took the early morning train to Atlanta on Independence Day, July 4, and arrived there at ten o'clock the same night. On the way to their room they met four men from the company, and Sallie was introduced to them for the first time as "my wife." They spent the last day of his furlough looking around Atlanta and the next morning he reported back to the company.

—⫷⦙⦙⦙⦙⦙⦚⦙⦚⦙⦙⦙⦙⦙⫸—

Sgt. Martin's new assignment was in the operating room. Once back on duty, he was allowed away from camp for the night on Wednesday, Saturday, and Sunday. Although it was necessary to get up very early to report back to camp on time, he described these as "sweet days . . . in spite of the inconvenience." The new-lyweds sampled services in the various churches of Atlanta, visited all the city's parks except one, and spent time with Musser and his new wife and with Ross at Emory. But it came to an end all too soon and in many ways seemed more like a dream than a reality. They had four weeks together before he was ordered to Camp Hill, the port of embarkation in Newport News, Virginia. When the orders came they said good-bye, and Sallie left for home on July 30. The next day William C. executed a new will naming Sallie K. Martin heir to his property and executrix of his estate.

The first leg of the journey to France was made on a slow train taking them to Newport News. Once at the camp in Virginia they were strictly confined, eliminating any possibility for Martin to get across the river to Norfolk where Bryce Cummins was at the Naval Training Station. Since the camp was located on the banks of the James River, the principal diversion available to the troops was swimming and boat riding. By talking to oyster fishermen William C. learned about their work and the tides.

The alert came on August 13 to be ready to move to the ship. After a restless night, they marched three miles to the dock and went aboard the *Aeolus*. Formerly of German registry under the name of *Grosser Herzog*, she was one of the largest transports in service. On this voyage she carried 4,000 troops plus her crew. The men of the 13th were assigned bunks in the hold, stacked three or four high "with barely enough room between them for one man to go." The 13th Evacuation Hospital with Lt. Col. Craig R. Snyder of Kimbolton, Ohio, in command, embarked with a full compliment of 34 officers and 204 enlisted men. NCO Sgt. William C. Martin, Second Platoon (serial number 753,924) was number 40 on the manifest. All commissioned officers in the Medical Corps were doctors.

Since Col. Snyder was the ranking army officer on the ship, the 13th was given a choice duty assignment. Due to crowding, the air in the hold was foul and it was uncomfortable to be below decks. With the colonel's seniority, the personnel of the 13th were assigned to lookout duty, which allowed them to stay on deck. There were forty lookouts on duty twenty-four hours a day. Martin was put in charge of one relief, and promptly got into serious trouble. Because of the sleepless night, the long march, and the lulling motion of the ship once at sea, Martin fell asleep while on duty and did not wake again until six o'clock in the morning. By that time the adjutant, Capt. O'Donnell, was looking for him. Upon reporting, he was summarily relieved of his duty as sergeant of the lookouts. "Not since I have been in the service have I felt as depressed as I did following that interview." Moreover, some of the other noncoms seemed to be pleased with his distress. "Again I have had it demonstrated that most people are ready to give a kick to the man who is down." He remembered a similar experience while at Hendrix. High achievers are usually in somebody's sights. He was placed on regular lookout duty and assigned to a post in the crow's nest on the forward mast. He liked it. From that vantage point he had a panoramic view of the sea, the weather, and the other ships.

On Thursday the *Aeolus* was joined to a convoy out of Hoboken, New Jersey, which consisted of three more transports, the cruiser *Seattle,* and one destroyer. One other transport scheduled to go with them had become disabled and turned back to New York.

Martin was fascinated by the sea. In spare moments he talked with members of the crew about navigation and life at sea, but there was not enough action to suit him. "I no longer regret that I am in the army instead of the navy. The life is too monotonous and has too little variety." He continued work on his French and read as much as possible. Since no talk was allowed on lookout duty, there was plenty of time for thinking and meditation. In the early morning hours one day William C. determined never "to allow anything to cause me to be downcast in spirit since this would mar my usefulness to the service." In keeping with the resolution he adopted rules for himself he had learned from a Y.M.C.A. lecture: look on the bright side, do a kindness for someone else every day, be content with where you are and make the most of it, be usefully employed, remember that God wants you to be happy.

August 23 the convoy was joined by six submarine chasers with balloons. The danger now was real and constant. On August 25 from his post in the forward crow's nest, Martin caught his first glimpse of France and they were soon anchored in the harbor at Brest. "The voyage was over and I can say with truth that in spite of its privations, I enjoyed it greatly." The army provided a printed "Soldier's Card" announcing "The ship on which I sailed has arrived safely overseas," which he promptly mailed to Sallie.

The troops were put ashore in small boats, and marched to camp. "As we marched along the streets toward the barracks, we were accompanied by great crowds of French children, some to sell fruit and nuts, some to shake our hands but mostly to beg for pennies and cigarettes. With them I tried out some of my French and it was understood better than I had hoped." For the next few days they rested, unloaded freight, and had their first look at France and the French.

Word came on August 28 to be ready to leave, and at 3:30 A.M. on August 29 they were put aboard a train equipped with the now famous "40 and 8" cars—"40 *hommes ou* 8 *chevaux.*" A platoon was put into each car and issued rations—half the amount of the usual garrison allotment—for three days. "We were literally packed in the cars. At meal time there was hardly room to eat but the real jam comes when we tried to sleep." Their route the first day took them through Rennes, Laval, and Le Mans. The next day they passed through Tours, Bourges, and Dijon. On Sunday the journey was interrupted in Is-Sur-Tille to allow time for rest and clean up, and then resumed to Toul. They arrived there in the early afternoon, waited two or three hours, and then moved to their final destination in the village of Chaligny where they were served coffee, bread, and syrup—Martin said he had never tasted anything so good. Afterward they pitched tents for the night and experienced their first air raid. They were warned to expect one every day since they were located only about twenty kilometers from the trenches.

The 13th took over a French evacuation hospital that had been operating for a month. It was necessary first to invoice their property and then to prepare the facilities to receive casualties. In addition to his regular duties, William C. began immediately to work as an interpreter for the unit, and although he had difficulty at first comprehending the rapid speech of the French, he was well able to make himself understood. During the next air raid when an enemy plane flew directly over the camp, he also learned that friendly antiaircraft fire scattered shrapnel and resolved to take cover during air raids "if for nothing else than protection from our own fire." Martin was put in charge of the wards. A sufficient number of tents were erected to care for an expected 1,500 patients from the offensive about to be launched against Metz. Engineers laid off a site behind the hospital for 800 graves. "It gives one a peculiar feeling to think that the graves have already been prepared for 800 American youths who are now sound and well but who in a few hours will be dead."

The 13th received its first casualties on Sunday, September 7. Although days were busy, evenings were usually free and Martin went often into the villages to make purchases and talk to the locals. "I lose no opportunity to learn more of the language." On one occasion just after arriving, Martin went with Lt. Frank Tannenbaum to inspect the local water supply and shared a bottle of wine with him at lunch. "I did not like the taste and was not affected by the small percent of alcohol it contained. However, I shan't drink any more of it." He received his first letter from Sallie on September 11, and the next morning at 0300 hours the St. Mihiel offensive began. They lost their first patient on September 13. Three days later they had seven deaths. "I have seen some terrible wounds during the last few days," he said.

After all the work getting set up in Chaligny, the hospital had been in operation only ten days when they received orders to move closer to the front. Their remaining patients were evacuated to Toul. In the now-expected fashion, however, the move was delayed, leaving more time to explore the countryside, eat in the restaurants, and anticipate what the future might hold. On September 23 they were finally relocated to Toul and housed in buildings that had formerly served as the dormitories of a military academy. "It is by far the best place I have been in since the war." For the first time since Camp Greenleaf days Martin shared quarters again with Sgts. Stark, Charles P. Sohn from Pittsburgh, Young, and Colbert. He wasted no time in touring the cathedral, and with Corp. Samuel Lang climbed a nearby mountain in the early evening. From the top they could see the flash of guns. Martin also made his first visit to the front where firsthand he saw the trenches and barbed wire.

William C. and fellow Sgt. Robert C. Loudermilch made a more memorable return to the front on October 2—"curiosity got the advantage of better judgment." It was exactly the circumstance that his family feared might get him killed. By walking and hitching rides they made their way to Flirey and then on to Bulainville, where they started into the trenches. In sight of Thiaucourt, "we met a soldier who told us that three men had been killed there the night before," and once in the trenches, "the shells from the German guns were whistling over us and bursting near by." Still unsatisfied they continued forward until they reached the town of Xammes, where they were warned "that if we showed our heads over this ridge the machine gunners would pick us off." They were on the literal edge of "no man's land." The night before 400 gas shells had fallen on the village. Loudermilch wanted to stay longer but William C. "pulled him away fearing the Germans would open fire again." Later he reasoned, "It was a great day yet too dangerous to be gone thru with again just from curiosity."

The family was concerned that Clyde might lose his life as the result of a foolhardy adventure, but if they had known what was actually happening they would have been better advised to worry about his friend Loudermilch. Four days after his trip with William C., Loudermilch persuaded Sgts. Colbert and Humphreys to go back to the front with him. On that excursion he was shot in the back by a sniper and seriously wounded. Martin's trip to the trenches had another result which was unanticipated—it convinced him that the war would be won by artillery and he promptly made application for officer's training in that branch, and as immediately found and started to read books on the subject. Col. Snyder, however, denied his request for a transfer and the subject was closed.

<hr/>

The unit moved again October 12, this time to the site of a former French hospital near Nancy. Martin was given a detail to build a latrine. He and the other noncoms now were housed with the enlisted men in a stone building that had formerly been a brewery. "It is a large bare room with a concrete floor and is anything but comfortable as sleeping quarters." Nancy proved, however, to be an interesting town and Martin enjoyed it. He went to mass at the cathedral and to the French movies, which he usually didn't like because of the "slowness of the action."

The hospital moved to Commercy on Halloween. This required relocating 150 patients, but put them close enough to visit the fortifications at St. Mihiel. They were set up and ready for patients by November 7, but the air was full of "peace talk," and there was optimism that hostilities would soon cease. Martin was caught up in it, too. "I worked this afternoon with a detail fitting up some wards that I felt sure would never be used." He was wrong.

By 11:00 P.M. November 9 they had 200 medical cases. The next day they received 200 surgical patients. "The operating teams were all busy and men that worked the day and night before were still working." Again Martin was in charge of the medical wards. His patients were mostly victims of a gas attack and almost all were from the 33rd Division. "From several of them I learned that the last charge had been entirely uncalled for. The men were forced over the top by officers who were greedy for personal glory. They were unsupported by our artillery and the attack had been largely a failure." The hostilities continued until the actual moment of the armistice at 11:00 A.M., November 11. "More patients came in all thru the day. Every available bed is filled. . . . This is a time for great rejoicing but we are too busy with other things to spend much time that way." The 13th eventually received a thousand patients and the work was intense for a week.

On November 20 Martin and two others found time for a long-anticipated trip to Verdun. Once there he realized "there was not a single house that was not literally riddled with shells." The cathedral "was barely hanging together." With this trip he had seen two of the main engagements of World War I, San Mihiel, and Verdun. November 25 was a unique day for Sgt. Martin—a first in his army career. "Today I shirked. Somehow or other I had a disinclination for work and I did very little of it." His problem was, however, that he was never able to enjoy anything that compromised his obligation to doing his duty. The next day he was stricken with guilt and "resolved to stay closer to the job." He might well have enjoyed it more had he remembered the words of Martin Luther's confessor, who in a somewhat similar situation urged the reformer to "sin bravely." Malingering was never one of Martin's strong points.

Thanksgiving and the armistice were celebrated with a good dinner, services conducted by the chaplain, and a talent show put on by the men, which was "excellent." On November 30, the 13th was relieved by a base hospital unit.

Having already visited Toul and Verdun, Martin wanted to see the site of another significant engagement, Metz. He made the trip on December 15 with Sgt. Allen, but they were able to see very little since the city was under strict control of the military police. After seeing what they could, they left the city in heavy fog. Shortly afterward, their train crashed into the rear of a French troop train, killing and injuring several soldiers. The sad irony of the accident was not lost on Martin. "It gave me a deep sense of sadness to consider that these men would have lived thru four years of hell only to be killed . . . by a railroad accident."

Christmas was spent with other noncoms and at a service in town conducted by Chaplain Gibson. The next day Sgt. Martin was in serious trouble for the second time in his army career. He was called to the office of the Commanding Officer, Col. Snyder, to explain what had happened to the valuables of three patients whom Martin had evacuated to Toul. When he arrived with the men, he had, in fact, given their property to a guard at the gate with instructions as to what should be done with it rather than deliver the items to the proper place himself. As a result he had no receipt to prove they had been received. When questioned about it, he misled the Colonel by telling him the property had been delivered to an office near the gate. The Colonel was suspicious because he did not have a receipt and sent him to retrieve the items. He was lucky. To his considerable relief, he discovered the guard had followed his directions and delivered the items to the proper place where they were waiting. The valuables were returned and a lesson re-learned. "The next time I am called into question about an action I shall tell the truth about it from the beginning no matter how careless the act may have been."

The men of the 13th Evacuation Hospital began the new year by being assigned to duty in the army of occupation in Walferdange, Luxembourg. "Our hopes for a speedy return [home] vanished immediately and a great wail went up from all over the camp." Twenty-five men requested an immediate discharge. All the requests were denied, but Martin requested and was granted a week's leave in order to visit Paris with Emil Frey and Charles Oliver. He read Jack London's *White Fang* on the train. Once in the City of Light they saw the regular sights and discovered what all visitors to Paris could have told them. "We found the prices quite high." Martin commented, "I imagine that few people have seen more of Paris than we did in the same length of time." Actually, they overstayed their authorized time in the city and found themselves in trouble with the military police when they tried to leave. "The M.P.," Martin said, "was quite harsh in his remarks about our staying over 24 hours longer than our passes allowed. He threatened to hold us but then decided to let us go." He told Sallie about their experience in a letter: "We left Paris at 8 o'clock after a little argument with an M.P. because we had overstayed our time in Paris 24 hours. We were told to leave at 7 o'clock following the night of our arrival at 11 o'clock but of course that would have been entirely too little time to be there so we took a chance and stayed until the morning." Once free to go, they moved on to the army recreation center at La Bourboule in the Auvergne mountains.

The mountains and countryside around La Bourboule reminded Martin of the area around Hot Springs in Arkansas. Although they were assigned to a room with three beds and no heat, the weather was beautiful, the scenery spectacular, and the people they met interesting and friendly. It was wonderful. One day they climbed to the top of a mountain knee deep in snow and saw the Roman ruins. Martin devoted the time available for reading to finish *White Fang*, read Arnold Bennett's *How to Live on 24 Hours a Day*, and for good measure Boswell's *Journal of the Tour of the Hebrides with Dr. Johnson.* "Truly a charming book and a most remarkable portrayal of a most remarkable character." On the way back to Luxembourg they, having learned a lesson, asked for and received permission to spend an additional eight hours in Paris. He and Frey had an argument on the train about whether the United States was justified in entering the war. Martin took the affirmative side.

While in Paris Martin purchased a "self-instructing" course in German, a watch fob and a crystal for his watch, and then stopped by the Y.M.C.A. headquarters in the Rue D'Elysee to get information about a program that he had heard was soon to begin. He said later that he did not remember where or when he first heard of it. College graduates or persons in the A.E.F. with college credit were eligible to apply for 2,000 places that had been made available for study in universities in France or England. It was the first step that would lead Martin to Aberdeen.

Back in Luxembourg, the travelers completed their journey with three hours of sight-seeing in the city and reported to the hospital at its new location in Walferdange. They found the 13th now located in the old summer home of the Duchess of Luxembourg. It was an idyllic setting. The enlisted men were living on the second floor of the barn. "The grounds surrounding the building are spacious, beautiful and well kept. It will be a lovely place in the spring." There was work to be done with more than 200 patients and the time passed rapidly. There were, on the average, one to three deaths each day.

⸻⚜⸻

January 25, 1919, William C. himself became a patient. He had not been feeling well and soon was hospitalized with a high fever. He was not finally discharged until February 5, but used the time to read seven books of Milton's *Paradise Lost*. He did not like the food. Less than a week later, February 11, a telegram came to the unit requesting the number of men who had as much as two years of college, their preferences for French or British universities, and the proposed course of study. There were twenty-five men in the company who were eligible. "I don't know what will come of it. Nothing most likely," Martin said.

He was enjoying himself. His work kept him busy and the more he became involved, the better he liked it. He wrote Sallie every night and counted the days until they would return home. "Every one that passes means just one less for us to be over here." The unit now had a chaplain, a native of Boston, whom Martin came to know well, as he did the French family with whom the new chaplain was living—a mother, Madam Kleis, two daughters, and an eighteen-year-old son. All but the mother spoke French. The chaplain, whose name the diary does not contain, was a good preacher and conducted a regular Bible study class on Thursday nights. Moreover, he had books that Martin could borrow. It was from him that he obtained Milton's *Paradise Lost,* read *Studies in Christian Truth* by H. R. Mackintosh, Gipsy Smith's *Your Boys,* and Bishop Moule's *Light from the First Days*. Martin began to keep a notebook on his reading, a practice he followed for years. The chaplain conducted a Bible study on the book of Amos in which Martin participated, and one of the Jews in the company, Abraham (Abby) Margules, started to teach him Hebrew. February 26, he had been in France six months. It was an especially good day since six letters came from Sallie.

98

Although William C. had no idea what was to happen, his time in Luxembourg and the leisure that went with it was soon to be over. Without advance warning, Sunday, March 30, 1919, orders came to report in England for assignment to a theological college. The orders required him to begin his travel the next day. "I had had so little faith in the matter that it was a great surprise to me." There was no time to prepare, and the prospects of leaving his unit aroused mixed emotions. "It was not without a feeling of sadness that I shook hands with the fellows this morning. Some of them I have been with since I first came into the army and I have found in them true friends."

In Luxembourg City he discovered there would be no train until two-thirty in the afternoon. There was, however, a French passenger train about ready to leave, but on which enlisted men were forbidden to ride. As he was pondering his situation, he happened to meet Alexander Buckley and Coleman Griffin, friends from the 13th, who were on their way to Ireland. After considering the matter briefly, they decided to take their chances and board the French train. They got as far as Lorraine, not far from Strasbourg, before a French officer came on the train and ordered them off. While they were "discussing" the matter with him, the train started from the station. Realizing he had left his bag on the train, Martin waited until the last coach was about to pass, tore his papers from the hands of the French officer, and jumped on board. "It was a narrow escape from loss," he said.

They were less fortunate in Nancy when at 2:00 A.M., an American military policeman put them off the train to stay. Martin decided to spend the night in order to visit the university, but his two companions took the next train. After a day in Nancy, a favorite city, he left on a slow night train sharing a compartment filled with French soldiers, with whom he had a delightful conversation. They were young, in high spirits, and going home. Reaching Paris the next afternoon, Martin checked in at the Y, left his luggage, and went to see *Pantheon de La Guerre,* a panoramic view of the leading figures, nations, and events of the war—"it is a wonderful piece of work."

At the Y.M.C.A. he was given the name of the individual in

London who was in charge of making assignments to theological colleges. He also managed a visit with the parents of the young Frenchman Alfred Eugene Casalis, whose letters Martin had first read while at Camp Greenleaf. "I expressed to them as best I could, what the writing of their son had meant to me." They gave him a copy of the French version of the book.

Leaving Paris, Martin arrived in Southampton in the early morning hours of Friday, April 4, spent a brief time walking around the city, and was in London by four o'clock that afternoon. Going directly to 50 Russell Square where he was ordered to report, he discovered the office closed for the day. Space was available at the American Y.M.C.A., "Eagle Hut" located in the Strand, and he checked in. In addition to ice cream, griddlecakes, pie, hash, and baked beans, the "Hut" offered a bed with clean linen for 18 cents a night. Reporting again the next morning, he discovered that J. Ross Stevenson, president of Princeton Seminary, who was working with the Army Educational Commission and the Y.M.C.A. in the program, was away until Monday. The delay caused by Stevenson's absence allowed time for sight-seeing in the city, services at Methodist Central Hall, and a mandatory visit to John Wesley's Chapel in City Road.

He was unable to see President Stevenson until Tuesday morning. His advice was to go to the United Free Church College of the University of Aberdeen. The college had a distinguished faculty that would welcome an American student. It is somewhat surprising that Martin appeared not to be impressed with the individual with whom he was talking. It could be that he was unaware of who the person actually was, but it is more likely that he was simply preoccupied with where he would be going. There is not much doubt that the president of Princeton Seminary had sufficient experience and information to advise a prospective seminary student where to attend school, but Martin was not willing to take his advice since he had his heart set on going to Oxford. Stevenson's warning that it would be expensive and hard to find a room would have to be tested. "I had always preferred Oxford or Cambridge on account of their traditions and I was not willing to give Oxford up without looking into the possibilities." Stevenson was willing for him to look and gave permission for Martin to go up to Oxford to see the situation for himself. He went immediately, but when he arrived virtually everyone he needed to see was away. The only person he managed to find was the Warden of Rhodes House, Mr. Wyle, who knew nothing about either the program or the expenses. However, he did know all of the men from Arkansas who had been Rhodes scholars and that was a treat.

William C. spent the night at a bed and breakfast on Cornmarket Street and, in his usual fashion, kept the receipt for the charge of 4 shillings. The next day he looked around the city and at the various colleges of Oxford University. In the afternoon he went to nearby Stratford on Avon where he spent the night. Although his time was limited, while there he managed to see most of the Shakespeare sites except for Anne Hathaway's cottage. On the way back to London he stopped again in Oxford and was able to talk with Capt. Bruce, who was in charge of the American students, and had breakfast with a soldier he knew from the 14th Evacuation Hospital who was studying English at Cambridge.

Once back in London on Friday, he told President Stevenson he was ready to be assigned to Aberdeen. Since orders could not be cut until the following Tuesday, he was able to enjoy another long weekend in London. This he spent making visits to St. Paul's Cathedral, Westminster Abbey—"Poets Corner" interested him most—the British Museum, the National Gallery of Art, the Tower of London, and the fish market. At the Eagle Hut he reread Macaulay's essay on Johnson, and reviewed a short history of England. By chance he met Griffin and Buckley, who had stopped on their way back from Ireland. There was an unpleasant experience, too. After leaving his billfold on a table in the reading room, he returned to find that all of his money was stolen and he had to get a loan of 9 pounds from the Red Cross. He resolved not to let the experience weigh on him, and with his new resources bought a ticket at the Old Vic to see a production of *Everyman*. Tuesday morning, April 15, he was on his way to Scotland. Had he not been sleeping when they passed, he could have seen the German fleet anchored in the Firth of Forth. By nine o'clock in the evening he was in Aberdeen and spent the first night of what was to be a life-transforming experience. Rooms were scarce but he managed to obtain one in the home of Mrs. Callie on Die Street. Aberdeen, a city of 163,000, was known as the "silver city by the sea." After finding a room, William C. went immediately to see the beach and the ocean, always an attraction to him. Dr. John Alexander Selbie, secretary of the college and chair of the Old Testament Language and Literature Department, helped outline a tentative course of study for him to follow. Once registered at the college, Martin reported to the officer in charge of the student detachment and was ready to begin classes. He prepared himself by beginning to read *Lady of the Lake,* better to appreciate his host country and its traditions.

The faculty of the Free College during the Easter term, 1919, consisted of four professors: Principal and Professor of New Testament Language and Literature, James Iverach, Professor of Church History, James Stalker, Alexander Selbie, and David S. Cairns, who was professor of Dogmatics and Apologetics. There were fewer than ten students enrolled, counting Martin. He took Christian Ethics with Stalker, Dogmatics and Christian Apologetics with Cairns, and New Testament with Iverach. He considered adding Hebrew in order to study with Selbie but decided it would make his course load too heavy. Iverach was the only member of the faculty who had ever been to America. He was especially fond of talking about "American characteristics and peculiarities." "Under the instruction of such a 'settled' man as this there is little danger of being led into the heresies of higher criticism," Martin concluded. Iverach was eighty years old, "but remarkably strong physically and mentally." Stalker was seventy-one, Selbie sixty-three; Martin estimated Cairns's age as fifty-seven, but he was actually only forty-four at the time, the junior member of the faculty by any measure. Professor Selbie was especially well known for his work with James Hastings on the various dictionaries of the Bible.

It was Cairns, however, whose influence on William C. Martin was significant and lasting. They kept in touch for two decades after Martin left Aberdeen. By 1918, Cairns had already written *Christianity in Modern Times* and *The Reasonableness of the Christian Faith*, but it was a later book, *The Faith That Rebels*, which Martin credited with renewing his passion for ministry. February 15, 1932, shortly after being appointed to First Methodist, Dallas, Martin wrote Cairns. The purpose of the letter was to tell his teacher "what a Godsend your book *The Faith that Rebels* was to me."

> The book came to me . . . at a time when·I was groping for a deeper assurance of spiritual reality. Almost like a clear answer to prayer it brought the statement of Christian truth I sorely needed and since that crisis, for it amounted to that, I have had an abiding confidence which has deepened and enriched my whole religious life. You are a prophet of a new day for progressive Christianity.

Cairns, Sallie remembered, said Martin was the best student he ever had.

Classes, which began the Monday after Easter, April 21, 1919, met every day from 10:00 until 1:15, except for Mondays when there was no class at 12:15. Afternoons were free for reading in the library and there was plenty of time for walking. The weather was colder than Martin had ever experienced at Easter. The week classes started there was heavy snow mixed with rain, but when the sun broke through later in the day William C. went for a walk on the beach. The people of Aberdeen were warm and gracious to the American soldiers stationed there, and provided many social events for them to attend. "The Scots are the most successful entertainers I know," Martin said.

Although he liked the Callie family, it was impossible there to have a room to himself so he moved to Mrs. Sinclair's on Crown Street. The private room cost about half the amount allotted to him for rent by the army. "I have a nice room all to myself and the food is good." He was later to change his mind about the food since it consisted of a steady diet of fish. He wrote Sallie in verse to tell her about it:

Since I was a boy on my grandfather's farm
It always has been my wish
to have my fill of the finny tribe
So madam, bring on the fish.

Mackerel, halibut, salmon and cod,
Gunplucker, seith and cat,
Sardine, trout, and the big speckled perch
Herring and flounder flat.

Star-fish, mussels, buckies and eels
Whether scales be light or dark,
Octopus, limpet, dolphin or whale
I really would tackle a shark.

Whether caught with a net or a hook and line
In rivers or in the sea
Whether brought to the shore in trawler or skiff
It's all the same to me.

Dried fish, smoked fish salted or canned,
Caught swimming alone or in schools
Dragged up from the bottom of ocean depths
Or found in the clear shallow pools.

You may fry them or bake them or boil them in oil
Serve them hot or cold
Fish is a dish we can eat every meal
And it never begins to get old.

For breakfast, dinner, supper and tea,
In bowl or platter or dish
Here's my request about the food
Please madam, bring on the fish!

A private room, unheard of in the army, made reflection and
meditation easy. The only disadvantage was that Mrs. Sinclair

insisted on bringing meals to him rather than allowing him to eat with the family, which he would have preferred.

The first mail came from Sallie on April 30. She did not know he had gone to school, and W. C. was somewhat uncertain what she might think about the possible delay it might cause in his returning home. She had, however, "written a number of times that she hoped I could go."

The janitor at the college, Mr. Fordyce, was asked to send a student to preach at Nethy Bridge, the home of the Grant Clan, and he invited Martin. After preaching in the morning at Nethy Bridge, he was taken farther up the Spey River to the Boart of Garten to preach again. On the way home he stopped in Grantown, climbed a mountain, and had dinner with a fellow student from Aberdeen. It was the start of a busy week. On Tuesday he went to Marichal College to hear the Gifford Lecture on "Personality and God," given by C. J. Webb of Oxford. "I have never heard a man so completely lose himself in a mass of technical and to me meaningless words." He decided not to go again. The next day he bought copies of Tennyson's "Maud" and read it.

On Thursday the full text of the peace treaty with Germany appeared in the press. The terms seemed severe to Sgt. Martin and he mused perceptively in his journal: "Whether the present treaty bears in it the seeds of another war remains to be seen." Friday afternoon he had tea with Cairns, "a privilege which I had looked forward to with anticipation and which I enjoyed."

Mr. Sunderland, the minister at Nethy Bridge, extended an invitation to Martin to preach at Kirkmichael, a town on the Avon River. The church's former pastor of more than thirty years, William Grant, had recently died of a stroke in the pulpit. The day was lovely and offered the opportunity to walk and climb another mountain. "Nothing could have been more beautiful than the view we got of the surrounding country from this mountain." Riding back to Aberdeen on the train, he finished reading *Beside the Bonnie Brier Bush,* "one of the most delightful little books I have ever read."

Martin's choice of reading material while in Aberdeen was eclectic, to say the least. He read Darwin's *Origin of Species* and

Childe Harold, "just to get the apostrophe to the ocean." To that he added Bousset's *What Is Religion,* Owen Wister's *Pentecost of Calamity,* a life of Goethe, and a collection of Hazlett's essays. After reading the chapters on tragedy in Stalker's book *How to Read Shakespeare,* he reread *Othello.* While thinking about the proposed peace with Germany, he read Thomas Aquinas on war in Latin because no translation was available.

Exams were taken the week of May 19, and on May 21 Martin received a bulletin from Southern Methodist University along with a letter from Hoyt M. Dobbs, the dean. "I am now very much of the opinion that it would be better for me to go there than to Vanderbilt." On May 25 he preached in Lagie Buchan to a large congregation that included the Earl of Caithness. His observation that "this was my first and no doubt my last time to preach to a member of the nobility" was not, in fact, to prove correct.

After exams there was time before classes resumed for a brief sight-seeing trip to Edinburgh. In addition to the regular attractions, he was entertained in the home of David Cairns's brother, a minister in the city. In early June he went over into the Scott country with a group of military and Red Cross personnel. There were cruises on the lakes and the mandatory visit to Loch Lomond. On that trip he heard James Moffatt preach in Glasgow—"His sermon was simple and practical." Monday he took an all-day cruise on the Clyde, but had to be up at three o'clock Tuesday morning to catch the train back to Aberdeen in time for class. Perhaps being overtaken with some pangs of conscience in the midst of such stimulation, beauty, and joy, he wrote Sallie on June 7 from Glasgow: "The only thing I regret about these trips is the remembrance that while I am seeing the beauties of nature and having a good time my little wife is at home waiting for me and maybe not having such a good time." No doubt about it. She was not having a good time living at home with her parents while her husband enjoyed the sights, and it is unlikely she could have appreciated this expression of his "concern" either.

Another weekend he visited Braemar, where he saw the summer home of the Prince of Wales and Balmoral Castle. "The whole region seems more like a fairy land than anything else." On the side of a mountain overlooking the Valley of the Dee, "all the bits of poetry came rushing to my memory. . . . Nothing but poetry will express one's feelings under circumstances such as these," and he resolved to memorize more of it.

The time passed quickly. He preached again in Kirkmichael and Cairns outlined a trip for him through the Sir Walter Scott country. Classes were over on June 27. "I shook hands with the professors and students for perhaps the last time." The next day he left for Abbotsford to see the places Cairns had chosen for him. His last day in Aberdeen was July 2. "I am to go tomorrow morning back into the restraining force of military discipline. . . . Farewell freedom until I am demobilized." In a bad mood he wrote Sallie with more than a touch of self-pity to complain he had heard nothing from her in more than a week. "I shall not hear from you now until I see you. . . . It is too bad," he continued, "that you were so sparing of your time and pains that you could have written once more and that I must be here for ten days without a word from you because you were in such a great hurry to stop writing." He concluded the letter with a few lines of verse describing his deep feelings upon leaving Scotland.

> Farewell, my bonnie Scotland
> I bid you now adieu
> I may forget the ruins of France
> But never so with you.

He and the others enrolled in British universities reported to Liverpool and went aboard the U.S.S. *Plattsburg* expecting to sail for Brest the evening of July 3. Their departure was, however, delayed by a strike of coalers thus allowing time to see Liverpool. It was more like an American city, Martin thought, than any he had seen while in Europe. He was also quickly reminded he was back in the army when forced to stand in line for everything. "This is the most disagreeable feature of army life." He was pleasantly surprised to meet Percy Herring, one of the Hendrix men with whom he enlisted, who had been in school in Dublin. They had not seen each other since Camp Greenleaf days.

The *Plattsburg* actually sailed for France on July 7 and landed in Brest on July 9. Martin noted Brest to be "the same filthy city it was a year ago."

Having received a telegram from Col. Snyder saying the 13th would be in Brest on its way home, and requesting his reassignment to the hospital, Martin quickly discovered their whereabouts and paid a visit. They were in high spirits to see him and in anticipation of leaving for home the next day. As it turned out, the time in school had not delayed his return home. The visit to the unit also gave him the opportunity personally to thank Col. Snyder for his influence in getting him assigned to study in Britain.

On Monday, July 14, they were unexpectedly ordered to the docks and put aboard the battleship *Minnesota*. Seventeen men could not be found and were left behind. They sailed the next afternoon. "The sun was shining brightly and our last view of France was one of beauty but there was no expression of regret from any soldier or sailor." The ship carried 1,200 troops in addition to her crew of 1,400. "The food was the best I have ever seen served to soldiers and there was an abundance of it." There was a band and an orchestra in addition to the movies that were shown nightly. Two weeks later they landed in the place from which they had sailed just short of a year earlier, Norfolk, Virginia.

Martin was discharged on July 31, and left for home on August 1. When he reached Memphis on August 2, he was ill with dysentery and, getting no better over the weekend, he was hospitalized overnight on Monday, August 4. When finally released the next day, he went up to Tipton where he was met by Uncle Perry and stayed with him for three days visiting relatives and taking care of business matters. He did not reach home until August 11, where he found Mamma, Papa, and Grandma Smith at the train station on their way to Oklahoma. "Found Sallie at home and well but somewhat out of humor because I hadn't come directly home."

3

Seminary and Grace Church, Houston

<figure>ornamental divider</figure>

The recently reunited Martins were at home in Arkansas just over a month before they packed their meager belongings and moved to Dallas for William C. to begin classes in the new seminary at Southern Methodist University. Though their time at home was short, there were plenty of things to occupy every moment of it. There was, first of all, the need to get adjusted to marriage and reacquainted with each other. They had, after all, been a married couple only thirty days before being separated for fifteen months. His help was needed on the farm with the hay, and chores around the house seemed endless. There was also "catching up" to do with the family, especially with Brice who was just home from service in the navy.

A protracted revival meeting opened at the church in McCaskill on Thursday, August 14, and William C. attended every service, preaching on Sunday and Wednesday nights. Another revival was going on in nearby Pleasant Grove and they asked him to preach there, too. It closed on September 19, and that night he and Sallie took the train for Dallas.

Consistent with two decisions he had made in France, Martin was on the way to enroll in the new school of theology at Southern Methodist University, and to take the full theological course leading to a bachelor of divinity degree. He made these choices shortly after arriving and while riding back and forth in a truck hauling medical equipment from Toul. The assignment allowed plenty of time to think about the future. He described it in the diary:

> I had some time to think and my thoughts turned to what I should do after the war. If we continue in as safe surroundings as we are now I have an excellent chance to get home. For some time it has been my plan to spend a year in a theological school and then enter the ministry. I had thought that it would be too late in life for me to spend more time than that but today the thought came to me that it would be wise for me to take the entire course.

Despite the fact that the school of theology charged no tuition, money was required to live, buy books, and provide necessities. Finances were a problem. Martin's original plan had been to borrow money on his Tennessee property, but he was unable to get a loan. Papa said he was willing to advance the money needed to live, and Martin was confident he could find a student appointment or secular employment that would supplement their income enough to get by. And with that settled, Will and Sallie began the journey and a new life together.

The new university in Dallas and Emory University in Atlanta were born in response to the struggle between the Methodist Episcopal Church, South, and the Board of Trustees for control of Vanderbilt University. The matter was finally settled in favor of the trustees by a decision of the Tennessee Supreme Court in 1914, but the Methodists had earlier decided to begin two new institutions and withdrew their support. Planning for the new schools began in 1912, and Southern Methodist University opened for business in 1915. The necessary money to create it came from the city of Dallas, the General Board of Education of the church, and the Methodists of Texas. By November 1914, the bursar of the university reported 15,000 people had made subscriptions which averaged $70 each. A special, separate endowment was created for the school of theology. Both Emory and Southern Methodist University remain the property of their respective jurisdictions in The United Methodist Church.

Led by a scholarly and energetic new president, Robert S. Hyer, SMU's new campus consisted of a stately main building named Dallas Hall; Atkins Hall, a residence for women, named to honor Bishop James Atkins, who had been the chair of the original commission that recommended founding a university in Texas; and three temporary dormitories for men. There was no housing on campus for married students. The school of theology's entire operation, including chapel, classrooms, faculty offices, and library, was located in Dallas Hall. SMU's permanent buildings were constructed in the Georgian style, and Dallas Hall was copied from the Rotunda designed by Thomas Jefferson for the University of Virginia in Charlottesville. That was as far as the similarity extended, however, for its location in a field of Johnson grass, a noxious weed which, along with the Southern Baptists, many folks predicted would take over the state, bore no resemblance to the rolling, wooded hills of Virginia. But hopes were just as high for its future.

The first dean of the SMU School of Theology, Bishop Edwin Mouzon, served in that capacity while continuing his episcopal duties. Although Mouzon had been elected to the episcopacy in 1910, he agreed at Hyer's request to organize the school of theology and become acting dean. The stately white house in which he lived still stands on University Avenue near the campus. Mouzon began the process of hiring a faculty in 1914. The first full-time dean was Hoyt M. Dobbs, the man who replied to Martin's letter from Scotland. Martin noted in the diary when the letter came.

> I have just received a bulletin from Southern Methodist University describing the courses and a letter from Dr. Hoyt M. Dobbs, dean of the theological department. I am now very much of the opinion that it would be better for me to go there than to Vanderbilt, tho I have received no answer to my inquiry from that school.

We know from his early journal that Martin also considered going to Vanderbilt for college, but decided to attend Hendrix. Since he was determined to attend a Methodist seminary, he was frustrated by the events that had in 1914 removed the Methodists from control of the Nashville institution. So far as schools of theology per se were concerned, he was only familiar with Emory, having visited the campus to see his Hendrix classmate and attend the General Conference while stationed in Atlanta. He had friends there, too, and considered attending it seriously. But in the final analysis Martin concluded that attending school in the Southeast would limit the scope of acquaintances with whom he would be associated throughout his ministry—it was the same reason that ultimately sent him to Hendrix.

Martin's first academic year, 1919–20, was a turbulent one at the fledgling SMU School of Theology. Dobbs served as dean only six months before illness forced him to resign. James Kilgore, who was to become both friend and mentor to Martin, was named acting dean. Kilgore had been a member of the Texas Annual Conference and was presiding elder on the Houston District when he agreed to join the faculty. During the same year Hyer, a brilliant academic, was forced out of office in favor of a more successful fund-raiser, Hiram A. Boaz, who was leading the Church Extension operation of the Methodist Episcopal Church, South, in Louisville. Paul B. Kern was named permanent dean in 1920, and remained in the office for six years. Kern was from Vanderbilt. Thus SMU had in its first five years two presidents, two deans of theology, and an acting dean. Martin first heard Paul Kern speak at the Pastor's School in Hendrix, and it was Kern who brought stability and maturity to the struggling institution. His influence on Martin was substantial at the time and lasting, and his role in southern Methodism conspicuous.

It is interesting how many of the persons associated with the early years of SMU's School of Theology later were elected to the episcopal office. In addition to Mouzon, who was already a bishop, Hoyt Dobbs and H. A. Boaz were elected in 1922, Paul Kern followed in 1930. Ivan Lee Holt, a Ph.D. from the University of Chicago who chaired the first faculty and taught Old Testament, was elected in 1938 with Charles C. Selecman, who had followed Boaz as president of SMU in 1922, and William C. Martin, the first alumnus of the school to be elected. Paul E. Martin, an undergraduate contemporary of William C. but no relation, was elected in 1944. At one time Martin claimed that during his lifetime he had met or known 172 Methodist bishops. Without knowing it at the time, he had met a fair number of those in two years at SMU.

Paul Kern's vision of theological education shaped the curriculum under which Martin was educated. Kern's father, John A. Kern, was on the faculty at Randolph-Macon College and Vanderbilt. Paul was educated at Vanderbilt and after two years on its faculty served churches in Tennessee. Martin described Kern as "small of stature—the height of John Wesley [5'2"]—with the courtliness of his Virginia background, he was so balanced and symmetrical in all of his bearings that it was hard for the boys to find handles to 'take him off' on 'Faculty Day.'" His pictures portray a face that makes it hard to imagine one so young in such a place of responsibility.

Kern, who served as dean from 1920 until 1926, hired a new and distinguished faculty. Robert W. Goodloe, an SMU graduate fresh from military service as a chaplain, taught in the academic year 1920–21, but left at the end of the year to enroll in the Ph.D. program at the University of Chicago. After completing his degree, he would spend his entire career as professor of Church History on the SMU faculty. Jesse Lee Cuninggim was professor of Religious Education during most of Martin's years. The father of Merrimon Cuninggim, a Rhodes scholar who became dean of the Perkins School of Theology in 1951, "J. L." became president of Scarritt College in Nashville, Tennessee. Kern hired Harvie Branscomb, a Rhodes scholar, to head the University's Department of Philosophy, but asked him to teach New Testament in the theology school after Frank Seay's sudden death. Branscomb had studied New Testament at Oxford, and went on to a distinguished career in that discipline at Duke and as chancellor of Vanderbilt University. He was the author of a widely used and popular textbook on the teachings of Jesus.

Kern's most controversial appointment proved to be John A. Rice, professor of Old Testament. A gifted preacher and scholar, Rice had been pastor of the large and prestigious St. John's Methodist Episcopal Church, South, in St. Louis. While there he had written a book, *The Old Testament in the Life of Today*, which was published by Macmillan in 1920. In this work, Rice made no attempt to hide the fact that he accepted the basic assumptions of the new, "higher criticism" of the Bible. He outlined the documentary hypothesis of the Pentateuch, wrote critically of the work of the prophets and sages, and rejected the idea of the literal interpretation of the Bible. His modern stance attracted the ire and indignation of conservative and fundamentalist critics, the most vocal of whom was J. Frank Norris, the pastor of the First Baptist Church in Fort Worth. Despite the fact that both faculty and students came to the defense of Rice when he was attacked, he resigned his position in October 1921. Bishop Mouzon appointed him pastor of the Boston Avenue Methodist Church in Tulsa. He is known today for the construction of the new sanctuary, the tower of which is a familiar landmark in that city. When he resigned, Rice's slot in the faculty was filled by John H. Hicks, a Ph.D. from the University of Chicago, who was to teach at SMU for thirty-three years.

James Kilgore was the senior member of the faculty. Although he did not have a Ph.D. degree, he had done graduate work at the University of Chicago before coming to Dallas. He taught Philosophy and Psychology of Religion, and courses in Christian Doctrine. A "utility infielder" in the faculty and administration, Kilgore, in addition to his teaching responsibilities, served briefly as acting dean after Hoyt Dobbs's illness, and again from 1926 until 1933. He was acting president of the university between the administrations of H. A. Boaz and Charles C. Selecman. Martin recognizes Kilgore as having the greatest influence on him as a student. In looking at Kilgore's career, it is difficult to imagine why he was never given a permanent appointment to the office of dean.

Although he did have one course under him, Martin had little real opportunity to know and study under the intellectual star of the faculty, Frank Seay, since he died in February 1920. Although Seay, like Kilgore, did not have a Ph.D. degree, in addition to his theological work at Vanderbilt he had done graduate work at Chicago, Harvard, the Universities of Berlin and Oxford. Like

Mouzon, he was recruited by Hyer from the faculty at Southwestern University in Georgetown to come to SMU as professor of New Testament and New Testament Greek.

Other members of the faculty during Martin's years at SMU were Walter B. Nance, who taught Missions in the fall of 1920; James Seehorn Seneker followed Jesse Lee Cuninggim as professor of Religious Education and like Goodloe and Hicks remained on the SMU faculty for three decades.

The mission statement of the SMU School of Theology declared its intention to equip "a man [they assumed there would be no women] spiritually, intellectually, technically for the work of a preacher of the gospel in the Methodist itinerancy." The school proposed to "keep the idea of Christian manhood squarely in the fore, to train the mind, and to develop skilled workmanship." All of the members of the faculty had considerable experience as pastors of local congregations. The curriculum was operated on the quarter hour system and the first year required two quarters of Old Testament and one of New Testament, two quarters of general church history and one of Methodist doctrine, three quarters of religious education, and three of sociology, two quarters of ministerial efficiency and one of missions. Three quarters of New Testament Greek were required. Hebrew was elective. Public speaking was required of all students but no credit was given.

The second year was much like the first: one quarter of New Testament, two of homiletics (preaching), one of Christian doctrine, and two of either philosophy or psychology of religion. The balance of the curriculum in that year was elective.

During this formative period of Martin's life, there is a dearth of information about what he was thinking and doing. Abandoning his earlier commitment to keep a diary, Martin kept only a sketchy record of his seminary years. The contrast between his account of the years in seminary and his experience in Scotland is stark, but the reasons for it are not mysterious. In addition to school, he now had a wife, a small church at which he preached on Sundays in addition to a part-time job, and he was about to become a father.

After riding the train all night William C. and Sallie arrived in Dallas about noon on Saturday, September 20, 1919. After checking into the Adolphus Hotel downtown, they went directly to the campus where they talked with the secretary of the school, Frank Reedy. He was not encouraging about their finding rooms but told them to come back on Monday and he would see what he could do to help. On Sunday morning they attended the services at First Methodist Church. Nowhere in their wildest dreams could they have imagined that just over two decades later William C. would himself stand in this prestigious pulpit.

All Monday was spent in search of a place to live, and late in the day they managed to find one that afforded "kitchen privileges" and was "fairly satisfactory." It was in the home of Mrs. Ford on McKinney Avenue, about twenty minutes by streetcar from the campus. Mrs. Ford, who lived in the house with a granddaughter and a female border, was the daughter of Isaac Webb, a pioneer settler for whom the first Methodist church established in Dallas County, "Webb's Chapel," is named. A main street on the western side of the city also bears their name.

The Martins lived—mostly on preserves and jelly that they had brought from home—with Mrs. Ford for only two months. "We lived pleasantly, for the most part, and worked with some diligence on the task of getting adjusted to each other and to our new environment," the new husband said. A source of some unpleasantness, however, was the necessity to use money that Sallie had saved while W. C. was in the army, and the dim prospects of his repaying it anytime soon. But they managed.

In November they moved from Mrs. Ford's to rooms with the Rev. and Mrs. Z. R. Fee, who had a large house on McKinney, two blocks nearer town. Fee, like Martin, was enrolled in the school of theology at SMU. His wife, Mae, remained their friend for life. Their rooms at the rear of the house looked out over a cemetery, but the dismal scene did not detract from their happiness. The house has long since been replaced by new buildings since McKinney Avenue now is the site of office complexes and fine restaurants, but the cemetery remains.

Sallie did the washing, with W. C.'s help, and they sometimes threw the clothes out the back window in order for him not to be seen carrying them down from upstairs. To meet expenses during the Christmas holidays, he took a job with the express company handling trucks and loading cars from 3:00 to 11:00 P.M. The work wasn't hard, he said, and he earned a much needed $40. Papa and Mamma came to visit at Christmas and he and Papa spent part of the time at Love Field watching the airplanes "go up."

Although their money was borrowed and scarce, from time to time William C. and Sallie managed to find an extra dollar to take in a movie, a favorite pastime for the rest of their lives, and, on rare occasions, even to go out to Fair Park for a musical or play. They discovered the great State Fair of Texas in October of their first year and rarely ever missed attending all the years they lived in Dallas.

The great flu epidemic hit Sallie, who was pregnant, in the winter of 1920. During most of that time she also thought she had tuberculosis, but such was not the case. Mamma came to help and stayed until Sallie was well. The flu was so widespread and so many students were out of school that William C.'s absences to care for Sallie did not cause him to get behind in his work. Nearly everyone was out. For virtually all of his life, William C. Martin was rarely sick, and seldom tired. Sallie, on the other hand, was often ailing in one way or another or fearful she might be. Her energy level, at best, was always low, and she was frequently depressed. Her mother, Nannie Beene, took to her bed in the middle years of her life and was cared for until she died by Sallie's brother, Brice, and his wife, "Jack."

In his first semester William C. enrolled in a course on the "Prophets of Israel" taught by Frank Seay. His required Greek course was "The Early Epistles of St. Paul" taught by Seay and James Kilgore. In it he earned the only grade of B that he received during his entire first year. James Kilgore taught the courses he took on "The Philosophy of Religion," and "The Philosophy of Revelation." Martin said that "in many respects" Kilgore was his favorite professor. He took Jesse Lee Cuninggim's course "The Modern Sunday School"; Paul Kern taught him homiletics and pastoral administration. Martin and the other students quickly learned it was "a given" that to get a good grade in Kern's course in homiletics one almost had to memorize John Kern's book, *The Ministry to the Congregation*. In addition to his B in the Greek course, during his first year Martin earned one grade of B+, thirteen A's and two grades of A+, one of which was given to him in the "Jeremiah" course taught by Hoyt Dobbs.

He enrolled in the Standard Training School, which was held at the end of the regular school year, because the credits earned there would count toward his degree. In it he took "The Social Teaching of Jesus" with Ivan Lee Holt, "The Basics of Religious Education" under Dr. Meyer, and "Stories and Story Telling," which was taught by Dr. St. John.

At the close of the spring term, Dr. Cuninggim went with his family for the summer to Tennessee to direct the encampment at Monteagle. The Martins were invited to "house-sit" while the Cuninggim's were away, and they moved their modest belongings from the Fee's in the early part of June. Their possessions were so few, in fact, that they moved them in one evening on the streetcar.

The Cuninggim's house was a well-furnished and comfortable place, and they were happy with the space. They especially enjoyed the cool nights on the upstairs sleeping porch. The stairs were, however, hard on Sallie. Nannie Beene came again in July to help Sallie, who was nearing the end of her pregnancy. On August 2, 1920, at St. Paul's Hospital, she delivered their first child, a son, whom they named Donald Hankey. Although William C. never actually knew him, Donald William Alers Hankey was a British soldier who was killed in action on the Somme October 12, 1916. He was the author of a collection of letters written during his military training and first published as articles in the *Spectator*. They appeared a year after his death in book form under the title *A Student in Arms*. Martin had read and admired the work. Hankey's first book was titled *The Lord of All Good Life*, and while recovering in hospital after being invalided from the front he wrote part of another volume, *Faith or Fear: An Appeal to the Church of England,* which also appeared after his death.

When Donald was six years old, Martin wrote Hankey's publisher to get the address of any of his relatives and was put in touch with Hankey's sister. He then wrote directly to her asking if she would be willing to tell Donald Martin something about the man for whom he was named. She soon responded with a long letter that told Donald something of her family and her brother's life. The letter was carefully printed and in words a first grader could understand. She told him their mother was a seventeen-year-old Australian at the time she met Robert Hankey. They married shortly afterward and moved back to England where they lived "in a big ugly sea-side town called Brighton, where there are too many houses and too few trees, and too little sand on the beach and too many stones." Their son, Donald, was born there in 1884, the youngest of six. He was, in fact, seven years younger than his next brother.

The family had a tradition of military service and Donald attended the Royal Military Academy at Woolwick, served six years in the army, and then went up to Oxford to study theology and then to Leeds for "clergy school." When the war began, he could easily have received a commission or served in the chaplaincy, but chose to go in the enlisted ranks. After being invalided home from the front the first time, he accepted a commission out of his concern for a shortage of officers. In his book, *A Student in Arms,* which William C. had read, he wrote of life in the army and of the people with whom he served. He was killed after his return to the front. C. H. S. Matthews wrote of Donald in the preface to the volume *Faith or Fear,* to which Donald was a contributor, "He faced death as gallantly as he had faced life, and, true disciple of his Master as he was, he made of death not a defeat, but the final victory of his life." And his life clearly impressed an American named William C. Martin enough to name a son after him.

Before the end of the spring term in 1920, William C. managed to find a job at the Y.M.C.A. working in the "physical" department. There he was responsible for taking care of the baskets in which members kept their clothes during workouts and for selling towels and athletic equipment. He worked from 3:00 P.M.

until 10:00 P.M. Sallie didn't like being alone until almost 11:00, but she sacrificed because they had to have the money.

About the same time he also began preaching in Lisbon, a small town six miles south of Dallas. The preacher there had given up the work and Martin was offered the place by Walter Johnson, the presiding elder of the Dallas District. The Methodists in Lisbon shared a building owned by the Presbyterians. This arrangement enabled them to have services on alternate Sunday mornings and evenings. They were willing to pay $25 a month to have a preacher. Although the amount is small, it needs to be seen in perspective. The Adolphus Hotel in downtown Dallas, where an evening in its now famous Century Room can easily exceed $100 per person, featured dinner entrees at the Japanese Roof Garden ranging in price from 60 to 75 cents and the noon plate lunch cost 35 cents. Martin's "Thumb-Indexed Pastor's Book" records on the first page that the stewards were R. R. Mills, Isaac Bowman, and Ellister Nix. Since they were responsible for collecting the salary from members of the congregation, two pages of "Receipts on Salary" faithfully record that payment of $30 was made by them for the months of September and October 1920. They managed to pay their new preacher $31 in December, and gave the young family an old-fashioned "pounding" of food and gifts at Christmas. Every dollar collected by the stewards is faithfully recorded in the book along with the date on which William C. received it. The final entry is May 15, 1921, just prior to graduation.

The Presbyterians in Lisbon proved to be as cordial as the Methodists to William C., and he ended up spending almost as much time in their homes as in those of the forty-eight "official" members of his flock. His practice was to catch the interurban early Sunday morning, preach, and visit with as many people as possible before the Sunday school session. He would then go home with a family for lunch, make calls during the afternoon, and preach again at the evening service. On occasion he would also hold afternoon services at Bonny View, a school house two miles away. He walked to make pastoral calls and to Bonny View so the work afforded plenty of exercise as well as income.

Although there were some long hours spent waiting for the interurban on Sunday nights, "my heart was light with the feeling that I was doing the Lord's work and helping to care for my family."

During the late fall of 1920 as he began his second year at SMU, Martin added to his jobs the pastoral oversight of the congregation at Webb's Chapel in the nearby town of Farmers Branch. He began his work there just after the first of January 1921. This required two Sundays a month and alternated with Lisbon. The arrangement was convenient and provided an additional $25 a month, too. His "Pastor's Book" carefully records the first $5 earned at the new assignment and the date, January 9, 1921. He remained there until May 22. For his work at Farmers Branch, he was paid a total of $169.60, more than he had been promised. The congregation's membership of seventy-six, sixteen of whom belonged to the Dennis families, was made up of some of the oldest settlers in the county and the fellowship was delightful.

While at Farmers Branch he began the practice, which he continued throughout his ministry, of recording the titles of every sermon and the date on which it was preached. His first sermon on January 9, 1921, was "Digging Out Wells," the second that same day was on "The Profit of Godliness." Later he preached on "The Bible," "The Joy of Christianity," and "Religious Education in the Home." His last sermon was "The Life that Jesus Brings." Because of the richness of the Martin archives, it is possible for most of Martin's life to know from his diaries what he was reading, and the titles of his sermons. In most cases, the outline from which he preached is also available. That is not the case, however, for his first efforts at Lisbon and Farmers Branch.

When the Cuninggims returned at the end of the summer, the Martins had to move again. This time they found a two-room apartment in the home of the G. J. Forshees on Dickens Street, near the campus. The Forshees had three children and with Donald the house was full. There is a favorite story in the Martin family about calming Donald when he would fret or cry while they were eating. They tied a rope to the leg of his crib and would push it away from the table and then slowly reel him and it back.

Along with nine other classmates, W. B. "Bill" Slack, E. E. "Red" White, Otto W. Moerner, L. Bowman Craven, Archie W. Gordon, Roy E. Faucet, Willard W. McConnell, J. C. Mann, and M. T. Workman, Martin received his bachelor of divinity degree on June 14, 1921. The caption in the *Rotunda* described him perceptively: "Modest and unassuming, 'W. C.' is a diligent seeker after truth. His many friends greatly appreciate his type and are rightfully anticipating a life of abundant service." It also reported he had been on the Honor Council, president of the Ministerial Association, to which virtually all of the theologs belonged, and president of the class during the winter term.

The transfer of credits from his work in Aberdeen and some "double credit" enabled Martin to complete the work for his bachelor of divinity degree in two, rather than the usual three years. The registrar, Nell Anders, reckoned that he had earned credit for 98 term hours in the school of theology. He had been given an additional 10.8 hours because of his high grades and 31 hours of double credit, which probably included the transfer hours and credits earned in the Standard Training School in which he took three courses in the summer of 1920. This brought him to the required 138 hours for graduation.

Although he did not plan it, completing the degree in two years dramatically changed the course of Martin's professional life. He had expected to return to Arkansas to receive an appointment in the fall, but circumstances over which he had absolutely no control were at work to keep him in Texas. One might even say it was providential.

⟞⟝

Just about the time of SMU's graduation, the pastor of Grace Methodist Church, South, in Houston, Dr. John R. Nelson, despite having been at the church only six months, was appointed presiding elder of the Memphis District in the Memphis Annual Conference. This created a vacancy at Grace that needed to be filled temporarily until a new pastor could be appointed at the meeting of the Texas Conference in November. Since Grace Church was the third largest congregation affiliated with the Methodist Episcopal Church, South, in the city of Houston, filling the vacancy in the middle of a conference year would have necessitated making a number of changes in other places, so the bishop and his cabinet decided to appoint an interim pastor to serve until conference met in the fall. Presiding Bishop William N. Ainsworth, who lived in Dallas, discussed the matter with James Kilgore, a longtime member of the Texas Conference, and asked his friend to recommend a student who might be able to assume the duties. Kilgore recommended Martin, and the Bishop immediately appointed him to Grace Church. Ainsworth's telegram, which was sent not to Martin but to Dean Paul Kern, on May 20, 1921, said "inform Martin appointed to fill out year of Nelson at Houston. Report at once." He wrote to Martin, incorrectly addressing him as "W. A." Martin, the next day to confirm the telegram and, once again, urged him to get on the job as soon as possible.

Grace Church was an assignment that under any ordinary circumstances would never have been open to a recent seminary graduate, and Martin fully understood he was expected to remain only until the Texas Conference met in November when he accepted the assignment. Even the temporary assignment was fortuitous since he could not be appointed in the Little Rock Conference until November anyway. The assignment in Houston gave him a good place to work, a house in which he and his growing family could live, and a salary. He was not, however, unaware of the magnitude of his task nor of his lack of experience, so it was with considerable anxiety that he headed south with Sallie and Donald. In fact, his doubts about his ability to do the job, he remembered later, became "quite an annoyance, quite a problem." Martin never thought of himself as being ambitious, though Sallie knew he was and told him so, but he was determined not to fail.

The first six months passed rapidly, his work was outstanding, and the folks at Grace were pleased if not overjoyed. In those days Methodist bishops seldom consulted preachers about their appointments, and the preferences or wishes of church members were given only slightly more consideration. The leaders at Grace, however, did not want to lose Martin and were willing to make their feelings known. As Bishop Ainsworth wrote Martin after he had been reappointed, "the brethren at Grace Church . . . were instant in season and out of season in pressing their appeal" for his return. They knew they had a good thing, but there is no doubt that Martin correctly understood the terms of his assignment and knew his chances of remaining at Grace, no matter what his members might say, were somewhere between slim and none. Bishop Ainsworth had, in fact, made it abundantly clear to him. Just prior to annual conference, he wrote Martin to commend him for his good work at Grace, and to inform him that "it is the general desire of the church to keep you for the next year." He had, he said, received a flood of telegrams and letters from members of Grace Church urging Martin's return. Unfortunately, this was not likely to happen. His letter of October 17, 1921, described his position clearly.

> I must, of course, give the preference to worthy men who have been in this conference for a long period of years, and the chances are that I cannot properly take care of the men without using Grace Church for some one who is already in the ranks. If it should develop that I can get all of the men properly cared for without using Grace Church, I will be glad to keep you there. This, however, is not probable.

The bishop did say he would be happy to have Martin join the Texas Conference and would "be delighted to ask for your transfer" if Martin wanted to come. Since there was little to encourage him about his chances of remaining at Grace Church, Martin saw no reason to leave the Little Rock Conference where he was already a probationary member. He thanked the bishop and declined the offer of a transfer.

In those days Methodist preachers reported on their work in person to the annual conference. Martin made the trip to Beaumont, where the Texas Conference was meeting, reported and, without waiting for adjournment, returned to Houston. There, in a short time, he sold his Ford automobile, packed the family's scant belongings, freighted them to Arkansas, and took the train with Sallie, who was pregnant again, and Donald for Pine Bluff to attend the Little Rock Annual Conference, where he expected to receive his next appointment. During the night, however, the porter woke him with a telegram from Robert Cole, chairman of the Board of Stewards at Grace Church, saying he had been reappointed. Not knowing what had happened or how to respond to the news, he got off the train at the first opportunity and telephoned Bishop Edwin Mouzon, who presided over the Methodist Conferences in Oklahoma and Arkansas, and asked him what to do. Mouzon told him he belonged to the Little Rock Conference, was a member on trial there, and would be given an appointment when he got to Pine Bluff. Obedient to his bishop, Martin went to the conference and there was ordained a deacon.

In the meantime, Bishop Ainsworth had gotten in touch with Mouzon to explain the situation in Houston and to urge him to allow Martin to transfer to the Texas Conference in order to remain at Grace Church. He also wrote Martin at the conference in Pine Bluff on November 29 and explained what had happened. At the last session on the last day of the conference, November 22, one of the preachers, Tom Morehead, against whom charges of sexual improprieties had been brought, was found guilty of immorality by the Committee of Trial. He was suspended for a year, making it necessary to shuffle the list of appointments before they could be read and conference adjourned. The bishop and his cabinet immediately adjourned to consider what could be done, and they decided that the preacher newly assigned to Grace Church should be sent to fill the vacancy created by Morehead's suspension. Bishop Ainsworth was clearly in a situation where the easiest course of action was to return Martin to Houston. It was, under the circumstances, a win-win opportunity. The people in Houston would be delighted to have Martin return and were urgent in pleas to the bishop to appoint him; Martin was doing a great work and would gladly accept the appointment; and the cabinet would be spared the necessity at the last minute to change a number of appointments to accommodate a conference member. The situation, as Bishop Ainsworth explained to Martin in his letter, made

> it necessary for me to send Brother Vance [who had been appointed to Grace] to take care of a very delicate situation in Orange [where Morehead was serving]. This opened the way for me to put you in Houston, and accordingly I announced you there, and wired Bishop Mouzon that I had so announced, and asked him for your transfer. This, of course, was a surprise to him, but it seemed the best way for me to handle a delicate situation in the very last moments of the Conference session.

Appended to this unusual letter in Ainsworth's bold, flowing hand, is a postscript saying, "I am leaving Saturday for Washington for ten days. I hope you will be safely in Houston before I return." George W. Davis, presiding elder of the Houston District, wired Martin on December 2, "INSIST ON MOUZON RELEASING YOU WANT YOU BAD." Bishop Mouzon knew himself to be trapped in a fait accompli, but in fairness he was willing to acknowledge that although he did not want to lose Martin to the Texas Conference he had nothing to offer him that was equal to Grace Church and agreed to his transfer.

In short order Martin and his family were on their way back to Houston for what turned out to be four happy and successful years. Grace Methodist Episcopal Church, South, is located on the corner of 13th and Yale Streets in a section of Houston called the Heights. The old sanctuary is gone, but the new one, facing the opposite direction, remains on the original site. The Heights was Houston's first suburban development, located just on the outskirts of the city. It was separately incorporated and when annexed its municipal restrictions, one of which prohibited the sale of alcoholic beverages within its boundaries, were accepted as a condition of the merger. It is still possible without too much difficulty to identify the corporate limits of the Heights by looking for liquor stores.

The Heights appealed to its residents not only because it was new and out of the city but also because, as its name implies, it was located on higher ground above Buffalo Bayou, which was less subject to flooding. While there are no hills on the Texas coastal plain, and none of the city of Houston is more than a few feet above sea level, the Heights were less prone to flood than some other parts of town. Grace United Methodist Church has problems keeping its basement dry because of the high water table but the land around it does not flood. To add to the convenience of life in the Heights, a streetcar line ran directly into downtown. These amenities caused the development quickly to attract a population of "up-and-coming" persons looking for a better life on the outskirts of the city. The wide and lovely Heights Boulevard contains many of the elegant homes they built during the 1920s and 1930s.

In 1921 the Heights was growing rapidly, and Grace Church, organized in 1905, was growing with it. Martin had, without much other than good fortune and talent to commend him, landed in the right place at an opportune time and made the most of it. Driving through the neighborhoods of the Heights, it requires little imagination to see the pleasant and appealing place it was when William C. and Sallie Martin served Grace Church. Their parsonage, which was next door to the church on Yale, was torn down and replaced in 1953 with a new one some blocks away. Sallie Martin would have liked the change since she disliked living next door to the church.

Grace's original sanctuary was designed in the popular Akron Plan style, which made it especially good for preaching, but its rapidly expanding membership demanded additional Sunday school space. Martin reported to the conference in Beaumont in November 1921, that Grace's total membership was 800. Although less than a third the size of First Methodist in downtown Houston, it was, nevertheless, a large, city congregation of the Methodist Episcopal Church, South. During that year there had been 133 additions on profession of faith and another 159 had joined by transfer from other congregations. The records don't indicate how many of these were added during the six months Martin was the pastor. After persons who left the church for various reasons had been removed from its rolls, the net growth for the conference year 1921 was 81.

Grace Church continued to grow at the rate of about 10 percent a year during all of Martin's ministry there. In 1921, the church owned buildings valued at $30,000, with total indebtedness of only $3,000. Sunday school enrollment was 772, the total budget was $11,532, and Martin's salary was set at $3,000—a significant increase over what he had received at Lisbon and Webb's Chapel. In terms of its buying power, the dollar in 1995 would have been worth 11 cents in 1925. Of the twelve congregations of the Methodist Episcopal Church, South, in Houston, only three, First Methodist, St. Paul's, and North Side, had larger budgets. Two of them paid their pastors a higher salary than Grace paid Martin.

After this stroke of remarkable and unexpected good fortune, Martin threw himself into his work with the full force of his almost boundless energy. It was at Grace that he established many of the practices that he continued through all his years as pastor of a local congregation. He thundered at breakneck speed through the streets of Houston in his car, bringing himself to the "official" notice of the police from time to time, and while the fines for speeding or running red lights and stop signs were not well received, he paid and kept going. Over the years the diary reports a fair number of minor accidents and fender benders. In his retirement years he seemed even to have improved his considerable talent for backing into cars. One might easily conclude that he was not an especially careful driver. The Martin children remember him as a good driver but "bold" when behind the wheel. As he roared down a street with a car about to enter the roadway somewhere up ahead, without slowing down their father used to say, "I know he won't pull out, he is too smart for that." Once in a while the driver wasn't.

When he reported to the annual conference at the end of his first full year at Grace in November 1922, the results were again impressive. Grace had a net total increase in membership of almost 10 percent bringing it to 879. Sunday school enrollment now reached 820. During the year, 187 persons had joined the church, and the total budget had grown to $14,116. John M. Moore was now his bishop; George W. Davis finished his final year as presiding elder and was replaced by Charles T. Tally.

One significant event involving the Martins went unreported to the annual conference. Their second child, a daughter whom they named Mary Katherine, was born on May 3, 1922. Mary was William C.'s favorite name for a girl and Katherine was Sallie's middle name. Although she decided later in life that Mary Martin was "just too plain" and began to call herself Mary Catherine (and spell it with a "C" rather than a "K"), during her early life she was known to one and all as Mary. Life was busy at the Martin household with a small boy and a new baby.

It might have been impossible, in fact, had it not been for the tender and loving help provided to Sallie by a member of the congregation, Mrs. T. A. Moore. Living on nearby Harvard Street, she was the companion and surrogate mother that Sallie needed, and the Martins stayed in touch with her for as long as she lived and regularly remembered her with a box of pears at Christmas. Mrs. Moore's granddaughter now attends Grace Church.

In what became his usual practice, Martin began to write down what he was thinking or reading in small notebooks. One of those, a "Blue Jay" tablet is headed "Thoughts, Houston and Port Arthur." The first entry, written in pencil in his clear hand, contains an admonition about the dangers of success.

When you get to feeling real proud of yourself and begin to consider how pious you are, what a wonderful success you have made in life and how much better you are than other people; when you reach the place where the natural expression of your thought would be the prayer of the Pharisee, "I thank thee that I am not as other men are"—when you reach that point the most wholesome exercise upon which you can enter is to ask yourself the questions, "What do I have that God hasn't given me?" Body, mind, Xn influences, educational advantages and a multitude of other blessings which come to you with no effort on your part. They are the unmerited gifts of God. Two results come from that sort of exercise: first, tolerance toward the frailties of others and second, the recognition of the fact that all things worth having have come from God and that I must use them in his service.

We don't actually begin to get a complete picture of Martin's work at Grace Church until he resumes keeping his diary in January 1923, but there is no doubt even without its record that he was a dedicated and successful pastor. Even after he was elected to the episcopacy and served there with distinction, Will Martin always said he considered himself first and foremost a pastor. He found it to be a challenging occupation. In a thoughtful entry dated January 29, 1923, he wrote about the difficulty faced by a pastor in keeping focused on the "primary purpose for which the gospel stands, namely, the regeneration of the human race." He wrote of the Bible in the Blue Jay notebook:

> The main objective of the Bible is not to furnish a complete basis for a world philosophy but to point the way to godly living. The preaching of today should follow that wise example. If the under-lying principles of true Christianity were taken for granted in our preaching we could present doctrines by indirection which is after all the best way to present it.

He confided that he thought "if he could afford it," that a "preacher should buy every book he knows he ought to read even though he does not have opportunity to read it at the time." In another entry he prayed, "Lord, deliver me from the ecclesiastical mind—from the tendency to consider everything and everybody from the narrow point of view of denominational loyalty." He thought about science and history, too.

> There is as much possibility of having too much history as there is of having too little. Unless history is read with intelligent discrim-ination the conclusions that are drawn from it may be false and misleading. The weaknesses of the past may be mistaken for its strong points and we may find ourselves attempting to reproduce that which ought to be forgotten.

There are entries which show that he was thinking about the relation of science and religion. The Scopes trial in Tennessee in which Clarence Darrow defended a biology teacher who dared to teach Darwin's theories in a high school classroom took place in July 1925. Although Martin does not mention it specifically at the time it took place, he must have read and thought about the larger questions it raised. "If materialistic science is permitted to have its way, it not only rules out the possibility of the miraculous but the freedom of the will as well. The two are simply different parts of the same whole and they stand or fall together."

In another entry on the same subject, he wrote: "There is a voice, deeper and more authoritative than the voice of reason—the voice of the deep, age-old, instinctive nature—the voice that cries out after God and declares its cry is not in vain even in a world in which a materialistic science is shouting, 'There is no God.' "

If Martin was prepared to warn against the appeal of "materialistic science," he was committed to mount the barricades and die on moral issues. He read articles on birth control and concluded the "prevention of conception by unnatural means is wrong socially and religiously." He was uneasy about the movies, held out staunchly against the liquor trade, although it was not a regular topic for his sermons, and heard with approval SMU's president, Charles C. Selecman, explain to the regular Monday preacher's meeting "what the university was doing to discipline students who participated in a recent disgraceful dance." He also left a play at the high school that was "pitched on a low plane," and included an "interpretive dance" that was "positively objectionable." He commented, "The insidiousness of sin is appalling." When he preached the graduation sermon at Heights High School for the third time in a row, his topic was "When Sin Comes In," but he had to admit "the material did not lend itself to use as I had hoped."

From the diaries Will Martin kept faithfully from January 1923 until almost the end of his long life, we can safely assume what he did in his first years at Grace and follow the daily routine that fills the diary's pages afterward. He generally got up at 7:00 A.M., although in April 1923, he bought an alarm clock and resolved to be up by 6:30, in order to be in the study by 8:00 A.M. Martin was a man who required a good deal of sleep and almost always was in bed by 10:00 P.M. Mornings were spent in the study, pastoral calls and errands filled the afternoon. Meetings were normally scheduled at night. He records in the diary what he was reading, and how his time was spent during the day.

He began recording the number of pastoral calls he made and continued this practice throughout his ministry in the local church. He made a great number of them, and as a presiding bishop required the preachers under him to report how many they made. As he did during his days as a student pastor, he includes the title of his sermons and a brief evaluation of his performance in the pulpit. When he spoke to the Y.W.C.A. cooperative home on January 4, he rated the effort "unsatisfactory to myself." He doesn't say how his audience responded. He preached on Sunday evening, January 21, "The Danger of an Unconquered Sin," "with some effect." The following week he did not do well and chastised himself for "insufficient preparation for the evening sermon." He soon resolved, "to let no Sunday come without a carefully written proposition for each of the two sermons and the principal thoughts committed to writing." The highest accolade was "as good as I am capable of doing at this time."

February 11 he preached the sermon, "That the World May Believe," to a full house and observed "How great things God must expect of an intelligent, well provided for people in this critical hour of the world's history." On Wednesday of the same week, while working on the church bulletin, which he did not enjoy, he confessed that for the first time he was "beginning to see the possible value of the church bulletin as a means of disseminating religious propaganda." Afterward, he began writing an editorial on some phase of the church's activity for each issue.

Following his resolution to learn from the example of great preachers, he began regularly to read either their sermons or something about their lives. In his "Thoughts" he wrote: "To read a sermon each day, to read a prayer a psalm or other devotional literature which will stimulate thoughts which can be used in prayers—these two things I am resolved to do each day." In January he read Alexander V. G. Allen's *Life of Phillips Brooks,* but found Brooks "so super-human in his intellectual powers as to awe rather than inspire one." He also noted that the "circumstances of his life were so entirely different from my own that I simply cannot understand him." He identified more with the sixteenth century Protestant reformer, Martin Bucer and devoured the writings of Bishop William A. Quayle. After attending the community revival services in Houston in which Charles L. Goodell preached, he read some of his books and arranged for a private conference with him. "Impressed that Dr. Goodell is a man who has proved in his own pastorate that evangelism can succeed in the midst of modern condition if the personal element is introduced." In his conversation on February 21, Martin "spoke to him about my personal religious experience and he advised me to test myself and use the opinions of others in adopting a plan for evangelistic work. . . . Gave me the names of a number of books he thought would be helpful." Martin had a unique capacity to soak up information like a sponge, was always in search of it with self-improvement as the goal.

Because his study in the morning was frequently interrupted, he began the practice of reading in the public library as many days a week as he could. He borrowed books from C. M. Bishop, pastor of St. Paul's Methodist and later a member of the faculty at the SMU School of Theology. Sick children at home sometimes interrupted sleep and study. Martin made pastoral calls in the afternoon and sometimes in the evening when he did not have meetings. Although he believed it to be an essential part of a pastor's work, he admitted that "I never begin an afternoon of pastoral calling but that I do it reluctantly; I never return from this work without rejoicing that I went." He met regularly with Robert L. Cole, chairman of the Board of Stewards and frequently with J. L. Rundell who was superintendent of the Sunday school. Rundell's son is still an active member of Grace Church.

In addition to weddings and funerals, there was a regular meeting on Monday mornings for preachers in the Houston District at which papers were read and discussed. It was here that he met the pastor of First Methodist Church, A. Frank Smith, who would later become his friend and colleague in the Council of Bishops. Martin also gave regular attention to completing the correspondence lessons and exams that were required for ordination and full membership in the annual conference. Sometimes Sallie would make calls with him in the late afternoon, but her time was almost fully occupied with home and children. When at leisure, he read Shakespeare and worked in the garden; he chopped wood when it was needed, and for exercise.

By 1923 he had sufficiently established himself in the city of Houston to receive a good many invitations to speak at special events and meetings and for the services at Grace to attract a crowd. On Easter Sunday, April 4, 1923, there was a sunrise prayer meeting that attracted a large congregation at 6:30; 653 people were in Sunday school that day, and a large congregation filled the sanctuary to hear his sermon. Unfortunately, the two choirs that "presented the best music we have had" also left little time for his sermon on John's vision on the Isle of Patmos. Determined to have it heard, the next Sunday night he preached "Where There Is No Vision the People Perish," but failed, he said, to "take enough time to develop it well."

The annual spring revival featured the preaching of S. S. McKenney of Beaumont; Baron de Ely, Jr., of Dallas led the singing, but "a spirit of coldness seems to persist." Part of it was his own, and he resolved during the evening service on May 3, "to see a manifestation of the spirit of God which would enable me to speak with confidence about his presence." It was the same old demon that haunted him from the time of his call to preach. And it got worse. He wrote in the diary on May 7:

> I have felt during this meeting the same spirit of depression that I have always felt during a revival. This is caused partly by my concern for those who are not Christians and partly by the fear that there is something lacking in my Christian experience which, if I had it, would enable me to reach these people. . . . I resolved to

allow nothing to turn me aside in my search after this experience. . . . I recalled my experience in Tennessee when I left off
preaching for a time in the conviction that I ought not to preach
again until I had had the blessing. . . . I trust that I may not long
remain in this condition of uncertainty.

The revival ended on Friday, May 11, without his having found
the assurance he so desired. That lack of assurance did not, however, hamper his success. Mother's Day, May 13, he received sixty
people into the church and baptized thirty-five. Good things were
happening.

On May 16 he began reading John Wesley's sermon "Witness
of the Spirit," and the next day noted "a morning which will be
far reaching in its consequences." There are, in fact, two sermons
by that title, plus another titled, "The Witness of Our Own
Spirit" in the *Standard Sermons* of John Wesley. The first two,
written twenty years apart, are preached on the text in Romans
8:16, which was quoted by Mr. Wesley to read, "The Spirit itself
beareth witness with our spirit, that we are the children of God."
The third uses the text in 2 Corinthians, 5:17. In the University
Edition, edited by Albert Outler, the three combined include only
about forty pages of text, and it is likely that Martin read all
three. While reading, the thought came to him that our relation to
God is much like that of a child to a father. "If this is true then
will not our knowledge of him and love for him be a matter of
growth and progression?" he asked. Wesley's understanding of
the witness, as Martin interpreted it, is an "abnormal" rather
than a normal experience. Most people have never experienced it.
It is growth and maturation, therefore, which is the norm. "Along
this line of reasoning I worked out, I believe under divine guidance, the most satisfactory conception of the whole problem I
have ever had. . . . Thanks be to God for his goodness."

He reviewed George Albert Coe's popular *Social Theory of Religious Education* for the regular Monday preacher's meeting and
"was presumptuous enough to offer some criticism, of his position
with reference to the chief task of the church"—evangelism. Once
again he does not comment on the response his colleagues made.

That same day he went to the "picture show" with Sallie to see *Robin Hood,* a "perfectly wholesome picture," but didn't feel comfortable being there. When *The Hunchback of Notre Dame* came out in 1924, he was "strongly inclined" to see it, "but decided that such use of the time would not help forward the work I am most vitally interested in." Sallie later said that he wouldn't go to the movies, and he wouldn't let her and the children go either, but he got over it. That is easily attested by the fact that they may have been able to lay claim to the record for having seen *Gone with the Wind* more times than any episcopal couple in America, certainly in the Methodist branch of it. Nor could the family drink root beer, attend the movies on Sunday, or have games in the house that could be associated with gambling. Mary Catherine remembers the hot summer evening when the chairman of the Board of Stewards in Little Rock came by to take them all out for a root beer. Martin protested that he never drank any variety of beer and was laughed out of the car by his lay leader, who explained the difference. After they moved to Port Arthur he came to terms with his feelings about the propriety of movies, but did not change his mind about attending them on Sundays, and he was always careful to avoid any which might be of questionable content. He would, in fact, inquire at the box office, "Is this movie suitable for children?"

May 27, 1923, Martin preached the commencement sermon at Heights Senior High School for the second year in a row. The sermon was titled "The Measure of Greatness." The first mention of a Friday fast day comes on June 1. Despite the fact that he considered fasting beneficial and resolved to do it years earlier, this appears to be the time at which he actually began its regular observance. He continued for a number of years with somewhat less than absolute regularity.

In the summer Sallie, who was pregnant again, took the babies and went off to Arkansas for a well-deserved change of scene and some rest. The parsonage was located next door to the church, as was the custom in those days, and Sallie was the first preacher's wife who made it available to the congregation. It was a mistake. "It liked to have killed me," Sallie remembered. "I kept the silver, I kept the keys to the church; they just came in and out. I couldn't keep the doors locked. . . . They were good to me but they would come in and take my things out of the ice box and put church things in. They would take every dish I had, everything I had in my kitchen." When she complained about it, never being reluctant to express her opinions about things that mattered to her, the response was, "Well, that parsonage belongs to us." She was willing to make any sacrifice, however, to support her husband and ensure his success. "He had to be a success. That was all there was to it; that was the burning ambition," she said. They shared it.

While Sallie and the children were gone he rode the train to Dallas to attend the annual Pastor's School at SMU. There he roomed with former Hendrix classmate, A. W. Martin, and spent hours walking and talking with friends. Albea Godbold was there as was Frank Musser, Harry Devore, C. E. Nesbitt; SMU classmates Theophilus Lee, Ed (Red) White, and Robert Jackson were there, too. One of the best things about the gathering was renewing old acquaintances. But there were classes, too. In the mornings he heard James Henry Snowden speak on "Psychology of Religion and Its Practical Application," took J. W. Perry's class "A Program for a City Church," Dr. Alderson's "Church and Ministry in Early Centuries," and James S. Seneker's "Introduction to Psychology." The courses also enabled him to complete the requirements for the fourth year of the Conference Course of Study and made him eligible for full conference membership and ordination as an elder. Afternoons were spent resting, talking, reading, and playing. He had a wonderful time. And, as always when he was in Dallas, he went on Sunday morning to hear George W. Truett preach at the First Baptist Church. "A packed house and a great sermon. . . . He continues to set forth an ideal of the ministry which is the most appealing to me of any I have known." A trip to hear well-known evangelist Bud Robinson in Fort Worth was disappointing—"a slap at most organized agencies of righteousness followed by an appeal to seek the second blessing. A good reward for curiosity." He did later list more than sixty expressions in a notebook on "conversion" that came from the evangelist so he must have gotten something from the experience.

When the school at SMU was over, he boarded the *Sunshine Special* for Arkansas to rejoin his family and enjoy a brief visit with the kinfolk. He, Sallie, and the children were all back in Houston on July 7. During this time he was reading *Les Misérables,* Paul's letter to the Romans, and Charles Reynolds Brown's *The Art of Preaching.* He read the poems of Wordsworth and Byron and wondered if Wordsworth was a pagan. There were drives with the family in the country, watermelons to eat, and picnics in the woods. William C. Martin loved the out-of-doors, and just being there had a therapeutic effect on him. Despite their power and prestige, he refused the invitation of the Ku Klux Klan to attend their meeting and worried once again about the time necessarily spent sleeping. "I have weighed the arguments with myself and my present conclusion is time spent in sleeping is profitably spent." As a responsible husband and parent, he purchased a $2,000 life insurance policy and a $25 weekly health and accident policy.

President Warren G. Harding died August 3, and William C. Martin began to read about Abraham Lincoln. He began with Frances B. Carpenter's *Six Months in the White House with Abraham Lincoln,* and John C. Nicolay's *Traits of Lincoln.* Lincoln became a lifelong interest, and Martin was rarely ever in the vicinity of the Lincoln country that he failed to take time to visit one of the sites of the president's childhood and early life. He became very knowledgeable about his life and work.

The Fourth Quarterly Conference came and went smoothly, and the conference year was over. Terry Wilson brought a rumor that Martin would be "sought" for Bering Memorial Church in Houston when conference met. He does not say what he knew about the rumor, but seemed to ignore all such possibilities and continued to work with relentless energy, sometimes making twenty-five pastoral calls in a single day.

In October, just prior to the annual conference, he went to Freeport to hold a meeting for Wesley W. Hardt. He did well and the meeting went well. At one service he preached "A Woman's Fall," making reference to the evil of dancing and other "popular forms of recreation." "About a hundred women committed together at the close of the service to stand against all forms of indecent recreation and to help promote the wholesome type." A child disrupted the closing service, and Martin asked the mother to take it out of the service—"not the best type of sermon for closing service. I have learned much here."

The demands of the revival caused him to fall seriously behind in his reading and he acknowledged his "store of ideas getting lean. I must read if I am to preach." The next day he went over to borrow books from Dr. Bishop.

November 19, the Monday annual conference was to begin in Cameron, Sallie went into labor in the early morning hours. "We went to the sanitarium at 7. I went to 1st Church to make report and later to town to collect Conference Claims. Baby was born at 2. . . . John Lee was given to the boy as a name. . . . Thanks be to God for his matchless goodness." Sallie and the baby did well and Will took the train to Cameron early Tuesday morning. Sallie's brother, Brice, and Nannie Jacob came to take care of the older children while he was away.

Grace Church reported to the conference 60 additions on profession of faith and 162 received by other means. The net increase of 87 brought the membership of Grace to 965. Its total budget had increased to almost $16,000 and the Martins were given a $300 raise in salary. The extra money would come in handy for a man with a new baby.

On Sunday evening, November 25, 1923, William C. Martin, King Vivion, and Wesley W. Hardt, father of a well-known member of the Texas Conference, Bishop John Wesley Hardt, were, along with ten others, ordained elders in the Methodist Episcopal Church, South. H. I. Robinson, who became a close friend and associate of Bishop Martin, was among those ordained deacon by the presiding bishop, John M. Moore (*Journal of the Texas Conference, 1923*, 68), "The end of a road which I had traveled for nine years," Martin observed with obvious satisfaction. At two-thirty the next morning he was on the train back to Houston to pick up Sallie and John Lee at the hospital and begin another year at Grace Church.

He resolved to study New Testament Greek five days a week, accepted the fact that he functioned better with enough sleep, and concluded, "This is not discounting God's power but cooperating with him." He also determined "I must have four hours in the study every morning except Monday [the Preacher's Meeting was that morning] if I am to live intellectually. I shall get up by an alarm clock so that it will be at the same time each morning." The very next Sunday, however, the babies interrupted his sleep, proving once again that the best laid plans of even the most disciplined cannot overcome the noise in families with small children. The last day of 1923 he wrote in his diary, "As it appears to me now, I am meant for a pastor and by his grace I shall strive to be the best pastor it is possible for me to be." The last page of the diary lists the names of sixty-five books he had read in full or in part during the year.

Planning for the new church school building occupied a great deal of Martin's time during his last two years at Grace. Mr. Silber, an architect from San Antonio, was engaged to draw the plans, and Martin confessed, "My head is now so full of building plans and financial plans that I can scarcely think of anything else." He was, however, forced to think about personal finances, for the budget at home was stretched to the point that he had to borrow $75 in January on his All Church Press stock just to make ends meet. "Sallie and I have determined to live within our salary, however it pinches. Many privations are involved, but it is worth the price." William C. resolved, but Sallie managed the money.

The trustees approved a recommendation to raise $15,000 to begin the building project on April 28, 1924. The men of the church at a dinner meeting "kicked off" the drive by pledging $7,400. "The question is now settled as to whether we will have a church building; it is now simply a matter of how soon it can be done." They broke ground on March 9. Just about the same time Sallie learned to drive the car. John Lee was not gaining weight nor developing as he should so the doctor put him on a diet of buttermilk which could be obtained only in south Houston. Sallie needed to be able to drive to keep it on hand.

News of Woodrow Wilson's death came February 3—"In many respects he was the world's greatest citizen," Martin said. That evening he preached "poorly" on the topic, "The Strength of Weakness," to a crowd made smaller by the presence of William Jennings Bryan, who was giving a lecture in town. He began seriously to think about gaining a comprehensive knowledge of the history of Methodism and thought with obvious nostalgia, "What could be more fascinating in all the world than to study church history in London."

Photographs of Will Martin in 1924 reveal a boyish looking man with a portly frame. He noted it, too. Early in the new year, February 16, he resolved to reduce by twenty pounds, but does not tell us what he weighed. He went to the library and read Copeland's *Overweight? Watch Your Health.* It was the first salvo in what was to be a lifelong battle against overeating and an expanding waistline which he waged with varying intensity and success. In 1928 he even began keeping a special notebook devoted entirely to his weight. When he began thinking about his weight early in 1924, he wrote that the three "outstanding centers of interest for me now are (1) living, including proportionate giving, within my income, (2) collecting books bearing upon Methodist history and (3) the study of diet and its relation to general health." The next week he lost four pounds. Later, after hearing Luther Bridges preach in a revival at St. Paul's Methodist, he got directly to the heart of his concern about weight. "A fat man's words respecting the deeper earnestness of the spiritual life are rather seriously counteracted by his personal appearance of complete comfort and satisfaction." Martin was a big man weighing between 190 and 200 pounds most of his life. He had a large frame, and massive hands and feet. Despite his dissatisfaction with the extra pounds and the need to lose them for his well-being and the effectiveness of his mission, William C. was never obese. He was a handsome man whose size only added to his imposing presence.

One of the most dramatic changes that Martin made during the first months of 1924 was in the method he used to prepare his sermons. On February 10, he began the practice of waiting until Sunday morning to write his sermon outline. "It has worked well and has given me a vigor and freshness of thought in delivery that I could not otherwise have had." The success of such a plan, he wrote, depended on "a well stored mind . . . mental alertness which depends largely upon physical fitness" and "a theme that is expansive enough to give one's thought processes ample range." He would select the topic some weeks in advance, read on the subject until time to preach, and then actually create a short outline which he used in the pulpit. He was not, however, averse to changing the topic if it seemed better at the last minute to preach on another subject.

For preachers everywhere, deliberately waiting until Sunday morning to prepare a sermon seems designed to strike terror into even the most stalwart heart. Almost anyone who has preached for as long as a year knows from experience the soul-rattling angst of coming to Sunday morning poorly prepared or, God forbid, without a sermon to preach. Waiting until the last minute surely opens the door to a Pandora's box of serious ills. What happens if the press of other duties leaves inadequate time to read? What if emergencies or other unforeseen events arise and fill the time set aside for planning or writing a sermon? While Martin did acknowledge that the Sunday evening sermon would require more advance preparation since both mind and body were likely to be tired, he himself was unable at times even to be fully ready for the morning. The last Sunday in August 1924, he "discovered that my material was entirely too inadequate and I had to dig like a Trojan." But on the whole, the practice suited him and he continued it throughout his years as a pastor. Sunday was not his only problem, however. Wednesday was, he said, "almost as busy a day with me as Sunday and the relief is almost as great when it is over." Prayer meeting required still another preparation. He continued reading Paul's letters in his morning devotionals.

The Martin archives contain hundreds of sermon outlines. Most of them are no longer than two pages torn from a steno pad, written in pencil, and folded into three sections. They contain little more than the salient points of his presentation and, for a current student, provide little real information about what was actually said. When in later years in Port Arthur the local newspaper published a summary of his sermons regularly, each Monday morning had to be spent writing out the sermon that he preached from notes on Sunday. In time he memorized the text of his scripture, no matter how long, and if he quoted poetry he did it from memory as well. He rarely used quotations from other sources but made frequent references to them. The backlog of reading provided resources, and thinking about the subject during the week kept his mind focused. When he told Albea Godbold what he was doing, however, he found little enthusiasm from him. It simply would not work for most people and spelled disaster for anyone who was less disciplined than he was.

Martin had sufficient interest in book collecting to read William Harris Arnold's *Adventures in Book Collecting,* but the person who nurtured and guided him in it was his "across the block neighbor," the remarkable E. L. Shettles. A retired preacher, Shettles was a bookseller and bibliophile of most unusual talents, and it was through him that Martin began to address his interest in collecting books on Methodism. Shettles capitalized on a real weakness present in the young preacher and encouraged Martin in his collecting. Once after having received a book from him, Martin confessed, "I can scarcely afford to own it and positively cannot afford to be without it." A month later Shettles sent him another batch. Martin did, however, manage to resist the salesman who was selling the *Library of Southern Literature*—"no way to afford it." Shettles provided the original collections to the SMU library when it was begun in 1915. Martin stayed in touch with him all his life, and would ride the train when he was pastor at First Church from Dallas to Austin just to spend the day with him. Throughout his life, Martin counted Shettles among the most remarkable persons he was ever privileged to know.

In the spring his old friend from Arkansas, Paul Quillian, and SMU classmate, Erwin "Bummie" Bohmfalk, came to hold a revival meeting at Grace Church. Quillian did the preaching and Bummie led the singing. They were a rousing success, and when it concluded on Easter Sunday Martin said, "the boys" "had captured our people." "Decision Day" on April 13 saw thirty-two people respond to the call to make decisions to commit their lives to Christ and thirty infants and small children were baptized. Later Bohmfalk served as a district superintendent and was a member of Martin's Central Texas Conference Cabinet.

About the time of the revival, Bishop Samuel Ross Hay, who was in town to speak to the Monday preacher's meeting, asked Martin if he would be interested in going back to Arkansas. He told the bishop "that I was here under what I regarded as a clear call and I thought it best to remain." But he talked it over with Sallie at length and they both agreed "it seems best to stay in Texas."

During the summer, after Martin suffered a round of colds and throat problems, Dr. O'Banion, the family doctor, recommended that Martin have his tonsils removed. It was done in the office, caused considerable pain for the next few days, and delayed his going to SMU for Pastor's School. When he arrived, as always, he heard George Truett preach, who, without a doubt, he said, "ministers to my spiritual needs more than any man I have ever heard." He went back in the evening and told Truett after the service "how I was accustomed to go for a whole year in the inspiration of his messages." The next Sunday he chose hearing Truett over Bishop Warren Candler who was preaching at SMU, and after hearing Bishop Candler in the evening decided "I did not regret having made the choice I did." An added bonus was gained from Truett's services being held in the Melba Theater while the First Baptist Church was being remodeled. The building was "artificially cooled." When he got home, he talked to an electrician about installing fans in Grace Church.

In August he decided not to vote in the gubernatorial election since he was "unwilling to be a part to making either of the candidates governor of this state." In that election Governor James Ferguson was ineligible to have his name on the ballot so he saw to it that his wife, popularly known as "Ma Ferguson," became the candidate. In the primary in which Martin refused to vote, she ran successfully against Felix Robertson, a conservative candidate backed by the Klan, and went on to defeat George C. Butte to become governor in the general election in November.

The coming of autumn, "the most glorious season of the year," brought happy memories of "school days, possum hunting, France, etc." It also brought, in November, the first experience of doing a baptism by immersion and the regular session of the Texas Annual Conference. That year it met in Mt. Pleasant, on the northern edge of the conference, and returned William C. Martin once again to Grace Church. "There is no more thrilling moment during the entire assembly than the time during the reading of the appointments." Grace Church now had 1,107 members and a budget of $21,086.

The year 1925 was to be the Martins' last in Houston, but William C. began it with enthusiasm. There was a surprise party given by the congregation to celebrate their return where "deep and genuine joy . . . was manifested." For some unknown reason Martin had for several weeks been under the impression that his former presiding elder, Charles T. Tally, had changed his attitude toward him. When confronted, however, Tally assured him that "there had been no change." He continued to read extensively and followed the same pattern of sermon preparation. Bishop Hay had not forgotten about the possibility of his returning to Arkansas, and in March Hay offered him an appointment in Jonesboro, Arkansas, to begin on May 1. Martin did not find it a difficult decision and promptly declined. In early September Bishop John M. Moore urged him to take an appointment to the University Methodist Church in Norman, Oklahoma. Although that decision was harder, Martin declined it, too, but it was clear that he soon would be moving somewhere.

The building campaign for the Sunday school addition ran into a roadblock when in July all the bids for construction, as usual, came in higher than any of the estimates. There were also problems in getting a loan and the building committee made a decision to postpone the project. The Board of Stewards thought the project too important and too far along to curtail, however, and voted to borrow $25,000 and go ahead with the building. The contract was signed on September 3, 1925. The very next week Martin's presiding elder, S. S. McKenney, talked to him about moving to First Methodist in Port Arthur. Martin always regretted that he left Grace in debt for the educational building that he had urged them to build, and after becoming a bishop returned to help them retire what remained of it. The announcement was made to the congregation on October 29 that Martin would not be returning as their pastor.

It was common Methodist practice not to allow a preacher to remain longer than four years—most did not stay more than three. He preached his last sermon as pastor of Grace Church, Sunday, November 11. A great party given four days earlier presented Will and Sallie with a variety of gifts including a quilt with 600 names. Martin's final report to the annual conference showed the membership at 1,267. One hundred and five persons had been received on profession of faith and the church had seen a net gain of 163 members. The budget had risen to $24,342. Under Martin's leadership Grace had surpassed St. Paul's Methodist Church and now was the second largest congregation in the Houston District. By any standards, his work at Grace was a remarkable record of accomplishment, especially for one in his first appointment.

Despite the success in the church, 1925 proved to be a difficult year for the family. John Lee continued to have problems and underwent surgery in October to remove his tonsils and adenoids. In early July, Martin finished a revival meeting in Gilmer and took the train to Arkansas to join Sallie and the children for a visit at home. Papa came with them to meet his son at the train. They celebrated the Fourth by watching a baseball game and going to Blevins to visit friends. The next day Papa was unwell, but on Monday he went to the mill and by his office. He failed to improve and in the early morning of July 8 had a stroke, which left him paralyzed on his entire left side. This episode caused the family to postpone their trip back to Houston, and Brother Cole assured Martin that the Sunday services would be cared for in a good way.

Martin's experience in the military hospital served him well and the advice of Major Tucker to "make it your first business to see that your patient is comfortable" came clearly to mind. "A feeling of depression was driven away by the suggestion that the primary purpose of life is not happiness." Every hour of the next few days was spent caring for Papa. In their conversations William C. spoke with his father about the Christian gospel of hope and salvation and read to him from the New Testament, but the diary fails to record his father's response. Father and son had their last talk the evening of July 15. "His interest in spiritual things is growing daily. There are yet many misconceptions of the way of salvation but may the Holy Spirit remove them all."

The Martins left for home without waking Papa and reached Houston the next day. The afternoon of August 10 a telegram came from Arkansas saying that Papa had died just after noon. The diary records gratitude for the final time together and a last prayer for his father.

How thankful I was for the last hours I had had with him and for the hope of salvation which he had expressed. Oh God, thou knowest that he loved the fellowship of thy people. Give him a home in which he need never be separated from them.

4

Moving Up:
Port Arthur and Little Rock

⸺⧼⧽⸺

The Texas Conference met in Jacksonville in 1925. As was often the case the appointment "grapevine" had the correct information, and when the bishop made it "official" on Sunday afternoon, November 15, W. C. Martin was moved to Port Arthur. It was a promotion and recognition for his good work at Grace Church, and they were looking forward to his coming. H. F. Banker, chairman of the Board of Stewards, wrote two days after conference closed "that more than 40 good loyal men comprising the Official Board are solidly behind you and in advance welcome you to our city." Martin was thirty-two years old.

The *1925 Texas Almanac* reports that Port Arthur, Jefferson County, Texas, was a city of just over 31,000 residents. Located on the banks of Sabine Lake and the Neches River, seventeen miles southeast of Beaumont, it was first settled in 1898, and grew rapidly to become a shipping and industrial center with a deep water harbor. Home then to five oil refineries, two of which were among the largest in the world, Port Arthur remains a center of the petrochemical industry. In 1925 it was the largest port in Texas, three times the size of Houston, shipping more than eight million tons a year. The harbor, which was equipped with excellent wharfs and facilities needed to export oil, grain, cotton, and lumber, handled over fifty million barrels of oil, with an aggregate value of $215 million. The city had one high school and six grade schools, with a total school enrollment of 7,950. There were four banks and 550 commercial establishments.

The Methodist Episcopal Church, South, in Port Arthur stood at the corner of Fifth and Nashville Streets. Originally organized in 1902 with forty charter members as the Trinity Methodist Episcopal Church, South, it had grown with the city. Construction on a new building was begun in 1922; the congregation moved into the Sunday school unit the following year. While the "auditorium" was being completed, worship was conducted in the educational unit, which itself remained unfinished. Martin's predecessor, H. W. Knickerbocker, reported to the annual conference in 1925 a membership of 1,661, the second largest of the twenty-nine charges comprising the Beaumont District. There were 1,055 enrolled in the various departments of the Sunday school; its budget of $58,271 was the largest in the district. Martin's salary was set at $4,200, a welcome increase since he had trouble living within his means in Houston and had been forced to borrow $50 to move. Despite the increase in pay and Martin's good intentions, by the first of the year his bank account was overdrawn and the church treasurer, H. H. Brown, had to come to his rescue. "Put me in a financial sweat box for a little while," William C. said.

In Port Arthur Martin continued the practices that had worked so successfully for him in Houston, and he added a few new ones, too. Following his pattern of beginning the day in his study with a time of meditation and prayer, he now began reading through a book of the Bible four chapters at a time. He opened 1926 reading the Gospel of Matthew, and got about halfway through the entire Bible before giving up. He read Matthew in January, Romans in February, and began 1 Corinthians in March. He continued his interest in John Wesley and Methodist history, reading Wesley's *Sermons* and *Journal*. Popular authors like Harry Emerson Fosdick were on his reading list, including Fosdick's *Modern Use of the Bible;* biography and books of sermons were always included in his reading. When he left Houston, he was reading the life of the nineteenth-century evangelist Dwight L. Moody, written by Moody's son. He continued to read extensively about Lincoln. Fiction was rarely on his reading list, and later in his life he admitted that perhaps he should have read more of it. Sallie encouraged him to include it because she thought he would be broadened by the experience. When he did read fiction, he usually read the classics such as Shakespeare and Dickens.

To have more time during the day he resolved to get up at 6:00 A.M. rather than his usual 6:30. Martin was not, however, an early morning person and he needed plenty of sleep to function, so the new plan did not help him as he had hoped.

As could be expected, his preaching in Port Arthur at first consisted of reworking old sermons written for Grace Church. Mary Katherine's bout with diphtheria, which she contracted just after they moved and during which the entire family was under quarantine, made the writing of new sermons difficult, if not impossible. She was very sick. Mary had taken malaria in Houston when she was a year old, and its regular recurrence made her susceptible to other diseases and complicated any that she contracted. She did not finally break the cycle of re-infection until she was ten years old, and during these years she was forced constantly to take quinine to control the chills and fever. The side-effects were not pleasant. Her illness so early in the new conference year also kept her father from making the number of pastoral calls he would have made ordinarily. To make matters worse, about the middle of February, Sallie became ill and was at home or in bed for almost a month. Although they had domestic help by now, the necessity for Martin to be available to help with the children curtailed his activities, especially in the evenings.

As the new minister in town he was invited to speak his way around the civic club circuit and was eventually persuaded to join the Lions Club, which met on Fridays, his regular fast day. He rationalized the decision by saying, "Had not planned to join a luncheon Club but there was no easy escape and it will give me contact with a great many men and will open up new avenues of life." Despite his reluctance to become involved at all, once a member he joined willingly in the club activities, including a "tug-of-war" against the Rotarians at the fair, and enjoyed the association. He was regular in his attendance.

The Port Arthur *News* often ran a summary of his sermon in its Monday edition. Since Martin used scant notes when he preached rather than a prepared text, Monday mornings had often to be devoted to getting the copy ready for the paper. Once, in March, he was angry because his sermon appeared next to the picture "of a lewd actress," but after a talk with the editor, who explained it was an oversight, Martin accepted the editor's apology and it didn't happen again. Tuesday was "bulletin day," and getting it ready and preparing the column it always included was a chore. Prayer meeting on Wednesday evening required another preparation and that always occupied part of the day.

There were the usual glitches in adjusting the style and wishes of the new minister to the established practices of the congregation. In Martin's fourth month as pastor, the choir director left the service in protest "because I made a change in the order of worship." The episode raised questions "which I considered, to my profit, during the day," Martin said. A number of preachers have had similar learning experiences. Whether he apologized or ever did it again—or even what he learned—we don't know.

He continued his observance of Friday as a regular fast day but steadily lost ground in the creeping "battle of the bulge." Family recreation in their new town mostly consisted of drives in a new Dodge "DeLuxe" sedan purchased at cost in July from E. P. Baker, a member of the church. Their usual practice was to drive late in the evenings and on Sunday afternoons, which Martin now set aside as family time. They went often to the nearby beaches—Port Neches was a favorite destination. Sometimes he caught crabs with the children at Keith's Lake or swam with them at McFadden's Beach. As they had done often in Houston, the entire family enjoyed taking a picnic supper to the park or beach.

He remained single-minded about the importance of evangelism and forty persons joined the church on Easter Sunday during his first year. He held a revival meeting a week later in Huntsville. When it was over, impassable, muddy roads made it necessary to return home by bus. He began reading Galatians the next day,

April 23, and moved on to Ephesians in early May. The construction of the "auditorium" was finally finished and the opening service held on May 2, 1926. The building itself, first begun in 1921, was built in four stages. H. F. Banker chaired the building committee. Although the Sunday school building was already in use, and had been used for worship before the completion of the sanctuary, it was not yet entirely finished—a task Martin would complete. President Charles C. Selecman of Southern Methodist University preached the morning of its dedication and S. S. McKenney, the presiding elder, came for the evening service. Although rain reduced the crowd and Martin admitted he was glad when the day was over, it was a grand occasion. The new pipe organ was installed later and inspected by the stewards on May 20; the inaugural recital was given a week later. Leo Bonnel Pomeroy of Shreveport played before 700 people who paid one dollar for admission. However, organs, old and new, have a psyche of their own and three days later at the Sunday morning service it refused to play at all.

In June Martin decided that his practice of skipping supper as a means to control his weight "is an example of a fad that doesn't work." But through the years this was only one of many which he tried. Martin was a big man who liked to eat, and he watched his weight carefully throughout his life. That summer he began taking a short nap in the early afternoon. He found that it restored his energy and after only fifteen or twenty minutes, he would awake refreshed. Later in his life, he always referred to it as a "siesta" and seldom missed a day without it.

The SMU Summer Pastor's School at the end of June was a welcome change. He took a course on the "Social Background of the City Church"; Paul Kern taught one he took on "The Minister's Message," and his friend from Houston, C. M. Bishop, now a member of the SMU School of Theology faculty, offered "The Gospel of John." As always lots of old friends were present and there was plenty of time to talk. "Am enjoying immensely the fellowship," he said. "The courses are stimulating. I think I shall put down this summer school as one of the things which I must make room for every year." He bought a book entitled *Walking as Exercise* and decided correctly "this is my best type of exercise." It was a decision from which he never wavered. Throughout his life, William C. Martin enjoyed walking; he walked, and encouraged others to walk with him, whenever and wherever he could.

When he returned home from Dallas, he and other members of the Ministerial Alliance began seriously to address what Martin described as the "moral conditions" in Port Arthur. The primary object of their concern was an area in the city known as the "reservation" where gambling, bootlegging, and houses of prostitution flourished. The opening salvo in this crusade was a sermon preached by C. W. Culp, pastor of the First Baptist Church, in which he challenged the twelve pastors of the city to unite to eliminate its vice. Specifically, he proposed that they raise enough money to hire a detective agency to keep them informed of the true happenings in the reservation district, but they began by having a conversation with the chief of police, W. W. Covington. The chief "promised to clean things up after the elections."

A single sheet of paper, written in pencil, outlines Martin's "Thoughts to drive the houses of prostitution out of Port Arthur." One of these "thoughts" concerned the role the members of the Ministerial Alliance realistically could expect Chief Covington to play in the effort. These "Thoughts" were not dated, but the diary has an entry for August 10 that reads, "considerable thought given to finding the best method of dealing with social vice in P.A." With respect to the Chief, Martin said,

Nothing more should be said to the chief of Police about the matter at this time. He has given his promise and if he does not keep it may be best for the cause. He is half hearted about it—the people are not aroused. If a clean-up is begun under such conditions it is not likely to be permanent and the whole thing will have to be done over again.

It will be better to get the question before the people in such a way that they shall be well informed concerning the evils of licensed prostitution.

It is not hard to imagine that the chief and his colleagues in law enforcement opted to take a pragmatic view of the situation. Any port city was likely to have prostitution and the presence of a "restricted" district gave the authorities some control over its activity and, at least, contained it in a given area. If the citizens were not up in arms about it, as Martin acknowledged they were not, the best thing to do was let well enough alone. There were twenty-five establishments in the district.

Martin was temporarily distracted from the cause when on July 17, a newspaper reporter called to give him the news that J. Frank Norris, pastor of the First Baptist Church in Fort Worth, the old enemy of the SMU School of Theology and especially of Dr. John A. Rice, had shot and killed a man in his office. "The work of the entire day was overshadowed with thought of the Norris tragedy which was given in all the papers as the most prominent event of the month." The next day it was front page, headline news in the Port Arthur paper, too. Norris, later acquitted, often discussed the event as a regular feature of his evangelistic radio broadcasts.

By July 30 the members of the Ministerial Alliance formed a committee to consider the subject of public morals and propose plan of action. As in the past, the center of their concern was "the restricted vice district." The day following their meeting Martin, who must have been given the responsibility, spoke with J. W. O'Neal, assistant county attorney, and on the next Sunday night weighed in publicly with his first attempt to "arouse" his people to action. He preached on the subject "Civic Righteousness." The announcement of his topic appeared on the front page of the newspaper on August 1, and 750 people came out on Sunday night to hear what he had to say. "People were with me . . . good was accomplished." Martin was convinced "the agitation against this form of evil will help to arouse interest in other movements looking to moral betterment." Martin told his congregation, according to the report of the sermon that appeared in the Port Arthur *News,* August 2, 1926, there were three groups of people who could not be expected to help remove the evil—the individuals who made a profit from its operation, those who patronized it, and the many, good persons who were indifferent. "They," he said, "are a parasite upon the social order and . . . unworthy of the name 'citizen.' " To arouse them to action was clearly the purpose of his message. The presence and location of the "reservation" was known to everyone. Any ten-year-old in the city, Martin said, knew where to find the houses of prostitution. He acknowledged that some persons thought it was simply the preferable way to deal with the inevitable, "the best way to handle social vice," but Martin told his congregation he knew and refused to believe any of the arguments offered in support of the existence of the "reservation." It had to go. The African Americans, in whose part of the city the district was located were being unfairly treated. They "do not deserve that we shall gather up the moral off-scouring of this city and thrust it down in their midst . . . thereby saying to them, 'You're a negro. We expect nothing from you but sin, therefore these things will not disturb you.' "

He then challenged the common wisdom that assumed the district was supported by sailors from ships visiting the port. If you stop them from coming, Martin said, the reservation will still go on. The people of Port Arthur have to want to stop it, and he concluded by challenging his flock to tell their public officials to close the district.

The sermon was designed to arouse the faithful and it did. Monday morning, following the sermon, he, together with his colleagues C. W. Culp and F. W. Langham, pastor of the Westminster Presbyterian Church, met again with Chief Covington and two of his detectives; immediately after this conversation Martin drove to Beaumont to talk to the district attorney, Marvin Scurlock. The preacher's meeting with the chief was front page news. Scurlock "promised to issue the injunctions on the evidence presented by Covington."

On Tuesday, Martin, armed with the statement of the district attorney, went back to see Chief Covington, who "reaffirmed his willingness to present the necessary evidence for injunctions." Although the officer was now more willing to listen, he continued to protest "that the people of Port Arthur do not want the reservation to be closed." It was a classic case of handing the responsibility from one party to another and the ball was now back in the preacher's court. Determined to test that conclusion for himself, Martin spent the rest of the day talking to "leading laymen" and they all told him, "Close it up." It is hard to imagine, however, that anybody would have been likely to tell the Methodist preacher, especially if they were members of his congregation, they were in favor of keeping houses of prostitution open. On Wednesday there was an offer of help from an unexpected quarter. The women of Mary Gates Klan No. 45 of the Ku Klux Klan wrote to congratulate William C. on his sermon, which some of them had heard, and pledged "our hearty cooperation in anything that you may undertake which would require the assistance of a body of women or individuals." The Klan in those years was a large and powerful political force. Since many of its members were also church members, it was not easy to ignore their offer of support. The same day detectives began to gather evidence against the "resort" operators, and the city attorney drafted an ordinance prohibiting their houses from having interior locks. This was designed to deter the destruction of evidence when the establishments were raided by the police.

Martin's overall plan, outlined in his "Thoughts," was to form an organization dedicated entirely to closing the brothels. It had to be led by "laymen of recognized standing and unimpeachable character." The organization would be responsible for getting information to the public and bringing "pressure upon public officials for the enforcement of the laws now on the statute books." An appeal would be made to every civic and religious organization in the city. Funds to support the work of the organization would be raised by public subscription, a portion of which would be used to employ a detective to gather evidence.

On Saturday all the Martins drove to Beaumont for a visit with former Presiding Elder Tally and his family, and while there William C. spoke again with District Attorney Scurlock. Judge R. G. Robertson of the City Court was invited to speak to the Monday preacher's meeting, and he expressed his approval and support for their plan to close the vice district. Afterward, the preachers discussed a strategy for "putting the question before our people." Perhaps being preoccupied with the topic or simply through carelessness, Martin only narrowly averted real tragedy as he left the meeting. He hit a small boy with his car "and came near to running over him." Fortunately for everyone involved, the child was not seriously injured. He and Sallie visited with the boy and his mother the next day and reconfirmed that he was not hurt. There was no mention of the accident in the newspaper.

Martin met again with Chief Covington but the diary does not mention the subject of their discussion nor the outcome; he also got a resolution passed for the second time by his Lions Club, "commending Chief Covington on his stand on social vice." This must have been part of a strategy to strengthen the chief's resolve to take some positive action. Martin personally agreed to take responsibility for getting the necessary papers signed to file an injunction against the brothels and talked again to the district attorney. September 17 he wrote an article for the *Texas Advocate* "on the relation of the preacher to social righteousness." The truth of Chief Covington's conclusion that the people of Port Arthur did not want the district closed may be indicated by the fact that the editorial page of the Port Arthur *News,* which treated a variety of topics, did not take any position on the minister's campaign to close the reservation.

<hr />

In the midst of all this, life went on. Donald started to school and Bishop Hay told William C. at a chance meeting that Bishop John M. Moore wanted him for University Church in Austin, but Hay said he was unwilling to discuss the transfer and the matter was closed.

Jeremiah was now the subject of his morning devotionals, and a biography of Brigham Young and one on *Henry Ward Beecher as His Friends Saw Him* made up his reading. Martin's personal feelings about biography are revealed in an interesting paragraph in his Blue Jay notebook.

I cannot read biography objectively and with the detachment of critical research. I am constantly reading myself into it. If the person about whom I am reading was engaged in any kind of religious work I am constantly without any intention to do so, comparing myself with the subject of the biography. When I stand in a reasonably favorable light in such a comparison there is a sense of gratification; if I fall too short, I am depressed.

Later he observed in the diary, "Beecher's life is having great weight with me just now. If I can only be able to get the good and pass over the bad."

During September he preached a series of four sermons on the Apostle's Creed, and did the preaching for the fall revival in his own church. He was pleased with the results. In preparation for these special services he spent considerable time studying the doctrine of the Holy Spirit. "There was never a real revival," he said, "without an appeal to His power." Frankie Whiteside replaced Myra Price as church secretary.

Like other good citizens in a Texas town, he attended high school football games, listened afterward to the reasons why they were won or lost, and supported local causes. Jubilee Sunday was observed in November just before annual conference with the largest attendance the church ever had. The offering totaled $1,352. The secretary of the Board of Stewards wrote Bishop Hay to report,

> By unanimous and enthusiastic vote of the Board of Stewards I have been instructed to write you with reference to the work of Brother W. C. Martin, our pastor for the past year. We feel very sure the right man was sent to us and the attitude of the Board and the membership at large is 100% for him and his return.

Speaking for the board, he acknowledged their awareness that Martin was capable "of caring for a much more important charge than this one," and told the bishop, "We did a little better by Brother Martin than for his predecessor and we are prepared to do a little better by him for the next year." The reference was to salary and they had, in fact, done better by paying him $4,500 instead of the $4,200 that was set at conference and by voting to increase his salary for 1927 to $5,000.

Martin's only comment about the annual conference was "The

bishop is rather autocratic." That, however, was not by any means an unusual trait among southern Methodist bishops, and he was probably not surprised. Following the usual custom, he and other members were entertained during the conference sessions in the home of a Methodist family. The J. T. Adams family hosted not only William C. but also W. B. Kidd and J. C. Handy of Palestine. Kidd was a local deacon in Martin's congregation. At the proper time, Martin, on behalf of his congregation, invited the conference to hold its 1927 session in their new sanctuary, and spent considerable time during the sessions "spreading all the propaganda I can" to help the cause. Three other places were nominated, but Port Arthur was easily the winner—a mixed blessing since it created a vast amount of work for him to do the following year. Sallie came for a day. Martin was elected secretary-treasurer of the Epworth League Board, which supervised the youth organization.

The Texas Conference *Journal* reports that 81 persons had joined the Port Arthur congregation during the year by their profession of faith and another 169 had united by transfer and other means. The total membership reported was 1,545, a net gain of 74, reflecting the fact that Martin had removed 167 persons from the rolls. The budget was increased slightly to $58,355. When the appointments were read on November 21, Martin was returned for a second year to Port Arthur.

It always seemed that the pattern in the Martin family was for someone to get sick at the beginning of every new conference year. In 1927 it was Mary again who did the honors by taking scarlet fever. The boys had to be given a vaccine, and "nobody slept much during the night." The Blue Jay notebook contains a note that could have been prompted by looking ahead at a new year and thinking about the ways in which it should be approached.

There may be value in the minister working as if he expected the end of the world to come tomorrow but the pastor who expects to remain more than one year had better not work that way. God doesn't so work and it is wisdom to follow God's method.

Christmas came, the children were excited about their gifts, and William C. and Sallie sent eighty-three cards to acknowledge gifts or greetings from Port Arthur families. Sallie, with Donald now in school and her domestic help, was somewhat freer from the responsibilities of home and children, and she accompanied her husband on pastoral calls, did a few on her own, attended the Women's Missionary Society, and helped with dinners and other events in the church. As not infrequently was the case, the women of the congregation earned extra income by feeding one of the civic clubs in the community. Together the Martins and the Port Arthur Methodists under their care had enjoyed a good and productive year. No New Year's resolution was made for 1927 except one to be more faithful in keeping the resolution made weeks ago to let the first thought of each morning be a thought about God and his goodness together with a prayer for his guidance through the day.

Martin began 1927 by reading Emerson's essay "Self Reliance," and making a trip to the bank with Sallie to begin "a new method of keeping the record of our expenses." This modification leads us to believe that a part of their frequent financial problems may have been due not just to a lack of funds but to poor record keeping. The Gospel of Luke now provided Martin's devotional reading. His concern for social issues resurfaced early in 1927 when he and the other members of the Preacher's Meeting signed a petition, written by Martin, to ask the school board to prohibit dancing in public school buildings. Always concerned about the evils to which he was convinced dancing could lead, he had a conversation with a female police officer at the end of the previous year on the subject of the relation of dancing to juvenile delinquency. As always, he was willing to act on his convictions, and on January 3, a woman came to protest his public rebuke of a private dance she held in her home. Her forceful reaction got his attention, and he later observed, "A lesson can be learned here but I cannot fail to warn the people against sin." Daughter Catherine later described it perceptively as "the beginning of the wisdom of the wisdom of life." He was opposed to boys and girls swimming together, too. He continued reading Emerson's essays, adding the one "Our Times" to "Self Reliance." Later he began Will Durant's *Story of Philosophy* and a biography of Charles Darwin.

Hearing George W. Truett preach in Beaumont boosted his resolve to become a better preacher and he wrote on January 17, "I got up this morning with a definite resolution to spare no pains in the effort to learn to preach effectively." Brother Shettles sent a box of books, including a set of Henry Ward Beecher's sermons. By now Martin was reading sermons by noted preachers, past and present, on a daily basis.

His daily routine, beginning with a time of meditation and devotion, now included an hour of practice on the typewriter, reading at least one sermon, a walk of two miles or more, and a thirty-minute nap at noon. Fasting on Friday was no longer a part of his week. He often took Donald to school or picked him up in the afternoon.

On January 25, 1927, Martin joined the Masonic Lodge and was given the degree of "Entered Apprentice." He became active in the work of the lodge and devoted considerable time to it during his remaining years in Port Arthur. While pastor of First Methodist in Dallas, he earned the 32 degree in the Scottish Rite as a gift from several of his members, but was never again as active in the lodge as he was in Port Arthur. In February he was awarded the Fellow Craft degree and took the exam on the work of a second degree Mason. In March he took the Master's degree. That same month he began Sinclair Lewis's *Elmer Gantry,* which he judged to be "a scurrilous thing," but resolved to read it anyway "to see what is in the man's mind." Later he said "every page is revolting," but he finished it.

By coincidence his reading of the novel coincided with a revival led by B. B. Crimm, a popular evangelist with unorthodox methods, including the use of profanity in his sermons. Crimm was preaching to 4,000 people a night in Beaumont. After giving the matter some serious consideration Martin refused to attend Crimm's services because he thought his presence would "endorse the methods." Sallie and her mother went to hear him and came home to report "I was much criticized . . . for not being present." He was labeled by some as "uncooperative," and admitted he had been "much embarrassed by not being able to cooperate in the meeting." His chagrin was heightened when nineteen people united with his congregation as a result of the revival. A few weeks later he did attend the Baptist tent meeting led by the Walker Brothers, but approved even less of them and their message. "More crass materialism could hardly be imagined." He came home from the service and read *Elmer Gantry* until eleven. After Easter he "made a resolution to visit fifteen homes where I have not called before, each week." He finished *Elmer Gantry* and was determined "to burn it." We don't know if he actually burned the book, but he did make the calls.

During February he preached the annual revival at Lon Morris Junior College in Jacksonville and talked for two hours about forgiveness with a student whose lover had been shot and died in her arms. Plans for completing the Sunday school building moved ahead and the stewards set the pace for the finance campaign with $15,000 in pledges. The next Sunday $22,000 more was pledged in the morning and $2,200 during the evening service. The financial report was the best in the history of the church. Another building project of smaller scale but closer to home was the construction of a sandbox and swing for Donald in the backyard. Later in the year, a hutch for two rabbits was added.

Just after the middle of March it was determined that Donald would need surgery to remove a growth under his chin. The surgery was performed at the Methodist Hospital in Houston on May 17. Although it took the surgeon, Dr. Charles Green, over an hour to remove the cyst, Donald did well and the doctor assured them there would be no more trouble. He did, however, have to undergo a series of X-ray treatments after returning home. William C. returned to Port Arthur as soon as Donald was awake and resting comfortably since he needed to help care for John and Mary Katherine. Once again family responsibilities limited his time for reading and sermon preparation. He and the children often read about trees and flowers together.

He writes in the diary, "[I] wrote in my notebook some observations on the relation of the preacher to place seeking."

It is an epochal day in a man's life when he makes up his mind to be himself and to spend no time in striving to be another. This does not mean that one should not use every means to increase his use-fulness and to fulfill his mission in life but it does mean that he should not be constantly measuring his effectiveness by what somebody else is doing. There can be no freedom or joy until one makes up his mind to do his best and then be content in the belief that the Father is pleased with that kind of service.

A few pages earlier he wrote:

If my fellow preachers are promoted more rapidly than I am, I shall take it as an evidence of their superior fitness and worthiness. I am determined to allow no bitterness to corrode my soul. When abler men are found I should rejoice rather than mope about it. There will always be an opportunity for doing all that I am capable of doing.

Three daily entries in Martin's diary in early May concern the mayor of the city of Port Arthur. J. P. Logan, a controversial figure and member of Martin's congregation, who had served several terms as mayor, and only at the last minute threw his hat in the ring for re-election after having announced earlier he would not be a candidate. His pastor opposed him both as a person and on the basis of his record as a public official. The first entry reports a visit with Police Chief Covington, "about a report concerning Mayor [J. P.] Logan." The next day Martin called on the mayor and "he agreed that it would be best for him to withdraw from the membership of the church." Near the end of the month the third entry says without comment that Mrs. W. A. Martin made him defend the action "of asking Mayor to withdraw from the church." Mrs. Martin was not the only voter who supported Logan, and after he was re-elected Martin admitted that he was "dismayed," and described the experience as "a humiliating blow." There was always something else to learn.

To improve his skills in conducting worship, he began memorizing the ritual for the services of the church by spending fifteen minutes a day reading them. It was a method he used in memorizing scripture, too. Promoting the building fund occupied great blocks of time, especially when the bids for construction came in

$5,000 above the estimates and more money was required. That "caused my sleep to be somewhat uneasy," he confessed. He also admitted to the diary that "everything seems to go at loose ends when I am off my schedule." He was a man who flourished in a routine that he could control. But the building moved ahead and work was actually begun the second week in June. They moved into the new quarters the first week in August.

During this period he read Rufus Jones's *Getting Acquainted: The Faith and Practice of Quakers,* but decided not to read *The Education of Henry Adams* after looking it over. Perhaps the stress of the last few months finally took its toll, for at a Rotary luncheon he reports "I had a sort of rigor . . . and went to bed." It turned out to be an intestinal disorder, which laid him up for almost a week and caused him to miss a Sunday. "Twice within 4 months I have been laid up for five or six days with an intestinal trouble. I must keep my body healthy if within my power to do it." He decided he could "avoid a recurrence . . . by watching my diet which I am resolved to do at whatever cost." It seems likely he might have needed to find ways to reduce the level of stress under which he was working, too.

⌁

July 2, 1927, a new and unexpected opportunity presented itself. That day a letter came from his former teacher and mentor, James Kilgore, who was now acting as dean of the SMU School of Theology. "I want to see you," he wrote, "and talk over some matters with you of importance to this institution and may affect you personally." Martin noted the arrival of the letter in his diary and admitted, "A letter from Dr. Kilgore aroused curiosity as to what he wants to talk with me about." Since Kilgore had not said the meeting was urgent, Martin waited until after the family vacation in Arkansas before he went to Dallas to see him.

The family vacationed at Mt. Sequoyah, the Methodist camp near Fayetteville, Arkansas, in July. In addition to taking courses being offered in the camp's Pastor's School, Martin found time to visit Goshen, where he had held a revival during his student days at

Hendrix, and the campus of the University of Arkansas, which brought back many good memories. He attended services in his old church in Fayetteville, too. "After an absence of 13 years the church looked much smaller than it did when I was a student." He read *Shepherd of the Hills* which he judged to be "the finest novel which has its setting in the Ozarks." He took long walks with the children in the woods, where they continued to enjoy their study of trees and plants under the guidance of their father. The family took drives to visit nearby places like Springdale, Rogers, Siloam Springs, and Bentonville. The preaching of Forney Hutchinson was memorable. "He has the most magnetic personality of any man I know," Martin said. Through the years there were many pleasant and enjoyable occasions with "Brother Forney."

At the end of the time at Mt. Sequoyah, he drove the family to Blevins to visit Mamma, Brice, kinfolk, and friends in the area. Leaving them there, he rode the train to Dallas on July 21 to hear what the dean had to say. After his meeting with Kilgore he went to Port Arthur and then rejoined the family for a memorable drive home on August 8. A flat tire caused the car to swerve from the road and almost caused a wreck. "It gave us a considerable scare and we were thankful to escape with no injury to ourselves or the car."

Martin was not as much in the dark about Kilgore's reasons for wanting to see him as the diary might suggest. For example, while at Mt. Sequoyah, he talked with one of the lecturers, Dr. John A. Rice, a former member of the SMU faculty, "as to what I should say about going into teaching work." The day he left for Dallas he pondered in the dairy "what my answer should be in case Dr. Kilgore offers me a place as a teacher."

Kilgore did exactly that when they met. "Before I went to bed . . . Dr. Kilgore told me he wanted me to take the place Rev. Spann's leaving will make vacant and teach the courses which Dr. Kern used to offer." While Martin was available on campus Kilgore brought Professors Wasson, Hicks, and Goodloe into the discussion and they all said "they were anxious for me to come." The diary on July 22 reports, "I feel very incompetent in the face of such a call" but acknowledged "the academic atmosphere has a strong appeal to me." The process of reaching a decision, however, was distracting enough to cause him trouble in preparing his sermon for Sunday. "Too much thought about whether I should go to SMU." Martin deliberated a week, during which he was also reading Emil Ludwig's *Napoleon,* before he wrote to Sallie and to Kilgore on August 1 and accepted his offer to join the faculty. The wording of his letter, however, betrays uncertainty.

> I have considered your offer of a place on the Faculty of the School of Theology at Southern Methodist University in the light of all the available facts and have not been able to find sufficient grounds for refusing to accept.

He gave Kilgore permission to submit his name to the SMU Board of Trustees for their approval and to contact Bishop Hay, who would have to agree to make the appointment. Sallie, he told Dean Kilgore, "concurs very enthusiastically in the decision." Obviously he had spoken with Sallie, but since she was in Arkansas during all his deliberations they must have discussed it earlier. He was not sanguine about what Bishop Hay might say. "If the bishop does not disturb the plans I shall soon be entering new and untried waters."

Because Bishop Hay had the power to block the move, Kilgore suggested they take advantage of the fact that he was out of the state and wait to approach him. Moreover, SMU's president, Charles C. Selecman, was out of the country until the first of September so they could easily use his absence as a reason to delay. In the meantime, Martin turned his attention to issues and topics of concern to a prospective member of the faculty of a school of theology. As usual, he wrote his thoughts in the Blue Jay notebook.

> It would be better to begin slowly and gain momentum as I proceed rather than the reverse. Here, as elsewhere my aim should be to be myself—my highest self, of course—but not somebody else. If this kind of procedure does not meet the demand, nothing which I could offer would meet it.

He went on to anticipate unspecified questions that might arise in his classes, especially the vexing ones of doctrine, which "will require a steady hand and deep consecration to the progress of truth and righteousness." He committed himself to spend time and effort in the cultivation of the spiritual life of theological students; chapel should be "devotional rather than critical." Evangelism should "be kept uppermost in all the process of training a minister." And he pondered the implications of the "great chasm between the academic atmosphere of a school and the practical, pragmatic atmosphere of life in the world outside the schools."

Kilgore's decision to delay Martin's appointment proved to be a mistake. As always, Martin had written to others for advice. One of his first letters went to his old friend and classmate, Albea J. Godbold. This extensive correspondence with Godbold, which began sometime around 1923 and was carried on during all the active years of Martin's pastoral ministry, provides a clear window into their thinking and development. The diary on August 10, 1927, records Godbold expressed such serious objections to his going to SMU that Martin lost sleep over them and "the things he mentioned struck me as being so sound," that he immediately wrote to Dr. Kilgore "asking for more time for consideration." He wrote Paul Kern on August 11 to seek his advice, too.

Although we don't know exactly what Godbold said, Martin credits his friend with helping him avoid a serious mistake. He wrote to Kilgore the same day he received Godbold's letter and told him,

I was too hasty, I now see, in accepting your offer of a place as teacher in the School of Theology of Southern Methodist University. . . . I have a feeling of doubt in my mind as to whether I did what I ought to have done.

Kilgore had certainly not expected Martin to change his mind, but he remained fatherly and understanding. He replied on August 13, telling Martin that he had similar feelings of uncertainty when he agreed to leave Houston for SMU.

The whole thing is psychological. . . . I had been in one line of work for a good while, and coming up here was a change in my line of work, and therefore entering into a new territory. The mind of man is so constituted that the contemplation of a change is pleasant, but when one actually enters upon a change there comes a reaction.

He reassured Martin that "there isn't a greater work upon which you could enter—either from the standpoint of your own development, or the standpoint of the service you can render." He concludes by saying, "I feel impelled, as your old teacher, to urge you to stand by your decision, which was your first impression and the best, and let the matter stand settled in your own mind."

By coincidence Albea Godbold came for a four-day visit on August 13, the same day Martin wrote his letter to Kilgore asking for more time. They undoubtedly talked the matter through carefully and Martin enjoyed, he said, "More real fellowship than I have had for a long time." Martin's letter to his former teacher Paul Kern on August 11 asked Kern to "tell me plainly and frankly whether or not you think I should go and why." He urged Kern to weigh "my own limitations in native ability and experience, the conditions which obtain at the school, the type of man that is needed there." He admitted to his former dean, who was now pastor of the Travis Park church in San Antonio, that the work "has a tremendous appeal for me but I have deep and serious misgivings as to whether it would be best for me or the school or the cause of the Kingdom for me to go." Kern's reply, written from Mount Sequoyah on August 19 began by affirming his confidence in Martin's ability to do the work at SMU. He then raised a number of questions that he thought had bearing on the situation: Who would be dean, and what would he teach? It would, he said, likely have to be homiletics and that might prove to be a problem. Kern suggested that if Martin were serious about teaching, he should return to school and prepare himself in a discipline such as philosophy or Christian doctrine. He then described what was going on in the "general administration" of the university as "a spiritual tragedy" and said it was one of the reasons he and Richard Spann had decided to leave. "I should be very glad to see you there for what I know you can do," but concluded, "and yet I am loath to see you leave a field in which I have high hopes for your success and far reaching influence. You have a gift for preaching no less than for teaching."

Martin quickly wrote his thanks for "your frank expression of your opinion regarding conditions at Southern Methodist University and the advisability of my going there," and said it "helped greatly in enabling me to decide that it would not be best for me, for the school nor for the cause in general for me to go." Kern acknowledged the letter with a brief note written September 10, 1927, that said, "I think you have wisely decided. . . . Stay with the preaching end of it."

Martin wrote Kilgore on August 22 formally to withdraw his name from consideration. "I am now thoroughly convinced that it would not be best, from any point of view for me to accept the place that has been offered." The reasons he gave are interesting. First, "I am not a scholar and am lacking in the ability for an inclination toward the application to the close, diligent research that is necessary for the attainment of real scholarship."

The second reason cited was lack of experience. "At the present time my experience is so limited and covers so short a period of time that I should not be able to speak any sure word of authority even here." None of this was, of course, news to Kilgore, but he was so disappointed and angry at Martin's decision that he now made no secret of his displeasure. Beginning his reply of September 3 by noting that Martin for some reason had failed to sign his letter, he wrote:

A letter from Port Arthur without any signature came to me several days since—although it had all the earmarks of having been written by you. I am not surprised at you for failing to sign it, for I think you ought to be ashamed of it. I wouldn't want my name signed to a letter like that.

Kilgore said he had discussed the situation with the faculty and they refused to look for anyone else. He concluded by observing "All the objections you raised could be raised against you doing anything."

While it appeared Martin had closed the matter, for some reason he could not let it die. In describing the situation to Godbold in a letter written on Halloween, Martin said, "My teaching fever has completely cooled,"

> but not until after another serious attack after you were here [August 13-17, 1927] . . . the relapse, to which I made reference, came a few weeks ago when I felt an "urge" to say to Dr. Kilgore that I would be willing to prepare myself through a period of special study, along with my pastoral work and then a year or two in school, for a place in Philosophy of Religion or Christian Doctrine.

He finished the letter recounting that after an all night session "with myself and what I believe was the spirit of God," he came to the conclusion "that the educational field is not the place for me. . . . The place for able bodied men is on the firing line."

And so he turned more energy to a new self-improvement project—learning to type. He proved not to have great aptitude for it and the hour each day he allocated to practice was insufficient so his progress was slow. But like most things William C. Martin attempted, he persevered until he learned to do it.

Rally Day, October 9, just before the annual conference, brought out 951 people. That month the question of the "restricted district" in Port Arthur also came up again, but this time Martin was not as involved as he had been earlier. What did require a great deal of time for the better part of a month was making arrangements to host the meeting of the annual conference. The church had adequate space to accommodate the actual sessions, but a place had to be found for every delegate to stay. He talked to Bishop Hay about the arrangements on October 26 and was told during their visit that he would be returning to Port Arthur for another year. The delegates began coming on November 15, which was also the day his youngest, John Lee, took the measles, causing Martin to be up all night. Bishop U. V. W. Darlington was the conference preacher and he did it well. Martin judged it to be the "outstanding feature" of the session.

Most of the time William C. was so busy with details related to entertaining the conference that he missed its sessions, but overall it went well and he was pleased. January 28, 1928, he wrote Godbold, who was now pastor of the Brevard Street Methodist Church in Charlotte, North Carolina, "nearly every delegate was kind enough to say that it was the best entertained conference he had ever attended." The weather was ideal and "no issues were raised to disturb the harmony of the sessions. Bishop Hay was as dictatorial as ever but the brethren of this Conference call him 'Sam' and don't take him too seriously." After Martin had finished making his report to the conference, he told Godbold that "the Bishop said, 'a certain Bishop got me out of bed the other morning over long distance and wanted Martin for a church that pays $6,500 but I said to him that Port Arthur would take care of Martin.'" The Bishop to whom Hay made veiled reference was H. A. Boaz and the appointment being offered was to the campus church of the University of Oklahoma, McFarland Memorial Church in Norman. The Port Arthur *News* put Hay's remark in bold face type on the front page "so all the folks who didn't hear it saw it." When the appointments were read on November 20, W. C. Martin was again "read out" to Port Arthur. He was glad to stay and he noted, "The people here seemed glad to have me back." They raised his salary to $6,000 to prove it.

With conference finally over Martin returned to his usual routine at home and in the office and reaffirmed his conviction, "There is nothing greater than being a pastor." He told Godbold, "Nobody could be happier in his work than I am here." The Lions Club honored him by elevating (or demoting?) him from his role as a Director to the office of "Tail Twister," whose auspicious duties included fining members who failed to wear their lapel buttons or address fellow members properly as *Lion* Jones!" He finished the year writing Shettles a letter on the typewriter, made one negative and reinforced several positive resolutions for the new year but failed to reveal what they were. He now was in the habit of walking from the church to town, on pastoral calls, and to the hospital. He preached New Year's Day, 1928, "The Gospel of a New Start," and in the evening "The Power of Endurance."

The Martin family began having morning devotions together at the table before William C. left for the office at 7:15. He continued to spend most mornings in his study, reading and writing, as he had for a number of years. He took a short nap after lunch and spent the afternoons visiting hospitals and calling on prospective members, and in the evenings conducted meetings. He set Saturday afternoons aside for the family and they enjoyed trips to the nearby beaches for picnics.

It was also in 1928 that Martin began keeping a notebook on the subject of his weight. The first entry was made August 9 when he confessed, "I am carrying too much surplus fat and [that] the only way to get rid of it is by eating less." He had gained seven pounds since April and weighed 199 pounds. He resolved to get down to 190 and, as always, developed a plan to achieve the goal: "to eat my usual breakfast, a normal dinner and not more than 300 calories for supper." On the days when he was forced to eat in the evening, lunch would be no more than 300 calories. He was not looking forward to the experience but stoicly said, "I need to test myself occasionally to see whether I am capable of doing a thing that ought to be done whether I want to do it or not." He admitted being concerned about developing diabetes, the disease that had killed his father. After nine days on his new plan he managed to lose two pounds, but on August 17 he fell off the wagon. "I can practice abstinence but I cannot practice moderation. Candy is my enemy and I have made a resolution to eat no more of it." In thirty days he had lost four pounds and accepted the fact that "there is little chance for a fat man to reduce by exercise."

At Martin's urging, the church added a second staff member as assistant to the pastor. When the board offered to raise Martin's salary to $6,000, he insisted they needed an educational director instead. As a compromise they agreed to pay Martin $5,400 and hire a director for $2,100. A young man in the congregation, Bascom N. Merchant, accepted the position. Mary Katherine, beginning the year in her now usual fashion with a health problem, had her tonsils and adenoids removed without complications. He began holding a weekly Teacher's Meeting on Wednesdays before the prayer meeting.

Preparing his sermons on Sunday just before going into the pulpit, a practice begun in his last years at Grace Church, worked well for him. "My present view of the best preparation for Sunday is as follows: a good night's sleep on Friday, a restful day on Sat. and an active mind on Sat. night." He told Godbold, "I am spending less and less time in specific sermon preparation. I have had some uneasy feelings as the hour for preaching approached but not once in a long time have I failed to get hold of a truth that fed the people in a life-giving moment." He continued reading sermons, both old and new, and could now type well enough to use the machine in writing to his friends. As he told Godbold in a letter he had typed, "I am not yet finding it a time saver, although I can write as fast on the machine, I think, as I can with a pen, but there is a great deal of satisfaction in knowing that when you write a thing it can be read" (WCM to Godbold, March 30, 1928).

His correspondence with Albea Godbold, unique and impressive since letter writing has now become an almost entirely lost art, is entertaining, informative, and revealing. They discussed books, ideas, events in their lives and congregations, filing systems, sermon preparation, church affairs, family life, people, and anything else of mutual interest. It was Godbold who encouraged Martin to read the *New York Times*. A sermon, "Why Nations Die," which Martin preached on January 8, 1928, was based on a *Times* article on the discovery and translation of Hittite records.

In February the Martins bought a Victrola, and the pleasure of listening to music enhanced family evenings; in addition they took long drives and enjoyed picnics together. William C. became even more active in the work of the Masonic Lodge and progressed rapidly through the various degrees.

March 1, Martin attended a Conference on Evangelism in Dallas. Twelve hundred preachers and laymen were present. A day earlier he represented the Beaumont District at a meeting to discuss a plan to unify church-related college interests in Texas. The goal was to eliminate their indebtedness. He told Godbold, "I had never seen so many Texas preachers together before," but went on to lament "the number of real leaders in our church is pitifully small." Although he enjoyed the conference, he was sick for four days afterward. In late April he decided at Godbold's urging to attend the summer Pastor's School at Union Seminary in New York rather than the one at SMU. It was to be the first of several trips.

———————

Southern Methodist University School of Theology was still determined to entice him to join its faculty. From his January 13, 1928, letter to Godbold, we learn that Dr. Kilgore and the university's vice president, H. M. Whaling, Jr., brought to the annual conference in November 1927, an offer from President Selecman for Martin to become associate dean "until I learned the work and then take full charge." He told them, "I was not open for this kind of work now and probably will never be." This was in response to Whaling's candid admission that they needed to find a money-raiser who could build endowment and scholarships.

SMU was not, however, prepared to accept "no," and the appeal came again in May 1928. Kilgore wrote him on May 24, "The president and I and the whole theological faculty are still insistent that you are the man to come here and take up the work in the department of ministerial efficiency." Moreover, Kilgore was convinced "that the situation is such that it is really the call of the Church and of the Lord."

Martin replied to Kilgore on May 28 and wrote Bishops John M. Moore and Samuel Hay for advice at the same time. Hay answered promptly on May 31 and encouraged him to go. By contrast, Moore's short, handwritten letter, which is also dated May 31, said he thought it best not to go. "I would be glad to see you in the School of Theology and some day I may advise you to come. Just now I believe it is to your interest and to the interest of the Church for you to remain in the pastorate." Martin had replied to Kilgore, however, before he heard from either, causing one to wonder if he actually wanted their advice. His first impulse, he told his former teacher, was to leave the matter closed, "but after further consideration I found that I could not afford to dismiss the urgent plea of a friend and brother with so little attention" (WCM to Kilgore, May 28, 1928). But on June 4 Martin wrote Kilgore the same answer he had given a year earlier. "I am thoroughly convinced that it would not be best for me to go up there at this time." He informed Bishop Hay of this decision the next day and added, "I have a positive feeling that the pastorate is the place where I can render the best service to the church." Kilgore was by now both out of patience and frustrated, and he told Martin in no uncertain terms he was making a mistake (Kilgore to WCM, June 8, 1928).

Martin's important letter of June 22 is missing from the archives, but his diary and a reply from Kilgore makes it certain that for some reason he opened the door again. Why we do not know. Based on Kilgore's reply of June 25, it is obvious that Martin raised the possibility originally suggested to him by Paul Kern of preparing himself to teach in the area of Christian Doctrine or Philosophy of Religion, rather than go into "ministerial efficiency." Perhaps Martin simply did not want to be dean. Kilgore correctly pointed out that Martin could more easily prepare himself to teach homiletics, and do it while on the job, but he did not discourage him from undertaking the other plan. "I most heartily urge you to begin work of that sort, for I don't think there is any possibility but that the administration in the future will be as anxious to have you as they are at present." He finished the letter by saying that Dr. Selecman "is ready to nominate you to the Board of Trustees for a professorship."

Martin wrote again to Kilgore on June 24 and tried to clarify his intentions. He was thirty-five years of age, and had been a full-time pastor for only seven years. Although he had not read Levinson's *Seasons of a Man's Life* since it had not been written, from a distance it seems he was passing from one "season" to another in his life and needed to do some "re-visioning." In a frank and introspective statement, he seems to recognize it.

There are too few things about which I am positive. I often think of myself as being little more than a bundle of uncertainties and perplexities. There are a great many things that I must get cleared up in my own mind before I try to make them clear to anybody else. The only hopeful thing about it for me is that I was never more anxious to learn than I am now, and from men like yourself. I am confident that I have secured the right start in many directions and I have an abiding resolution to follow the search until I find something that I can present with the clear note of certainty.

With this on his mind, in early July Martin set off for New York to attend the summer Pastor's School at Union Theological Seminary. On the train to Charlotte, where he was to meet Godbold and G. Ray Jordan, he had the misfortune to have "talked with a man who seems to have been everywhere and to know everything." From Charlotte they drove in Godbold's car to New York which afforded "plenty of time to have fellowship about the things of the Kingdom." They took their time passing through Virginia and visited the sights in Washington D.C., which Martin pronounced "a city worthy of being the capital of a great nation." Paul Quillian joined them there. Martin had time for a visit with Dr. William F. O'Donnell, formerly Capt. O'Donnell of the 13th Evacuation Hospital. The "vets" spent a pleasant evening talking about the men they knew and remembering the experiences they had shared in World War I. The four arrived safely in New York City at 6:00 P.M. on July 9.

Lectures began the next day at Union. Martin heard Henry Sloan Coffin on "The Cross and Preaching," Dr. Bell of the Episcopal Seminary at Alexandria, Virginia, on "The Nature of Life," and Hugh Black on "Expository Preaching." He paid visits to Henry Ward Beecher's Plymouth Church in Brooklyn and to Wall Street. At lunch one day he broke a tooth and had to go to the dentist instead of a baseball game with the rest of the group. Throughout his life Martin spent hours in the dentist's chair. It was one aspect of his overall health that started badly and deteriorated steadily as he grew older. When Pastor's School was over, they drove up into New England, visiting Yale, Harvard, and Brown University along the way. Going home they stopped at Drew Theological School in Madison, New Jersey, and Princeton Seminary. Martin finally reached Port Arthur and home on July

27. Sallie and the children met the train. It had been a hot summer for them during which they had sought and found relief from the heat by attending a lot of movies.

While Martin was in New York, he received a letter from Bishop John M. Moore that reopened the question of becoming associate dean at the SMU School of Theology. Although Moore's letter is missing, we know from other correspondence that he wanted him to take the job in September. Martin rejected the idea and wrote to Albea Godbold about it on September 21. "Judging from what he [Moore] and Dr. Kilgore have written me about it, the search for another man has been abandoned and they are counting on me to come up there a year from this time." A letter from Martin to Bishop H. A. Boaz in October confirms it. He wrote Bishop Boaz: "For more than a year, Dr. James Kilgore, acting Dean of the School of Theology at Southern Methodist University, has been urging me to join the faculty of the school with the idea of becoming Dean as soon as I am familiar with the work. More recently Bishops Hay and Moore have joined him in that request."

Martin's July 17 reply to Moore's letter contains a counter offer—he would accept the position but wanted to come later. Martin said, "If the school can be carried on for another year under the present management and if, at the end of that time, no one better fitted for the work has been found, then I would undertake it." He suggested that Umphrey Lee, Paul Quillian, King Vivion, and Angie Smith were persons they should consider in the meantime. He knew, in fact, that Paul Quillian had already been approached and turned down the job. The letter also reveals that Martin's interest in theological education had prompted him while in New York to have a conversation with President Henry Sloan Coffin of Union "as to where he thinks the emphasis in theological training should be placed."

Moore talked to Kilgore, who agreed with Martin's request to come in 1929, and wrote to him on August 25, "We are delighted that you have determined to join us at the end of your next year at Port Arthur or wherever you are sent." He also reminded him that the description of a man bound for heaven is one "who sweareth to his own hurt and changeth not." Kilgore did not

want to repeat his earlier experience. Martin did not hear immediately from Moore, but when he did, in an undated letter, one of
the bishop's less helpful habits, but written soon after September
3, Moore made it clear that his preference was for him to assume
the post "at once." "However" he wrote, "I will not persuade
you against your will. We have felt out the situation sufficiently
to know you would be thoroughly acceptable to all parties concerned." The letter to Godbold written September 21, 1928,
which has already been mentioned, expressed again Martin's preference for having had "ten or twelve more years of practical experience before I went. . . ." But, he said, it seemed "to be one of the
inevitable things of life so I suppose I had as well go on and get
into the work."

SMU's president, Charles C. Selecman, wrote in early September 1929, to invite him to preach the university's opening sermon
at the end of the month and added a paragraph that said the occasion would "afford us an opportunity to talk over matters of interest and will give you a fresh, up-to-date contact with the University
group" (Selecman to WCM, September 2, 1929). Martin was
unable to accept the invitation to preach but sent yet another
acceptance letter to Kilgore a week later. He would come in a year
(WCM to Kilgore, September 11, 1929). He asked for help getting
prepared and opined, "If I were a Presbyterian I would be inclined
to believe that I was fore-ordained to the life of a teacher but I am
Baptist enough at this point to believe that the decision to go came
largely from the 'perseverance' of one of the 'saints' who may later
on regret his choice" (WCM to Kilgore, September 11, 1929). Kilgore was pleased and replied, "The saints up here are rejoicing at
my perseverance" (Kilgore to WCM, September 22, 1929).

Following Kilgore's advice, Martin wrote Bishop Sam Hay to
explain the plan and ask him to make the appointment, but added
a paragraph in his September 28 letter to his bishop that he had
not shared with the dean. "My preference," he said, "still remains
toward the pastorate but if in the judgment of those who are in
authority in the Church I can render a larger service in some other
field I will make no protest against the appointment." The plan
was now firmly in place for Martin to join the faculty in 1929.

The ink was hardly dry on Kilgore's letter when events unfolded that would allow Martin's preferences for the pastorate to win the day. October 5, a night letter came from Bishop H. A. Boaz and James Thomas, presiding elder of the Little Rock District.

FIRST CHURCH LITTLE ROCK WILL BE OPEN AT CONFER-
ENCE WILL YOU CONSIDER ACCEPTING THE PASTORATE
AT SALARY OF $7500 SPLENDID PARSONAGE AND ASSIS-
TANT AND SECRETARY WE ARE ANXIOUS TO HAVE YOU
LET US KNOW AT ONCE.

This was exciting news. It was a significant affirmation of his success in the local church, a validation of his prior commitment to the work of a pastor and carried both larger responsibilities and an increase of $2,100 in salary. Once again the preacher information network had anticipated the move. His good friend Paul Quillian, who was pastor of Winfield Church in Little Rock, wrote Martin in September to say that he was being considered.

Martin wrote President Selecman and Dean Kilgore on October 5 and wired Bishop Boaz immediately to say "transfer would be agreeable." He enclosed a copy of his letter to Bishop Hay, with the paragraph about his preference to remain in the pastorate, and told Kilgore "a little more time in the pastorate would enable me to present certain matters to students somewhat more authoritatively, and it ought to leave me in better financial circumstances for providing a place for my family to live." Afterward he wrote letters to Bishop Boaz and Presiding Elder Thomas of the Little Rock District to inform them of his agreement to go to SMU the following year, and said he expected to honor his commitment. But he also quoted the paragraph in the letter to Bishop Hay expressing his preference for remaining in the pastorate. He concluded by expressing his complete willingness to be subject to the appointive power of his bishop.

I have always felt that the chief strength of our form of church government lies in the fact that it looks primarily to the welfare of the church as a whole rather than to that of the individual or of the local congregation. In the long run, the two interests are, of course, identical. My case is in your hands and I shall make no effort to influence the appointment one way or another.

The diary entry for October 10 says, "Letter came today from Dr. Thomas in which he wrote as if the L.R. appointment were as good as made." It was not, however, as certain as Thomas seems to have thought. The next day Martin talked with his presiding elder, R. A. Adams, who advised him that Bishop Hay did not want to release him to go to Little Rock. Hay confirmed his position to Martin on October 14, and the same day Bishop Boaz wrote to tell him of Hay's opposition. "Your telegram and letter are very satisfactory but a letter from Bishop Hay is not quite so good. I wrote him that we wanted you over here but he writes that you are to remain where you are." Boaz went on to say, however, that if Martin himself were to ask Hay to release him, he would agree and do it (Boaz to WCM, October 15, 1928). In the meantime, Boaz had told Selecman he thought Martin would be available after General Conference in 1930 to go to SMU even if he moved to Little Rock (Selecman to WCM, December 19, 1928). An unsigned letter dated October 15, but undoubtedly written by Presiding Elder James Thomas, urged Kilgore to let him accept the appointment to Little Rock. After assuring the dean that Martin was not "self-seeking" and would do whatever the "appointive powers" decided was in the best interest of the church, he urged him to "acquiesce to the plan of his coming here [Little Rock] for one or two years." If he would, Thomas told him, "I believe it could be arranged." The pressure was on Martin from both Dallas and Little Rock, so on October 15 he wired Bishop John M. Moore for advice.

BISHOP BOAZ WANTS ME FOR LITTLE ROCK BISHOP HAY WILL RELEASE ME ONLY ON MY REQUEST WHAT DO YOU ADVISE WIRE COLLECT AT ONCE

The bishop did not answer immediately, so Martin telephoned him and was advised to seek the release from Bishop Hay and move to Little Rock.

The next day, Tuesday, October 16, he went to Houston, where he met with Hay and secured his transfer. Hay dictated the letter releasing him to Bishop Boaz while Martin was in the office. "I have just had a conversation with Brother Martin and I cannot afford to stand in his way of going to First Church, Little Rock. . . . I regret very much to let Brother Martin go" (Hay to Boaz, October 16, 1928). Martin thought the experience strange for a Methodist preacher, and wrote Godbold on November 11 to tell him about it. "I was virtually put in the position of making my own appointment, a responsibility which I had supposed a Methodist preacher had shifted to other shoulders when he joined the conference." Although Hay told him the matter was settled, Martin continued to be uneasy and made no preparations to move until after the meeting of the Texas Annual Conference. He did, however, confide to some of the leaders in his congregation that he expected to be leaving. "They had confidently expected me to stay for another year—just as I had—but they said 'We will not do anything to stand in the way of your advancement.' " Although the negotiations with SMU had always been considered to be confidential, Angie Smith, pastor of Trinity Methodist in El Paso, wrote congratulations to Martin on his appointment to Little Rock and added, "I presume this means you will not accept the deanship at Southern Methodist University" (Angie Smith to WCM, December 5, 1928).

The 1928 Texas Conference met in Lufkin. Martin and King Vivion were assigned to stay in the home of a young lawyer, John Redditt. Making his final report both as pastor of First Church in Port Arthur and as a member of the Texas Annual Conference, Martin finished the year in Port Arthur with a membership of 1,910, 988 enrolled in the Sunday school and 110 young people in the Epworth League. In his last year Port Arthur raised $45,479 for all causes. Under his leadership the congregation in three years had a net increase in membership of 439. While he was their pastor they had moved into a new sanctuary and completed their education building.

The sessions of the conference did not change his attitude toward Bishop Hay: "I do not rate Bp Hay as the best type of presiding officer," he wrote Godbold, "because he does not beget, by precept and example, as high a degree of dignity as should be felt, in my judgement, in such an assembly as an Annual Conference." He did say, however, that Hay had lost "almost entirely" the "dictatorial" spirit he had two years ago. He does not say what caused it. There was a farewell party on November 14 when the congregation presented William C. with an expensive leather club bag and Sallie with a silver tea service.

After a stopover to visit the family in Blevins, they arrived in Little Rock on November 21. Although "home folks—relatives and friends seem to be rejoicing at our appointment," he said, when they reached the parsonage it was locked and by the time the keys were found it was too late to get the trunks containing their bedding from the freight office so their first night in the city was spent in the New Capitol Hotel, "The Popular Priced Hotel." He wrote a long letter to Godbold from the hotel that night.

Martin followed Dr. H. D. Knickerbocker in Little Rock who, he confided to Godbold in his November 21 letter, "did not get on well at this place from the first." Bishop Boaz had forced the congregation to keep him a final year, but at the end of that time "the people demanded a change." Knickerbocker had been appointed presiding elder of the Oklahoma City District. When he moved, however, the Board of Stewards took the opportunity to reduce the salary from $10,000, which they had paid Knickerbocker, to the $7,500 they offered Martin. Martin did not take the reduction personally, but regarded it, as he told Godbold, "simply an inflated condition and it is the usual thing for a congregation to go back to the 'pre-war' salary after Knickerbocker leaves." In any event, he received a sizable increase. The Board of Stewards had 102 members, about half of whom, Martin told his friend, were active. About half a dozen of them had been his classmates at Hendrix. One of the premier appointments in the Methodist Episcopal Church, South, Little Rock boasted a total membership of 2,449 with a Sunday school enrolling 1,150 in all departments and a church building and parsonage valued at $280,000.

The parsonage into which the Martins moved was a lovely, new $25,000 two-story house, "which rather frightens us," in an exclusive section of the city across the street from the Arkansas School for the Blind. The Martin children remember listening to the clock, which rang the hours for the students. When the school was closed, the present governor's mansion was built on the site. Martin commented, "How can we manage three young animals in a place like that?" Since the house was twelve blocks from the church, Sallie usually took William C. to the office in the morning, kept the car for her own use, and picked him up again at noon. Until Martin came the only pastor's study was in the parsonage, but he quickly set one up at the church. Given his family situation, that is easy to understand. He liked to spend Monday, Wednesday, and Friday in the church office and the other three days in the study at home. He attempted to keep Tuesdays and Thursdays as clear as possible for "serious study."

Although Sallie had finally reached a place where she no longer had to live next to the church, as she had in Houston and Port Arthur, she quickly learned that there were disadvantages. A good many of their members had expectations for her as the first lady of a prominent congregation, which made her uncomfortable. They made formal calls on her at home and expected her to return them. They attempted to direct where she should go, whom she should see, what she should do, and told her what to wear, too. Keeping quiet was not easy since Sallie was never one who appreciated being told what to do.

Her husband got his share of advice, too. Even before he got to town, he was told he was expected to preach in a "cut-away suit," which featured what some folks used to call a "frock tail coat" and striped trousers. He managed to get one before he moved from Port Arthur. Among the members of his new congregation were the Governor of the state and his wife, two former governors, a federal judge and a justice of the state Supreme Court, plus a host of lesser officials. Since Little Rock was the headquarters of the conference and the home of the presiding bishop, a number of denominational officials, retired preachers and, most impressive of all, the bishop's wife were also members. The morning service was well attended but "almost nobody goes at night," Martin discovered. No critic in the audience was more demanding than the preacher himself. On Whitsunday morning he preached on the subject, "A Modern Pentecost," a "good sermon," he said, "rather poorly" preached. The more he thought about it during the day "the more humiliated I became and I felt bad all day about it." He gave his first talks on the radio in Little Rock.

With the responsibility for a large congregation, his reading reflects the issues that were clearly on his mind. He now read books almost exclusively on preaching and pastoral administration. He read Gladden's *The Christian Pastor,* Broadus's *The Preparation and Delivery of Sermons,* Beecher's *Yale Lectures on Preaching,* and a new book by DuBois, *Some Problems of the Modern Minister.* He had also to reallocate his time to care for the administrative details associated with a large congregation. He never became as active in the Masonic Lodge as he had been in Port Arthur and gave up going to the public library to read almost entirely. He continued to devote most afternoons to calling and visiting the local hospitals. There were, however, more of both than he had ever had before. He increased his walking, too—to and from the parsonage to the church, from the church to town, on pastoral visits, but bought a new Buick after having a round of car trouble with his Dodge. He paid $1,513 for it and was given $400 for his old car as a trade-in.

He and Paul Quillian began the new year by attending a missionary conference in Memphis and later the same month one in Fort Worth for pastors of large churches. One of his greatest joys in Little Rock was the association with Paul Quillian, who was pastor of the nearby Winfield congregation. They truly loved each other. They were soul mates. If William C. Martin had a true friend on the earth, it was Paul Quillian. Since Winfield Church was only a few blocks away, they managed to be together almost every day. They talked over their personal problems, shared concerns, gave each other advice, discussed theology and church related issues, and, with their families, ate meals and spent leisure time together. They were very different personalities—Quillian would attempt to get Martin to look around and smell the roses and William C. tried to get Paul "to slow down" because, as he told Godbold, "if he doesn't . . . he will kill himself before he is fully matured." And that is almost literally what happened.

A thousand people gathered at the missionary conference in Memphis, January 1-3, 1929, to hear E. Stanley Jones, the famous Methodist missionary to India. "I had gone primarily to hear him and I was not disappointed," Martin said. "His grasp of Christianity is vital and comprehensive." Evangelist Billy Sunday's famous colleague, Homer Rodeheaver, led the singing. There were 11,000 reported cases of flu in the city when they arrived and Martin had a sore throat. The next day, however, he felt better and went through the busy program without problems. Martin was always an admirer of E. Stanley Jones. Jones's son-in-law, James K. Matthews, would be a colleague of Martin's in the episcopacy.

It is difficult to imagine why the move to Little Rock did not immediately put an end to the prospects of becoming dean at SMU, but it did not. In Memphis he talked with Bishop Moore about SMU and was told that he should plan to begin there "this fall." Martin responded again that he didn't agree. He had breakfast with Paul Kern, who remained steadfast in his advice not to go at all. Martin told Godbold that Kern believed Selecman would be elected a bishop at the next General Conference and that the SMU vice president, H. M. Whaling, Jr., would become president. If that happened, Kern told Martin, he would be "so out of harmony with the administration that there would be no joy in it for me to be there" (WCM to Godbold, January 8, 1929). Martin now said that he thought it might be best to stay in Little Rock three or four years before going to Dallas, but in a somewhat bizarre way he reaffirmed his commitment to go. That afternoon he talked with Dr. Selecman, who could see the value of his staying longer in Little Rock, and he had a helpful conversation with Paul Quillian as they walked up and down through the train on the way home. Back in Little Rock, he talked with Presiding

Elder James Thomas and learned from him that Forney Hutchinson had been "besought to go" to SMU but declined.

At the end of January, Martin and Paul Quillian attended another meeting with thirty pastors of large churches invited by the Layman's Board of the Church, South, to discuss "The Men of the Church." It met in Fort Worth with well-known pastors such as Forney Hutchinson, Paul Kern, Carl Gregory, Eugene Hawk, S. S. McKenney, and Al Freeman in attendance. The fellowship with these pastors, some of whom Martin had not met previously, was pleasant, and the proximity to Dallas afforded an opportunity to speak again with Selecman and Kilgore about SMU. Kilgore told him there was no need to assume the position, "for two or three years."

But by the middle of March, Martin was rethinking his commitment, but hoped the problem would just work itself out. He told Godbold in April, "I am hoping that somebody else can be found for the place. . . . However, if nobody else is found and the leaders over there continue to insist on my going, I suppose I shall accede" (WCM to Godbold, April 13, 1929). The fact that things were going so well in the new church had decidedly diminished his enthusiasm for moving to Dallas.

There were always problems with which Pastor Martin had to deal. He went to see Governor Parnell, a member of his flock, to protest a bill allowing Sunday baseball games. The governor said he would not sign it, but four days later he did. Knickerbocker had left a badly divided congregation at First Church with a $60,000 debt and Martin made his first attempt to reduce it on April 1. He asked for $10,000 and actually got $10,500 in pledges. His goal, he said in his appeal to them, was to eliminate the debt entirely by the 100-year anniversary of the church in 1931. Palm Sunday and Easter he received seventy persons into the church and baptized eighteen babies. In April he held a twelve-day revival meeting for former classmate Roy Fawcett in Nashville, Arkansas, near his hometown of Blevins, and on June 2 preached the commencement sermon at Hendrix College, where the next day he and Paul Quillian were given honorary doctor of divinity degrees by their alma mater. It was the first of several both men were to receive. The same day Martin was elected president of the Hendrix Alumni Association. The Arkansas Pastor's School followed commencement and Martin taught a course "The Program of Work for the City Church."

Earlier, Bishop Moore, probably sensing Martin's rising uncertainty about going to SMU, pushed him for a firm commitment. "I want to see you. I will come by Little Rock next Wednesday" (Moore to WCM, May 4, 1929). The diary reveals Martin knew exactly what the bishop had in mind and talked it over with Paul Quillian who told him he "had as well go to SMU." Moore came and "renewed his plea that I go to SMU." Three weeks later, with the support of Dr. Selecman, Moore sent a formal offer for Martin to become dean of the SMU School of Theology at a salary of $6,000, less than he was making and without a house provided. Moore acknowledged the sacrifice involved but promised "there will be high service" (Moore to WCM, May 24, 1929). Martin responded on May 28, saying, "I am inclined to accept the invitation to come to Southern Methodist University on the condition that I be allowed to complete my full year's work here." Moore replied immediately and the diary on May 31 says, "my offer to come to SMU after end of this year would be accepted." As it turned out, however, Moore, Selecman, and Kilgore were not all on the same page.

He had seen Selecman in Conway at Pastor's School and talked with him about several items related to SMU. Martin reported their conversation to Bishop Moore and told him he would be at the University of Chicago to attend its Pastor's School during July. Moore enclosed a letter of introduction to the dean of the divinity school, Dr. Shaler Matthews, and advised him to discuss the SMU appointment with nobody but Bishop Boaz, since the bishop would need time to make a new appointment for First Church.

When the teaching assignment in Conway was finished, the Martin family took some much-needed vacation at Mt. Sequoyah. Martin preached in Bentonville in the morning and Mt. Sequoyah at night, and then took the train to Chicago for the ten-day Pastor's School (July 16-28) where he heard the young Wilhelm Pauck—"a real scholar," J. M. P. Smith, Morton Scott Enslin, William Warren Sweet, and Robert Cushman. Shirley Jackson

Case spoke at chapel. On a trip to Garrett Biblical Institute in Evanston he heard Murray Leifer and Harris Franklin Rall. As he told Godbold, he decided to go to Chicago because he thought its Midwest perspective would be more relevant to his work than Yale's. While there he used Moore's letter of introduction to discuss theological education with Dean Shaler Matthews. On his birthday, July 28, he wrote Moore to say that he would like for his election to be deferred until November 15, the end of the conference year. Moore agreed to Martin's request and in his letter promised that "Dr. Selecman and I will . . . probably call on Dr. Kilgore and acquaint him with what is to be done. That would be but fair" (Moore to WCM, July 28, 1929).

He was back from Chicago to meet the family in Fayetteville on July 29. After a brief stop in Eureka Springs they reached home on August 2. In September there was a brief family trip to Randolph for the first time in over three years. Uncle Perry killed a pig to barbecue and Uncle Dick's family came for the evening. Fifty-five relatives came for lunch the next day. William C. preached in the Randolph church to a packed house. They were home the next day and he observed in the diary, "Strange that I should have come out of the past into the present in so short a time." It was the first trip Sallie and the children had ever made to see his Tennessee relatives.

Shortly afterward, the wheels finally came off the SMU wagon. Dr. Selecman revealed that Acting Dean Kilgore did not know what was planned. In August, however, Martin had, despite Moore's admonition to keep the arrangement confidential, leaked it to Kilgore. Martin also told Godbold in early September that Bishop Boaz and Presiding Elder Thomas were now insisting that he stay in Little Rock until the meeting of the General Conference in May 1930. Angie Smith, as usual, had the entire story and wrote on September 19 to confirm that Martin would accept the deanship after Christmas (Smith to WCM, September 19, 1929). A year earlier Martin had written Godbold after a similar experience, "Angie Smith has a way of finding out more than almost any preacher I know."

As late as September 26, when Kilgore wrote Martin again,

Moore had still not spoken with him. Martin replied that although he was supposed to come following the meeting of the annual conference, at least in his mind, it was all contingent "that such a plan would be in line with your convictions about what should be done, and I insisted that they [Moore and Selecman] talk with you about it." Martin told his former teacher almost everything but did not tell him he was coming to assume his position as dean. On October 3 Selecman wrote to Martin that he was prepared to go forward with Martin's nomination as dean at the Executive Committee meetings the following week (Selecman to WCM, October 3, 1929). Martin received the letter on October 5. Ironically, he had the day before received a letter from Kilgore saying that he had contracted Umphrey Lee and Harold Cooke to teach and in so doing "nearly all the income for the year has been appropriated." Martin was not needed, and Kilgore had no money left to pay him.

Martin wrote Selecman and Moore nearly identical letters on October 5 and sent both special delivery. He asked Moore to release him from his agreement to become dean because it "was based upon the belief that I would go under such circumstances and now that I find they do not exist you will readily see my position and be willing to release me from the agreement to go at this time" (WCM to Moore, October 5, 1929). He wrote Moore again later the same month to reiterate, "I would not be willing to go to SMU without the full approval of Dr. Kilgore" (WCM to Moore, October 22, 1929). The same day he heard from Bishop Moore, and the diary entry for the day says "they must have a dean now, and he wants to know if I will take the place." Martin replied via special delivery. "I had not realized . . . to what an extent you consider the selection of a dean at the present time essential to the success of the financial campaign."

Martin's letter reached Moore while he was presiding at the New Mexico Annual Conference. His reply was brief and blunt: "The School needs you and it needs you right now. If you can come and will come we want you to declare now that you will." Martin could not agree.

The year 1930 proved to be a difficult one for the Martins. Sallie was ill when the year began and on January 29 she had surgery to correct an undisclosed problem. The surgery took only an hour and the doctor was confident there would be no further complications. She was hospitalized for two weeks, made a slow recovery, and did not leave the house until February 24. Martin took the children to school in the mornings and arranged his schedule to spend Saturdays with them. In May, Sallie "was growing despondent" and William C. took her to Hot Springs for a series of treatments with Dr. Scully, which included taking the baths for which Hot Springs is famous. She was there for two weeks.

Martin himself was also having a difficult time. He had, for some reason, moved into a kind of "dark night of the soul" which he remembered long afterward and described in an interview in 1975 as "dry ground—in so far as having any thrill in the ministry." He went on to recall "I was doing my work, I guess, with a fair degree of satisfaction with the congregation, but I wasn't getting the sense of joy out of it that I felt I ought to have." He recalled in the diary, the same day Sallie left the house for the first time, having talked with Paul Quillian about the problems he was having "holding to the supernatural in religious faith." He went on to say, "Something of vital importance seemed to have died in me and I walked in sort of a dull maze." He expressed it in poetic form in his diary.

> Faith had fallen asleep,
> I heard a voice "Believe no more"
> And heard an ever-breaking shout
> That tumbled in a godless deep.

"February 24," he wrote in the diary, "marks one of the crises of my life." What changed him was the writing of a professor he had met at Aberdeen, David S. Cairns. On the recommendation of James Kilgore, Martin had read Cairns's book *The Faith That Rebels* a year earlier. A study of the miracles of Jesus, it sought to give a contemporary interpretation of the gospel. "And that book, under God, gave me a new hold on the sense of the transcendental element of the Christian life, and that experience . . . has remained with me as a continuing blessing, my source of light and strength."

He described his experience to Cairns in a letter written in February, 1932.

> The book came to me, when I took it for the second time more than a year ago, at a time when I was groping for a deeper assurance of spiritual reality. Almost like a clear answer to prayer it brought the statement of Christian truth I sorely needed and since that crisis, for it amounted to that, I have had an abiding confidence which has deepened and enriched my whole religious life.

When he first read Cairns's book in 1929 he naturally recommended it to Godbold, who said he enjoyed it but did not find it as helpful as Martin had claimed. "If I can read Cairns' mind . . . he just insists on holding to the miracles because he believes they ought to be conserved in the Gospel story." Martin admitted later to Godbold, "I find that I am not able to go all the way with him—I almost wish I could—but I am very thankful for the book." He went on to say, "The point of view he takes, when seriously considered, will help to check the blatant denial of certain liberals of the reality of every occurrence that cannot be fully accounted for in terms of its physical antecedents."

Sallie's illness caused him to spend more time with the children, especially Donald, his oldest. They climbed mountains and went for long walks in the woods. He always referred to the peak that was their favorite as "blessed Pinnacle." They hunted rabbits together in the snow, too. In the evenings he read to the children and to Sallie. One Saturday they even flew kites on the grounds of the capitol. A favorite place was the farm of the McAllisters, who had two boys of their own, and they went often. There they planted vegetables, pitched horseshoes and enjoyed the companionship of supportive friends. He took John Lee to kindergarten on his way to work in the mornings and picked him up at noon.

As was now their custom, they went to Mt. Sequoyah in August for vacation and for Martin to preach. But after only five days Sallie decided it was too noisy and that she wanted to go home. In accord with her wishes, they packed and left the next day. The impact of the economic depression now sweeping over the country was being felt, and on November 17 the American Southern Trust Company in Little Rock closed its doors, throwing the city "into a panic." Hard times were at hand.

Conference met at the Lakeside Church in Pine Bluff, where Martin reported the membership of First Church had grown to 2,644. Despite his personal problems and the financial difficulties imposed by a worsening economic climate, the church continued to do well under his leadership, and the congregation was glad to have him returned. Thanks to the generosity of one of its members, a lovely new pipe organ graced the sanctuary. It was to remain there until the day after Martin's memorial service in 1984 when it was dismantled and portions of it rebuilt to be incorporated into a new instrument.

President Selecman invited him to SMU to hold the annual campus revival in February. Since attendance was required, he had a good audience. On Monday nights he tried to listen to "Amos and Andy," and he heard Will Rogers whenever he was on. Nannie Jacob was in poor health and trips were required to Blevins to see about her. Sallie's health had not improved significantly. She was in church for the first time during the entire year on March 15. Together they enjoyed going to the movies and went more often. Once, however, he took the family to see a film titled *The Smiling Lieutenant,* and when it proved to be "disgustingly suggestive" he took them all out. The children remember that moment well. He never, however, missed a Will Rogers film. In July he performed a wedding and for his services was given a $100 bill—"a new high record." His offer to the Finance Committee in April to reduce his salary was, however, rejected. The family vacation in the summer of 1931, which was a good one, was spent at Gulfport and Biloxi, Mississippi, rather than at Mt. Sequoyah.

In October, President Selecman outlined yet another plan for him to go to SMU, but other opportunities took precedence. A letter came on October 24 from Bishop Boaz, saying, Martin "was wanted at First Church, Dallas." William C. preached in Dallas for the first time on November 8. The family said good-bye to Little Rock on November 17 and began what were to prove their long years in Dallas.

James Marion Martin,
Clyde's paternal grandfather

John Harmon Martin,
Clyde's father

Leila Ballard Martin,
Clyde's mother
(C.M. Dome, Prescott, Arkansas)

William Clyde Martin

Clyde and his father

Jack Martin's saw crew in East Texas

*Clyde with maternal grandparents, J.W. and second wife,
Ellena Berlin Ballard*

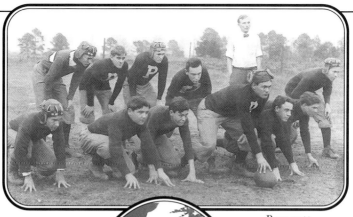

Prescott,
Arkansas, High School,
1911.
Clyde is the center
(his hand is on the ball)

Honeymoon, in
Memphis, Tennessee,
July 1918

Pvt. William C. Martin,
1918

The pastor of Grace Church, Houston,
with Sallie, Mary Katherine, and Donald

The active bishops of the
South Central Jurisdiction, 1942.
They are from left to right:
Charles C. Selecman, Martin,
Frank Smith, Ivan Lee Holt,
and John C. Broomfield

A visit to the Air Force
in Japan,
Christmas, 1953

Korea, 1953

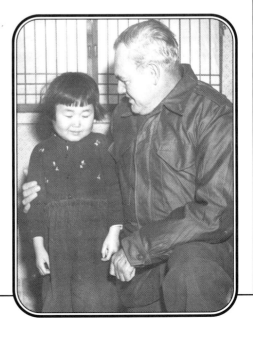

Getting acquainted,
Korea, 1953
(official photo)

*The President of the National Council of Churches
with President Eisenhower at the White House, c. 1953*

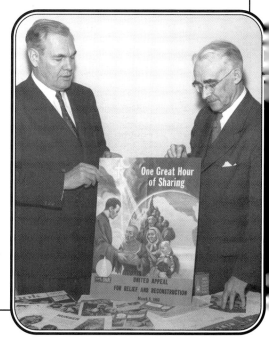

*With Samuel McCrea Cavert,
general secretary of the
National Council of Churches,
c. 1953*

*In India, 1958,
to attend the
World Council of
Churches third assembly*

*Martin and Sally are welcomed
to the Jordon Home for
children in Moradabad, India*

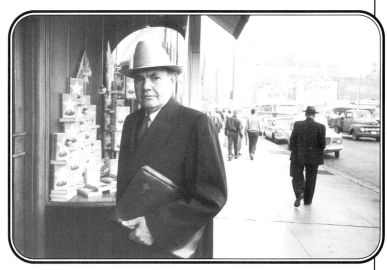

*1910 Main, Dallas, Texas.
The bishop arrives for work at his office*
(photo from *Together* magazine)

*Honors from the
University of Denver,
August 28, 1953*
(University of Denver
photo by Ed Maker)

*At work in his
Dallas office*
(photo from *Together* Magazine)

*Twenty-fifth anniversary
in Episcopacy*

5

Dallas

Although late in his life William C. Martin stated that the most "satisfying" years of his ministry were spent in Little Rock, it is hard to imagine why he did not make that judgment about Dallas. In every way, the years at First Methodist Church in Dallas were the high watermark of his pastoral ministry as well as the springboard into his service in the episcopacy. Altogether the Martins lived in Dallas for almost three decades, with William C. in the roles of student, pastor, episcopal leader, and teacher. It was there that they developed most of their closest and most lasting friendships. Had it not been for the need to be near family in their advancing years, it seems likely they would have lived out their retirement years in the city.

Dallas got Martin when he was at his best. He was thirty-eight years old and had three very successful pastorates behind him. With coal-black, wavy hair and his father's piercing black eyes, William C. Martin was an appealing man with a magnetic personality. Although he remained vigilant about his weight he was never a fat man and carried his almost 200 pounds on a frame that was as massive as the personality of the man himself. His hands and feet were large; his shoulders and chest broad. The adjective most often used to describe Martin by the people who knew or encountered him was "big." When asked about Martin, those who knew him often respond by saying, "He was a big man." But that was not all that he was. Eight-year-old daughter Mary Katherine remembered that many women found him attractive and flirted with him "openly and extravagantly." He remained utterly unaware of his appeal to women, in fact he paid them no attention, but Sally, as she now spelled her name, noticed and resented their interest in him. She herself was an elegant and beautiful woman with good taste who dressed accordingly. Although she could be difficult at times, as any mortal can, she was also vivacious and fun and people responded to and liked her. The new pastor of First Methodist and his wife were an impressive couple. His energy was boundless and was exceeded only by his commitment to the task. His life was the church, and what he was willing to do for it and its mission hardly knew any bounds. Over and over again he told his children that "duty is the sublimest word in the English language."

By this time the negotiations with SMU, which had gone on for so many years, were finally over, and he was entirely focused on his role as the pastor of a large and well-known congregation in the Methodist Episcopal Church, South. Although circumstances had enabled Martin to begin his ministerial career farther up the ladder than his seminary peers, Martin had matured and demonstrated in every situation that he was equal to the task. His preaching had improved; his experiences in dealing with all kinds of people had expanded his tolerance; in every way he was prepared to be a big city, "high steeple" pastor. And he knew it. In a letter to W. P. Daman of Dallas, who wrote to congratulate him on his appointment and welcome him to the city, Martin said, "I regard First Methodist Church, Dallas, as being, in many respects, the greatest church in the Southwest and I hope that my appointment as its pastor may be reasonably justified."

Despite having learned much of "the wisdom of the wisdom of experience," Martin continued to hold steadfastly to some convictions he had held from the beginning of his ministry. He opposed the remarriage of divorced persons and refused to officiate when asked; he remained outspoken in his opposition to gambling and to any games that could be associated with it. For years

he would not allow cards in the house, but he liked to play dominoes and even came to appreciate the Texas variety called "Forty-
two." He was adamant in his opposition to drinking and the
liquor trade. Although not so rigid as he once had been about the
evils of dancing, he opposed its introduction at SMU. He would
not allow the children to attend the movies on Sunday, but they
enjoyed them at other times, as did he and Sally. As Mary
Katherine described it, Martin underwent a real "growth spurt"
in Dallas.

There is nothing that indicates that Martin expected to leave
Little Rock, despite the fact that it was no secret that Carl
Gregory, the pastor at First Methodist in Dallas, expected to
move to Travis Park Methodist Church in San Antonio. As usual,
Martin and Godbold shared conference "gossip," but if Martin
knew that Dallas would be open, he must have thought he had no
possibility of being considered and does not mention it. The first
part of the letter was written in mid-September, but was broken
off and resumed on November 15 after the appointment to Dallas had been made. He told Godbold in the early section that
"Bishop Boaz writes to the *Texas Advocate* that 'this is a good
time to stay.'" Quillian expected to return to Winfield for another
year, Al Freeman had gone back to his appointment, and even
Forney Hutchinson, who wanted to leave St. Luke's in Oklahoma
City in order to become the pastor of Boston Avenue Methodist
in Tulsa, admitted he was uncertain about it, though he told Martin he expected to go. Forney's problem was that C. M. Reves, the
pastor in Tulsa, had earlier told Paul Quillian that he expected to
return. Hutchinson did leave St. Luke's, but moved to Mt. Vernon
Methodist Church in Washington, D.C. The usual time for the
sessions of the Little Rock Annual Conference had been postponed from late October to December 2 in order to allow the
churches to get their financial houses in order. To help First
Church, Little Rock, "pay out," Martin had increased the amount
of his own contribution by $500. This was accomplished by
reducing the amount of his salary.

The call to Dallas came in the form of a letter from Bishop
Boaz, which arrived in Little Rock on October 24, the day after

Martin and Paul Quillian returned from an ecumenical conference in Atlanta. The letter must have come as a surprise since Martin told Godbold at the time of the Atlanta conference President Selecman and Bishop Boaz were still insistent that he become Dean at the SMU School of Theology. Boaz had left Atlanta before Martin arrived, but in a long conversation with Sally "he painted a glowing picture of the opportunities at SMU." Martin told Godbold that he did not know whether "the possibility of a later transfer to SMU entered into the appointment." After receiving Boaz's letter, Martin talked the situation over with Paul Quillian and immediately wired Bishop Dobbs, "IF WANTED IN DALLAS I AM AGREEABLE TO BEING TRANSFERRED." He wired Boaz at the same time.

Since the move required a transfer from one annual conference to another, Martin needed the permission of two bishops. Bishops Boaz and Dobbs had discussed it before Martin was notified. Dobbs had at first refused to allow the transfer and notified Boaz in a telegram that he would not release Martin. As a result, the same day Boaz wrote Martin (October 22) he also wrote Bishop Dobbs protesting his decision.

> Your telegram came and was a great disappointment to me. I can readily see your attitude of mind, yet I believe you will pardon me for being more or less insistent in this case.
>
> First Church, Dallas, is unanimous in their desire to have W. C. Martin to succeed Dr. Gregory. This would be a great promotion for Martin, and I am sure you would not willingly stand in the way of his promotion.

Boaz then requested permission from Dobbs to make a trip to Little Rock to see Martin, and his presiding elder, Dr. Thomas, "to discuss the matter." "I am still hoping," he told Dobbs, "that arrangements can be made to take Martin to Dallas."

Boaz was candid with Martin about Dobbs's unwillingness to release him. He told Martin of his desire to come to Little Rock for a conversation and reminded Martin he had experienced similar difficulties when trying to appoint him to Little Rock.

You remember the difficulty I had in securing you for Little Rock. It seems the way may be blocked in securing another promotion for you. I wanted you as Dean of the Theological faculty, but First Church is a better chance for the present. I know you are a loyal Methodist Preacher and subject to those who are in authority. It may be necessary for you to make your wishes known in this case.

Once again Martin found himself in an uncomfortable position between two bishops. Having already told Boaz he was willing to transfer, he was now uneasy that it might appear to his bishop that he was trying to make his own appointment. He wrote Bishop Dobbs on October 31 and asserted his innocence.

I thought it worth while to make clear to you . . . that I was expressing willingness to being transferred only because Bishop Boaz had written to me asking me to let you know how I felt about it and had enclosed a copy of his letter to you in which he said, "First Church, Dallas, is unanimous in their desire to have W. C. Martin to succeed Dr. Gregory."

The last paragraph in Martin's letter hints that Dobbs's real concern might have been finding a suitable successor to Martin in Little Rock rather than opposing his promotion. Near the end of his letter to Dobbs, Martin expresses confidence that "Dr. C. M. Reves will be cordially received at First Methodist Church, Little Rock and I am sure he will have a satisfactory ministry here." The plan was to transfer Reves from Boston Avenue, Tulsa, in the Oklahoma Conference. Despite the optimism he expressed to Bishop Dobbs, Martin's diary contains expressions of concern about his successor and also notes "an unfortunately frank" telephone conversation with Reves on November 3. The likelihood is that the candid exchange was a discussion of the opposition to Reves's appointment, which had surfaced among influential members in Little Rock about which Martin must have felt obliged to tell him. Reves, in fact, probably was already well briefed on the subject. An earlier entry, October 29, mentions Martin's having lunch with Dr. Thomas and a visit from one of the stewards who came "to protest against appointment of a certain preacher to succeed me if I go."

In about a week, however, Dobbs agreed to the transfer and a gleeful Bishop Boaz telegraphed Martin on October 31, "DELIGHTED TO APPOINT YOU SUNDAY NIGHT TO FIRST CHURCH DALLAS."

Since Carl Gregory had already left, the officials and members of First Church, Dallas, were anxious to hear their new preacher and invited him to come to preach on November 8. After talking it over with his officials in Little Rock and learning they could see that his absence would make little difference in the long run, Martin took the train to Dallas and preached for the first time. When he arrived on Saturday there was a crowd at the station to greet him, including a photographer from the *Dallas Morning News*. He told Godbold "about 75 people were at the train at 7:45 A.M. to meet me and that spirit of warm hearted welcome was manifested all during my visit." David A. Lacy, Jr., then Chair of the Board of Stewards, welcomed him on behalf of the congregation. Dave and Pauline Lacy were to become close personal friends and strong supporters. Saturday was spent meeting with the staff at First Church, having lunch with his old friend Perry Knickerbocker, and touring the parsonage at 4403 Rawlins Street. He soon learned that it took forty-two minutes to walk from home to the church, and he did it frequently in good weather and bad. Bishop John M. Moore lived in the next block, and next-door to him was the parsonage of the Oak Lawn Methodist Church.

On Sunday morning, Martin chose Psalm 121—"I will lift up mine eyes unto the hills, from whence cometh my help"—for the responsive reading and had the congregation sing "Come Thou Almighty King," "Break Thou the Bread of Life," and "O Jesus I Have Promised." His sermon was an old standby, "The Faith of a Preacher." At the evening service he preached on the subject "The Christ We Need." He concluded to Godbold, "From all I could gather the people were reasonably well pleased with the new preacher." Gregory, he said, had done a good job in preparing the way for him.

After the Sunday night service, Martin returned to Little Rock to finish his work there and get ready to move. He preached his final sermon on November 15, baptized two babies and received a dozen people into the congregation. He and the family left for Dallas two days later. They stopped in Blevins where Nannie Jacob, who was ill, was found to be worse. They reached Dallas on Thursday. Before Martin's arrival the Board of Stewards had elected Dr. A. V. Lane as chair, George E. Drewery as vice chair, Richard T. Morrison as secretary, and George W. Moore as treasurer. He met with them for the first time the day he arrived and they set the salary for the new pastor at $7,500, a reduction of $1,500 from the amount they had paid Gregory. It was, however, to be the largest salary Martin ever earned while pastor of First Methodist. Because of the effects of the depression, the following year the salary was lowered to $7,000, in 1933 to $5,000, then moved back up to $6,000 for the following two. He was earning $7,000 when he was elected a bishop.

First Methodist Church, Dallas, reported a membership of 3,422 to the annual conference at which Martin was appointed. The church school had a total enrollment of just under 2,500, and the large facility standing on the corner of Ross and Harwood in downtown Dallas was valued at $700,000.

Before Martin could finish the letter he had begun in September, Godbold had heard of his appointment to Dallas and written to him. "I rejoice with you," he said, "believing that at Dallas you have an even greater opportunity than at Little Rock. If your success there is as striking as I predict that it will be, you will be prominently mentioned for bishop soon." Godbold also announced that he and Ray Jordan had figured out why Martin was chosen, but would like to hear the reasons directly from him.

The Martins were cordially received in Dallas, "almost too good to be true," he told Godbold. He was pleased with the staff and grateful to Carl Gregory, his predecessor, for his good work in paving the way for him. Estelle Barber headed Christian education and Hattie Rankin was the church visitor. Martin thought her visitor's organization was the best he had ever seen. She was sufficiently astute to notify Martin even before he arrived in Dallas of a death in the family of Mrs. G. W. Morris. In usual fashion, he wrote condolences on November 13, two days before he preached his last sermon in Little Rock. Soon after arriving in Dallas, Martin began the practice of having lunch with E. Gordon Perry, superintendent of the church school, on Tuesdays. With the family he discovered the Farmer's Market and the vistas around White Rock Lake. It became their spot for afternoon drives and picnics. Every Saturday he took Mary Katherine to the "Expression School" run by Mrs. Cocke.

The chief problem the congregation faced was the accumulated debt on their building, which amounted approximately to $200,000—a large sum in the declining economy of the day. The repayment schedule was set up so that every February $23,000 was due on the principal plus accrued interest. The total payment each year was $30,000. The church had never raised enough money in any previous year before Martin arrived to make the payments above their current expenses. That meant the entire amount had to be raised in addition to the budget. His first year, however, it was deceptively easy since the City of Dallas had purchased property from the church to widen Ross Avenue and $18,000 was available when he arrived to apply on the debt. The security was fleeting, however, since the city had also assessed the congregation $23,000 for the improvements and increased value of their land. It was added to the debt and payable over fifteen years. At its May meeting the board insisted that the budget be balanced and recommended reductions in the staff. Martin told Godbold that he would have been prepared to accept a reduction in his salary, and he successfully pleaded to retain the staff in order to get the work done. Every year was a challenge, and it was not until Jesse Lee Johnson came up with a creative financing plan that the burden of the debt was eased.

Sally was ill most of the first half of 1931. After surgery in Little Rock, against which one of her physicians advised her husband, she had to have nurses around the clock. She did not improve after arriving in Dallas. Martin's diary describes her condition as "heart trouble," and in one entry he makes reference to a "heart attack."

She clearly did not suffer what generally is known as a "heart attack" but was unable to function and was depressed. Sally Martin, despite being light-years beyond her mother in emotional stability, like her was often ill and troubled with mood shifts that left her depressed and unable to function. In midlife Nannie Jacob took to her bed and lived with Brice and Jack, who cared for her until she died. Katherine reported she could not remember ever seeing her grandmother out of bed. Her mother was often there, too. After the move to Dallas Sally was unable to come downstairs to join the family for the first Christmas dinner in their new home. She finally was well enough to join them on January 8, 1932, and the family celebrated by going together to see Marie Dressler in *Emma* at the Palace Theater in downtown Dallas. Martin went with her a week later to see Cornelia Otis Skinner and Maud Adams in *The Merchant of Venice* at Fair Park.

Because of Sally's slow progress to recovery under the care of Dr. J. S. Davis, it was decided that she should enter the sanatorium in Marlin, Texas, south of Waco, run by Dr. Torbett, for an extended period of rest. She was admitted on February 15, 1932, and was there for a month. Although the diary records that she improved during the early part of her stay, she was still "not doing well," Martin told Godbold, in May. No indication is given of the nature of her treatment, and it likely consisted largely of rest. Mrs. Walker came from Little Rock to stay with the children while Sally was away. Martin wrote to her every day, but not one letter he ever wrote to Sally exists in the archives. If she saved them, they were later destroyed. There is almost no mention of her condition in the diaries either.

At about the same time Mary Katherine became ill again and was confined to bed for two months. The children are reasonably clear, as are many of the people who knew her well, that Sally sometimes used her illness to avoid doing things she did not want to do or for control. She nearly always seemed to be physically able to do the things she wanted to do. They use the word *hypochondria* in describing her condition. Although she was a person with very low energy, frequently ill, and often depressed, Sally Martin lived to the ripe old age of ninety-seven.

In addition to his problems at home, Martin soon discovered he had trouble being heard in the sanctuary of First Church, especially by those seated under the balcony, which surrounds three sides of the room, and he determined to learn to use his voice more effectively. The sanctuary seated just less than 2,000 people. He rated his first Easter sermon in Dallas a poor effort—"was out of touch with the congregation most of the time." In July he went again to the University of Chicago for the Pastor's School. There, in addition to the regular courses, he took private voice lessons from Hubert Greaves of the Department of Public Speaking. They were designed to help him improve his audibility and reduce the strain caused by what he characterized as "screaming." He also went to the movies instead of the opening banquet and visited the planetarium, where his lifelong interest in astronomy began.

He bowled for the first time on March 1 while attending a meeting in Memphis and congratulated himself on doing "quite well in the second game." He bowled frequently thereafter and enjoyed the pastime for many years. He was, in fact, bowling at the time he was elected to the episcopacy.

On Saturdays, as he had in Little Rock, he spent time with the boys; they played baseball, and he and Donald hunted rabbits in the Trinity River bottom. Recreation with Sally continued to include many trips to the movies. Will Rogers and the Marx Brothers were among his favorites. Ever a menace with the car, Martin managed to run over the family dog "Snoozy" in May. Donald, the oldest, was almost twelve at the time. Although the diary records the event, it makes no comment about the reaction of the children to the death of their pet.

The Martins found a comfortable cottage for $10 a week in Bella Vista, Arkansas, for the family vacation, and while there Martin and the boys began hunting arrowheads. They found about sixty. John was somewhat hindered in doing his part, having fallen out of a tree a month earlier and breaking two bones in his left arm.

Like most Americans, Martin listened to Franklin D. Roosevelt when he spoke on the radio, and he had Thanksgiving dinner with friends Dan and Brownie Otstott. At the end of his first year in Dallas, he was invited to preach at both the North Texas Annual Conference and the Little Rock Conference but was forced to decline the latter because of conflicts in his schedule.

The first meeting of the North Texas Conference that Martin attended as a member met in Gainsville October 27-30, 1932. It was a stormy session. He reported the congregation at First Methodist had grown to 3,494, although the 79 persons admitted on profession of faith was the smallest number in any year of his ministry. Sunday school enrollment was up to 2,715. Conference apportionments had been paid in full and a grand total of $70,000 raised for all causes. The indebtedness, however, had not been reduced. Nevertheless, he summed up the year in a letter to Godbold saying, "I have read some stimulating books during the fall and have never had more joy in my work." Among the books was the autobiography of Elwood Worcester, *Life's Adventure*. Reading the autobiography of Sir Oliver Lodge, *Past Years*, caused him to read Stoltz's *Pastoral Psychology* and *Body Mind and Spirit* by Worcester and McComb. In addition he read *The Pastoral Ministry* (Adams), and Oliver's *Psychiatry for Ministers*. He read Canon Raven's *Jesus and the Gospel of Love,* and then Raven's autobiography, *A Wanderer's Way*. A. C. McGiffert's *History of Christian Thought,* "a hefty book" written by a "cold blooded" man "I think wholly in error in many of his interpretations," was "a fine book to read." He read a book on the history of surnames to help him remember names and others on practical matters like revivals, missions, evangelism, and church programs. "I have grown during the year," he said. "Elwood Worcester and Canon Raven have brought me most light and Sir Oliver Lodge, A. C. McGiffert and several others have helped greatly."

During the annual conference, five members of the SMU Board of Trustees, including the chairman, R. H. Shuttles, resigned to protest the policies of its controversial president, Charles C. Selecman. Two of the five members who resigned were Martin's members at First Church. Paul Quillian wrote Albea Godbold during the summer before the conference, "Discontent with the policy of the present administration resulted in an attempt to oust the President some time ago. When this failed an attempt was made to override his policies. This also failing they resigned." After Shuttles had tendered his resignation, a motion was made by R. G. Mood asking him to withdraw it. Shuttles read a paper outlining his reasons for resigning and in the ensuing debate Selecman made an unfortunate reference that sparked a floor fight. Adjournment at noon interrupted his rebuttal speech, and over lunch Martin took the opportunity to urge Selecman "to keep the issue away from personalities." After conference resumed, Bishop James Cannon, Jr., spoke on prohibition, and when Selecman was allowed to continue his rebuttal he seems to have taken Martin's advice and spoke in a more conciliatory tone. At least on the surface, harmony was restored.

There apparently was also trouble between Selecman and "the leadership" of Highland Park Church, too. Umphrey Lee, the pastor, had been given study leave to spend time in Europe until the summer of 1933. Robert Goodloe, a professor in the SMU School of Theology would preach in his absence. Evidence indicates that Lee was prepared to leave and Paul Quillian appears to have been approached about coming in his place. In a letter to Albea Godbold, Quillian wrote that "the controversy between the head of the University and the leadership of the Highland Park Church was one of the prime factors influencing my decision to go to St. Luke's Church, Oklahoma City rather than to Highland Park." Quillian would rather have gone to Dallas, he said, "but the conditions existing there I found would make impossible a fair chance for me," so he took the advice of Bishop Arthur Moore and Bishop Hoyt Dobbs and accepted the assignment in Oklahoma. Quillian speculated that Selecman would have a hard time carrying "forward the program of the University with any assurance of success." In 1938 there was a consensus that Martin's election to the episcopacy had been aided by the determined efforts of the opponents of Charles C. Selecman to keep him out of the office.

Martin made 1,769 pastoral calls his first year in Dallas. He walked to make many of them. More important, however, he grew and he knew he had changed. He decided he could do the work in Dallas. In early December he wrote in his diary, "One of the fears from which the Lord has helped me to escape is the fear of my job." He continued, "I am beginning to believe that God has a special work for me, and I am in position to accept it now as I was not even six months ago."

The financial problems of his congregation had, however, gotten worse with the increasing depth of the depression. Two weeks before Christmas 1932, the chair of the Board of Stewards, Dr. A. V. Lane, came to tell Martin that he was unable to get an extension on the bonds from the lenders, and the Finance Committee was forced to raise the entire $19,000 to make the payment by the deadline on February 15, 1933. It had not been put into the budget since it could not have been raised there. They began by reducing expenses. They discontinued the position of the church visitor, who had resigned, and the church paper, *The Dallas World*. A decision was made to pay all budget items on a proportionate basis, including staff salaries. All members of the staff agreed to the proposal, though "somewhat reluctantly in some cases." Godbold opined that church debts "have a way of squeezing all the religion out of a congregation," so it is hardly surprising to learn that finances were constantly on Martin's mind. On December 17 Martin examined his situation frankly in the diary:

> There may be trying times before me in this church and conference. I shall be sustained by these facts:
> 1. I did not seek to come to Dallas. I was willing to come if I was needed and am willing to stay as long as I can do the work as well or better than anybody else available.
> 2. Nothing can be done to prevent me from giving to my fellow Christians the best I have. Whatever my own limitations may be I represent an irresistible power and so long as I can keep myself in line with His plan for my life there can be no failures.

His final comment for the year 1932 echoes the same theme:

I have learned this year:

1. That the heaviest load in the world is self. Not that I had not learned it before nor that I have been guilty of gross selfishness but the significance of this fact had never been so real to me before. When I am most Christian in my attitude about preferment, etc. then I am first to devote myself wholly to the work of the kingdom. When I refuse to seek for worldly honor I have on my side the wisest and best man who ever lived. God helps me to keep out of my heart all worldly ambition and all sense of bitterness and disappointment when it does not come. God's guidance is dependable.

2. I have been accustomed to eat from 30%-50% more food than was required to sustain my body. The excess became a burden upon the system and reduced my efficiency. I have materially reduced the amount of food consumed.

He decided that when his weight undressed exceeded 180 pounds, he would skip dessert and eat a light lunch. The Martins' youngest, John, had the opposite problem. He was unable to gain weight and was hospitalized in April for two weeks to see if his problem could be addressed. Today a man as large as his father, John regards that experience as "useless." The Martins, like all loving and responsible parents, wanted only the best for all their children and were acting on the basis of the best medical advice available to them at the time, but in two weeks John did not increase his weight.

The children that Christmas enjoyed less expensive gifts than in the past, and during the holiday season Martin wondered "when this whole season of want [is over] what will the poor think of the rich . . . ?"

Ever the organizer, Martin attempted to set up a round robin letter with Godbold, Ray Jordan, and Paul Quillian. They would pass their letters around and add to them when they came. Godbold demanded that Jordan and Martin use a typewriter for their letters since Jordan's handwriting was "execrable and Martin's is fast degenerating. There is no reason," he continued, "why I should have to take off half a day to decipher manuscripts from either of you." The good idea never got off the ground since Quillian admitted in April that "the series of letters stopped dead still when they reached me." By December, Martin declared the experiment a failure and closed it out. Quillian and Jordan were good friends but poor correspondents.

At the beginning of the January quarter 1933, Martin finally began teaching a class on preaching at SMU. It met three days a week—Tuesday, Thursday, and Friday. In return for this teaching he received the services of two seminary students five afternoons a week. One of those who worked from 1936 to 1938, Alonzo Monk Bryan, later became a bishop. The annual campaign to raise the February debt payment began three days later. Sally started the year in Methodist Hospital with "heart irregularities."

By now William C. had joined and was attending the meetings of Chi Alpha, a discussion group composed of Dallas clergy and a few members of the SMU School of Theology faculty. They met in homes every month for dinner and talked about books that were assigned to the sessions. In January 1933, Martin reviewed Norman Thomas's *America's Way Out* "poorly." C. M. Bishop, his old friend from Houston days and a member of the New Testament faculty at the SMU School of Theology, wrote Martin of his experiences in Chi Alpha in 1935 after he moved to St. Louis. "I have never been associated with any group," he said, "which so thoroughly met my own needs for fellowship spiritually and intellectually." Although Martin never gave such expression to his own feelings about the group, he seldom, if ever, missed its meetings.

Mary Katherine had her appendix removed on February 20, 1933. She was in the hospital for a week. Her illness necessitated going to Dave Lacy for a loan of $100. Lacy gave Martin the money but insisted on making it a gift.

In addition to his usual routine of mornings in his study, pastoral calling and sick visits during the afternoon, and meetings almost every evening, he began riding the train to Fort Worth for a day alone. On those outings he often visited the library, wrote, read, and sometimes went to a movie or bowled. These trips provided a renewing change. During the spring quarter at SMU he taught the course "Pastoral Administration," which had an enrollment of only five students—"a disappointment under which I smarted during the day but did not become bitter over it." E. Stanley Jones came to lecture at SMU and Martin got him to autograph his books. "To be with him was a heavenly benediction." On election day he tried to vote but discovered, as he had in Little Rock, he was not on the tax roll. A few days later, just before Palm Sunday, news came that his predecessor, Carl Gregory, had committed suicide. The tragedy affected the entire congregation and made it difficult for Martin to preach.

In May he was asked by President Selecman to serve on a committee to interview prospective SMU School of Theology dean candidates. One of them was Eugene B. Hawk, who was later appointed to the job. The same day he met Hawk, Martin decided to purchase 1/128 interest in a Louisiana oil well, but he discovered he could not borrow the money he needed on his insurance and backed out. "It would have been a foolish move," he later said. Later his good friend Dr. Knickerbocker tried to sell him lots in University Park, the new elite suburb of Dallas in which SMU is located. He decided they would be too much trouble to own and declined. That, however, was a mistake, for the value of houses and lots in the Park Cities is, on the average, in the hundreds of thousands of dollars. His children and grandchildren would have been grateful for his taking the leap. Mary Katherine remembers that she once spoke to him about the joys that might come to them from riches. He responded that money never, by itself, did anybody any good nor brought happiness, and that was especially true in the case of persons who had not earned the money themselves through honest effort. In truth, Martin never really gave money very much consideration. Sally managed their finances, although Martin did balance the bank statement. He was so little concerned about it that he readily accepted reductions in his salary or the lowest allowances provided by the church.

During the hot Texas summers, William C., Sally, and the children moved their beds outdoors and slept in the backyard. In the summer of 1933 there was a special vacation when they drove together to Chicago to see the great World's Fair. On the way

Mary Katherine suffered a recurrence of her malaria and was ill, as was Sally. Once there, however, after they saw a doctor and obtained some medication they set out to see the fair, tour the museums, and hear the evangelist Gipsy Smith preach. During the day, while the family enjoyed the city, Martin attended the Pastor's Institute at the University of Chicago, as he had the previous two summers. On the way home they drove through the Lincoln country and finished up in Arkansas for a few days of fishing and hunting arrowheads. As has been the experience of many a preacher, he arrived back in Dallas "in a mood of desperation for sermon material but pulled through by the grace of the Lord."

Sally began teaching in the Primary Department in October and Martin held a not-too-successful revival meeting at First Methodist Church in Lubbock for his SMU classmate, J. O. Haymes. His state of mental health was poor when he went out and on the way he confesses, "woke up while we were passing through the desolate country south of Post and felt homesick and alone." He felt better once in Lubbock, but few people joined the church.

At the North Texas Conference in Denison, where delegates to the 1934 meeting of the General Conference were elected, he received 55 votes on the first ballot but "a thoroughly organized group elected its ticket straight through" and he wasn't on it. The controversy from the previous conference in 1932 had spilled over into 1933 and the anti-Selecman forces, who now added Martin's friend Frank Richardson to their list of enemies, had made careful advance preparation and elected their delegates. By contrast, Paul Quillian, like Martin a transfer from the Little Rock Conference, was elected on the third ballot in Oklahoma. Bishop Boaz was in the middle of the fight and managed, as Martin told Godbold, "to punish his severest critics by taking two of them off districts and sending one out of the conference." Martin was uncertain whether Boaz had done the right thing but was sure he believed "that men who showed such disloyalty to an officer of the church, even though they did not like him . . . should not be kept in places of leadership." Presiding elders were, after all, an extension of episcopal power. Rumors were circulating that the bishop would be charged at the next General Conference with maladministration, and at the end of the session a decision was made by his supporters not even to offer the *pro forma* resolution of thanks and appreciation for his episcopal leadership "lest the discussion might be more embarrassing than the resolution would be pleasing." The question of whether bishops should be elected for a limited term rather than for life was before the denomination. Martin's early inclination was to favor limiting the term bishops could serve.

Even though Martin was not elected to the General Conference, more than four hundred people attended a "Welcome Back" dinner at First Methodist and bought the Martin family an electric refrigerator to celebrate the occasion of their return, and that felt good. When he first moved to Dallas, Brownie Otstott, in her usual enthusiasm had written in a letter of welcome, *"You'll like us! And we expect to like you."* Her words were prophetic. They did.

Dr. Martin ended his second conference year having made 1957 pastoral visits. The congregation had grown to 3,567 members and the debt had been reduced by $17,000. They had promised him $6,000 in salary but paid only $5,000, a portion of which was raised in early November after conference was over. He told Godbold that he had to borrow money to live during the middle of the year since he received only 60 percent of his regular salary. He was forced to drop some of his insurance, but on the whole the family managed comfortably on $5,000 and thought themselves fortunate by comparison to many others who had far less than they or were out of work entirely. First Church Dallas missed paying its apportionment to general and conference work by $1,353 and raised a total of $67,574, which also reflected the financial difficulties.

Although 1933 had in many ways been a difficult year for the Martins, the conference, and the First Methodist congregation, their pastor closed it out when he preached "with joy and, I think, effectiveness" on its last day. During the year he had taken advantage of lectures at SMU on the depression and had finished the year reading Bishop Francis McConnell's book, *Christianity and*

Coercion. It set his mind, he said, "to work as to what the church should do about the economic situation." He was also reading the work of the great theologian of the social gospel, Walter Rauschenbusch. "I am convinced," he said, "that if the church is to minister to the people in the largest way it must show more interest in their material welfare." When the year was over, he gave thanks to God "for a hungry mind. It accounts very largely for whatever capacity I have had for preparing sermons that were interesting." During 1933, he had also read from Wesley's *Letters*, Dickens, Browning, and O'Henry. He discovered *Time* magazine that year and continued regularly to read the *Christian Century*.

He began 1934 by taking part in the union service on New Year's Day, which was attended by 1,800 people. He also reviewed his progress in the battle with his waistline. His weight had crept up to 190 pounds and it was proving difficult to shed the extra pounds. "Getting rid of a few pounds of weight, once they get settled, is a difficult process." He resolved to eat less at the evening meal, and to omit jelly, sweet potatoes, candy, cold drinks, and ice cream entirely. Controlling his weight was not the only challenge he faced in 1934. There was the usual struggle to meet the debt payment and near the end of January he had to decide whether to give permission for Donald, who was now fourteen, to join the North Dallas High School R.O.T.C. unit. He decided to let him make the choice, because no matter what happened it was "a lesser evil than having him regarded as being odd. He is scarcely martyr material." Donald was later to serve with distinction and valor as a bomber pilot in the South Pacific during World War II.

Mary Katherine once said that "the only thing which kept our father from being pompous was a neurotic wife and three awful children." They opposed him when they thought he was wrong, argued when they disagreed with what he was saying, disobeyed him when he was unreasonable, and teased or laughed at him when he became self-righteous. He encouraged them to think for themselves, praised their successes, and allowed them to fail. They got into trouble when they disobeyed or made their mother feel bad, or if they were unkind to other people. Like all children they were sometimes an annoyance and embarrassment to their parents, fulfilling adequately the stereotypical role assigned to "preacher's kids." There were cherished family customs to observe and traditions that they all valued and enjoyed. One of these was established because they often forgot the key to the door and locked themselves out of the house. John, the youngest, Sally once said, spent so much time being lifted in and out of windows that she had some concern that he might be attracted to a career as a burglar. As a result, when the family would leave on a trip, they developed a routine that was faithfully followed. At the top of his voice Martin would ask, "Children, is the key outside the house?" They would respond, "Hanging on the nail by the light, Daddy." Sally often said she hoped nobody was listening to that exchange when they were so obviously on their way out of town.

At the church there was the never-ending challenge to pay the debt, and the looming deadline for the February payment produced "long and gloomy" sessions of the finance committee and an all-out effort in the congregation to raise enough money to get by one more year. Writing about it later, Martin said, "No money raising method was overlooked . . . in fact every device was resorted to except bingo and lottery—and some were strongly tempted." But in 1934 Jesse Lee Johnson, an insurance man in the congregation, came up with an idea that would provide a viable, permanent solution. Martin remembered that Johnson used to say, "This building is worth more than the debt simply as a commercial property. We can issue and sell our own bonds." At first people were reluctant to endorse the idea, but by December a "Bond Committee" had been organized and serious consideration was being given to Johnson's proposal. The necessity, once again, of making the debt payment in February created the sense of urgency that was needed. Johnson's idea prevailed and the entire debt was refinanced. The bonds paid 6 percent interest and were issued to mature serially over a period of fifteen years. They were purchased mostly by members of the congregation. The refinancing scheme enabled them to reduce the size of the payments and include them within the regular church budget. More important, for the first time they could be assured of covering the cost every year. Selling the idea and going through the necessary steps to issue the bonds took a great deal of Martin's time, but it may well have saved the congregation from financial ruin.

Early in the year 1934, Martin splurged and purchased the complete works of Dickens "in a beautiful edition," which Donald eventually received. There were an enjoyable twelve days with Paul Quillian in Oklahoma City when Martin held his spring revival at St. Luke's Church. Martin, who was intentional to a fault, had a steadying influence on Quillian and Paul had a liberating influence on Martin. They were very good for each other. The revival was not, however, much of a success. "We did not make much of a stir; in fact if it had not been for Paul's words of encouragement I would have marked it down as a pretty flat failure," Martin said. But it was a good time, he told Godbold, "just being together."

During the summer, while Sally and Mary Katherine went to visit the Beene family in Arkansas, William C. took the boys and drove to El Paso. On the way out they visited the caverns at Carlsbad—Martin always loved a cave. Coming home they stopped to tour the campus of McMurry, a Methodist college in Abilene. Afterward he made a brief visit to Tennessee and then took a longer vacation with the entire family in Arkansas. There wasn't money available for a more elaborate trip, but in addition there was the usual time at Mt. Sequoyah for Martin to lead a discussion group on "What Can We Preach Today?" Bishop Kern urged him not to lecture, but to "guide" the discussion.

For recreation at home, he continued to hunt with the boys in the Trinity River bottom and shot ducks on the Doggett farm. Recreation with Sally still included drives around White Rock Lake, frequent trips to the movies, and a yearly trip to hear the Weaver Brothers and Elviery when they came to town. In the fall the entire family enjoyed the SMU football games.

The greatest pleasure the Martins enjoyed was derived from going to the homes of friends, like those who were members of the Supper Club, Layton and Clara Bailey, Jim and Pauline Hubbard, Ode and Del Mason, Edla and Frank Martino, along with the Bookhouts, Freemans, and George Drewerys. These were the people who knew them best and loved them anyway. They laughed with them (and sometimes at them, too), knew well that Sally was not just Dr. Martin's wife, and that he was not some icon. At one of their gatherings, Martin admitted that he felt "uncomfortably self conscious when all the other men left the room to hear a radio report of a prize-fight but I stood my ground." The women in the group got together for lunch, shopped, and talked on the telephone. They spent many summer evenings doing things as families, went on outings together, and later became "families away from home" when Mary Katherine and John enrolled as students at SMU. Others, though not in the Supper Club, were good friends through the years—Dave and Pauline Lacy, the Norrells, whose brandy-laced fruitcake at Christmastime was a special favorite of William C.'s, and the Edwin Doggetts—he was elected Chairman of the Board of Stewards during the year. Doggett and his wife were both killed in a tragic automobile accident near Waxahachie in March 1939. Martin held their funerals. There were preacher friends, too. The family was especially close to Paul and Elizabeth Stephenson and the Glenn Flinns.

Making good friends, which was difficult for William C., was easy for Sally, and she kept the ones she had through all the years. The children of these Dallas friends called Sally regularly even after she had moved back to Little Rock and were with her at William C.'s funeral. Even with those closest to him, he was inclined to withhold a part of himself. But as never before or again, he was able to relax with this Dallas circle of friends and they enabled him to become a more understanding person. As pastor and friend, he shared their good and ill fortunes. He celebrated with them the various rites of passage—attending graduations, officiating the marriages of their children, and baptizing their grandchildren; and he stood at the sickbed and graveside with them. Among his circle of male friends, Martin was closest to the journalist Lynn Landrum, with whom he often had lunch and in whose home he and the family frequently were guests. This friendship, however, was to be sorely tested during the anti-communist crusades of the Cold War.

The Martins' attendance at the movies was made easier by the fact that the operators gave them a pass each year. During 1934 they saw Will Rogers, one of William C.'s absolute favorites, in *Mr. Stitch, David Harem, Judge Priest,* and *Handy Andy;* Frank Buck in *Wild Cargo,* along with assorted Wallace Beery, Laurel and Hardy, and Amos and Andy movies. He thought *The House of Rothschild* with George Arliss was a great picture, but Sally did not share his opinion. They also saw Arliss in *Disraeli.* He saw *The Count of Monte Cristo* with the boys.

That summer of 1934 was unusually hot and dry even for Texas, and as usual they moved out of the house to sleep in the yard. Several preachers in town had prayed for rain, but Martin allowed to Godbold that "most of us have not had quite enough confidence in the soundness of our judgement to attempt to take the weather in hand." There were numerous weddings and funerals, as is always the case in the life of a busy pastor. He increased his already full schedule of pastoral calling and made 2,032 of them during the year. Bishop A. Frank Smith, the new bishop in the Dallas–Fort Worth Area, asked him to consider becoming presiding elder of the Dallas District, but he knew he had no interest in such an appointment and respectfully declined. "I do not think I am called to be a presiding elder," he said in the diary. He was even more direct with Godbold. "The presiding-eldership has fallen into such disrepute that I have serious doubt as to our ever being able to reinstate it."

The ordinary work of a pastor was challenging enough. Members of his congregation, H. H. Tucker, Jr., and W. F. Tyree, were charged and convicted of using the mails to defraud. Tucker was sentenced to four years in Leavenworth and Tyree fined $1,000 and sentenced to a year in El Reno. After visiting both men in jail Martin went to the Court House and talked unsuccessfully with Judge Atwell about getting Tyree's sentence suspended.

Paul Quillian held the fall revival in Dallas in 1934 and, as always, Martin was overjoyed to have his company for a time. Throughout the year Martin also enjoyed conversations with Umphrey Lee, the pastor at Highland Park Church near the SMU campus. In some of them they discussed the chapters of Lee's new book on John Wesley. Martin appreciated the ability and talent of the man who was destined to become president of SMU. "He is thoroughly brotherly and I get more joy from talking with him, which I don't do very often, than from anybody else here." The General Conference in May 1934 elected Martin to the SMU Board of Trustees as a representative of the Methodist Episcopal Church, South, and SMU named him to its Executive Committee, giving him an active role in the affairs of the university, and free tickets to the football games. He continued his opposition to any form of dancing on the campus, and for a time he and its opponents prevailed. Martin's mind could be changed, but there were a good many things about which he remained steadfast. He ended the year with the frank acknowledgment that

> my interests are never concentrated at the same place for a very long period of time. This is probably a defect which will limit my achievements but I shall try to look at the positive rather than the negative side of it. It gives me the advantage of a wide range of interests which has its value for the preacher. Knowing this limitation as I do I should always guard against buying materials, books, etc. and making plans as if it did not exist.

The year 1935 opened with a joint New Year's Day communion service organized by a small group of ministers including Martin, Floyd Poe, pastor of City Temple Presbyterian, and W. W. Phares, pastor of South Dallas Christian Church. It became an annual event and the following year almost 2,000 persons attended the service. Selling bonds to refinance the debt at First Methodist got off to an early and busy start. February 3, a called session of the Quarterly Conference ratified the bond issue, but

Johnson's idea still lacked full acceptance and support in the congregation. There was, in fact, considerable pessimism in the Bond Committee about the possibility of selling all the bonds, causing Martin considerable anguish and some lost sleep, something he rarely did.

About mid-January, Martin, who had for many years been tempted to begin a serious and systematic study of John Wesley, gave up the idea entirely. He said in the diary that he had two reasons for doing it: "I cannot afford to put so much time and attention at one place in the history of the church, and the reading of very much of Wesleyan literature has a depressing influence on my spirits." A fair number of seminary students would join him in that conclusion. Perhaps he was also led to give up the idea because of his close association with Umphrey Lee, whose area of expertise was Wesley and Methodism. Lee was a scholar in every sense of the word. By comparing himself to Lee, Martin easily would have seen that he had neither the inclination nor the commitment for such an endeavor. Moreover, through their conversations, Martin was fully aware that Lee's new book, *John Wesley and Modern Religion,* which appeared in 1936, was well along and would eliminate the need for a new study of Wesley.

Once having decided he would not undertake serious Wesley study, Martin got in touch with E. L. Shettles and told him he would like to sell all his Wesley books. Shettles questioned the wisdom of such an act, but finally agreed to do what he could and thought he might get $25 or $30 for them.

Martin continued to be troubled about his responsibility "for expressing my convictions concerning social justice." Late in the previous year he had allowed his signed response to a survey sent out by Kirby Page affirming his conviction that "socialism may be the way" out of the depression to be quoted. He was fully aware of the implications of his stand and thought there would be repercussions, but apparently there were no significant consequences.

In March he was bothered by a throat infection and decided that his lack of good health and feelings of "mutual depression and general unworthiness" were due to the lack of exercise. He decided to set aside one afternoon a week for recreation and determined that he would plant and cultivate a vegetable garden. One of his members, George Drewery, had a farm on the outskirts of town and offered him a plot of ground to work. With Donald in tow, he selected the spot and began to lay out a vegetable garden. Lacking their father's enthusiasm, both Donald and John, nevertheless, were included in the new exercise regimen. Earlier Godbold had recommended gardening to the members of the round robin, but with little positive results. Paul Quillian wrote Martin that "Godbold's suggestion that we take up gardening in our spare hours makes me laugh." He continued, "Feeling a religious urge to return to the soil, I have two or three times before been induced to spade up unoffending ground and plant flowers and radishes, etc. I didn't enjoy it, and the flowers and vegetables didn't seem to appreciate it, for they refused to blossom under my touch."

But in Martin, Godbold found a convert. He was no doubt pleased when Martin wrote, "I have adopted your hobby, gardening. But I go in for something to eat." He went out to Drewery's farm, about ten miles away, at every opportunity, and Sally would often join him late in the evening and bring a picnic supper. He and the boys planted corn and beans, and when Martin felt cross or depressed, he nearly always resolved to take more exercise and went to work in the garden. By late April the produce was growing nicely, and in May they began to harvest the fruits of their labors. SMU honored Paul Quillian's labors at its commencement that month with an honorary degree. Martin did not receive his honorary degree from SMU until 1957.

On June 19, 1935, word came from Blevins that Nannie Jacob, "Mamma," had suffered a cerebral hemorrhage and was in critical condition. They hurried to her bedside. She continued to weaken, and early in the morning of June 23 she died. The funeral and burial were in Prescott, where "a tired body was laid to rest by the side of Papa's." That afternoon he and Sally walked together over the home place and picked berries. Brice was named executor of her estate. The Martins returned to Dallas two days later and discovered that good friends had dinner waiting for them when they arrived.

The second week in July Martin took the *Sunshine Special*,

now boasting air-conditioned cars, to New York to attend the Pastor's School at Union Theological Seminary. There he heard James Black of Edinburgh—who was substituting at the last minute for the popular New York preacher, Harry Emerson Fosdick—Bruce Curry, Paul Scherer, and Harvie Branscombe, his old SMU professor, and found time to see *Tobacco Road*, which he judged to be "a scurrilous libel, for the most part, but enough of truth to make a Southerner squirm." He prowled the used bookstores in the city, toured Riverside Church, Rockefeller Center, and the Music Hall, and saw *The Children's Hour*, a play "which had little meaning." He stayed two extra days in order to hear theologian Reinhold Niebuhr and Bible scholar James Moffatt. On the way home he stopped again in Washington where he visited both houses of Congress in session and saw many of its familiar sights again. He took time while there to visit with former SMU classmate Angie Smith, who was now the pastor at Mt. Vernon Church. His advice for traveling: "Always have a definite purpose in mind when you travel and when that objective has been accomplished, move on. Don't loiter. Life is too short for any part of it to be spent 'killing time.' And, besides, it's dangerous." He got back to Dallas on July 26 and went to visit his garden after supper.

In August he fulfilled his usual teaching assignment at Mt. Sequoyah—a course on Evangelism—despite John's coming down with the mumps during the session. How many people he managed to expose to the disease is unknown. As was now their custom, Martin and the boys hunted arrowheads while in Arkansas, and as a result of their success he resolved to help the boys follow up on their interest in things related to Native Americans. When they got home, he, Donald, and Mary Katherine marched in the anti-whiskey parade through downtown. The next month he went with Sally to see *Becky Sharp*, their first "all color" picture which he did not enjoy, but anyway, as he said, "it was too wet to go to the farm."

Methodist preachers did not usually stay long in their assignments during the 1930s. So before conference in the fall of 1935, Bishop Smith talked to Martin about his willingness to serve longer at First Church. "He knew of no reason why I should move and I told him I was willing to remain." But he also told the bishop, "I thought it was the exception when a preacher should stay longer than six years." He also heard the rumor that he and a Texas Conference preacher, Bob Goodrich, were to exchange pastorates. Goodrich was to serve First Church, but it would be years later when he came.

Italy invaded Ethiopia "in spite of the protest of the civilized world," on October 5, moving it one step closer to war. Conference met in Wichita Falls where Martin was entertained in the "spacious, luxurious" home of the J. J. Perkins family. Joe and Lois Perkins and J. S. Bridwell were later to become the largest contributors to the SMU School of Theology, which was renamed the Perkins School of Theology in 1946 in recognition of their gifts. "Brother Forney" Hutchinson preached. Once again the congregation was elated with Martin's return, and despite the hardship imposed by the depression a committee began negotiations to purchase him a new car. On Christmas Day 200 people called to extend good wishes and greetings.

In looking back on the year 1935, now in the depths of the depression, and reflecting on his own life, Martin mused about the changes that had taken place in one generation. "What justification is there," he wrote, "to being taken out of the workers' class, to which my fathers for generations have belonged and put into the thinkers' class?" In another entry he concluded, "When we seek a course in life so simple and direct that there will be no difficulty in making decisions and determining where truth lies, we seek what cannot be found. Life is simply more complex than that." It seems fair to say that William C. Martin was never really comfortable with ambiguity, and the truth of his own profound observation was never easy for him to accept though he knew it to be so.

The lavish entertaining and good eating of the Christmas season proved, once again, to be his downfall, and shortly after the first of the new year, 1936, he consulted Dr. David W. Carter about his weight. Carter gave him a metabolism test and a restricted diet. After sixty days on the new diet he had lost ten pounds and accepted the inevitable: "I am now convinced that I have been too lenient with myself in the matter of establishing a standard of normal weight out of deference to my larger bone structure. It is evident to me that my excess weight is not on my limbs but on my abdomen." He took possession of the new Lafayette automobile that the stewards had purchased for him on January 22.

Events moving the world ever closer to war and the Great Depression in the United States had been greatly on his mind for some time. What was his responsibility and that of his large congregation in the area of social justice? He began 1936 thinking about it even more seriously than before. Sally started the new year in bed with "exhaustion." By the end of January she was in Methodist Hospital under the care of a psychiatrist. He "thinks it will require 3 months for her to get well," Martin wrote. While Martin carried on his work at the church and saw to the needs of the children and affairs at home, Sally did not get better. In his prayer for the sick one Sunday morning he admitted in the diary that his "voice broke." A new treatment was begun, and the entry on February 15 notes that Dr. Watt, the psychiatrist, asked him not to see her again for a few days. Sally, however, asked him to come and he went. A week later the doctor made the same suggestion, and this time Martin respected it and did not see her until March 4. Although Sally's emotional state and progress toward health continued to go up and down like a roller coaster, on March 14, she was allowed to come home. While she was in the hospital, Martin held a revival meeting in Shreveport.

Although at home, she was not well and her emotional state was fragile and had to be guarded. In fact, when he brought her home, Martin wrote in his diary "she was at hospital nearly seven weeks and did not make much progress." During the first part of April she and William C. went for long drives almost daily and spent hours in conversation alone. When at home, Sally was in bed most of the time for the next four weeks. Just after Easter he drove her to Hot Springs, a favorite spot of theirs. They picked violets on the mountain and went to see Shirley Temple in *Captain January*. Sally remained there alone for a month. Martin described her condition to Godbold near the end of April as "a case of complete exhaustion."

Life and work in Dallas went on much as usual. Now president of the Ministerial Alliance, Martin worked with a committee of "colored preachers" to ensure there would be no discrimination at a meeting that was to feature the noted Japanese Christian leader, Toyohiko Kagawa. "A delicate situation which was harmoniously worked out." There were trips with the boys to the Drewery farm to put plants into the garden and a nostalgia trip with them to Houston and Galveston in conjunction with a preaching assignment in Port Arthur. On the way home they stopped in Austin and climbed to the top of the dome of the Capitol building.

Sally returned home from Hot Springs on May 5 much improved, but was not feeling well three days later. The diary, though obscure, clearly reflects his distress about her. May 21: "Sally in despondent mood. . . . Faced a dark outlook." The next day, "Not much sleep last night. . . . Out of my distress I cried unto the Lord and he heard my prayer."

He preached at the graduation ceremonies at Hendrix College, which were held in the sanctuary of First Methodist Church of Conway where Albea Godbold was now pastor. The trip afforded an opportunity to enjoy two delightful days in Godbold's company and lifted Martin's spirits. At home he had a major role in planning an all-city revival that was to feature the famous evangelist, Gipsy Smith. The Texas Centennial celebration was in full swing, and despite the opposition of the Ministerial Alliance to the presence of Sally Rand and her "Nude Ranch," Will and Sally went often to the fair and took visitors when they came. Among them were Aunt Stell and Uncle Martin Nelson and Albea Godbold. In August the family vacationed in Albuquerque and Santa Fe. On the way home they covered a record 525 miles in one day's drive. This was yet another bone of contention with Sally. She liked to stop; he saw every mile as a personal challenge to be overcome in the shortest period of time. One evening after they got home, he and the boys went to the farm where they slept on the grass in the pasture in order to see the stars.

Hearing theologian Walter Marshall Horton at the SMU Pastor's School in the summer tweaked a renewed interest in British theology. Writing of him to Godbold, Martin perceptively observed, "Dr. Horton is your age and is a very intimate member of that small group of younger theologians like [Robert Lowery] Calhoun and [Henry Pitney] Van Dusen and [John] Bennett and Aubrey who are destined, I think, to have a large share in directing the theological thought of the liberal element of Protestantism in this country during the years just ahead of us."

The Gipsy Smith all-city revival began at First Baptist Church the morning of September 20, and followed with a service in the afternoon for men only. At every event there were overflowing crowds. "Rumored that 2,000 people were turned away from G.S. service in eve" on October 2. When he and Smith were introduced, they shook hands and Smith told him, "I am expecting great things of you. You can do the work I am doing." They were together frequently during the revival and Martin liked him and enjoyed his company. He described the evangelist as "a marvel for continued vigor and youthfulness," but Godbold was not so impressed. "No doubt he has done some good work through the years, but I regard him as too old now. [Smith was 76 at the time of the Dallas revival.] Also, he seems to be unaware of what religion is up against in this modern world."

An almost fatal accident marred the days of the revival. John Lee, the Martin's youngest son, was on his way to town with a friend. They had ridden partway on a city bus and were running to catch a streetcar when John, without looking, darted in front of the bus and was struck by an automobile. Someone had called to him as he got off the bus, and in turning to see who it was, he exposed the left side of his back. The door handle of a passing car tore through his back and emerged just under his armpit. Although the driver, Mrs. Wallace, did not stop and carried John for some distance impaled on the door handle, he is clear that she was not at fault except for leaving the scene of the accident. He was critically injured and might well have died had not a passerby taken dramatic and bold action. Mr. Fry, a plumber, was passing and stopped to see what had happened. He asked if anyone had called for an ambulance, and, amazing as it seems, no one in the sizable crowd of people who were standing around had thought to do it. John's chest was crushed from the back and his left lung was exposed and collapsed. Martin later wrote Godbold that "the outside handle of the car door tore its way into his chest from the back." After seeing his condition, Fry realizing that John might not survive if they waited for help to arrive, carefully picked him up, put him in his truck, and drove as fast as he could to Parkland Hospital, the nearest medical facility. He had, in fact, done so in violation of the law that prohibits moving the victim of an accident, and his willingness to take that risk may have saved John's life. When things calmed down, Mr. Fry came to the house to explain to the Martins why he had done what he did and later William C. took John to meet him. On the way to Parkland, John regained consciousness and upon arrival was able to give the attendants the names and telephone numbers of his parents. He still remembers them.

His injuries were so severe that it seemed to the attendants in the emergency room that he was unlikely to survive and they simply sewed him up. John said that the suturing caused no pain since all the nerves had been cut, but he does remember the sound of the sutures as they closed his chest cavity. By chance Martin, who was out making pastoral calls, had gone back to the church to pick up more addresses and was there when the call came from Parkland about 4:15. Although Martin reports that the doctors assured them there was a "fair" chance for his recovery, the danger from infection made John's situation critical. Sally remembered the doctors telling her there was virtually no hope for his recovery. When X rays could be taken, it was determined that six ribs and his collarbone were broken, a lung collapsed, and the lower part of his chest was so filled with fluid that it was pressing on his heart. His father admitted that when he saw the pictures, John's chest "was so badly broken up that I was unnerved by it." And that was the judgment of one who had seen severely wounded men in a World War I evacuation hospital.

Martin spent the next twelve consecutive nights with his son at Parkland Hospital. SMU theology professor Dr. J. T. Carlyon preached at First Methodist in Martin's absence and members of the church took over the business of closing out the conference year. Sally quickly rallied to the situation and was strong throughout the entire ordeal, too. Frances Bookhout, Pauline Hubbard, and Clara Bailey shared a constant vigil with her at home. She often said later that this single act of friendship meant more than anything ever done for her. In the days that followed, fluid had to be drained from John's chest a number of times, but he somehow managed to avoid infection and made rapid progress.

With John still in the hospital but finally out of danger and healing, William C. felt free to leave for Houston the morning of November 4 to attend the joint session of the six Texas annual conferences. As if writing his own version of the corollary to Murphy's Law (when things go wrong they get worse before they get better), Mr. E. M. Edwards, one of his members at First Church Dallas well known for sitting on a front pew and sleeping through Martin's sermons, rose during the session formally to charge Martin with heresy and distributed a paper full of accusations. No real notice was taken of Edwards or his charges and Bishop Smith gave clear evidence of his confidence in Martin by asking him to preside at one of the conference sessions. Preaching at Grace Church, and the warm reception that he received there, made things much better as did the presence of so many of his close and supportive friends.

Martin arrived back in Dallas on November 10 and took John home from the hospital that same day. "His recovery has been like receiving him back from the dead." He described it to Godbold as "near an approach to the miraculous as anything I have witnessed." John came to the table for dinner on his birthday and was fully dressed for the first time on Thanksgiving Day. Writing about the experience much later, Martin said, "We shall always believe that the prayers of the congregation for him were a decisive factor in his being spared to us." He also credited the power generated by the Gipsy Smith revival as crucial. "Mrs. Martin and I were particularly grateful for the experience of this meeting because of the inner courage which it gave us to face a trying ordeal." Although the Martins were strongly advised to sue the driver of the automobile to recover their medical costs and to compensate John for some of the pain and suffering he had experienced, they decided just before Christmas "that we will not be parties to a law suit in connection with John's injury, either in our own name or for him. This course is not in accord with Judge Frank's advice but it squares with our own consciences." What certainly must have been a wonderful Christmas gift to Mrs. Wallace gives further evidence of Martin's feelings about money and coincides with John's recollection that she was not at fault.

It seems as if John's brush with death enabled Sally to move to a new level of focus and health in her own life, and in 1937 she was greatly improved both emotionally and physically, often making calls with her husband or taking part in other activities at the church. She was teaching regularly in the Primary Department. But, almost as usual, she began 1938 sick again. William C. began it teaching a course on evangelism at a Pastor's School in Tucson, and when he got home Sally was in bed with influenza. In a week Mary Katherine was infected as well. While in Arizona he was able to spend time with Robert and Ruby Beene, Sally's cousins who lived in Tucson. Early in February he described himself in the diary as "irked" by a statement and picture in the *Dallas Times Herald* that linked him to the episcopacy. But he could not have been surprised. Friends had mentioned the possibility of his election, too. His reply was consistent. He truthfully told anyone who asked that he did not seek the office and believed firmly that his best service would continue to be rendered in the local congregation, but he did acknowledge that he had always considered himself ready and willing to serve wherever the leaders of the church thought he could best be used. If the church required his service in another arena, he was ready to obey its mandate, but he was not going out in search of new responsibilities. "If my peace and happiness were dependent upon what others say to do it would be most insecure," he wrote.

The farm continued to be a pleasant diversion and at times he and Sally went fishing together. Both were competitive to the core, and William C. kept a record in the diary of who caught the most fish—"I caught 3 and S. caught 1," he said in March. He didn't say when she caught more than he did, however. The children recall that Sally often beat her husband at games, and loved to do it, and that he would practice before they played to avoid the experience. She did the same. Neither liked to lose. As was now his established custom, he and the boys tilled the garden plot and planted onions and corn in the early spring.

Easter Sunday 1937 saw the largest crowd attend services at First Methodist since Martin had been in Dallas. The evening crowd also set a record. April 15, thanks to the generosity of a group of his members, he completed the necessary requirements to become a thirty-second degree Mason. "I am now a 32 degree Mason. May its highest teaching be exemplified in my life and may I add to it a higher degree of Christian fervor," he wrote in the diary. In May he returned to Grace Church in Houston to hold a revival meeting. It was a time filled with preaching to an overflowing audience and renewing pleasant associations from the past, as well as an opportunity to be again with Paul Quillian, who was now the pastor at First Methodist Church, Houston. Between the services there was also time for leisurely trips to Galveston to swim, walk on the beach and enjoy the ocean. He told Godbold, "It was a very happy experience and I was delighted with the results." The one that pleased him most was helping to raise $6,000 to reduce the debt on the Sunday school building, which had been planned and begun when he was pastor. "I had always felt a sense of responsibility about the debt since it was incurred during my stay there and on my recommendation . . . so I was glad of the opportunity to have a share in helping to get them out of the woods." When he got home he discovered John had suffered a blow to the head while playing baseball and was in the hospital for observation. It was determined he was not seriously injured, but Sally was frightened for him because of his earlier accident. He remained in the hospital overnight for observation.

Edwin Doggett took Donald and William C., along with Marshall Steel, his son, and another boy, to the Koon Creek fishing camp for a two-day outing. They managed to catch forty-three fish "big enough to keep," mostly bass and white perch. They had such a good time that Doggett called Bishop Moore and arranged for Martin to miss the SMU Board of Trustees meeting to stay an extra day. At the end of school, Donald left on the train to spend the summer with Uncle Brice and his wife, "Jack," on the farm in Arkansas. John went in July. Both Will and Sally believed it was important to stay close to the land and her brother, Brice, gave each of their sons the responsibility for making a crop on the old home place.

Teaching in the Pastor's School at Southwestern University in Georgetown afforded Martin the opportunity to spend most of a day with E. L. Shettles in nearby Austin. "When I come near to Bro. Shettles I am irresistibly drawn into his interest in books, particularly his books on Methodism. I found myself resolving to read more of these first hand accounts of our beginnings as a church." Shettles was a truly remarkable human being and he had an influence on Martin. He was also impressed with Southwestern and noted, as parents are wont to do, "Would like for D[onald] to come here."

As usual, when the heat of a Texas summer got into full swing, he and Sally moved their bed into the backyard. Lots of nights were spent at the farm where the plentiful harvest of vegetables and the pleasant surroundings provided occasions for picnic suppers with good friends. The Glenn Flinns went out often. As always Martin had a self-improvement project, and this summer it was learning shorthand. Fortunately for his biographer, he learned only a few symbols before giving it up as too time consuming and unrewarding. Had he been successful, using the diaries that covered the next fifty years of his life would have been even more of a challenge than the already formidable one of reading his handwriting in the later years of his life. His attorney continued to press them to sue Mrs. Wallace for the injuries John had sustained, but he and Sally were steadfast in their earlier decision not to seek legal redress. Martin said they had trouble in getting Judge Frank "to understand why I refuse to bring suit," but in their minds it was simply the wrong thing to do. John agreed.

After William C.'s usual trip to teach at Mt. Sequoyah, the

Martin family summer vacation in August 1937 was spent at Lake Junaluska, a Methodist conference center near Asheville in the Great Smoky Mountains of North Carolina. It was their first time to visit the popular assembly ground. On the drive over they made a brief stop in Tennessee to see the kinfolk and to walk over the farm. They also made a brief stop at Shiloh to see the battlefield, and then at Chickamauga Park, where Martin had been stationed for training in World War I. He planned to show the children the camp, but "so many changes had been made I could hardly find where our tents had stood." They arrived in Lake Junaluska August 9 and went to hear Bishop Arthur Moore preach that same evening.

The children recall being told by their mother that it was Arthur Moore, one of the most prominent leaders in the Methodist Episcopal Church, South, who encouraged the Martin vacation in the center of Methodism in the Southeast. Although there are no letters from Moore or Martin which collaborate this memory, perhaps it was an attempt on Moore's part to enhance Martin's visibility in that portion of the Methodist Episcopal Church, South, where he was not well known, and, if so, thereby to enhance his candidacy for the episcopacy. That the trip was unique and not like any they had taken before is obvious, but that Martin was thinking about the episcopacy when he went is not. Self-promotion was simply not a part of Martin's personal agenda. Besides, the Doggetts, Johnsons, and Bullocks from First Church, Dallas, were also vacationing in Asheville, and there were many pleasant times with them. They too must have encouraged the Martins to consider taking their vacation at Junaluska. Furthermore, Martin loved the mountains, and he and the boys climbed as many of the ones surrounding the lake as they could. One was the Eagle's Nest in Waynesville, where they climbed to the summit and "got good view of the surrounding country from the top." They also climbed Mt. Mitchell, at 6,711 feet.

While at Lake Junaluska, they made side trips to Henderson and Raleigh in order to visit relatives of Sally who were members of the Reavis family. Sally was making application for membership in the Daughters of the American Revolution, and it was through the Reavis line that she sought to establish her eligibility. On the way home they drove through the Great Smoky Mountain National Park, visited Nashville, and made another stop with the relatives in Arkansas. They arrived safely home after 3,500 miles of driving just at the end of August. The first Sunday back, Martin preached in the newly air-conditioned sanctuary. He judged it to be "working fairly well."

In anticipation of the formation of a united church in 1939, a new hymnal had been prepared, and William C. and Sally spent many evenings going over the hymns looking for ones that he judged "useable." Martin had a good singing voice and loved music. Although he eventually came to support the idea of unification, he was not convinced at the beginning that it was a good thing. His friend Paul Quillian, however, led the movement to get it approved in the Southern church and Martin eventually joined in supporting it, too. The Methodist Episcopal Church, South, existed for the better part of a century and during its life grew and flourished. Moreover it became one of the most effective organizations in preserving Southern life and culture after the Civil War. (See Christine Leigh Heyrman, *Southern Cross: The Beginning of the Bible Belt* [New York: Alfred A. Knopf, 1997].) A group of laypersons and a few strong leaders within the clergy, such as Bishops Warren Candler and Collins Denny, steadfastly opposed unification until the end.

As leaders of a prominent congregation, the Martins were often invited to take part in welcoming important persons to Dallas. In September, William C. and Sally were invited to the Adolphus Hotel in downtown Dallas to a luncheon honoring comedian Bob Burns. Martin's comment in the diary makes his attitude toward the celebrity clear: "My poor opinion of him was slightly modified," he wrote. He was more interested in the purchase of a new Buick, in which he and Sally drove the family to Houston to spend Thanksgiving with the Paul Quillians. No doubt he and Quillian discussed the upcoming conference and General Conference and their chances for election as delegates.

About conference time Martin also began taking a series of exercises every morning. They took about ten minutes "and have helped me greatly," he said. November 1, 1937, he weighed in at 197½ pounds and was, once again, facing the problem of how to maintain a positive mental attitude without putting on weight in the process. He determined that he would "put less dependence upon my body and my moods and more upon that part of my nature which is above them." From his youth, Martin was dedicated to self-improvement and he sought constantly to educate himself in areas he thought were important, like economics or the proper use of language; and he worked hard to control his impatience and temper as well as his weight. From time to time he even adjusted the hours devoted to sleep in order to have more time for things he thought were important.

Before any Methodist gathering at which bishops are to be elected, there is always lots of talk and groups with a political agenda working diligently to aid the Holy Spirit to ensure the election of a favored candidate. There is no question that Martin's name was being mentioned for the episcopacy, and he knew it. He talked with Selecman "about his preference concerning the episcopacy" before the annual conference opened the last of October, but he does not say what he learned. The first order of business on the opening day of conference, as it is in any year preceding the quadrennial General Conference, was the election of clergy and lay delegates to the upcoming conference in Birmingham. This quadrennial conference is the policy-making body for the denomination and was, until the formation of The Methodist Church in 1939, the site of episcopal elections. It was and is a delegated assembly composed of equal numbers of lay and clergy members. Following the Methodist pattern, separate elections were conducted in the annual conference with clergy voting for clerical delegates and laypersons for lay delegates. Voting is done by secret ballot without nominations. All clergy members in full connection are eligible to be elected; lay delegates must be beyond a minimal age and have been members of a local congregation for at least five years. It is a process in which politics is never much below the surface, and Martin was well aware of its influence from his first encounter with the North Texas Conference. Unlike the situation four years earlier, however, one faction was unable in 1937 to prevail. "The group which was very greatly in the majority four years ago had more aspirants than the wagon would carry so there was a division of forces which let in some men who had been in the minority," Martin wrote Godbold. Ryan, Barnes, and Groseclose were the only clergy delegates elected who had attended the General Conference in 1934. Barnes had, in fact, led that delegation that year. There was strong sentiment both for and against the president of SMU, Charles C. Selecman.

On the first clergy ballot 197 ballots were cast. A majority is necessary in each case for election. Ten ballots were found to be defective, usually due to too many or too few names being included, or because ineligible persons were named. Once the invalid ballots were eliminated, it took 94 votes to elect. Paul Martin, presiding elder of the Wichita Falls District, received 111 votes, becoming the first elected and, therefore, the leader of the clergy delegation. He was joined in the delegation on the first ballot by H. G. Ryan, pastor of the Travis Street congregation in Sherman, Charles C. Selecman, and S. A. Barnes, pastor of Dallas's Tyler Street Church. On the second ballot there was only one election, J. H. Groseclose, superintendent of the Methodist Hospital in Dallas. After the memorial service for deceased clergy, a third ballot was ordered and William C. Martin received 90 votes and was elected. "I had not expected to be elected as a delegate to the General Conference, which opinion I held until the results of the first ballots were announced." But he was pleased to have been chosen. It was the only time, in fact, he was ever to attend General Conference as a clergy member. One additional delegate, S. H. C. Burgin, Martin's presiding elder, was elected on the sixth ballot to fill out the delegation of seven persons to the last session of the General Conference of the Methodist Episcopal Church, South.

Following the adjournment of the North Texas Conference, Martin preached at the Little Rock Conference. He and Sally were welcomed back to Dallas by their friends and parishioners at a dinner and were given eight sterling silver goblets to mark the occasion.

Finances as usual were far behind as the end of the year approached. Reflecting on his work, he wrote, "About the most hopeful element in my religious experience is my awareness of my imperfections." But there was no disputing the success he had achieved in Dallas despite them, and his career in the pastoral ministry of the church was rapidly drawing to a close as 1938 began. During his years as a pastor in Houston, Port Arthur, Little Rock, and Dallas, Martin preached more sermons on subjects related to the Christian life than any other. The register of sermon topics and texts that he maintained until 1957 contains 408 different sermons on topics related to it. The next largest number is on the general subject of evangelism, including a good many on stewardship.

⚯

The diary for the significant year, 1938, is unique because the original volume which he began at the first of the year was in a bag which was taken from him on the train. Although he immediately began a new one, the first six months, including the account of his election to the episcopacy, are reconstructed from his memory of the events. We know from it that he held revivals in Denton for Wesley Hite, and in Paris, Texas. The one in Denton exacerbated his weight problem, but, as he told Godbold in explaining why he did it, "by no means a negligible factor was the $325 which I was given for my work. With a boy in college . . . I do not know how we would have made ends meet without it." Donald had graduated from North Dallas High School and, despite his father's earlier preference for Southwestern University in Georgetown, enrolled as a freshman in Hendrix College at midterm. Having chosen to attend Hendrix, he, according to his future wife, Ernestine, found life on a campus of 400 students in the quiet town of Conway to be vastly different from what he had known in Dallas and had to adjust.

William C. and Sally left on the train on April 26 to attend the General Conference in Birmingham, Alabama. Joining in the popular pastime of predicting the outcome of episcopal elections, early in the month Godbold wrote to tell Martin he was convinced that if as many as five are elected, "you are likely to be one of the group." He went on to say that he was fully aware that

Martin was not seeking the office, but "I am hoping that if you are elected you will accept the office," for, he continued, "in the event of election I think it is wise for a man to trust the judgment of his brethren." Martin replied to his friend with candor. "You have me placed exactly . . . in the matter of my lack of desire for the office. It is, for the most part, a hard, thankless job and will become, I think, increasingly so." He continued, "I love the church and with me it has no rivals in its demands upon my time and attention. But with all that, I would not like to think it and talk it and eat it and drink it and sleep it and dream it every day and night of the year, even for a period of four years. And yet, if I should be elected, particularly if it was not at the end of a long drawn out wrangle, I would not decline." He did some speculation of his own and told Godbold he thought that J. N. R. Score, pastor of First Methodist in Fort Worth would, along with Selecman and Ivan Lee Holt, a pastor in St. Louis, be elected and they "will about fill the quota from the West." He concluded by saying, "I shall be greatly pleased to be left alone and I think that will be done." He would be happy, he told his friend, if it proved possible to spend ten more years in Dallas, which "has grown on me constantly."

Every shred of available evidence leads to the conclusion that Martin was doing little, if anything, to promote his own election. To anyone who wrote pledging support, and there were many who did, he replied much as he had to Godbold. He was honored by their expressions of confidence but believed his best arena of service to be the pastorate.

He and Sally arrived in Birmingham about midafternoon on April 27. The outcome of the vote committing the Methodist Episcopal Church, South, to join the Methodist Protestants and the Methodist Episcopal Church in creating a new denomination to be known as The Methodist Church was the greatest topic of conversation—not far behind was the upcoming election of bishops.

In short order: On May 1 Martin was struck by an intestinal infection and on May 3, Mary Katherine's birthday, he was elected a bishop. Two persons had been elected on the first ballot taken early that day: Ivan Lee Holt and William Walter Peele of

North Carolina. A second ballot was taken and sealed to be announced after lunch. Martin spoke to the SMU luncheon and then "went bowling with some friends [Paul Stephenson] in perfect confidence that there would be no disturbance of my career as pastor. . . . We were all sure that President Selecman would be elected and the Conference would certainly not choose two men from the same delegation." He was almost right. When the results of the vote were announced, Clare Purcell, Charles C. Selecman, John Lloyd Decell and, by a margin of three votes, William C. Martin of Dallas were declared elected. Martin received a total of 233 votes. "I could see Sally in the gallery and she did not seem too happy." That did not even begin to describe her feelings. He was escorted to the platform by Bishops John M. Moore and Paul B. Kern, and as he wrote later in classic understatement, "From that hour my ministerial life has flowed in a different channel." His SMU classmate, Angie Smith, who was the pastor of First Methodist Church, South, in Birmingham said, "Will was elected, not only because of his own innate ability, but because of the opposition of the people who were in such rabid opposition to Charlie Selecman." In a final election William T. Watkins became the last bishop ever elected in the Methodist Episcopal Church, South, and kept Martin from being the youngest bishop in the Council. Bishop Watkins was two years younger than Martin who was about ninety days shy of his forty-fifth birthday. But it did not prevent him from being the first graduate of Southern Methodist University and the first of Hendrix College ever to be chosen a Methodist bishop.

Sally was, indeed, not happy. She reported in an interview years later, "I went back to my room after he was elected . . . and cried my heart out. And I knew some people who really wanted it." She was not the only bishop's wife who wept after an election, for it made a sudden and radical change in all their lives. The salary of $6,600 was small. The allowance of $125 a month was all that was available to cover housing, office, and travel expenses. There was no episcopal residence. If it had not been for the courtesy extended by the railroads, which enabled clergy to ride without charge, it would have been difficult, if not impossible, for Martin or any of his episcopal colleagues to cover the areas assigned to them. And in a final stroke, he was assigned to California, and the church did not even pay moving expenses. With Donald already in college and Katherine ready to begin in a year, they were at a time in their lives when their expenses had reached a peak. Although Martin had seldom received more than a prorated share of his salary during the last years in Dallas, he would have to take a cut in his new assignment.

Sally, Mary Katherine, and John, moreover, after May 3, 1938, would be alone even more of the time. Sally was a person who needed the support of close friends, and she had lots of them in Dallas. Unlike her husband, she was not caught up in the work of the church, and as the spouse of a bishop she did not receive the satisfactions it provided to him. She knew she would be lonely. Later on, in fact, she discovered she enjoyed the freedom provided by her new role—more by far than she ever had experienced as the wife of the pastor of a local congregation. Their new life was not all bad.

Along with the others who had been elected, Martin was consecrated a bishop at a worship service the next day, May 4, 1938. The practice in the southern church was to wear cutaway coats and striped trousers on formal occasions, and Martin had not thought to bring his. As Angie Smith put it, "No one in the southern church used a gown except to sleep in, and then he didn't always sleep in that." After some hurried scouting around, Martin's friends arranged for him to wear Angie's.

John M. Moore preached the ordination sermon. Paul Martin and J. D. Hammons presented Martin for consecration; Bishop Frank Smith and Paul Kern joined Bishop Moore in laying hands on his head to bestow the office. Afterward Paul and Eula Quillian came by their room for a long talk. Although Paul Quillian was probably one of the people Sally had in mind when she spoke of those "who really wanted it," he was never elected to the office despite his distinguished career.

General Conference adjourned on May 6, but the Martins stayed over to get some rest and took the train home the next day. They managed a brief visit with Donald when the train stopped in Little Rock, and there were lots of friends to meet them when they arrived in Dallas. A flood of telegrams reached them in Birmingham, and the one from his colleague Estelle Barber summed them all up: "I HAVE NEVER BEEN HAPPIER NOR SADDER." The resolution passed by the Board of Stewards of First Methodist in Dallas carried the same sentiment. "We rejoice at his merited recognition, but how greatly we will miss him we cannot express."

Godbold wrote afterward to remind him, "At Birmingham you expressed the determination not to allow the office of bishop to interfere with your friendships. It seems to me that within bounds you should find this entirely possible, but as time goes along it may not be altogether easy for you." He told his good friend what A. J. Weeks had said to Bishop Mouzon after he was elected in 1910. After Mouzon expressed the hope to Weeks that their relationship would continue as before, he replied it would be impossible since "the office in the very nature of the case sets the man apart." Godbold went on to say that people could take advantage of the friendship of persons in high office or even expect different behavior, but pledged, "Personally I shall endeavor to refrain from subjecting your friendship with me to such strains."

Martin was assigned to the Eleventh Episcopal Area of the Methodist Episcopal Church, South, which comprised the Arizona, Pacific, Northwest, Western Mexican, and California Oriental Mission Conferences. Its boundaries extended from the Pecos River in Texas to the Canadian border, and in one way or another touched the states of Texas, Arizona, Nevada, California, Oregon, Washington, and Idaho. There is a smaller, modern version of this in the Rocky Mountain Conference, which is part of the Western Jurisdiction of The United Methodist Church. It includes three states, Colorado, Wyoming, and Utah. A story says that the bishop of that area died, and while the body was being viewed one person was heard to remark, "He looks terrible. What did he have?" The answer was "Colorado, Wyoming, and Utah."

The first Sunday after his consecration Bishop Charles C. Selecman preached at the morning service at First Church, "the congregation to which he last ministered as a pastor." His topic was

"Eternal Goodness." Bishop William C. Martin preached in the evening "When Youth Marches with Christ." His last sermon on May 29 was titled "This One Sermon." After a host of parties and celebrations with friends, including a banquet sponsored by the Scottish Rite to honor Martin and Selecman, farewell meetings with Chi Alpha and the Supper Club, the Martins left Dallas for California on June 8.

Martin left First Church, Dallas, having performed 232 weddings and 256 funerals. He had baptized 218 infants and 172 adults. Members of the present congregation will quickly tell you that he baptized them (and their children), received them into the church, performed their wedding, and buried parents and other loved ones. They will also confirm that Martin never failed to be present when people were sick or needed him. There is simply no getting around the fact that he was a great pastor with extraordinary talent and dedication. Under his leadership 481 persons had joined the church on profession of their faith and another 1,516 had transferred from other Methodist congregations and from other denominations. The total membership of the congregation when he left was 3,532; the debt had been reduced to $148,000, but it was not finally removed until 1944. The record itself is remarkable, but it does not even begin to reflect the love and affection in which he was held by this congregation.

6

California

———∘⦚∘———

All of the Martins, including Donald, who was now a student in Hendrix College, and Amy, their housekeeper, baby-sitter,
and friend, set out for California on Tuesday, June 7, 1938. A few
friends gathered at the Rawlings Street parsonage for some final,
sad good-byes, and afterward they were on the way. What was
before them was not just a move to another part of the country,
nor just another assignment from the church. It was a radical
change in the lives of Sally and the children and in Martin's ministry. They would no longer have the responsibility or support of
a single congregation, and they would not have a place guaran-
teed by his position as a pastor waiting for them in the community to which they were moving. They would also be coping in
difficult economic times with a lower salary and additional
expenses, including paying their moving expenses to California.
Once there they would also face the necessity of finding a suitable
place to live, whereas in the past comfortable, and sometimes elegant houses were provided and waiting for them. The most dramatic result of his new status, however, was from that point on
for the next sixteen years, Bishop William C. Martin, husband
and father, would be gone most of the time, and Sally and the
children would be left to cope without him. There was no period
of transition; the new pattern of life began for them immediately.

They reached Glendale June 14, and Martin left June 19 to preach
at the youth assembly of the Pacific Conference. In the six months
between then and the end of the year 1938, he spent seventy-
seven nights away from home.

John Lee was ill when they left Dallas, but they thought he was
well enough to make the trip. On the way they stopped for nights
in tourist camps, spending the second night in El Paso to allow the
new bishop to visit some of the property of the Western Mexican
Conference, now under his supervision. Amy, who was African
American, was passed in the segregated tourist camps as the family "nanny" and allowed to stay with them. When they reached
Tucson, Arizona, on June 10, John was running a temperature.
After seeing a doctor, he was declared unfit to continue and
stayed with Sally's cousins, Ruby and Robert Beene, until he was
well enough to join the family. The next day, in the company of
the presiding elder, O. L. Walker, and the conference missionary
secretary, C. L. Cartwright, Martin visited six congregations,
spoke at lunch and dinner, and got back to the Beene's at 10:30
P.M. He wrote Godbold later that the one-day trip had required
driving 600 miles. The next day he preached in University
Church, Tucson, in the morning, visited St. John's Church in
Patagonia in the afternoon, and preached again in Nogales in the
evening. It was a foretaste of the schedule that he would almost
routinely follow for years.

The Martins left for California on Monday. During a stopover
in Phoenix they had lunch with two preachers, and Bishop Martin began his steep climb up the learning curve by "talking out of
turn" about Dr. Coleman's appointment. Nobody, however, ever
found William C. Martin to be a slow learner.

They reached Blythe and the land of a "Thousand Wonders" in
time to spend the next night. As they crossed the state line they
were quizzed by the authorities, and the car was searched for agri-
cultural products. Daughter, Mary Catherine, who had made
most of the trip wedged into the backseat, was holding her dearest possessions in a small makeup case on her lap. The inspector
was determined to learn if she had cactus in the case, and her attitude quickly became as prickly as the plants in question. She told

him in clear terms that she would not have been holding a cactus all the way from Dallas, and besides, there were cactus everywhere. If she wanted one all she would have to do was reach out and take it. The food they had in the car had to be eaten since it could not be taken into California and the family was not about to waste it.

They drove into Glendale exactly a week after leaving Dallas and spent their first night there in another "tourist camp." The next day they began the search for a house and ended up taking one that had been identified by a friend of a Dallas preacher before they arrived. It was the first place they saw—a furnished house at 1254 N. Cedar Street. The house still stands. One of the reasons it was selected was that it had a bedroom and bath downstairs in addition to three bedrooms upstairs. The arrangement gave Amy a place of her own and all of them some privacy. Mary Catherine was delighted to discover it also had a yard full of olive trees. Olives, a favorite food of hers, in the Martin family were considered luxury items that appeared only at special times of the year like Thanksgiving and Christmas. In an effort to take advantage of the bountiful harvest and to please Catherine, Amy attempted to preserve them in brine, but the experiment turned out to be a dismal failure. Since their household goods had not yet arrived, the pastor of Broadway Church, Alec Nichols, helped them get sufficient cover for sleeping the first night in the house, and also offered to provide the bishop with space for an office at the church.

Without missing a Sunday, Martin preached in the morning service at Trinity Church, Los Angeles. He and his family were given a warm welcome, but they later united with a congregation closer to home. That afternoon he left on the train to attend the youth assembly at Mt. Hermon. He went from there back to Arizona, beginning the round of his "official" travel. At that point he confided to Godbold that "so far the duties of the office have been very pleasant. There will be difficulties and unpleasant situations to deal with," he acknowledged, "but they are bridges to be crossed when I get to them. I am not in this place by any choice of my own, but being in it I am going to find whatever joy there is in the chance for Christian service which it offers" (WCM to Godbold, June 19, 1938).

If it had not been for the established practice of the railroads to provide clergy with passes allowing free train travel, there would have been no way for him to meet his responsibilities. Fortunately, as he confided to Godbold, "I do not dislike that feature except the necessity it involves of being away from home so much" (WCM to Godbold, August 4, 1938). Martin was fortunate to be able to sleep well on the train, and the time en route enabled him to read and do the necessary correspondence associated with his new work. For many years, Bishop A. Frank Smith did not even maintain an office in Houston, but did his work on the train and met his appointments on the mezzanine of the Rice Hotel downtown.

The Eleventh Episcopal District of the Methodist Episcopal Church, South, to which Martin had been assigned, was vast in size, beyond anything that would constitute an episcopal area in the church today. Altogether it contained five annual conferences, but they had few congregations. The Church, South, was sparsely represented on the West Coast. There were only twenty-two "effective" or active clergy in the Arizona Conference and about twenty-five churches; there were seventy-three clergy who were full members of the Pacific Conference. It was composed of three districts, Los Angeles, Sacramento, and San Francisco. The Northwest Conference had two districts, Portland and Spokane. The Spokane District took in not only the western portions of the state of Washington but also several appointments in Montana. Martin always wrote to welcome new members of the episcopacy upon their election, and his usual reference was to their having joined "the fellowship of the riders of the long trail." His first one was long, indeed.

On June 28 Martin had lunch with Methodist Episcopal Bishop G. Bromley Oxnam at the University Club in Los Angeles. This meeting marked the beginning of a long, meaningful friendship and association. After Oxnam's death Martin wrote to his widow, Ruth, and remembered the occasion. "I had, of course, known of the varied aspects of his ministry and had read his books but it was not until the summer of 1938 that I met him."

He went on to tell her of his "feeling of special admiration and affection for him:" "His remarkable gifts of administrative skill and his boundless energy were a constant source of inspiration to me" (WCM to Ruth Oxnam, April 17, 1963). He expressed to her his hope that "you and the children can find a person who is capable of writing a full-length biography with a style and comprehensiveness that will be worthy of its subject."

Surely one of the most powerful if not arguably the most influential bishop in the soon-to-be-organized Methodist Church, Oxnam was about as different in temperament and background from Martin as can be imagined. He was a wealthy man with a Ph.D. degree. Oxnam and Bishop Francis J. McConnell were regarded as the most talented students of the great Boston University theological liberal, Edgar S. Brightman. Oxnam's biographer, Robert Moats Miller, dubbed him the "Paladin of liberal Protestantism." A native Californian, one year younger than Martin, Oxnam had made his name as the pastor of the Church of All Nations in Los Angeles and then later as president of DePauw University in Greencastle, Indiana. He was elected to the episcopacy of the Methodist Episcopal Church in 1936 and assigned to the Omaha Area. In the soon-to-be-created Council of Bishops of The Methodist Church, Oxnam served as secretary for sixteen years and from that position controlled its agenda, committee assignments, and deliberations. Nothing came before the council without Oxnam's approval. He served The Methodist Church in Boston, and the New York and Washington, D.C., Areas.

Oxnam was aristocratic and autocratic. A theological and social liberal, it was he, in his role as secretary of the Council of Bishops, who began the practice of having bishops visit overseas outposts of the church in order for them to be better informed about its worldwide operation. Active in the National Council of Churches and its forerunner, the Federal Council of Churches, and eventually one of the officers of the World Council of Churches, Oxnam was in the forefront of the ecumenical movement of the 1950s and 1960s, and it was directly due to his influence that Martin became involved in the movement and eventually became president of the National Council of Churches. A severe critic of Senator Joseph McCarthy during the Cold War years, Oxnam eventually requested to appear before the House Un-American Activities Committee. His spirited defense is outlined in a book appropriately titled *I Protest*. In 1939, William C. followed Oxnam as bishop of the Omaha Area of the newly created South Central Jurisdiction of The Methodist Church. Their meeting over lunch in 1938 was truly an auspicious occasion, foretelling a long and productive association.

Shortly after the family was settled in Glendale, John took a job delivering the *Glendale News Press*. While on his route one day he fell into conversation with the servants at one of the large houses, some of the few black citizens of Glendale. He told them about Amy and asked if they "would be a friend to my Amy." They, in time, did become her friends, and because of their influence Amy stayed in California rather than move with the Martins to Omaha the following year. When Mary Catherine was taken by her mother to enroll for her senior year in Glendale High School, the principal extolled to them the advantages the school could offer and mentioned in passing that Glendale was an entirely white community. He knew, he said, that was the case because it was "illegal" for a black person to spend the night in the city limits. Sally Martin, who could speak her mind clearly, assured him it was not an all-white community and told him why. Catherine remembered his shock and surprise.

⚌⚏⚌

With the bishop on the road and without the obligations a pastor's family has to a congregation, Sally, Catherine, and John experienced a type of freedom they had never known before. They enjoyed eating out and went to places entirely of their own choosing. One of their favorites was the old Brown Derby Restaurant (the one that really looked like a hat) where they delighted in having Sunday brunch. They went often to the movies. Sally shopped in Bullock's Wilshire and other similar stores in Beverly Hills and took elocution lessons. With John's help she learned to play Chinese checkers, and when the bishop came home she beat him soundly. Reflecting on such experiences years later she said she needed to "puncture his ego" from time to time. Sally loved southern California and would have been delighted to stay. John had a wonderful year, made friends in the junior high school he attended, and enjoyed discovering new attractions such as the beach and the observatory. Catherine, in her last year in high school, missed her Dallas friends and had a more difficult adjustment. She does not remember the year so fondly. Later, however, she returned to California to become a permanent resident.

Reflecting on the new work Martin had been assigned, Sally told an interviewer that she "supported him in his work to the extent that I don't think I ever called on him to stay at home for an illness or anything when duty called in a way that I thought meant more than what he would have accomplished had he stayed at home. I always felt equal to taking care of my family." And with a flash of the wit for which she was well known, she added, "I often said that if the children amounted to anything I was going to take the credit and if they didn't it was his fault."

It never seems possible to move without falling victim to some catastrophe, and the Martins were no exception. In July the family went to visit San Francisco and attend the World's Fair. Martin said they would, in fact, have enjoyed living there had its location been more central to his work. On the way home on the coast highway, they had a near head-on collision with a car whose driver had fallen asleep. Martin saw the car in his lane at the last minute, started honking the horn, and awakened the other driver, who swerved in the nick of time. Fortunately, both cars had slowed to a virtual halt when they hit broadside. The seawall on the right prevented Martin from driving off the road and avoiding the collision entirely, but no one was seriously injured. Their car, however, was badly damaged and had to be towed into Ventura for repairs. The offending driver accepted full responsibility and paid for the work. Sally said that W. C.'s physical strength, which enabled him to hold the car, kept them from going over the cliff and all being killed. A nearby Methodist preacher provided transportation back to Glendale. Martin speculated to Godbold in his letter of August 4, that "with 450 miles between San Francisco and Los Angeles it seemed almost the guidance of fate that we should have been at that particular spot at the exact moment" (WCM to Godbold, August 4, 1938).

Though causing considerable inconvenience, the accident did not deter any part of the bishop's schedule. The next day he preached at Carpinteria in the morning and in Reseda in the evening. He and Sally were guests for dinner in the home of a Korean pastor on Monday evening, and the entire family was honored at a large reception at Trinity Church, Los Angeles, on Tuesday night.

A Methodist bishop's primary work is with clergy, and the business of getting acquainted with them is a high priority for any new episcopal leader. Most customarily begin their service by visiting all the churches in the area, but in Martin's case it simply was not possible. So he made the rounds as best he could. The invitations flowed in: to get better acquainted, dedicate churches, celebrate their anniversaries, preside over ground breakings, preach for ten days in special services, and to address gatherings from the "Protestant All Church Convention" in Maricopa, Taft, and Fellows, California, to one at Goodwill Industries. He agreed to speak at the commencement ceremonies of the College of the Pacific. They would pay an honorarium of $50, something he did not always receive and never asked for. A week of preaching at another time netted $76.73, with a specific notation that the amount included car fare. Requests came from churches in the Methodist Episcopal Church, too. He accepted all he could work into his schedule. When Martin was elected to the episcopacy, Bishop Frederick D. Leete of the Methodist Episcopal Church wrote to congratulate him and offered advice he had been given at the time of his own election in 1912. "Your tendency," he said, "is to accept all opportunities for service. You will now get many invitations to appear here and there. You do not have to take them all, and ought never to do so unless you seem to be able to make adequate preparation." He continued, "Remember, from now on you represent the whole Church when you speak, and do not allow yourself to attempt more than you can do with credit."

It was not, however, advice that the new bishop was able to hear at the time, and he moved constantly from one place to another, filling every moment of the day, accepting every invitation.

After a trip to Lake Junaluska for a Layman's Conference and meetings in Nashville, on August 25, Martin called the session of the Northwest Conference to order. He was naturally nervous about presiding, but considered himself fortunate in not having responsibility for a large conference so early in his career. There were only about twenty preachers. Riding the train to Coquille, Oregon, where the conference was to meet, he wrote in his diary that "such time as I had at home was spent in preparing to leave again. This job allows almost no time for home life."

There was not much time for writing in the diary either, and many of its pages that year are blank. But in this remote place in the Northwest he began his long years of presiding in annual conferences. To keep a record of them, he created a notebook in which he recorded on loose-leaf pages the name of the conference, the dates when it met and its location, the names of the district superintendents, the names of persons ordained, and the number of appointments he made. The Northwest Conference is first; there were thirty-one appointments. The ninety-first, and last, was the Central Texas Conference held June 2-5, 1964. There were 351 appointments at that one. From 1938 to 1964 the notebook reveals he ordained 922 deacons, and 714 elders. Every one of these persons is named in the notebook with the simple inscription stamped in gold on its leather cover, "Conferences." In twenty-six years he made 27,308 appointments. It is a record that no current or future bishop is likely to equal.

The page on which the record begins contains a comment: "My first conference. No special difficulties. Excellent cooperation from all of the members." Part of this was surely due to its small size and the desire of its members to please a new bishop, but it should also be seen as testimony to Martin's talent and ability as a presiding officer. He was skilled in the chair and prepared himself well for the sessions. He had taken the time to learn Robert's Rules of Order and could use them appropriately to facilitate rather than hinder the proceedings. He was kind and courteous in his demeanor, patient with those under his direction, but there was never a question about who was in charge, and he was always firm. In time he was able to guide the deliberations of the General Conference, too. Experienced conference watchers at the General Conference can usually predict which bishops will have trouble presiding over those large and often feisty sessions. In addition to almost a thousand delegates seated at tables in a large arena, the procedures of the conference are complex and the more controversial the issue the more likely the presiding officer is to have trouble. Majority and minority reports from committees are brought to the floor, motions are amended, and substitutions are made; delegates vie with one another for recognition by the chair, attempts are made to close or extend debates, and there are always points of order and appeals to a large body of rules. A committee makes the assignments of the presiding officer for each session, and the good ones, Martin always among them, are chosen for the sessions in which there is likely to be trouble. Martin, from the beginning, was exemplary in his performance as a presiding officer. After he had completed his entire first round of conferences, he told Godbold, "The members of the conferences have been cooperative and brotherly to the last degree and there has been no effort in any single instance to take advantage of my unfamiliarity with the job" (WCM to Godbold, November 17, 1938).

Sometime later in his career, Martin reflected on "conferences" in a notebook that is appropriately labeled "Thoughts." The section begins with the bishop addressing himself on the subject of meeting conferences and small groups and the need "to agree with myself upon certain principles which I should follow." He lists five of them: (1) "Become as familiar as possible with the matters to be dealt with before the meeting begins." (2) "Be on time for the meeting, remain until it is over, and give undivided attention to the questions under discussion." (3) "Do not consider yourself under obligation to speak unless the emphasis which you are certain should be made has not been expressed by another." (4) "It is important at all times that your interest be given to the business in hand rather than to the impression concerning yourself which will be created in presenting it." (5) "The parliamentary procedure is important." Later he added one more: "In directing the affairs of a conference, the presiding officer must see to it that attention is fixed upon issues and not upon personalities. This applies to himself as well as to members of the conference."

The Northwest Conference was divided into what Martin characterized as "two straggling districts" spread over a geographic area as large as the one encompassed by four annual conferences of the Methodist Episcopal Church. He confided to Godbold before the conference that the Church, South, had "been in such steady retreat in that territory that unification is the only thing that could have saved us" (WCM to Godbold, August 4, 1938). At one time there had been three conferences of the southern church. At unification in 1939, the Northwest Conference was dissolved and its congregations incorporated into the annual conferences of the former Methodist Episcopal Church.

Among the major reasons leading to the formation of the Methodist Episcopal Church, South, in 1845 was a basic disagreement about the nature of episcopacy that had existed for some time between the northern and southern branches of American Methodism. The southern conferences adhered to the idea of the episcopacy and the General Conference as co-equal branches of church government. For a time after 1850, they even gave to bishops the right to veto legislation passed in the General Conference that they thought to be unconstitutional.

The northern conferences, on the other hand, believed bishops to be officers of the General Conference and entirely subject to it. The conflict that divided the connection in 1844 centered on Bishop James O. Andrew, a southerner who owned slaves. Bishop Andrew had violated no laws of the church nor had he been charged with any wrongdoing. He had never been tried for any offense. Yet the General Conference forced him to cease his work in the episcopacy so long as he continued to own slaves. The basis for their directive was the conviction of the majority of delegates, mostly from the North and West, that episcopal power was derived entirely from the General Conference, and thus they were authorized to do with its officers anything thought to be in the best interest of the church. Although they did not believe General Conference had the power to remove Andrew's credentials as a minister, the episcopal office that it had given to him could be taken away. The analogy was to other officers in the church such as Sunday school superintendents, the officers of a congregation, or leaders of boards and agencies.

As a result of these divergent understandings of episcopacy, different traits and talents were sought in the individuals who were elected to fill the office in the two branches of episcopal Methodism. The southern church became well known for its strong and autocratic bishops. This is not to say the Methodist Episcopal Church did not have some who operated in the same fashion, but as a group southern bishops did not expect either their judgment or leadership to be challenged. Warren A. Candler is a classic illustration of that style of leadership. During his years on the faculty of Emory at Oxford College, his students recorded in the yearbook what they had learned from "Shorty." They said they had learned that "what Shorty does not know has not been found out. Shorty did not make the earth, but was put there to run it. That Shorty is sorry for those that disagree with him, for they are wrong."

Candler's biographer says of the episcopacy in the Methodist Episcopal Church, South, "During his youth and early manhood [Candler was born in 1857] it was expected that bishops should be autocratic, and not often did the strong bishops of that period—and sometimes the feebler ones, which was worse—fail to rise to the occasion. . . . Democracy was slow in making its way into the Methodist Episcopal Church, South" (Alfred M. Pierce, *Giant Against the Sky* [New York: Abingdon Press, 1943], 98). Although he epitomized the southern style, Candler was joined in its practice by others like Collins Denny and U. V. W. Darlington, just to name two obvious ones. Denny, probably the best legal mind in all of American Methodism, was so opposed to reunion in 1939 that he refused to sign the documents or take a pension from The Methodist Church even though he was entitled to it. Near the time for his retirement from the episcopacy in

1964, Martin was interviewed by Robert Sledge for a book he was writing on the history of the Methodist Episcopal Church, South. In that interview Martin said that a new episcopal style was introduced into the church in the 1920s and 30s, and with it a different type of personality. He named Paul Kern, Arthur Moore, and Frank Smith among those who brought a new measure of democratic leadership to the episcopacy. Although Martin certainly was too modest to include his own name among these innovators, he richly deserves to be included among them.

Martin quickly discovered temptations and pitfalls on the episcopal circuit that played havoc with old weaknesses. Just before the session of the Pacific Conference, he visited six congregations in the Los Angeles area. Sally went with him and was exhausted when she got home. He described it as "a serviceable day." Although he rarely complained of being tired, the travel, which interrupted his exercise, and lavish church dinners immediately affected his weight and it climbed to 193 pounds. Everywhere he went there was food, good food—lots of good food. He quickly determined he had to find a way to diet without being conspicuous about it, and to eat lightly without calling attention to what he was doing. He accepted the fact that he could not eat anything between meals. "I must regard over-eating as a drink addict should regard liquor," he said.

The Pacific Conference met after the Northwest Conference. Its sessions ran from October 19-23, 1938. A larger conference with three districts and ninety appointments, it was the first conference in which Martin ordained elders—Edwin Mouzon Conn, named for the bishop who ordained William Clyde Martin an elder, Karl Kenneth Heilman, and William Vickrey Dougherty. It was also his first experience speaking to a delegation from a local congregation intent on persuading the bishop to move their pastor. In the sessions he was confronted by Points of Order related to the uniting conference and was asked to address a group of restless younger pastors who were uneasy about their future in the light of the impending union. When it was over, he went home and went to bed at seven o'clock. Although he became accustomed to presiding and meeting the annual conferences, it was, throughout his ministry, a stressful experience. All of the conferences that first year elected delegates to represent them at the Uniting Conference scheduled to meet in Kansas City in May 1939.

In short order Martin presided over the California Oriental Mission, with eleven appointments to be made, and the Western Mexican Conference, which met in El Paso. The Mexican Conference extended over parts of Texas, New Mexico, Arizona, and California. Its only district superintendent presided over the El Paso–Los Angeles District. There were thirty appointments. It would be hard to imagine a more diverse and unique episcopal assignment than the one that Martin was given by the southern church in 1938. By November 11, he had lost three pounds, too. His diet regimen called for "no cake, pie, candy nor butter. One piece of bread at a meal."

The Arizona Conference met in Safford, Arizona, after the Western Mexican Conference was finished. He continued the practice of giving the morning devotions that he started at the first conference. This was something he was to do in all his annual conferences, and preparing them was a task that occupied a considerable amount of time during the year. He gave the same set of devotions in all the conferences. In 1938 his first was "The Authority of the Bible," followed by "The Place of the Bible in Modern Christianity," "The Place of the Bible in Christian Preaching," and, finally, "Giving the Bible a Hearing." He finished the sessions, read twenty-seven appointments, and headed home. He and Sally celebrated by going to a movie.

He got around to writing Godbold in November after he had held all the conferences. "The round is now completed and I have found it to be a more delightful experience than I could have imagined." He went on to acknowledge that he was fortunate not to have been assigned to a larger conference. "I have needed the opportunity to learn some things about presiding in the sessions of the Conference and making appointments under circumstances that did not permit me to do too much damage by my inexperience" (WCM to Godbold, November 17, 1938). His reading, he said, was centered mostly on biographies of persons who had been bishops—he named William Wynans of Mississippi and John B. McFerrin of Tennessee (neither of whom was ever a bishop)— because he was "naturally interested in finding out all I can concerning the best methods for fulfilling the requirements of the office." He also said again, "After six months in this office I am grateful for being able to say that it has proved to be much more interesting and delightful than I would have thought it could be. Strange how we adjust ourselves to new situations and find life full of activities which are fascinating in their demands for attention." In truth, he could hardly have been more immersed in his work than he was as a pastor. His life was the church.

After the delegates were elected and the conferences adjourned for the last time, the denominational meetings to prepare for the uniting conference in Kansas City began. There was much to be determined, for the two episcopal Methodisms had existed separately for almost a century and the Methodist Protestants since 1827. The church, in good Methodist fashion, was united by being reorganized, and the key element was the jurisdictional structure. It had been first proposed in 1911 by the Joint Commission composed of representatives from the Methodist Protestant Church, the Methodist Episcopal Church, and the Methodist Episcopal Church, South. Bishop John M. Moore was convinced as early as 1916 that the jurisdictional feature was essential if reunion were ever to take place. The actual plan was proposed by Edgar Blake, secretary of the Sunday School Board of the Methodist Episcopal Church, who later became a bishop. It was designed both to address the concerns of the southern church about the existence of a powerful General Conference and to provide a solution to the racial composition of the united church. Moreover, it was designed to create decentralized, regional control of the episcopacy by electing the general superintendents of the church in the jurisdictions.

Under the Blake plan, there were to be five geographic regions—jurisdictions—and one that was organized entirely on the basis of race. All African American members of the new Methodist Church were to be members of the Central Jurisdiction. They would, as was the case in the other jurisdictions, elect their own bishops, whose service would be restricted to the Central Jurisdiction. On the positive side, it gave African Americans an added voice in the new church, but negatively it institutionalized segregation. It cannot be overlooked that no delegate from any of the traditional African American Methodist conferences voted for the Plan of Union in Kansas City. They either left the meeting before the vote was taken or they abstained. Yet, more than 300,000 black Methodists joined The Methodist Church as the best available alternative.

As decisive as the creation of the Central Jurisdiction was in the life of The Methodist Church, the jurisdictional structure had an even more basic and dramatic impact on the episcopacy. Electing the bishops in the jurisdictional conferences changed the nature of the episcopacy and also the type of persons who were chosen to fill the office. Prior to unification, bishops in both the Methodist Episcopal Church and the Methodist Episcopal Church, South, had all been elected by the General Conference. A successful candidate had to gain visibility throughout the denomination, and the largest groups of persons selected were editors of church papers, college presidents, secretaries of the boards, and other holders of churchwide offices. Few pastors were chosen. By contrast, in The Methodist Church the high road to the episcopal office ran from the pulpits of large congregations. Not even district superintendents (presiding elders in the early years) were chosen. William T. Watkins was the last bishop in episcopal Methodism to be elected in a General Conference. There is no doubt that the selection process determines the type of leader selected, and that reunion changed the episcopacy.

The bishops of the uniting churches met together in Nashville on November 29-30, 1938, for the first time in almost a hundred years. Thirteen hundred people attended a banquet to celebrate the occasion. Methodist Protestant leader James H. Straughn and Methodist Episcopal Bishop Edwin Holt Hughes spoke. Before the meeting concluded, however, Angie Smith, Martin's successor at First Methodist, sent word that Martin was needed in Dallas to conduct the funeral of A. V. Lane, longtime friend and loyal supporter during his ministry there. He went immediately, but on the way was able to stop in Little Rock briefly to meet Donald, who was back at Hendrix, for a "delightful and encouraging visit."

He and John marked the end of their first six months in California and the end of 1938 with a visit to the Mt. Wilson observatory to look at the moon and constellations. Maybe it wasn't written in the stars, but they knew it had been a momentous year.

Because of the impending merger, Martin and his Methodist Episcopal Church counterpart, Bishop James C. Baker, had to work out arrangements for combining the conferences of the two former episcopal Methodisms in the West. He first met Bishop Baker on October 15, 1938, and found him to be "brotherly and easy to get acquainted with." Baker had the distinction of having been the one hundredth person elected to the episcopacy in the Methodist Episcopal Church, and through the years Martin and Jim Baker became close, personal friends as well as genial colleagues. But it was obvious to everyone that making the necessary re-alignments, sometimes by combining congregations, would create a surplus of pastors, leaving some without appointments, and would not be easy. After an interview with one individual caught in that situation, Martin observed, "It is an unpleasant feature of this work that in the process of absorbing men in overlapping territory some men will be reduced and others left without appointments."

The real basis of power exercised by Methodist bishops has always been the authority given them to station the preachers. The appointive system, existing in American Methodism from the days of Francis Asbury, has been employed to send clergy to their places of service. Whether done without consultation—Asbury stationed virtually all of the preachers in America for most of his thirty-two years of episcopal service by himself—or by a process involving congregations, clergy, cabinet and bishop, the final decision about who goes where remains with the bishop. Although all of them make appointments, each bishop is expected to develop a system that suits his or her style and preferences.

Just as he had reflected on the principles by which he would work with his conferences, Martin also reflected in the "Thoughts" notebook about making appointments. Here are the "rules which he evolved:" (1) "Don't become impatient"; (2) "When a pastor has served a church for a quadrennium see if there is sufficient justification for his remaining"; (3) "Never speak lightly of the work of making appointments"; (4) "Make sure that the name of every clerical member of the conference appears on the list of appointments"; (5) "Don't be forward about discussing appointments with men; talk rather about how to fulfil the present obligations"; (6) "In so far as they can be obtained, all the facts relating to men and churches should be taken into account in the making of appointments"; (7) "Undue anxiety about the making of appointments is not conducive to the exercise of the best judgment." The last suggestion was that care should be taken to help pastoral relations committees in local congregations "to understand more fully the Methodist system of making appointments."

Martin used the Cabinet Working Sheets—printed forms supplied by the publishing house of the denomination, in making his first appointments in the Northwest Conference. Now among his papers in the Bridwell Library, they list the names of the charges, number of rooms in the parsonage (not filled in for the Portland District that year), number of preaching places, current salaries, present pastor, number of years in the assignment, and the appointee for the coming year. It was common practice to move a pastor at least every three years. The highest salary in the conference in 1938 was $1,500 a year, paid by Stevensville in the Spokane District. Coquille, Oregon, and Spokane, Washington, each paid $1,300. Almost no congregation projected an increase in the pastor's salary for the coming year. Times were hard. By the time Martin held the Pacific Conference the last of October, he had devised his own form. His listed the charges, pastors, salary, and asked whether the salary would be paid. He included a column with three boxes, one of which should be checked by the presiding elder—"should remain," "uncertain," "should move." These formed the basis for deliberations in the cabinet. He continued to use a variation of this same form throughout his epis-copacy. In addition, Martin created a supplementary notebook that contained the service record of each pastor, the pastor's edu-cational background, family information, and other pertinent data he could turn to in making appointments.

The usual practice in the early years of Martin's episcopal ser-vice was for the cabinet to meet for one or two days immediately prior to the opening of the annual conference sessions and then to complete their work during the conference. An elder would pre-side over the sessions when the bishop was meeting with the pre-siding elders. The appearance of a cabinet member on the floor of the conference to signal a preacher to leave was always enough to convey a strong message that changes were being considered and activate a new round of conference gossip. Appointments were not announced until they were read by the bishop on the last day, and they were usually not finished until just before they were read. Clergy and their families sat literally with bated breath wait-ing to hear their names read with their new appointments.

No matter how carefully assignments are made utilizing any system nor how patient, fair, and informed the bishop may be in making the decision, there are always those who believe they have been slighted, abused, or misled—if not lied to—by the bishop and the cabinet. Even in the "old days" there were always preach-ers and laypersons who wished to inform the bishop of their opin-ions, interests, and needs, and congregations that were equally determined to let their bishop know their collective wisdom. By the time he had been in office six months, Martin was receiving the kind of mail all bishops receive.

The added difficulty of making appointments in 1939 because of the necessity to re-align the conferences has already been men-tioned. There were simply not enough churches to go around. The Northwest Conference was eliminated entirely. The Pacific Con-ference of the Methodist Episcopal Church, South, was joined with portions of the former California Conference, Southern Cal-ifornia Conference, and Western Norwegian-Danish Conference of the Methodist Episcopal Church to create the California Con-ference of The Methodist Church. The Arizona Conference of the southern church was united with portions of the Southern California Conference of the Methodist Episcopal Church to create the Southern California-Arizona Annual Conference, something Martin told Godbold should not have been done. "It was a mistake," he said, "for our group [The Methodist Episcopal Church, South] to have dissociated themselves from California but many of our men have shown a genuine spirit of heroism there." The new conference was composed of five districts, one of which comprised all of the former southern congregations in Arizona. Final decisions establishing the boundaries of all the annual conferences of The Methodist Church were made by the Uniting Conference at its meeting in May 1939, but some fine-tuning was necessary afterward. The first meetings of the new conferences were held in June 1939. They elected delegates to the upcoming General Conference in 1940, and organized the various conference boards and agencies.

Almost everybody who dealt with the bishop had an opinion to share or wanted something. W. J. Lee wrote from Walla Walla, Washington, to protest the rumored appointment of his new presiding elder. There were certainly not enough of these positions to utilize all the current occupants of the office, and everybody was concerned about who would be appointed. Lee said that he first heard the presiding elder himself, P. D. Hartman, say he would likely be given a district in the united church. "I was embarrassed with the possibility," Lee stated. Lee outlined the injustice he and his wife had suffered under Hartman and said, "It naturally makes us fearful now as I near conference." In another letter written earlier he appealed for "a Presiding Elder, above the average in preaching ability, evangelical and sanely honest, both with the pastor and people."

Petitions came in from congregations. The stewards of the Eastmont Methodist Church in Los Angeles asked for the return of their pastor, T. A. Ray. He was appointed to Ventura, St. Johns instead. Fresno wanted Warner Bonner back and got him. The superintendent of the Sunday school at Park Place Methodist in San Diego, along with the San Diego Methodist Preachers Association, wrote to protest the efforts to move Moffett Rhodes, who had been there since 1932. "I should think Bro. Rhodes would be happier in another environment," Sunday school Superintendent Charles Read wrote his bishop, "but if he and his family want to return, they should have that privilege." Martin must have agreed with his first judgment, for Rhodes was transferred to the California Conference and assigned to Woodland in the Sacramento District, a long way from San Diego. W. H. Nelson, who was moved from Woodland, candidly wrote Martin that he felt after their conversation that he would be given a small appointment and hoped it would be no worse. In a sarcastic tone he reminded his bishop, "Of course you do not, and never will, have the problem of caring for one of your children in the high school on $450 a year." He concluded, "I wish you would write me just what sort of an appointment you think I can get, and if you are really willing to help me in this." When nothing was found for him, he retired.

There were plenty of volunteers to move to the sunny climes of southern California. Brother G. C. Rector said it was time for him to leave his current assignment in Linden if "a better man can be found to take my place." He continued, "I believe I could do some good work somewhere in sou. Calif." In another letter he told the bishop he could not afford to take any charge that paid less than $1,200 a year, but, unfortunately, most of them failed to meet that minimum. He went to Wesley Methodist in Anaheim. R. Orman Roberts, who was serving in Arizona, reluctantly agreed that he would accept the appointment to Willows, California, but "wondered if you have ever thought of me in terms of Southern California. . . . I could make things hum there," he said. Roberts may have been less concerned about the location of his appointment than about the situation in Willows. They had requested by a unanimous vote in the Board of Stewards that their pastor, A. I. Townsley, should be moved. He was not without supporters, however, and Dr. William Walker, M.D., wrote to say that he opposed the move during the discussion but did not vote against it. He wanted Martin to know that in his opinion, "Mr. Townsley was successful in the administration of his work, that he is a fine sermonizer and had he been given a fraternal Christian chance this situation never would have arisen." Obviously life was not harmonious in Willow Methodism. Brother J. Alvin Crawford, in his second year at Visalia, on the other hand got a warm endorsement from his board. Mrs. E. C. Snell, however, wrote to say that the only hope of a successful union of the Methodist congregations in their town would require both preachers to be moved. Crawford was moved to Tracy in the newly formed California Conference.

And so the story went. At best it is difficult enough to make appointments that satisfy preachers, their families, the congregations and the leaders of the church. And when those appointments not only must be made, but must accommodate a new organization and re-alignment of churches, as it was in 1939, it is doubly challenging. Martin worked closely with Bishop Baker and his leaders to re-draw the lines of the various conferences, combine some congregations, eliminate others, transfer or sell property, and effect a complete reorganization in their committees, boards, and agencies. During this time his once voluminous correspondence with Albea Godbold dried up almost entirely.

Traveling through his conferences, Martin promoted the cause of union, spoke many times on the importance of evangelism, preached every Sunday, and in his limited spare time went to the movies with Sally, to Forest Lawn, and to other sights in the area, including Universal Studios. He began to read in the Huntingdon Library in Pasadena and eventually applied for a reader's permit, but his time there was too limited.

His friendship with Gipsy Smith, begun in Dallas, was nurtured by several conversations during the year. When Martin went back to Texas to preach in a simultaneous revival organized by sixteen Methodist congregations in Houston, he wrote in his diary that "the sight of Texas made me realize that I have been a wanderer in a strange land." Paul and Eula Quillian met him at the station, and the congregation at Grace Church welcomed him back like a long lost son. Following the revival he preached in Holy Week services at Spokane. Between the two engagements he had a three-hour stop at home to pick up clean clothes, the only time he was to be there until after the conclusion of the uniting conference in Kansas City. He told Godbold that "if I did not have one of the best wives in the world she would institute divorce proceedings for such treatment as that" (WCM to Godbold, April 5, 1939).

He began to speak on the radio and recorded his first talk for a delayed broadcast. Like most persons who have had that experience, he did not recognize his voice when he heard it.

In addition to the preaching engagements, there were meetings of the bishops and the Board of Missions in April; he found time while riding the train to read the prospectus of the proposed *Discipline* of The Methodist Church. In St. Louis other bishops, including Arthur Moore and Bishop Darlington, got aboard. A brief stop was made in Louisville to meet with the Board of Church Extension before going on to Nashville. The primary business of the bishops was to approve the Episcopal Address to the uniting conference. The address had been written in large part by Martin's former neighbor, Bishop John M. Moore. Between the meetings, he managed to find time to visit Vanderbilt University and to have dinner with the Cuninggims, too. To his credit, and perhaps in genuine concern about the possibility of divorce, he also remembered to send a birthday gift to Sally. As he became more exposed to the variety of issues facing the church and its leaders, he took in a Shirley Temple movie in the early evening to relieve the tension and recorded his conclusion, "Don't be a reformer if you can keep from it."

Without returning home he went to Kansas City on April 20 for the Council of Bishops meeting and the sessions of the uniting conference that followed. On April 29 the question of assigning the bishops to areas took most of the morning. It was referred to a committee, but Martin and Bishop Baker had lunch together and, no doubt, discussed their situation. Martin had told Godbold in August that it was likely he would be returned to the South Central Jurisdiction, but he would have been happy to stay in California. The topic of episcopal assignments continued to be at the top of the agenda, and Martin acknowledged that on May 3, the bishops "talked about assignments with some disturbance." He bowled for relief and recreation, sometimes with Bishop Selecman.

The world situation was also creating tension and in one of the sessions of the uniting conference in which the delegates were attempting to approve an official stand for The Methodist Church on the subject of war, Governor Alf Landon, who was one of the delegates, lost his temper. On May 8, the assignments to the new areas were announced to the bishops—the Martins were going to Omaha, Nebraska. Bishop James Baker was assigned to California. Later they were announced to the conference, and Martin received an enthusiastic welcome from the Nebraska and Kansas delegations. His own response—"I was not too jubilant." Paul Root came to Martin's room and they talked past midnight. Godbold wrote on May 13 that he was very interested to learn of Martin's assignment because the talk in his part of the jurisdiction (Arkansas) was that Martin would be going to Arkansas and Louisiana. "Whatever that situation may be, I take it," he said, "that the committee in charge of assigning bishops thought that you should not return to preside over your home conference within a year after being elected bishop." He also acknowledged that perhaps Martin's success in working with the Methodist Episcopal Church in the Northwest had prepared him to continue working with the former members of The Methodist Episcopal branch in the northern reaches of the new South Central Jurisdiction of The Methodist Church. Unfortunately the real reason remains unknown.

It is interesting that Martin made little comment about the uniting conference in Kansas City. He does not mention the issue of race or the debates on the subject of war and peace in his diary, but he does react to his new assignment. He was disappointed about being given the Nebraska Area. Although he expected to be reassigned to the new South Central Jurisdiction he preferred an area closer to home. Nebraska and Kansas were formerly Methodist Episcopal Church territories and before being elected a bishop Martin had served his entire ministry in the Methodist

Episcopal Church, South. Bromley Oxnam, a former member of the Methodist Episcopal Church, had been their bishop for three years. Practically speaking, it was inconvenient and expensive to move anywhere after only one year, and it certainly was a long way from California to Nebraska. Moreover, there was a problem of finding a suitable residence in Omaha—the Oxnams had been living in a hotel. Sally was happy in Southern California and she would have been glad for them to stay.

Martin had received many letters and telegrams urging his continuation in the West, and they would have been pleased to have him in that area, too. But let it never be said that Bishop William C. Martin was not a loyal son of the church. The day after the creation of The Methodist Church was celebrated at a great gathering in the Municipal Auditorium in Kansas City, Martin was on the train to Omaha to spend a day talking with Bishop Oxnam about the transition. Bromley and Ruth Oxnam met the train when it arrived and took Martin to breakfast. They talked until noon about the work in Nebraska. Afterward the two bishops were joined by seven conference leaders who discussed with Martin the outline of its program and advised him on some practical matters like locating suitable space for an office.

He took the 11:00 P.M. train for California and got off both in Cheyenne and in Salt Lake City to walk and think. When he arrived, he "Found F [family] well but considerably upset about going to Omaha." That can be read primarily to mean Sally and John were upset. Sally was later to say, "I didn't know Nebraska was in the United States." John later made a comment about the experience, which was quoted in a "This Is Your Life" celebration. "Mother," he said, "we fought the battle of Omaha together." Catherine was at the end of her senior year in Glendale and planning to enroll in Southern Methodist University in the fall. She fortunately was spared another adjustment prior to leaving for college but did have to leave her boyfriend. Things must have been tense around the house because two days after arriving home, Martin took Sally to lunch at the Brown Derby and to see a double feature, *Dodge City* and *I'm From Missouri*. It probably helped both their feelings, but couldn't solve the problem.

On the last day of May, having given the commencement address in Tempe, Arizona, Martin took his first plane ride back to Los Angeles and "saw the world as God sees it and 'It was good.' " The various annual conferences met on schedule and without too much conflict. In San Diego he was taken deep sea fishing off Coronado Island—"a delightful experience"—and toured the aircraft carrier U.S.S. *Yorktown* as the guest of the chaplain of the Naval Training Station.

His last official duty in the West was assisting Bishop Baker in the organizational meeting of the newly created Southern California–Arizona Annual Conference. It met in Long Beach the last week in June. Martin enjoyed the occasion. His limited responsibilities left plenty of time for doing things in the area. The members of the former Arizona Conference honored him and his family with a reception, and Paul Quillian was there as the conference preacher. Eula came with him. Their hotel was on the beach and Martin commented that "sleeping within the sound of the waves is a luxury." It turned out to be one of their happiest weeks as a family. "We saw and heard more of the sea than ever before." It was always a toss-up whether he enjoyed the sea or the mountains more.

And then it was on to Nebraska. Martin went directly by train when his duties in Long Beach were finished; the family returned to Glendale to pack. He met the Nebraska Conference cabinet and looked over the apartment in Omaha. "Wired Sally about it," he said, but he does not tell us in the diary what he said. It could not have been good. The weather was July hot, but in four days he visited eighty-three churches, "met nearly all the active and retired preachers in the district, preached three times, spoke informally five times, traveled a thousand miles." He loved it. Life was good.

Two days after he got back to Glendale, just over a year after their arrival, they loaded up the car again and headed for Las Vegas. They arrived there by 1:45 P.M. In order to drive across the desert at night to avoid the heat, they rested during the afternoon and left at midnight. This enabled them to reach the Grand Canyon by three o'clock the next afternoon. Sally and Catherine were both unwell, but William C. and the boys hiked to the rim to hear the National Park ranger-naturalist lecture. Afterward they drove through the Painted Desert and to Cameron by nightfall. From there they drove to Albuquerque, where during a brief stopover John's camera was stolen, and on to Pueblo, Colorado, for the night. John left them in Raton, New Mexico, to ride the bus to Dallas to visit friends and from there to travel on to Arkansas to spend the summer with Brice and Jack on the farm. "If he had been going to Europe we could not have made over him more." In Colorado Springs Martin, Catherine, and Donald drove to the top of Pike's Peak before going on to Boulder for the night. From there they drove through Estes Park and the Rocky Mountain National Park, spent their first Nebraska night in Sidney, and reached Omaha on July 21.

Their new home was the Knickerbocker Apartments, where they would live most of their first year in Omaha. The real estate agent opened the apartment for them. Speaking of the living situation in his diary, Martin admitted, "S & C were greatly disappointed with it and the result was a miserable night. But it was a delightful trip of 2550 miles." The next day he wrote, "Long talk with S in afternoon which brought light and peace." We don't know what concessions were offered or what compromise might have been reached, but having done whatever he did, he left immediately on the train to speak at a Bible Conference in Lake Okoboji. The household goods they had shipped arrived on August 3.

For the second time in just over a year, the new bishop began the process of getting acquainted with pastors and visiting churches. He taught in the Pastor's School at Mt. Sequoyah in Arkansas, as he often had in the past, and on September 12 called the first session of the Nebraska Annual Conference into session. Although it was not his first time to preside, it was his first experience of presiding alone in a large conference. The Nebraska Conference had eight districts with 357 appointments.

The Conference met that year in Lincoln at Trinity Methodist Church. Martin admitted to Godbold that he was apprehensive before it started, but things went smoothly (WCM to Godbold, September 22, 1939). He began meetings with the cabinet the day before conference officially opened. From the diary we learn that their evening sessions sometimes went until 2:30 A.M. "Brother Forney" Hutchinson was the conference preacher. In addition to presiding in conference when the cabinet was not in session, Martin did five morning devotionals on Romans 8, and addressed the class of persons to be ordained, the Wesleyan banquet, and the conference young people's assembly. He was not satisfied with his address to the youth group, and described it in the diary as "poor." Sunday morning he preached and in the afternoon conducted a service of dedication and celebration for the union that had formed The Methodist Church. The appointments were read just after noon on Monday. There were "no great surprises or disappointments" in them. "I felt a trifle wearied, but a few extra hours of sleep made me 'as good as new.' " At the time, America stood, once again, on the brink of war. Just over a week before on September 3, 1939, England and France declared war on Germany. The College of Bishops of the South Central Jurisdiction met in Oklahoma City on September 8. Mary Catherine was getting ready to leave for Dallas to begin school at SMU, and on September 10 she and her father had their "goodbye talk." Donald went back to Hendrix. Sally was not feeling well.

Immediately following the conclusion of the Nebraska Conference Martin presided in the Southwest Kansas Conference for Bishop Charles L. Mead, in the Southwest Missouri Conference for Bishop Broomfield, and then assisted Bishop Frank Smith with the Mexican Conference in Dallas. In accord with the directives contained in the Plan of Union, he and Bishop Mead organized the Central Kansas Conference in Salina on October 5, 1939, by uniting the Southwest Kansas Conference and the Northwest Kansas Conference. Martin later told Godbold that "the knowledge of the men which I gained may be of value to me if there is a change of area boundaries in 1940." Five days after its adjournment (October 10, 1939) he opened the Southwest Missouri Conference in St. Louis. His old friends Bishops John M. Moore, Ivan Lee Holt, and Charles Selecman were there to assist in the organization. "The spirit of unity could not have been finer," but it was a busy and stressful time.

He reached home again on October 16 and immediately started a round of district rallies which Sally attended with him. She only went part of the way, however. He spoke in Harvard, Lincoln, and Cambridge, and spent a day in the Holdrege District. He reached Sidney on the day pheasant season opened—"thousands of hunters" and was not home again until October 28. When he got back he took Sally to see *Mr. Smith Goes to Washington,* which the bishop judged "not too good." He was off again the next day.

The assignment to assist Bishop Smith in the Mexican Conference provided the opportunity for Sally's first trip back to Dallas since leaving for California. The old friends were waiting and overjoyed to see them again. They had lunch with the Bullocks, went to the SMU–Texas University football game in the afternoon, and then had a reunion with the "Supper Club" at the J. B. Hubbard's. The next day they had breakfast with the Virgil Walkers and visited with the Doggetts. Martin preached to a full house at First Church and had lunch afterward with the Drewerys. Sally's old and dear friend Alta Gibson went with them in the afternoon. Someone in Dallas once said that red-haired Sally Martin and raven-haired Alta Gibson were the two most beautiful women in town. They had grown up together in Arkansas. The old group was together again for supper at the W. H. Marshalls'.

SMU inaugurated Martin's friend Umphrey Lee as its president on November 6; William C. gave the invocation. Mrs. Walter Fondren of Houston, widow of the founder of Humble Oil and Refining (Exxon), helped to make the occasion even more special when she promised to provide $25,000 to furnish the central library, which bears the Fondren name. The visit ended with dinner at Dave and Pauline Lacy's and a reception for Lee at SMU's Dallas Hall in the evening. It was a wonderful whirlwind of activity and renewed friendships; Sally stayed another week to enjoy more of it when Martin returned home. He found John had fared well on his own, and Sally's absence gave them an unusual opportunity to be together. Their outings included movies and bowling. One day they "drove into the country and climbed over the bluffs and threw sticks in the Missouri River." John went with him to Beatrice, where he was preaching, and then back to Lincoln for a pheasant dinner at Vernon Thompson's home. Sally was back on November 13. Martin noted, "She was not tired out by her strenuous schedule."

At the end of November Martin attended the meetings of the Board of Home Missions of the former Methodist Episcopal Church in Philadelphia. The major item of business for both was to combine the various national boards and agencies of the former branches of Methodism into one. Martin was one of four representatives from the former southern church. Bishop Selecman and Elmer T. Clark, editor of the *World Outlook*, were also present. In addition to attending the meetings of the board, Martin managed to visit Independence Hall and Old St. George's Church, the oldest Methodist church in continuous use in the country.

The meetings adjourned on November 30, and Martin and Selecman took the train to Detroit where they were to meet the Board of Foreign Missions of the former Methodist Episcopal Church. The proximity to Canada allowed Martin to make a brief, first visit. There he saw a group of volunteers preparing hospital supplies, "a grim reminder that Canada is at war. . . . I thought I detected a note of reproach that we are not in it with them." Bishop Francis J. McConnell was president of the Board of Foreign Missions—"He is always stimulating to me," Martin told Godbold. Ecumenical leader John R. Mott was there, too. The longtime secretary of the board, Ralph Diffendorfer, impressed Martin with his grasp of the world situation. Former southern bishops Kern, Frank Smith, Arthur Moore, Purcell, and Peele joined them in Detroit.

Martin preached on Sunday morning in Detroit's Metropolitan Church, where John R. Rice had been pastor for more than twenty years. He heard Bishop Selecman and John R. Mott speak in the afternoon and Arthur J. Moore in the evening. Afterward they talked into the night. Martin told Godbold that "The Methodist Church has not produced in this generation quite another so effective a preacher within his realm as Arthur Moore" (WCM to Godbold, December 4, 1939).

When the meeting in Detroit was over all of them moved on to Chicago for the first meeting of the newly organized Council of Bishops of The Methodist Church. Martin described it in the diary as "one of the outstanding events of 1939." Frank Smith of Houston was elected as its first president. Bishop Edwin Holt Hughes called on Martin for the devotions, and he confessed in the diary, "I was so frightened my hand trembled." They were, indeed, a formidable group and he was one of the youngest and newest members. Only William Watkins, elected at the same time as Martin, was younger. At a banquet honoring the bishops in the evening, Tom Henrix, Martin's second school teacher, introduced himself after the adjournment, and they enjoyed talking over old times. Henrix was a minister in the Chicago area. Bishop Martin's first official assignment from the Council of Bishops was to write the resolutions of thanks for those who had hosted the meeting, especially Garrett Theological Seminary and Northwestern University, both in Evanston. At the end of the session, he preached in Wilmette and took the train for Omaha.

The newly organized Council of Bishops quickly ran into procedural difficulties in its operation. All retired bishops were eligible to attend its meetings, and in the beginning also to speak and vote. Outnumbering their active colleagues, a few of these older brethren so dominated the sessions that at the insistence of Bromley Oxnam a rule was passed that allowed them to attend and speak, but not to vote. Sometime later Bishop Frank Smith offered the opinion they had made a mistake—"should have let them vote but not speak," he said. Today retired bishops still attend the council's twice yearly meetings at church expense, and are still allowed to speak in the sessions. They do not, however, vote. In the membership of the council they not infrequently outnumber the active bishops.

Martin managed to be home only a week when he had to return to Nashville for a meeting of the Board of Education. Paul Quillian was there, too. They ate, talked, and bowled together, always a pleasant and renewing experience for them both. Martin presided in the sessions on December 20—another first in his long career. The train ride home provided an opportunity for reading Lord Charnwood's biography of Lincoln (Godfrey Rathbone Benson Charnwood, *Abraham Lincoln*, Makers of the Nineteenth Century series). Train travel was always useful for thinking, catching up on correspondence, and resting, as well as for reading.

Snow began to fall on December 23 ensuring a white Christmas in Nebraska. Catherine came in from SMU after having ridden in the baggage car of a crowded train all the way from Kansas City. Donald had come earlier from Hendrix. Sunday, Christmas Eve, carried the usual busy schedule, but in the evening there was time with the family. Sally cooked the Christmas dinner, and the evening was spent with the Phillips family. He was the pastor of the First Christian Church in Omaha and lived across the street from the Martins.

Obviously thinking about what he had recently read of Lincoln, Martin closed the year with thoughts from the Charnwood biography. Lincoln "was big enough to sacrifice himself for the sake of a cause. He was unwilling to be identified with the Abolitionist agitators. The supreme importance of faith in God's individual providence. When we neither go before it nor lag behind it there is a mighty undergirding for life's conflicts. He could afford to be patient as God is patient." Applying the example of the president to his own life, Martin said, "Whatever good qualities a man has in him will find the opportunity for expression even though they may be overlooked for a season. Patience is a great Christian virtue."

As always, Martin raised questions about self-improvement: "How can I keep my body in fit condition? How can I enlarge the borders of my mind? How can I help my soul to grow?" And with these thoughts 1939 and the first Christmas in Nebraska came to a close. Donald and Catherine returned to school on New Year's

Day. Sally began 1940 with influenza. William C. heard she was in the hospital only after he arrived in York for a meeting, but he fulfilled his speaking engagement and met the cabinet on the way back. He was not home again until two days later, but he found her "slowly improving." He left again almost immediately for a series of services at Holdrege and was not back until January 21. "S. has improved slowly," in the interim, he said.

⟞⟝⟞⟝

Episcopal service provided Martin opportunities for travel and experiences that in the past he could only have imagined. In February 1940, he took part along with all the other bishops in a preaching crusade called the Methodist Advance, designed to promote the newly united church. This consisted of a series of mass rallies held around the country in which all the bishops participated. The Advance also included an emphasis on the Sunday school with an "Each One Win 3" campaign. Another feature of every rally was a luncheon meeting for men only. The bishops were assigned outside their areas to preach at the large meetings. Martin, along with Bishops C. W. Flint, J. C. Broomfield, and W. T. Watkins, went into the Northeastern Jurisdiction. On the way to Albany, New York, for his first preaching appointment, he arranged to stop in New York City and hear Harry Emerson Fosdick preach in the Riverside Church. Having read Fosdick's books of sermons for years and listened to him on the radio, Martin described it as "the end of a pilgrimage & the fulfillment of a long hope. . . . A great sermon and service." He spoke in Albany with Bishop McConnell, and went on to Utica and Syracuse and then to Buffalo. He spent more than an hour at Niagara Falls seeing them for the first time in their winter beauty. From there he moved on to Pittsburgh and then Charleston, West Virginia, before concluding his part of the effort in Cleveland and Cincinnati. He reached home on February 17 after being gone for fifteen days. During the Advance he participated in ten meetings in which thirty addresses were given, located in two jurisdictions, four episcopal areas, and nine annual conferences.

In March he and Sally began the search for another apartment, but eventually ended up in the Blackstone Hotel. They moved the day before he left for the meeting of the Council of Bishops in Atlantic City just prior to the opening of the first General Conference of The Methodist Church.

The council sessions began with a Communion service on April 24. The council was to make Atlantic City the site of its meetings for many years. Much of the time was spent on the Episcopal Address, which had been prepared by Francis J. McConnell. He read it to the conference on April 25. Sally arrived that day, too. It is the practice of the General Conference to use the bishops to organize the various legislative committees and to preside in its plenary sessions. Martin was assigned to oversee the Committee on Conferences. Bishop Straughn, elected by the Methodist Protestants in Kansas City, ran into trouble presiding in one of the morning sessions and Martin noted he "had much difficulty in getting through. Almost nothing done." Martin was not among those selected to preside.

He was assigned to preach at Paulsboro, Pennsylvania, on Sunday, April 28—only a hundred people turned out to hear him, but the day was a great triumph because of a "thrilling ride home through the golden sunshine." Folks in Nebraska don't see too much of that during its long winter months. Sally came down with a cold on May 2 and went to bed for two days.

The conference adjourned on May 6, and in the company of Bishop U. V. W. Darlington, William C. and Sally started home by way of Washington, D.C. There they rented a car and enjoyed seeing the sites on "a perfect spring day." They reached home on May 9, just in time to visit the high school to talk with two of John's teachers. He was in trouble because he had corrected a mistake made in class by his history teacher. When that was satisfactorily resolved, Martin resumed his demanding schedule.

The week of May 12 was typical. That day, a Sunday, he left in the morning for Page to preach at their sixtieth church anniversary. After lunch there he drove on to O'Neil, where he preached again in the afternoon and had refreshments with the pastor. He was in Randolph for the evening service and supper. After church he was driven to Norfolk, which he reached at 11:30 P.M. to spend the night. He was up the next morning in time to catch a 4:00 A.M. train that arrived back in Omaha at 7:45. From the train station he went directly to the office. Sally met him for lunch, and then it was back to the office until 5:45. With little more than three hours sleep the night before, he described himself as "sleepy and morose." Many days were like that.

The news from Europe was more and more gloomy, and he described these reports in one entry as "terrifying." Sally left for a visit in Arkansas, and William C. took time to bowl most evenings with John. They enjoyed these rare times together.

After working through the various actions of the immediately past General Conference, Martin reflected in the diary about his own work. "Sometimes I feel that it is a pity that every preacher cannot be a bishop; at other times I feel that it [is] a rank injustice that anybody has to be one."

The first sessions of the newly organized South Central Jurisdiction Conference of The Methodist Church opened on May 28 in Oklahoma City. In The Methodist Church these regional conferences were given power to establish boundaries of the various conferences, to organize them into episcopal areas, and to elect the bishops of the church. Bishop Ivan Lee Holt read the bishops' address to the delegates. The next day, in an uncharacteristic outburst Martin wrote in the diary, "Bp [Wilmer Emery] Hammaker preached a worn-out sermon which the conference unwillingly endured." He and the other bishops made their reports to the Episcopal Committee and "heard our characters passed." Dean Lynn Harold Hough, of Drew Theological School spoke and created considerable controversy in response to his "hawkish" views on war. When the areas were re-aligned, as Martin had thought they would be, the newly organized Central Kansas and Kansas Conferences were added to the Nebraska area. This gave Martin responsibility for three large and widely scattered conferences in two states.

Catherine came home from SMU on June 6, and despite a distressing admission to her parents that she did not attend church regularly, they were glad to see her—"a lovely girl," Martin wrote. That same day Martin gave the commencement address at Nebraska Wesleyan College and received his second honorary degree, Doctor of Laws. Catherine and Sally were shortly to leave for Boulder, Colorado, to attend the summer session at the University of Colorado. The rest of the family would join them there for the first of their many Colorado vacations. They all loved the mountains.

In the meantime, Martin had to preside in the opening session of the Pacific Northwest Conference meeting in Tacoma, Washington. It was a difficult time since he was suffering from an infection in his mouth caused by bad lower teeth. Throughout his life he was to have serious problems with his teeth and eventually had to have all of them removed. In spite of his discomfort, he went directly from Tacoma to the Oregon Conference in Portland. This provided him with his first, and then unique, opportunity to ordain a woman to the office of deacon, Gertrude Boyer. The appointments in both conferences proved difficult to make, and when he finally got home again he discovered he had sixty letters waiting for an answer.

Since Sally was with Catherine in Boulder and John was at the farm in Arkansas, William C. took the opportunity while he was alone to bowl almost every evening. He also looked for a more suitable apartment, and leased office space in room 512 of the Omaha National Bank Building. Edna Kahnt was hired as his first full-time secretary. For the first time in two years, he was able to unpack all of his books. Monk Bryan, his seminary student assistant at First Methodist in Dallas, had packed them when he left there and they had never been opened. Years later Bryan, as Bishop Monk Bryan of The United Methodist Church, also served the Nebraska Area.

The balance of the summer was consumed with the usual trip to lecture at Mt. Sequoyah and one to Chicago for the organizational meeting of the Board of Missions. Bishop Arthur J. Moore was elected its president. Martin was assigned to the Women's Division of the board. He continued on from there to the meeting of the Board of Education where he was assigned to the Division of the Local Church.

On August 7, he rejoined Sally and Mary Catherine in Denver.

He records a cryptic comment after a long conversation with Sally—"Registered a solemn vow." He does not say what the vow was. After ten days he returned to Omaha to meet some engagements and then was back in Boulder on August 20 where John and Donald had come to join the rest of the family. They stayed until August 28. While there they visited Estes Park, Grand Lake, Idaho Springs, Central City; they drove up Mt. Evans and saw the grave of Buffalo Bill. While visiting Mt. Evans, Martin climbed with the boys from the parking lot to the summit. Although it was not a long climb, the elevation was above 14,000 feet and the air was thin, making the walk difficult. Sally always thought this exertion was one of the causes of her husband's subsequent heart problems. William C. and John climbed to the foot of the Flatirons near Boulder too. He was home in time to begin meeting with the Nebraska Cabinet in preparation for annual conference, and to make a tour through a portion of his new conferences in Kansas. In early September he was the preacher for the Illinois Conference in Bloomington.

And then it all caught up with him. He opened the Nebraska Annual Conference in Omaha on September 17. After giving the devotions the next morning, he "felt sharp pains in upper chest from slight exertion." Despite the fact that the pain continued, he did not stop anything he was doing and met with the cabinet that evening until midnight. He remained in pain and experienced shortness of breath all the next day but did not finally see a doctor until Sally sent Dr. John C. Sharpe to meet him at the Methodist Hospital, where Martin had gone to talk with the district superintendent of the Norfolk District, William A. Albright, who was ill and considering temporary retirement. The doctor's tentative diagnosis was angina pectoris and his urgent advice was for Martin to cancel all his engagements. Martin flatly refused. The next day he preached at eleven o'clock—he said in the diary that he "never preached better"—conducted the ordination service in the afternoon while feeling "sharp pains in upper chest," and met with the cabinet until midnight. He told Godbold he simply could not make appointments in a hurry. He read the appointments the next afternoon.

One thing did change. To the "Weight Notebook" begun years earlier was added a "Heart Notebook." It opens:

I was not shocked or frightened when the Dr. made his announcement to me. I had felt, at times, that I would, one day have trouble with my heart but I had certainly not expected it at this age [forty-seven]. My pulse had been faster than is normal since an attack of pneumonia when I was in High School at Prescott, Ark. in 1910. Possibly this was the case before but I had not noticed it. There had been various sensations of discomfort in the region of my heart for a long time. I had considered myself to be in the very finest of good health and had done a considerable amount of climbing during the summer preceding at Fayetteville and Boulder. After a steep climb I would have to stop and pant for breath but I thought that was normal. The symptoms that led to sending for the Dr. were gripping pains in the upper part of my chest when I had walked for only a few blocks. It was getting worse as the days passed and the strain of work with the conference increased.

The doctor insisted that he needed rest, but Martin was unwilling to cancel the conferences in Kansas. He and Sally considered several alternatives, and he finally agreed to cancel several speaking engagements and to check into the Pickwick Hotel in Kansas City for some rest before the conferences opened. The doctor gave him advice on things to avoid—overloading the stomach, lifting objects, taking cold showers, and rushing. Martin acknowledged in the heart notebook that "there has been a degree of nervous and muscular tension during every working minute and in preaching, speaking or even presiding at a conference the strain would be intense." He decided that his exercises, sit-ups and leg lifts done first thing in the morning, were too strenuous and discontinued them. He resolved to keep the problem a secret from any who did not already know about it, and few did. Godbold inquired about his health after learning Martin had canceled a speaking engagement in the Missouri Conference, but was only told in a brief letter written the first week of November that "I came out of the Nebraska Conference so worn down by the long and sometimes difficult sessions during a period of intense heat that the doctor insisted I take out a few days for recuperation" (WCM to Godbold, November 4, 1940). The fact that he did not disclose the true nature of his condition to one of his oldest and most intimate friends illustrates the strength of his resolve not to let it be known.

After spending a day in bed at home, he took the night train to Hutchinson on September 24 to meet the Central Kansas Conference cabinet and then went on to Kansas City the next day. He stayed in bed until noon the next day and then walked with some discomfort to a nearby public library to read about angina pectoris. He followed pretty much the same routine each day, which enabled him to do a lot of reading—W. P. Paterson's *Conversion,* Lewis Mumford's *Faith for Living,* and Walter Marshall Horton's *Can Christianity Save Civilization?* He called Sally every night at seven to report on his condition, and began forming a plan for the future.

> When I return to Omaha I will have a cardiogram made. I will take the best care I can of myself in discharging my duties and if I hold up I will go through the year. Another cardiogram will be made and compared with the earlier one to see how much deterioration there has been. If it proves to be so rapid that the continuation of the work would mean a complete break in health then I should feel compelled to ask for relief. If I am holding my own I will go on through the quadrennium. If I am still holding up I shall continue in the office; if not, I shall resign and attempt to find some kind of work in the church which I am capable of doing.

A revealing entry, cast in the form of a prayer and dated September 29, follows. It is prefaced, "Still in search of encouragement with respect to recovery and not finding anything definite to pin my faith to." In that spirit he prayed:

> Oh Christ, my Savior, thou healer of bodies and souls, I do not want to ask of thee that which I should not have. I do not seek immunity from any pain or privation which I should bear. And yet I do not want to keep out of my life work by any lack of faith or

trust on my part any gift which it is thy will to give me. I do not want to be weak when I might, by asking in faith, be strong. I put my care into thy hands. Do thou for me what is best. Give me gratitude for the healing or courage to bear the pain without complaint and enable me to use them both for thee. Amen.

He noted that Emerson's "Compensation" "will be a greater source of comfort and courage to me than ever." On September 30 he was able to take a longer walk without discomfort and "felt jubilant and hopeful."

The next day he managed to go through a long session with the Kansas Conference cabinet without symptoms or exhaustion. Pushing his luck the next day he toured churches in the area and felt numbness in his left arm during the night. He went home on October 3 and saw Dr. Sharpe, who gave him a cardiogram that was "almost normal" and an encouraging report. He had not needed the nitroglycerin tablets he had been given.

He and Sally left to drive to Topeka the afternoon of October 6. It was a beautiful autumn day. After spending the night in Topeka they drove on to Hutchinson where the cabinet meetings began in the afternoon. The Central Kansas Conference opened October 9. They presented Sally with thirty red roses as a token of their appreciation for her and the family. Umphrey Lee was the conference preacher; Roy Smith, a member of the conference and soon to be editor of the *Christian Advocate,* delivered the address at the memorial service—"such an address as only he could have given," Martin observed.

As usual, cabinet sessions often lasted past midnight. He preached Sunday morning on the topic "The Eternal Word in a Confused World." After the appointments were read in the early afternoon, Martin drove immediately to Manhattan, Kansas, to preside in the Kansas Conference. It opened on October 16. In each conference he followed his usual routine of making the devotional addresses in the morning, meeting with the cabinet when he was not presiding in the sessions, conducting the ordination services, and preaching on Sunday. A number of changes had to be made in the Kansas Conference, and making the appointments was difficult because there were no openings in the upper level appointments. His sermon on Sunday was "The Christ Who Holds Life Together." The cabinet that day met until 2:00 A.M., and reconvened to complete the appointments at eight in the morning. Martin read the appointments at noon and left for home by midafternoon. The night was spent in Hiawatha. He was back in Omaha on October 22, bought a new suit of clothes, and received another encouraging report from his doctor. A week later he was back in Kansas to speak to the students at Baker University in Baldwin City. "Tired. Too many meetings," he wrote in the diary when it was over.

He summarized the pace of his schedule in a long letter to Godbold written on September 30, 1940.

> The Central Kansas Conference meets next week in Hutchinson and the Kansas Conference the following week in Manhattan. A few days in the office, a three day area council with the 20 DS's [district superintendents] and other conference administrative officers present, a week of revival services, a youth workers conference, Board of Missions in New York, Board of Education at Nashville with the Bishop's Council sandwiched between and then Christmas and another year.

Hardly what one would have prescribed for a heart patient.

Election Day, November 4, Martin voted against Roosevelt's bid for a third term. Sally did not vote, but ever the loyal Democrat and supporter of Roosevelt, she was angry at her husband for breaking ranks. He took the train to Topeka and learned after he arrived that the president had been re-elected. In Kansas, he continued to see Governor Landon. Landon was governor of Kansas from 1933 to 1937 and ran unsuccessfully against Roosevelt in 1936 as the Republican candidate for President. The two got better acquainted through the years and Martin was sometimes the governor's guest for meals. They met in his home on November 7 to consider the possibility of merging Baker University with Washburn. The idea was rejected.

The Board of Missions held its annual meeting in Philadelphia the week after Thanksgiving and Martin spoke at the Memorial Service—"about as good as I am capable of doing," he mused. Afterward he spent two pleasant days in New York City before going on to Atlantic City for the meeting of the council of Bishops. While in New York he went to see *Bitter Sweet* at the Music Hall and *Life with Father*. The council meetings went well under the joint leadership of Frank Smith and Bromley Oxnam.

Martin reached home again on December 7 but was on his way to Chicago a week later for the meeting of the Methodist Committee on Overseas Relief. He was embarrassed by making a motion that did not receive a second. Bishops quickly become accustomed to having their motions ratified by someone.

Mary Catherine and Donald came home from college for the holidays; as was their custom, begun in Little Rock, Martin read Dickens's *Christmas Carol* aloud during the evenings. He closed an eventful year with this thought:

> The secret of successful living is to believe in life. Lord, give me a Gospel always in which I can believe supremely and let me preach it enthusiastically. Before Christ I must always confess myself to be a sinner but I follow after. An individual loyalty is the only abiding source of confidence. I believe therefore I speak. If I must die for a cause I want it to be big enough to be worth dying for. My understanding of the law of compensation is a source of comfort and strength. This is a Christian fatalism.

7

The War Years

The year 1941 began in good style for the resident bishop of the Nebraska-Kansas Area of The Methodist Church: listened to the "Big Red" of Nebraska play Stanford in the Rose Bowl. Nebraska lost. Catherine and Donald went back to college and John began his year by being arrested for driving the family car with an expired safety sticker. William C. and Sally went to see the Marx Brothers that day, too.

Martin's routine now required shuttling back and forth to attend to the needs of two Kansas conferences as well as extensive travel in Nebraska. Many people were looking carefully at the world events and realized the inevitable nature of American involvement. Despite isolationist sentiment in the Congress, Roosevelt had, in fact, been making preparations to put the nation on a wartime footing for some years. The Lend-Lease program, which had supplied war materials to future allies was just one example. Governor Ratner of Kansas asked Martin's opinion about opposing the pending lend-lease bill. Unfortunately, we don't know what he told the governor.

On January 25, Martin left in a snowstorm to fulfill speaking engagements in Emporia only to receive a telegram on the train that everything had been canceled—"400 miles for nothing but there was no need to worry about it." He spoke during the religious emphasis week at Nebraska Wesleyan, participated in a successful campaign to raise $220,000 for Southwestern College in Winfield, Kansas, made a visit to a salt mine, and spent a day in bed to rest in early February "at Sally's direction." He recorded an entry in the "Heart Notebook" on January 9, 1941.

> There seems to be no change in the condition of my coronary artery from the time the defect was first discovered nearly 4 months ago. I feel perfectly normal until I walk two or three blocks. Then the feeling of being acutely out of breath develops. . . . I am like an engine that has a governor to control its speed; when I stay below the level of a certain amount of physical activity I am all right; when I exceed that limit the discomfort begins.

Still he did not alter his schedule. Shortly after his enforced day of rest he was on his way to Cleveland for the National Missionary Conference. He arranged to stop off in Chicago long enough to visit the Methodist bookstore at 740 Rush Street and while there was given a tour of Jacob S. Payton's private library. It was, Martin said, "an ecstatic experience. American Methodism, biographical and historical. What a rich collection." Payton was then editor of the *National Methodist Press* and covered Washington for the New York *Christian Advocate*. His weekly column, "Washington Observations," was widely respected. At the missionary conference Martin had lunch with missionary E. Stanley Jones, whom he had first heard in Memphis. Jones was one of the people for whom Martin had great respect throughout his life.

The evening of February 17, Martin preached in the Church of the Savior in Cleveland, "a great Gothic sanctuary" in a former northern "high church" and wore a robe for the first time—a real concession from a southern Methodist. He preached on the topic "Great Faith" and got "as good a response as could be expected in such a setting." It is probably fair to say he was not entirely comfortable. In a letter to Godbold he mentioned preaching in the three largest Methodist churches in Cleveland but failed to tell him how he felt about the experience.

On the way home he left the train long enough for a trip to

Chicago's Blessings Bookstore, a favorite place of his. He reached Omaha at 9:00 A.M. and left again to preach in Atchison and Leavenworth, Kansas, two and a half hours later. Back on the old schedule, he did find time with Sally to see *Western Union*, starring Claude Rains and in technicolor. After doing his income tax he discovered he had to pay $160, up from $48 the previous year.

In early March he was on the *Rocket* bound for Chicago again. The Council of Bishops held a joint meeting with the Commission on World Service and Finance and the Council of Secretaries. His first stop in Chicago, now as usual, was Blessings, but he also found time to tour the largest printing plant in the world where *Liberty Magazine* was produced. He was fascinated with the process by which books were bound. That same evening he ran into Gipsy Smith at the hotel. He was in town to hold a meeting, and gave the devotional at the Wednesday afternoon session of the Council of Bishops.

Martin was home again on Thursday morning and went directly to the office from the train—"almost caught up with correspondence," he noted. The next week he began a series of sermons at Lowman Church, Topeka. Sally went with him. While there he had lunch with Governor Alf Landon and toured churches in the area he had not seen. And so it went day after day in the life of a busy church leader. There were times when Sally said she delivered a suitcase of clean clothes to his office, but never saw him when he came through.

He was pleased to discover he was now able to bowl without discomfort for the first time in six months, but he was still having difficulty keeping his weight down. "Watching diet but hard with church dinners," he confessed on March 29. He taught "Christian Philosophy of Life" at the Pastor's School in Kearney, Nebraska, and then went on from there to attend the Regional Educational Conference in Kansas City. Godbold was on the faculty, Bishop McConnell spoke. Martin enjoyed both. He had written to Godbold earlier to express his hope they could find time for a conversation and told him he would be staying at the Robert E. Lee Hotel across the street from the meeting site. In the letter he said, "Surely we can find time for some kind of a visit."

But in the next sentence he told his friend, "I shall be meeting at odd hours with the Cabinet and the Commission on World Service and Finance of the Kansas Conference, but we can find some other odd times" (WCM to Godbold, March 18, 1941).

An April entry in the diary reveals that he was "gradually filling out [his] collection of books by and about the bishops." His interest had been stimulated after he began reading from and about them shortly after his own election in 1938 and collecting photographs, letters, and other written materials by nearly all of the men who had been elected in any part of the church. At that time he also began corresponding with Bishop Frederick D. Leete, a Methodist Episcopal Church bishop who was serving as president of the Ecumenical Methodist Council. Bishop Leete had been collecting memorabilia related to bishops for a long time and was the expert on all things related to them. In that process, Leete had assembled an extensive collection of Methodistica. It was his custom to write every person as soon as he was elected. Martin's letter requested a signed photograph, a letter written entirely in his hand, and a copy of a sermon or sermon notes, preferably written by hand and signed. Bishop Leete's collection, housed in the Bridwell Library of the Perkins School of Theology since 1956, is there largely because of the association and friendship that Martin cultivated with Bishop Leete through the years they traded books, memorabilia, and letters related to bishops. Their correspondence makes it clear that Martin's sensitive urging and influence was crucial in Leete's decision finally to place his library in Dallas. In the beginning Leete had no connection with the Southwest and no intention of housing his prized collection at Perkins; he had, in fact, given it first to a church in Indianapolis. When this proved unsatisfactory to him, he sought another place and largely in response to Martin's suggestions, it came to the Bridwell Library. At the time he moved it to Dallas, the Leete collection contained some 4,000 letters of Methodist bishops, a number of their ordination certificates and even more signed by them. There are more than a thousand books and pamphlets written by bishops and eighty letters written by John Wesley in addition to a stunning edition of his *Christian Library* bound in red morocco leather. Martin's collection of similar materials, housed with his papers in the archives of the Bridwell Library, was never as extensive as the one assembled by Bishop Leete, but it fills several archival boxes and contains something from most of the bishops in the history of The Methodist Church in America. His extensive correspondence with Bishop Leete is also there, and it reveals the joy they shared in a common interest in American episcopal leaders.

⟨⟨⟨⟨ ⟩⟩⟩⟩

May 13 Martin reached what he described as "a turning point." That day he found in the bookstore at the Union Station in Kansas City a book written by Victor H. Lindlahr titled *Eat and Reduce.* "I read all of this book before I read anything else and found it to be a sane guide to the loss of excess fat. I was weighing 200 lbs undressed and was becoming discouraged in my efforts to get below that mark. Lindlahr's method is not different, in principle, from the plan I had been following for 3 or 4 years but his reducing menus are exactly what I needed." After only two and a half weeks he was down to 193. "I am very jubilant over the outlook," he said, and then added, "The death rate for angina pectoris doubled for overweights."

Ignoring the fact that stress is also a significant contributor to coronary artery disease, he attended and spoke at the Pastor's School at Baker University during the summer. Boston University School of Theology professor Edgar S. Brightman, along with the former missionary and president of Scarritt College, Hugh C. Stuntz, were the featured speakers. Martin had a long conversation with Brightman "about miracles and philosophical books." From Baldwin City he went directly to Dallas for the SMU Pastor's School and to see Bishop John M. Moore who was in the hospital. He preached twice a day but found time for meals and conversations with the members of the Supper Club, the Glenn Flinns, Paul Quillians, Marshall Steel, Otstotts, and others. He left Dallas for Arkansas on June 27. There he found that John was having a good summer farming with Sally's brother, Brice, and his wife, Jack. He walked over the field, and went to bed that night "after sitting under the stars and remembering." When the Layman's Day speaker for the church in McCaskill failed to appear on Sunday, Martin preached in his place. He had lunch with Uncle Martin and Aunt Stell Nelson in Blevins, a few miles down the road, enjoyed an afternoon nap and preached in the evening in the home church in Blevins.

There were always more trips to be made and appointments to be kept, but his leisure time continued to be heavily invested in the movies like *The Reluctant Dragon*—"most of the show was a dead loss of time"; *The Big Show*, with his favorites, the Marx Brothers was a hit—"they always amuse me," he said. He preached at the Lakeside Assembly in Sandusky, Ohio, and met one of his old army buddies, Kellar Lewis, who was present.

A pleasant August was spent in a rented cottage in Boulder, Colorado. The Bookhouts from Dallas were there, too, and many friends were nearby in Estes Park, a popular vacation spot for Texans. Along with spending time with the family, he drove to see the now-familiar sights again, walked, read, worked on an article, went to Ringling Brothers Circus in Denver, and began to make preparations with Sally for Donald's wedding. Donald, who had turned twenty-one on August 2, 1941, had fallen in love with a Hendrix classmate, Ernestine Anne Matkin. Born in the small farming community of Gregory, Arkansas, Ernestine and her family had moved to Little Rock when she was eight. Because of the depression, she had at first decided to attend Little Rock Junior College, but her staunch Methodist family insisted that she go to Hendrix, and with the aid of a scholarship and a job she managed to obtain the money to enroll. She and Donald met during their freshman year but did not begin to date until they were juniors. A letter from L. W. Groves, executive vice president of the Texas Employers' Insurance Association and William C.'s last chairman of the official board at First Methodist, reveals that Donald in 1940 had considered leaving school to marry and asked Groves for a job. Ernestine recalls that it was during the spring of 1940 that they, after having been friends from their first year in Hendrix, discovered they were in love, but she says at no time did she consider marriage in the summer of 1940. The thought was clearly on Donald's mind, however. Groves wrote the bishop to tell him, "Don is apparently very much in love with the young lady he has talked so much about, and I am convinced that his real purpose in trying to get the work is to enable him to marry" (L. W. Groves to WCM, October 23, 1940). With his letter to Martin, he enclosed a blind carbon of his reply to Donald with specific instructions that he was never to know about it. He urged Donald to stay in school, and cited his experience as an example of what not to do. He had left the University of Missouri at the end of his junior year and always had been sorry for having done it. "How wrong it may have been," he wrote Donald, "I have no way of judging, but in looking back on my life I am fully persuaded that in any event the direction of my entire future was radically changed by reason of that decision. Whether for better or worse I know not, but I am confident in my own mind that it was for the worse. I have never yet met a man who, if he had common sense along with it, had too much education." Although his younger sister and brother readily acknowledge Donald as being the most intelligent among them, he was not always challenged in school and at one time was described by his father to Albea Godbold as "plodding" along at Hendrix. Ernestine remembers his performance as "uneven." He did graduate from Hendrix, finishing with a major in English and a minor in history. Following his discharge from military service at the end of World War II, he began doing the work of a civil engineer for the Missouri Pacific Railroad and by taking courses and examinations became a registered professional civil engineer in the State of Arkansas and a Fellow in the American Society of Civil Engineers.

Martin left Boulder on August 28 "with the feeling that it has been a profitable vacation." After spending the night in Trinidad, he was on his way to Raton, New Mexico, for breakfast when he ran out of gasoline, not an altogether unique experience for him. Once the tank was filled, Sally and William C. drove on by way of Dallas to Arkansas to pick up John at the farm. Sally and John stayed with the family while William C. made a quick trip back to Omaha to meet the cabinet and the Commission on World Service and Finance. He was back in Little Rock the morning of September 6 for the wedding. Donald, Ernestine, and others met the train, and there, for the first time, Martin met his future daughter-in-law. "I had heard so many fine things about her that I was prepared to be favorably impressed. Was not disappointed."

The wedding was at five o'clock that evening in the Pulaski Heights Methodist Church. Martin performed the ceremony with the help of the pastor, Fred Harrison. John was his brother's best man. Cora and Ernest Matkin, the parents of the bride, hosted the reception in their home. The newlyweds established their first home in Hope, Arkansas, where Ernestine had found a job in the school and Donald one in construction. Two days after the ceremony, Martin was in Hutchinson, Kansas, to meet the cabinet in preparation for opening the annual conference.

The Nebraska Conference opened on September 17 at St. Paul's Methodist Church in Lincoln. Martin's devotionals were based on the Gospel of John. When it was over he reported, "Am tired but not so much as last year," but he stayed in bed the next day until past noon. Reflecting on the conference he wrote at the end of the year:

> I awoke early one morning after a rather restless night and found my pulse beating at the rate of nearly a hundred. A sense of discouragement came over me. A little later there stole over me a sense of peace and quiet which remained through the days. It grew out of two assurances: I did not seek this place but was assigned to it by the church, and I am not pouring out more of myself in seeking to establish the Kingdom of righteousness than some men are in an effort to enslave their fellow-men.

He said he had learned "some lessons" about presiding, too. "Never get panicky no matter how impossible the situation may appear. Never get short-tempered no matter what the provocation." And as a tidbit of homiletical wisdom, "never use a long poem in a sermon." As usual he and Sally celebrated the end of conference with a movie, *Dr. Jekyll and Mr. Hyde,* but he said he found it "overdrawn toward the sex side."

The Central Kansas Conference convened in Wichita on September 30. Appointment making was difficult, but he and Sally were made as comfortable as possible by being housed in the Governor's Suite at the hotel. As a rule hotel accommodations for the bishop were provided without charge. Bishop Edwin Holt Hughes was the preacher. Despite a rocky beginning, the appointments were ready by Tuesday night, "But," he said, "we were confident that not all of them would hold." They didn't.

The Kansas Conference opened in Topeka on October 8. Henry Hitt Crain was the speaker. The Martins, along with the members of his cabinet and their wives, were entertained by the governor at the Executive Mansion. The conference was memorable because during one of the sessions the conference lay leader, Professor W. J. Williams of Baker University, was stricken on the floor with a cerebral hemorrhage—he died seven hours later. Last-minute problems delayed finalizing the appointments—Grand Island refused to put its salary at a level that would allow the man appointed to accept; a last-minute refusal of their new preacher by a congregation held up reading the appointments and delayed adjournment. Martin gained some practical wisdom there, too. "Never talk to a pastor in definite terms about a transfer to another conference without letting him know that the exchange is conditional upon certain conditions being met." That could probably be paraphrased as, "Where other persons are involved, be careful never to promise more than you can deliver." He also learned to "get all possible light on matters relating to a ruling before it is given. See to it that the former deceased Bishop is properly memorialized. Get as many administrative affairs as possible cared for in pre-conference sessions in order that the cabinet may not be disturbed during conference." Governor Ratner and his wife and Governor and Mrs. Landon were present for the ordination luncheon along with the cabinet.

In his dealings with individuals, Martin continued to learn valuable lessons, too. He outlined the following as "fundamental principles": "Never become impatient. Never speak from the mere desire to be heard. Always deal with the larger issues. Someone else will look after the details. Take the most charitable attitude possible toward those who are not in agreement with your position."

On October 15, Sally, W. C., and John Lee moved out of the

Blackstone Hotel and into the Glendale Apartments, #5. "We think we shall like it," he said for all of them. We don't know what Sally said. The plan was to stay through the winter. His health continued to improve and he was back in full stride. In early November he preached at the North Georgia Conference and had his overcoat stolen for his trouble. With either a stroke of genius or just good fortune, at the end of that month he and Sally purchased a 1941 Buick. It cost $830. Unlike many Americans who nursed their old cars through the war years, the Martins started with a new one. December brought the usual meetings of the Board of Missions. On the way he stopped to hear Harry Emerson Fosdick at Riverside Church. This time he introduced himself to Fosdick when the sermon was over. He also saw *Sergeant York* and said he was pleased with the role played in it by the church. No doubt he could identify with Alvin York, too.

Martin heard Fosdick the morning of December 7, 1941. Afterward he did some sight-seeing in the cathedral of St. John the Divine and took in a music program at "St. Barts." At the end of the service "the rector announced that Japan had attacked American possessions and called us to prayer. A solemn and subduing moment." America was finally at war.

Martin heard Norman Vincent Peale in the evening at the Marble Collegiate Church and spent part of the next day at the offices of the Federal Council of Churches. The Council of Bishops met in the Cloister Hotel, Sea Island, Georgia, on December 9. Bishop Selecman introduced the following resolution on the war which was seconded by Bishop Leonard, approved, and sent to President Roosevelt at the White House.

> The Council of Bishops of the Methodist Church in session at Sea Island, Georgia, desires to assure you, in this hour of peril, of our profound sympathy and loyalty, and above all of our earnest prayers that in this national crisis you may have divine guidance and support.

Bishop Oxnam moved to create a special committee to consider race discrimination in the defense program. Bishops McConnell,

Jones, and Martin were named. There was a discussion on the subject of conscientious objection. Many persons declaring that position during World War I had been subjected to abuse and imprisonment. "I spoke in favor of a statement that would give to him the same consideration as to the soldier. That position which had adequate support, prevailed." The statement read:

> It is the judgment of the Council of Bishops of the Methodist Church that all churches and religious agencies seeking to secure support for Conscientious Objectors should unite in proper representation to the Congress of the United States to the end that the same support shall be provided by the Government for draftees assigned to work of national importance under civilian direction as is provided for draftees assigned to other categories of service, and that the Council express its willingness to join in such representation, as well as its intention to proceed in such representation on its own authority.

A Commission on Chaplains was authorized, to be closely related to the Council of Bishops, and a wartime message drafted and issued to the church. On the way home Martin stopped off in Atlanta where he visited 77 W. Baker Street, the address where he and Sally began housekeeping during another world war. He tried to visit Camp Gordon, but bad weather kept him from going. His mind was clearly on the war.

Christmas Day 1941 was a somber one. The Brooks family came for lunch, and the realities of a world at war came with them to the holiday table. "Their son, Culver, is in the Philippines and the outlook there is gloomy," Martin recorded. "A quiet day with us in a world at war." Brooks was later taken prisoner by the Japanese. Martin preached December 28 on the topic "The Gospel of a New Start." New Year's Day 1942 dawned cold and snowy; he and Sally went to see *How Green Was My Valley*.

The last day of January he began "serious work" on what began as an article but evolved into a small pamphlet titled

"When Temptation Comes"; he finished it by the middle of April. Published by the General Board of Lay Activities of The Methodist Church, it was distributed in large numbers to recruits in the camps. Martin said in the introduction that he wrote it after seeing a soldier say good-bye to his family and sweetheart at a railroad station. "I hope he comes back to them. I hope he comes back whole—whole in body and in heart." As he watched him leave, Martin said, "I felt an urgent desire to say something to him that might help . . . something which I recalled from the experiences of another World War." It is printed in a pocket-size edition and begins with the scripture account of the temptations of Jesus in the Gospels of Matthew and Luke. "Temptation," Martin began, "finds the weak spots. . . . All of the real temptations of life are rooted in the instincts of our nature," and they are more powerful because nobody is apt to know if one gives in. But he remembered when his unit left France in 1919, somebody told them, "The one thing which not a man of you will leave over here is himself." Jesus, he wrote, won the victory over temptation because of his inner resources. He had a strong body and disciplined mind; he was not confused and had strong ideals given to him by background and religion. A life with a worthy purpose and a goal will not fall to temptation. Nor will one which remembers that there are a host of people who care. The eighteen small pages closed with "A Young Man's Prayer in Time of Temptation." Part of it said, "Keep before me the memory of those who love me and whose lives are united with my life. May the fires of Thy refining love burn in my heart with a hotter flame than the fires of temptation that burn without." It was Martin's first contribution to the war effort.

He was on the road a great deal during February and early in the month admitted he "was so emotionally exhausted that I was like a bear," and sleeping badly. But he kept going. There were preaching missions, debt reduction campaigns, hours and hours on the train overnight to attend meetings during the day and fill speaking engagements. He spoke to students, to Lions, Rotary, and Kiwanis Clubs, and at the chapel at Garrett Seminary. He preached a Holy Week series for Paul Quillian in First Church,

Houston. Its closing service was, he said, "the greatest service of its kind I ever witnessed."

On the way to Houston, Sally and John stopped over in Dallas for a visit with the Bookhouts, Baileys, Masons, and Drewerys at the farm. Umphrey Lee was there, too. Martin went directly from Houston to Arkansas to see Donald and Ernestine. They were all aware that Donald would eventually be called into the service. Family time was precious so Mary Catherine and John came from SMU to join them.

April 9, 1942, Bataan fell—"a dark day in our American history." The stress was showing. It seemed to be just "one thing after another." A visit with Dr. Sharpe produced a good report on his health except that, once again, he was overweight. A "sour" picture of him appeared in the Christian education magazine and kept him upset all day despite knowing his response was "silly." Tooth trouble, plus the possibility of having a case of trench mouth (the common name for Vincent's gingivitis, the symptom of which is swollen, bleeding gums caused by an infection) forced him to cancel speaking engagements, something he never liked to do. He was treated in Bethany Hospital in Kansas City, got better, and took the train to St. Louis. By May he was able, once again, to walk at his usual pace without chest pain or discomfort and pronounced himself "on the way out of my physical troubles." He preached for Godbold on May 24 in Godbold's new appointment, St. John's Methodist Church in Memphis. While there Martin baptized the Godbold's daughter, Margaret Eleanor, "one of those delightful occasions which make life so abundantly worth living." Uncle Dick Ballard, Cousin Horace Ballard, and other relatives were in the audience, too. John graduated from Omaha's Central High School on June 5. There were 432 in the class. Nearly all of the men in the graduating class, including John, were shortly to be inducted into military service, but until his call came, his immediate plan was to enter SMU in the fall.

Martin assisted Bishops Cushman and Kern in the joint sessions of their annual conferences in Minnesota, June 10-14. Going home he was unable to get a berth and rode in the chair car until he reached Salina, Kansas, at 5:15 A.M. Wartime restrictions on travel, made worse by overcrowding in public accommodations, would complicate his already demanding travel schedule. Arriving in Lawrence, Kansas, he was unable to find a room at the hotel so he went directly to Baldwin City where the Pastor's School was being held at Baker University. Sally was by now happily ensconced in Boulder with Mary Catherine and John, who were enrolled in the summer session of the University of Colorado.

The usual meeting in Chicago of the bishops with the Council of Secretaries of the national boards and agencies, produced "much discussion, few results." Following what was now his custom when in the city, Martin went to an all news movie and then to see *King's Row,* which he judged "impressive." With the family gone, he was able fully to indulge his movie habit. In less than a week he saw Kipling's *Jungle Book, The Magnificent Andersons,* and *Mrs. Miniver.* He was in Chicago when the city underwent a blackout drill, but its lights were not actually dimmed. He was reading H. Sheldon Smith's *Faith and Nurture* and judged it to "help in the clarification of my thinking more than any I have read for many a month."

When his schedule was completed, he was able to join the family in Boulder on August 2, but he admitted feeling guilty about being there in such a world of turmoil. "It seems almost like the part of a shirker to be in this quiet place while so many decisive things are being done in the world." Relaxation and leisure were never easy for Martin and his excessive energy, which enabled him to keep a pace that would have been impossible for most other men, caused him to be restless when out of his routine. He did, however, take time to spend an entire day with John just looking at the mountains. On August 8 he and Sally took a cabin at Grand Lake and enjoyed an evening just talking "before an open fire." "I discover anew," he said, "that my inner peace depends upon my doing whatever is in hand with a purpose, even though it be play or resting." Even when at leisure, Will Martin was as intentional as he was when fully engaged in the work to which he was called. He spent most of the days reading in the University of Colorado Library and writing. He and John spent one night at Flagstaff Hill outside Boulder in order to get up at 3:40 to watch the sunrise and climb over the mountain. It was a "memorable" night. The next day John left for Arkansas to spend the rest of the summer on the farm with Uncle Brice and his family.

Only once during the month were official duties permitted to interrupt the vacation—he was obliged to drive into Denver to hear a report from two persons charging one of his preachers, E. G. Cutshall, with immorality. But as soon as possible he was back in the university library where he had begun reading the writings of Alfred North Whitehead. They proved, he said, to be "a real discovery."

Along with philosophy Martin allowed himself time to indulge his passion for astronomy with the magazine *Popular Astronomy;* and he found time for more reading on his other favorite subject, Abraham Lincoln, too. He read again "The Lincoln-Douglas Debate." During this portion of his life, the study of Lincoln and astronomy almost totally consumed his leisure interests, along with the movies he enjoyed. He saw *Mrs. Miniver* again with Sally. In a fitting celestial tribute, the night his vacation ended there was an eclipse of the moon. He was on the way home to another year of hard work on August 26th—Sally and Catherine stayed until September 2.

Donald was called for military service on September 4, 1942, and was given ten days to report. Ernestine telephoned a day later to tell the Martins he had decided to volunteer for the air corps rather than be inducted. Donald wanted to fly, and when he volunteered he expected he would be ordered into flight training immediately if accepted. As it turned out, however, there was already a backlog of persons available to begin pilot training. He lacked only one semester to complete his degree at Hendrix and the recruiting officer wisely urged him to return to school and graduate since he might have as long as six months before he had to report. Donald went back to Conway, and his parents gladly lent him money to pay his tuition. This change in Donald's situation made unnecessary the trip Will and Sally were planning to Arkansas to see him before his induction. Mary Catherine went back to SMU on September 11, and John arrived from Arkansas to begin his freshman year there.

Despite the war, life in many ways went on normally. The Nebraska Conference opened on September 23. Martin's devotional series was titled "The Christian Ministry of Healing." Roy L. Smith, now editor of the *Christian Advocate,* did the preaching. Smith was sometimes known, in the popular fashion of the time, to entertain his audiences by telling jokes about Eleanor Roosevelt. Sally was an admirer of the President's wife and made it clear to the presiding bishop that she did not intend to tolerate any disrespect of the First Lady or her work from the conference preacher. Smith got the message. With the insight gained from his now considerable experience as a presiding officer, Martin judged it to have been "one of the best conferences I have ever held."

The Kansas Conference, meeting in Ottawa, followed immediately. It was over on October 4, "another load lifted." With only a week in between, the Central Kansas Conference opened in Salina. When it was over, Martin drove to Muskogee, Oklahoma, at 35 miles per hour, the wartime speed limit, and then on to Conway to see Donald and Ernestine at Hendrix. He and Sally watched their son drill with the other students and, perhaps, remembered the time when they allowed Donald to decide whether to join the R.O.T.C. at North Dallas High School. The consequences were much more significant now.

At the end of October, Sally left for Dallas to see John and Mary Catherine at SMU, then went on from there to visit relatives in Arkansas until after Christmas. Ernestine was expecting the Martin's first grandchild and Sally wanted to be on hand for the big event. Martin's time was taken up with a series of district conferences in all of his annual conferences. Because of the vastness of his area, everything involved a great deal of travel and large amounts of time.

With Sally away, a trip to St. Louis in November made it convenient to visit the Ballards in Randolph. "Poverty, squalor & ignorance" was what he saw when he was there. He spent the night with cousin Horace, and walked with him to the bottom field and across the farm. In a quick and radical change of scene, the next day he was taken into Memphis where he met Bishop John Decell at the Peabody Hotel for dinner. The previous August

Godbold had been moved to yet another St. John's Church, this one in St. Louis. He would remain there for the next seventeen years. Godbold was waiting at the station when Martin arrived and in the time available they toured the church facility. The regular meeting of the Board of Missions and the Council of Bishops was held in Cleveland in December. Martin had a difficult time getting a berth, but still arranged to stop over in Chicago long enough for a trip to the planetarium. It turned out to be a wonderful treat. When he proved to be the only one present for the lecture, he was allowed to choose the subject and enjoyed a special presentation on the constellations. He was able to take the lecturer to lunch, too.

By now all travel was adversely affected by the war, and Martin, like other travelers, had to stand in long lines to obtain a ticket; he was often unable to get a berth and had a ride overnight in chair cars. The trains were frequently hours late since passenger traffic was diverted to sidings in order to allow higher priority traffic to pass. After a trip to Kansas to fulfill speaking engagements, he left for Little Rock on December 21 to join the family for Christmas. He waited six hours for this train, was unable to get a berth, and rode a chair car filled with soldiers on leave and their families. Donald met him at the station and took him to the hotel where Sally was staying. John and Mary Catherine came the next day from Dallas, and Christmas was a "good day with all the family together."

Once again he and Sally were living in an apartment in the Blackstone Hotel when they welcomed the new year, 1943. "In a mood of prayer I commended myself and my work to God for the New Year." He also noted something which many leaders have never discovered. "It is possible," he wrote at the end of the year, "for any man to do a great deal of good in the world provided he is not too much concerned about who gets the credit for it."

John was classified 1A by his draft board on January 16, 1943.

Catherine sent her parents the news in a telegram from Dallas. Because of his previous injury, however, it seemed very unlikely he could pass the physical to be inducted. Will and Sally took advantage of Minister's Week at SMU the first week in February for a brief visit with him and Mary Catherine. Costin J. Harrell, pastor of the West End Methodist Church in Nashville, Ralph Sockman, pastor of Christ Church in New York, and Henry Sloan Coffin of Union Theological Seminary were the speakers. February 10, Sally, who was with Ernestine and Donald, called to say that their grandson had been born and was named William Clyde Martin II. Mother and baby were doing well. Martin was not able to get away until the next day, but as soon as possible he was on the train to greet his first grandchild and namesake, who would be called Bill from kindergarten on. An unexpected dividend was meeting Joe Louis, the famous boxer, on the train.

In February there was also a special and unique meeting of the Council of Bishops in Washington, D.C. Arranged by Bishop Oxnam, the bishops spent five days hearing and talking with government officials, labor leaders, and international figures like Madame Chiang Kai-Shek, wife of the Chinese Generalissimo, and President Quezon, who was in exile from the Philippines. The subject was the moral and spiritual elements of a lasting peace and postwar planning to make it possible. All but six of the active bishops were present. As could have been expected, Martin recorded summaries of the addresses he heard in a small, spiral notebook.

The bishops first heard Secretary of the Interior, Harold Ickes, express his concern that America not fall into isolationism, as it had following World War I, but "have a stake, as a nation, in helping to hold the world together." Ickes also told his audience that protective tariffs were "a divisive factor in our international life." Paul V. McNutt, who later chaired the War Manpower Commission, had either failed to read (or understand?) what the bishops wanted to discuss and, Martin reported, "did not give a very enlightening address." McNutt, Federal Security administrator, did tell them that "the spirit of unselfish sacrifice which we appeal to in war time must be relied upon in the post war world if we avoid serious reactions." Former governor of New York, Hubert H. Lehman, director of Foreign Relief, discussed plans for relief efforts and rehabilitation after the end of the war, and affirmed the role the church could play in it. Milo Perkins, administrator of Surplus Marketing, spoke to them on Monday afternoon and William Green of the A.F. of L., C.I.O. addressed them in the evening.

The next morning they heard Secretary of War, Henry L. Stimpson, reaffirm what Ickes had told them the day before, "isolationism is no longer possible." Sumner Wells outlined the problems that he thought would plague the postwar world—order, food, medicine. The morning concluded with an address from Adolph A. Berle, Assistant Secretary of State, who expressed his hopes that the United Nations would be a beginning of "a world fellowship of nations," but warned them of the upcoming difficulty in dealing with the Russians. The author and economist Leo Paswalsky finished the day by discussing trade agreements. Afterward Martin and Charles C. Selecman walked to the House office building to talk with representatives they knew. They saw Howard Buffett.

The next day began auspiciously at the White House where they heard the wife of the leader of China, Madame Chiang Kai-Shek and then President Franklin Roosevelt. Madame Chiang told them, "I have always believed that the church should be interested not only in the after life but in better conditions for living in this world." The president shook hands with each of the bishops and then spoke informally. He had no prepared remarks but talked of how soldiers overseas were attending religious services without regard for denominational affiliation, and urged the bishops to make an overseas visitation. He said Bishop Adna Wright Leonard would be a good one to do it. Later Leonard went and was killed in a plane crash. Roosevelt reminded the bishops that although everyone hates war, "it does appear that some good things come out of war." Frank Knox, Secretary of the Navy, had more directed thoughts for them. Knox told them that the postwar world had to be concerned about two things, (1) establishing security that would protect the freedom of air and ocean, which he believed would have to be shared jointly by the

United States and Great Britain; and (2) avoiding erecting tariff walls. "We must not attempt to impose our ideas upon others" he said, but give them access "to work out their own destiny." Responding to a question about Russia, the secretary said he hoped "she will stay in her borders." Jesse Jones, Secretary of Commerce, reminded them that it would not be good to think too much about the postwar world until the war had been won.

John L. Lewis, the controversial head of the United Mine Workers, was pleased to have been given the opportunity to speak to them. Calling the church "one of our chief anchorages," Lewis chided the bishops about not having done more. Organized labor, he told them, lacked strong leadership and was divided. He said there was no way to help labor without appearing to be partisan, and labor was largely indifferent about the church except in individual cases. President Quezon of the Philippines was introduced by Bishop Lee and told them of the situation in his homeland. "For every American killed in Philippines, there were 6 or 7 Filipinos." The long day ended when John R. Steelman, a labor arbitrator and a graduate of Henderson-Brown College, told them that labor arbitration is largely a matter of applying the Golden Rule.

Secretary of Labor, Frances Perkins, told them "the ideal in economics toward which we strive is that each person may maintain a decent standard of living as the result of his own labor." She then discussed social security legislation, the problems with transportation, and told the bishops, "It is your obligation to see to it that those of us who are in places of governmental responsibility are guided by ethical principles." Following her address the Secretary of Agriculture, Claude L. Wickard, described the postwar problems of feeding the world's growing population.

Between speeches and meetings of the council, Martin managed to see the house where Lincoln died, the Lincoln Museum and Memorial, Jefferson's Memorial, and the National Cathedral. The week, which featured twenty-two addresses plus the fiftieth anniversary celebration of American University, concluded with speeches from Charles W. Elliott, Vice-President Henry A. Wallace, Associate Justice William O. Douglas, and Philip Murray, who was at that time head of the Steel Workers Union and later of the C.I.O.

Murray warned them that at the close of the war "labor will make mistakes and will doubtless be severely criticized but it is seriously trying to find its way through to a better level of living."

Before leaving Washington, Martin was driven to Baltimore to see Mt. Vernon Place Methodist Church, which was built on the site of the Lovely Lane congregation where the Methodist Episcopal Church in America was organized in 1784. He also saw the Mt. Olivet Cemetery where Francis Asbury and other famous early Methodist leaders are buried. But the highlight of the trip for him was a talk with his army buddy from World War I, Sgt. Charles P. "Don" Sohn, who was operating a drugstore in Baltimore. They spent so long together that the bishop missed his train. He was, fortunately, able to catch another one an hour and a half later, and the time with Sohn was well worth the inconvenience. Once again he stopped in Chicago long enough to visit the planetarium. Five days later, however, he looked at all the things he was doing and decided, "I must shorten the line. My interests in astronomy and Lincoln must be restricted. The pastoral function with special reference to evangelism and missions will be my chief field of research and effort." Quoting the words of Robert E. Lee, he affirmed again that "duty is the sublimest word in the English language." It was something he often told his children.

By now he and Sally had discovered the Old English Inn in Omaha and dined there often. It became a favorite place for them both. He spent March 15, 1943, sitting up in the chair car all night to reach Little Rock in time to baptize William C. II the next day. He declared him to have "grown off marvelously." Despite the fact that Bill cried during the ceremony, they got through it in good form. A number of Little Rock friends were present for the occasion to make it even more special. Martin took the train back to Omaha the next day. Donald left a week later on March 22 for Santa Anna, California, to begin pilot training. He was assigned from there to Thunderbird Field in Phoenix, Arizona, for primary flight instruction. Ernestine left the baby with her parents in order to be with Donald as long as possible, and she quickly found a job working for an insurance company in Phoenix. Today the field, once owned by actor Jimmy Stewart and some of his friends, is the campus of the American Graduate School of International Business, known the world over informally as "Thunderbird." One of the original hangars is still standing on the campus.

John Lee was attending summer school at the University of Colorado when he became eighteen and had to register for the draft. As a result, despite being in school in Dallas, all attempts to transfer his registration had been denied and he remained under the jurisdiction of the draft board in Boulder. He was inducted into the army on May 5, 1943, at Fort Logan, Colorado. At the time of his call, both Japan and Germany were on the move and virtually everyone who reported was accepted. In a bizarre turn of events, John was not given a chest X ray in his pre-induction physical nor in any of the subsequent examinations. As a result the injuries received when he was run over by the automobile were never discovered. In fact, John never mentioned his condition to anyone and was thrilled to have been accepted even though he was given a "limited service" classification because he was underweight. A premed major at SMU, he was assigned to the infirmary at Fort Logan and taught to give shots and examine inductees for obvious physical defects. However, by early July, William C. and Sally became concerned about him. "From the tone of J's letters I have become uneasy about him, and having a day to spare, I decided to go see him." After arriving in Denver, Martin went directly to Fort Logan but had a difficult time locating his son. After walking about two miles from the main gate, he managed to find the proper area, made contact with John, who promptly obtained a pass and spent the rest of the day with his father. They enjoyed the day together and Martin left greatly relieved about him. "It was a happy day. He is in good health, physically and morally." They made pictures to show Sally, ate lunch, and talked.

John could probably have remained at Fort Logan for the duration of the war, but he was anxious to be sent overseas and convinced the chaplain to help him. He was first sent to Fort Dodge, near Des Moines, for basic training and then assigned to the station hospital as a night orderly in the surgical ward, an assignment like the one his father had in World War I. When a call for volunteers for an overseas posting came, he signed up. Once again he passed the physical examination even though he had to slump in order to disguise his height and minimize his underweight condition. Military service, which suited Donald to such an extent that he considered making it his career at the end of the war, did not elicit a similar response from John, and he was sometimes in trouble for failure to comply with its rules and regulations.

⚊⚊⚊

Mary Catherine completed SMU and graduated with her proud parents in attendance on May 31, 1943. The next day Martin went along to assist her in finding a job. She was quickly employed as a cashier at the gas company. As was their custom when in Dallas, he and Sally got together with friends from the old Supper Club; Bishop John M. Moore and First Methodist Pastor Angie Smith and his wife, Bess, joined them for the evening. His time in Dallas was brief, and Martin had just reached home when he received word that Sally, who had stayed longer, had discovered a lump in her breast and was scheduled for surgery at the Methodist Hospital on June 16. Changing various appointments, he returned to Dallas on June 14. The surgery was delayed for one day, but when Dr. Thompson operated, the cyst, to everyone's relief, was discovered to be benign. The bishop returned to his duties in Kansas the next day and Sally made a rapid recovery in Dallas. As usual, he rode the train all night to get there. Traveling at night enabled him to do a full day of work when he arrived at his destination. He almost never complained of any difficulty sleeping on the train, even on those occasions when he had to do it sitting up, and flourished under the routine. For men like Martin, the train was a haven providing a place for rest, reading, and catching up on correspondence—an ideal way to travel.

A week later he went back in Dallas to pick up Sally, who had been released from the hospital, and to recommence the job search with Mary Catherine. "She did not make good as cashier at the gas company," he wrote. Together they went to see Lynn Landrum and Harry C. Withers, managing editor of the *Dallas Morning News,* who hired Catherine as a reporter and assigned her to the social page. The Landrum family had been members of First Methodist for two generations and strong supporters of Martin when he was their pastor. Lynn Landrum was one of Martin's closest friends. During the 1950s, however, he became the author of a regular column titled "As I See It." Highly intelligent, Landrum was a conservative, single-minded man who championed the cause of ultra-Americanism during the McCarthy era and became a severe critic of the National Council of Churches during the time Martin was its president. He sorely tried the patience and friendship of the bishop and their correspondence was voluminous. It is ironic that despite being one of the few individuals who properly could be described as an "intimate" friend, Landrum has the distinction of being the recipient of the harshest letter in the entire Martin archives. Mary Catherine worked for the Dallas paper until 1945, when she moved to Topeka where her parents were then living.

After completing his primary flight training in Arizona, Donald was reassigned to Pecos, Texas, for basic flight instruction. Once again Ernestine joined him, this time with Bill. The two of them lived on a converted sun porch in order to be with Donald on the weekends. His rate of military pay was $75 a month.

While in Chicago in July, Martin took time to have a medical exam and was pleased when the cardiogram revealed "no organic trouble." He also attended a National Council of Churches meeting on July 20. In only a few years he was to have a prominent role in its work. A district evangelism rally in Tuscaloosa, Alabama, took him through Birmingham where he spent a moment of re-dedication in the auditorium where he was sitting when his election to the episcopacy was announced. "Five years have been full of rich experiences," he noted. His final sermon to his largest evening congregation in Tuscaloosa, he said, was "not very satisfactory. Must work on this sermon." But he ate watermelon afterward, one of his favorite foods along with ice cream and cantaloupe, and felt better. He was there for almost two weeks. He went home through Memphis and managed to get a room at the Peabody "only through the good offices of bell captain." From there he went on to Little Rock where he met Sally, and together they went to see Bill, who was living with his Matkin grandparents while Ernestine was with Donald. They found him in good spirits, had his picture made, and went shopping for a baby pen. Bill spent the night with them at the hotel. They stopped in Blevins for Martin to preach on Sunday, had a visit with Brice and his family, Uncle Martin, and Aunt Stell, and gathered watermelons and apples. From there they went on to Dallas where they learned the sad news that Pauline Hubbard's brother, a bomber pilot in the Aleutian Islands, was missing in action. Martin helped Mary Catherine open a bank account, tried unsuccessfully to see Dave Lacy and went with the family to Fair Park to see *Babes in Toyland*. Returning to Nebraska alone, Martin arrived in Kansas City at midnight, was unable to find a hotel room, and boarded the next train on to Omaha.

He freed time for another brief trip to see John who was now stationed in Des Moines. He discovered that he seemed "to have incurred the displeasure of the Lt. in command." He also spoke with a Roman Catholic chaplain, Willard Smith, who happened to be from Texas. It was Smith who helped John get posted overseas.

And then it was conference time again. The Nebraska Conference opened at First Methodist Church, Lincoln, on September 8. As usual the cabinet had begun its meetings days earlier. The devotional series that year was titled "Resources for an Effective Ministry." It had three parts: "Jesus Christ Is Lord," "That I May Know Him," and "I Have Learned This Secret." Paul Quillian preached. It was a good conference and only four appointments caused real difficulty.

Martin left at three o'clock the day the conference adjourned to drive with Sally to Topeka to begin meeting with the cabinet of the Kansas Conference, which was scheduled to open in the City Auditorium in Emporia on September 29. It adjourned on October 2, and he and Sally drove directly to Hutchinson to prepare for the Central Kansas Conference. In the three conferences Martin made a total of 797 appointments. "What a relief," he confided to the diary, "to have the appointments made." Back in Omaha, he and Sally moved into Apartment 320 in the Logan Hotel and the next day they drove over to Fort Dodge to spend the day with John. They found him still asleep after being on duty all night but managed to be with him through the afternoon. He was well, and "likes his work as well as we could hope."

In November Martin preached in the Little Rock Conference and managed to stop over in Dallas for a brief visit with Catherine who, he said, "was not going with her boy friend any longer and is planning to devote herself to journalism." He had lunch with Jim and Pauline Hubbard and Frances Bookhout, and talked with Paul Quillian, who was attending the Jurisdictional Co-Ordinating Council, until two o'clock in the morning. Every day was filled with appointments, meetings, travel, and duties related to his office.

John was able to get leave to spend Thanksgiving at home with his mother and father and in the evening they all went to hear Marian Anderson sing in the City Auditorium. In December Martin attended the first meeting of the Board of Missions, held in Buck Hill Falls, Pennsylvania. "Delightful place for such a meeting," he recorded. The board was to make this lovely and rustic place the site of its regular meetings for years and Martin, along with the other members, always enjoyed and looked forward to being there. On that trip he also went to see Paul Robeson in *Otello* at the Met. The music was wonderful, but he admitted to the diary that he did not think Otello was a Negro. He took time to hear theologian Reinhold Niebuhr preach in the chapel at Union Theological Seminary, too.

The Council of Bishops meeting was in Princeton but Martin arrived with the flu and found the "steady grind of routine business" tedious. He barely endured it, but going home he had his first ride in a "bedroom" compartment on the train. That afforded both a comfortable place to rest and time to work on a statement promoting church school attendance that had been assigned to him by the council, but he worried about the expense. The train, however, was late arriving in Kansas City, causing him to miss a scheduled appointment in Hastings—"first appointment I have missed for a long time." Finally arriving home, he was surprised to discover Sally had been in the hospital for three days with a hemorrhage. She was better, but weak.

Donald had by now been moved to La Junta, Colorado, for advanced flight training. The family made arrangements to join him there for Christmas. At the last minute, however, the ration board refused to provide additional gasoline coupons necessary to drive, so Will and Sally hurriedly arranged to go on the train. Donald, Ernestine, and Bill were waiting at the station and took them to their hotel where the first order of business was to purchase and decorate a Christmas tree. In crowded wartime, Ernestine and Bill were sharing a two-room house with the wife of another cadet and her baby and had no room for one. At 10:00 A.M. on Christmas Day, Donald and his family arrived to open presents and eat lunch. The Martins were elated when John was with them. He had caught a ride to Omaha on a special plane and taken a train from there to Colorado. Not having told his parents he was coming, his presence was a delightful addition to their celebration. They had Christmas dinner at the Country Club, and John was on his way back to Des Moines early the next morning. Donald was flying at night so he asked the base chaplain to show Martin the parts of the airbase that were open to civilians. While Donald flew, Will, Sally, and Ernestine talked until 10:30 on New Years Eve and later heard the bells ring in the new year, 1944.

During 1943, Bishop Martin calculated he had traveled 43,979 miles on a variety of always crowded and frequently unreliable forms of transportation. He had been paid a total of $1,160 in honoraria for such extras as the revival in Tuscaloosa. Along with a host of other material directly related to the church and its work, he had read Wendel Wilkie's *One World*, John M. Moore's *Long Road to Methodist Union*, discovered the work of biblical scholar John Knox through his book *The Man Christ Jesus*, and British theologian H. H. Farmer's *Servant of the Word*. He read all or parts of Lloyd Douglas's *The Robe*, Sholem Asch's *The Apostle*, The Lincoln-Douglas Debates, Shakespeare's *Richard III*, the *Merchant of Venice*, and *Toward an Abiding Peace*. Despite inconvenience and sometimes after sitting up all night, he preached 127 times, attended untold meetings, and held three annual conferences, all without any apparent detriment to his health. It was truly an eventful year.

Donald graduated, was commissioned, and given his silver wings on January 7, 1944. Sally was with Ernestine for the ceremony. From La Junta he was sent to Columbia, South Carolina, to be joined with those who would make up his crew and receive additional instruction in the operation of the B-25 medium bomber. His crew bonded in a unique manner, and till this day Ernestine stays in touch with its three surviving members.

The major item before the Council of Bishops at its first meeting in the new year was its "Crusade for a New World Order." The bishops had been organized into teams to speak at rallies, much as they had been during the Methodist Advance in 1939. Martin was assigned to be in Lincoln, Nebraska, Topeka and Wichita, Kansas, Boise, Idaho, Portland, Oregon, Seattle and Spokane, Washington, La Crosse, Wisconsin, St. Paul, Minnesota, Bismarck, North Dakota, and Kansas City. Other bishops on his "team" included Charles C. Selecman, who had two weeks earlier suffered the death of his wife, Ivan Lee Holt, John Calvin Broomfield, Ralph Cushman, and Raymond Wade. Between meetings he read Gordon Seagraves's popular book, *Burma Surgeon*. Martin left Omaha on January 10 and was not home again for twenty days. For virtually all of his career in the episcopacy William C. was gone most of the time and Sally Martin was alone.

In February the regular meeting of the SMU Board of Trustees and the Fondren Lectures, featuring his friend Bishop Bromley Oxnam, brought Will and Sally back to Dallas. They kept up their movies, too, and the Layton Baileys hosted the supper club before he took the 10:30 train for Omaha. In late February word came from John that he was to be sent overseas soon. He was now at Camp Phillips in Salina, Kansas, assigned to the 186th General Hospital. To be on the safe side, Martin did something that he almost never did. He canceled his Sunday preaching engagement to be with John. Martin saw his son on March 5 for what he expected to be the last time until he returned from overseas. Sally found a room at Special Services on the base and remained until he left. John told her she would know he was gone when one evening he did not appear to take her to dinner. When the 186th left, they moved first to Camp Kilmer near New York City for embarkation, providing John his first look at the city, and then went aboard an English vessel for the fourteen-day voyage across the Atlantic. An air raid caused them to divert from their scheduled destination at Bristol to Cardiff, Wales. Eventually they were sent to Fairford, Gloucestershire, to set up and operate a general hospital. While doing concrete work, John was injured and for the first time in his army career was x-rayed. He was ordered to report to the orthopedic clinic but did not comply for fear of being sent home; D-day came a month later and when the wounded began to pour into the wards nothing more was said.

Driving to Topeka on March 24, Martin had yet another narrow escape in an automobile accident. This time a man crossed into the wrong lane and smashed into the car in which Martin was riding as a passenger. Fortunately, nobody was injured, and Martin preached on schedule at eleven o'clock, and met a Parish Relations Committee from Manhattan in the afternoon.

The weather sometimes made travel difficult during the winter months. It was always cold and snow was a problem in both Kansas and Nebraska, but Martin seldom missed an engagement. When he had a choice, he preferred to ride the train to a central location where pastors or superintendents would meet him and take him to his appointments. When the schedule would allow, he spent as much time as possible in the office, but correspondence was always a problem, and he was not infrequently behind. In April he did a preaching mission in Corpus Christi, Texas, which warmed both his spirit and body. He preached to standing-room-only crowds on Easter.

By now Sally and Will had become friends with the widow of a doctor who was their neighbor in the Blackstone Hotel. Mrs. Wood was a kind and generous friend, and after they left Omaha they always took time to see her whenever either was in town. As a token of this friendship, Wood presented the bishop with a signet ring containing a large diamond that had belonged to her deceased husband. A friend in Dallas says that the bishop wore the ring only once, was sharply criticized for its ostentation, and never wore it again. Subsequently, he gave it to Donald, who also wore it only occasionally. The "Wood" ring was passed on to Bill as the oldest grandchild when Donald died in 1991.

General and jurisdictional conference meetings were held in 1944. The bishop's responsibility related to these gatherings began after Easter with the meeting of the Council of Bishops at the site of the General Conference in Kansas City. Much of Martin's time was now taken up with meetings of what came to be known as the Committee of Twenty-one. In anticipation of the General Conference, this committee, chaired by Bishop Paul Kern, had been given the responsibility to create a four-year program for the church. What finally evolved and was presented to the conference for action outlined five main objectives: the first was to continue what began earlier as the Crusade for a New World Order. The bishops had launched it with "The Bishop's Crusade." It was this effort that took Martin into the Northwest for twenty days earlier in the year. A second objective was to raise $25 million in 1945 for world relief and reconstruction. This was to be directed to the literally hundreds of Methodist schools, colleges, churches, hospitals, orphanages, and other institutions that had been damaged or destroyed by the war. The third, to be launched in 1946, was a nationwide evangelistic campaign. Training conferences were to be held, literature prepared, and 200,000 workers organized for an all-out effort to add new members. The fourth was a program of stewardship education that was to continue throughout the entire four years of the Crusade. The last was an effort to address the loss in Sunday school membership and was conceived to address a larger goal of combating the spiritual illiteracy of the American people. The committee was jointly composed of laymen and women and representatives from the Council of Bishops. Bishops Lowe, Hammaker, Jones, Kern, Purcell, and Oxnam served with Martin on this committee. His colleagues in the council also elected him to the Commission on the Course of Study, which set the curriculum for persons wishing to be ordained who had not attended seminary, and appointed him to the church's General Commission on World Peace.

Martin presided at a General Conference for the first time on May 2. "The conference," he said, "was generous in dealing with me and I had no difficulty in presiding. Thanks be to God." And thanks, he might have added, were also due to his knowledge, experience, and skill as a presiding officer. During the conference, he and Sally were honored at a luncheon given by the Nebraska-Kansas Area where there was "large attendance and a warm spirit of fellowship." In the evenings there were visits with the Paul Quillians and other friends and a movie or two. They saw *The Adventures of Mark Twain* and *Jane Eyre*.

When Martin got back to Omaha he checked with an osteopath about the discomfort in his shoulders and neck he had been feeling for three months. The doctor thought it was neuritis and treated it with heat and massage. Nothing actually helped, but the pain didn't keep him from bowling three days later. There is no indication that it might have been related to the earlier problems with his heart. May 21, Martin preached the baccalaureate sermon at Baker University and was given an honorary LL.D. degree at its commencement, his third. Ernestine called shortly afterward to say that Donald expected to receive orders for duty overseas between June 1 and 15. Will and Sally planned to enjoy one last visit with him, but there did not seem to be time before he left. Had they actually known what would happen, however, there was more than enough time to go.

After completing training and additional hours flying the B-25 bomber in South Carolina, Donald and his crew were sent to Savannah, Georgia, in early July 1944, where they picked up a new airplane they ferried via Hawaii and various islands in the Pacific to northern Australia. From Australia, they were sent to Port Moresby, New Guinea, to join the 5th Air Force as part of the 822 Bomb Squadron, 38th Bomb Group.

During the next year, as the Japanese were pushed north or simply bypassed, the 38th Bomb Group followed. From Port Moresby their base was moved to Nadzab, New Guinea, Biak, Mortotai, and eventually to Luzon in the Philippines. Donald flew a total of forty-six missions and was awarded the Air Medal with two Oak Leaf Clusters and a number of other citations. After a mission against the Hatetabako air strip on December 4, 1944, his plane was so badly damaged by anti-aircraft fire that he had to make an emergency "wheels up" landing. Donald flew the plane skillfully and everyone on board escaped without serious injury. Two days later he wrote to Ernestine: "Tonight I am going to prayer meeting. I will say prayers . . . for those of us that fly, that we may return. And for all of us that must fight and kill, I pray that faith will ever be strong; that killing will not make us killers; that we may live to be the creators of beautiful things." On January 31, 1945, Donald and his crew sank a Japanese destroyer off the southern coast of Formosa.

While Donald flew, Martin represented the Council of Bishops at the meeting of the Northeastern Jurisdictional Conference and was back in Tulsa for the South Central Jurisdiction Conference meetings where his old friends Angie Smith and Paul Martin were elected to the episcopacy. During the consecration service William C. joined Paul Stephenson and Paul Quillian in laying hands on Paul Martin. He and Sally were reassigned by the Committee on Episcopacy to the Topeka Area. Although the conferences in the area were not new to Martin, the headquarters was to be moved from Omaha, necessitating their third move since his election to the episcopacy in 1938. Once again Sally was unhappy they were to remain in the northern part of the jurisdiction, but the next day they were on their way to Topeka to look for a house and office space. They made several trips before finding suitable accommodations. Martin's secretary, Miss Kahnt, moved with them.

For the first time in years, the diary indicates a change in Martin's regular routine to include time for what he always described as a siesta in the early afternoon. He seldom neglected it. As was now their custom, they spent the month of August in Colorado. "This is an excellent opportunity," Martin said, "to absorb enough of the sense of permanence of the mountains to keep me steady during the difficulties of the day in the valley." By the end of August he said he was, once again, "prepared to break the ice" on another round of annual conferences.

He started meeting the Nebraska Conference cabinet on August 24. During the time he was away attending these meetings, his car was stolen from the garage in which it had been stored in Topeka. "It was reported to me only yesterday although a check-up showed it had been gone for more than a week," he wrote in the diary. The word must have gone out quickly across the entire criminal element in Kansas to look for a bishop's car to steal since it was likely that it might be weeks before he discovered it was gone. The Nebraska Conference opened at its usual time in the second week in September with a bishop who did not have transportation. Edmund Heinsohn, pastor of University Church in Austin, Texas, preached. Martin's devotionals were titled "This Inescapable Reality," "This Our Foundation," and "Unconquerable Hope." A meeting of the Jurisdictional Executive Committee interrupted moving to Kansas to begin preparation for the conferences, but when the Martins finally arrived, Kansas gave them a warm welcome. Four hundred people turned out for a reception in their honor at First Church, Topeka. Both Kansas conferences went well.

Just before Thanksgiving, Will and Sally purchased their first house, a two story model located on Birchwood Lane. "A vitally important decision to us and one I think we shall not regret." Sally loved the house. She had carefully saved their money through the years in order to be able to make the down payment. Persons who knew Sally remember she had good taste and lovely things. She always took great care to harbor their limited means and made careful purchases to ensure that her selections were of good quality and high style. The same was true of her clothes. Ever since Dallas, she had bought and worn expensive clothes—often from Nieman Marcus—but she purchased many of them on sale and had a limited number of selections. While in Topeka she became well known for her hats, too.

There was the annual and pleasant meeting of the Board of Missions at Buck Hill Falls, Pennsylvania, where Martin was now able to enjoy the company of Paul Martin. They loved to walk in the snow through the woods surrounding the rustic inn. On the way home he stopped in Chicago long enough to be examined by Dr. Latimer, a heart specialist, who found him to be fit. At year's end he resolved to be more regular with his devotions, to walk more, to diet, and to "get the most out of each moment of the day." During the year he had worked hard, traveled widely, and read more than usual. Among the authors he had read were New Testament scholar Frederick C. Grant, theologian Reinhold

Niebuhr, C. S. Lewis, missionary E. Stanley Jones, historian William Warren Sweet, preacher Harris Franklin Rall, and homiletics professor Alfred E. Luccock. He had also read Ted Lawson's *Thirty Seconds Over Tokyo*. Of special interest to him was the fact that Col. Doolittle's raid had utilized the same type of bombers Donald was flying in the South Pacific.

After a trip to Kansas City to consult with the interior decorator and buy furniture, the Martins moved into their Topeka home in early January 1945. It was the first time in their almost thirty years of married life they had owned a home. Sally was overjoyed, but Martin did not spend his first night there until January 29. He described it as "a happy experience," and he and Sally talked until midnight. He did soon learn, however, that home ownership demands a great deal more than living as a guest in a hotel, and the diary soon notes various "chores" about the house, "odd jobs at home," mowing the lawn, and the like. While the snow was still deep on the ground, Martin planned his garden and bought tools for use in spring planting.

<hr />

By 1945, with the prosperity created by the war effort, a new, regular item of local church business was appearing frequently on the bishop's calendar. It was a celebration to mark the retirement of long-standing debts, often incurred during the depression, and symbolized by the burning of mortgages. The next stage in this progression was a flurry of new facilities being constructed after the end of the war and the dedication of new churches, educational buildings, and parsonages.

SMU was no exception to this. At the meeting of the Board of Trustees on February 6, 1945, Mr. and Mrs. J. J. Perkins of Wichita Falls announced a gift of $1,320,000 to the SMU School of Theology. It was the largest gift that had ever been made to a theological school at the time, and in their honor the seminary was renamed the Joe and Lois Perkins School of Theology. Paul and Mildred Martin, who had been the Perkins's pastor in

Wichita Falls, were instrumental in securing this gift. Joe Perkins once said that if all the money they had given could produce one other preacher like Paul Martin, it would have been worth it. The gift provided sufficient funds for the construction of a new quadrangle to house the school and increased the endowment.

Martin was troubled again with chest pain, which he diagnosed as "pleurisy," but the doctor said it was a soreness in the muscles of his chest. He treated it with mustard plasters. At the same time he was having tooth trouble and had to have another extraction. Mary Catherine came to live with them in their new home on March 13, and she soon found work as a reporter on the Topeka *Journal.* Less than a month later Ernestine and Bill joined them, too. Coming home from an engagement the day Catherine arrived, Martin slept through his stop at Topeka and had to spend the night in a hotel in Herrington. "Another travel lesson," he said. Home-owning lessons abounded, too. He had gone to attend the meetings of the Board of Lay Activities in Chicago when "S called to say the basement was leaking and I went home."

John wrote in early April with the dismal news "that he had been sent to the front." Martin recorded that a few days earlier John had written "that he had been demoted but did not tell the reason." This had, in fact, happened two months earlier when he and a friend got what they thought was a two-day pass to Bristol, and returned to learn they were "absent without leave." He was demoted from corporal to private and sent back to the wards. He was also given the choice either to stay in England for basic training as an infantryman or to be sent immediately into combat as a medical corpsman. He chose the latter since he did not want to go through basic again, and was sent to LeHavre. There he moved from one replacement depot to another and eventually ended up in Marburg, Germany. In that process he also met Chaplain Wilson Canafax, who would later officiate at his wedding. He was in Marburg when V-E Day came. Given another physical examination, he was told he should never have been inducted in the first place and assigned to the library. It was there, with plenty of time available, that he read Shapley's *Thesaurus of Science* for the first time and learned of the potential power hidden in the atom. But in spite of his disability, in good army fashion he was not sent home but to Aix-en-Provence to join the 49th Field Hospital, which was awaiting transportation to the Pacific. Fortunately for John, the war was over before they could go.

News of Roosevelt's death came on April 12. Mary Catherine called her parents from the paper to tell them. Like most Americans, they all listened to the radio most of the evening to hear the reports about it. The death of Adolf Hitler was confirmed less than a month later and false rumors abounded that Germany had surrendered. The surrender took place on May 8 and a great service of thanksgiving was held at First Church in Topeka. Will and Sally kept Bill the next evening while Catherine and Ernestine went to a movie, something they liked to do often.

Bishop Martin preached the commencement sermon at SMU and while in Texas filled a week-long preaching engagement in Lufkin, which is near the site of the old Lindsey Springs Lumber Camp at which he had lived with his father. It was also close to Ryan's Chapel and "after a long search we found the grave of my baby half-brother," which was "well marked and kept." He visited Diboll and from there located the site of the Lindsey Springs Camp. "It was all clear to me again as I walked over familiar ground, almost holy ground. A good day." Paul Quillian came over for a good visit, too.

Ever the pastor, when Martin reached home he learned that a parsonage family had lost a son in the war and went immediately to offer his condolences. He later held the memorial service.

Planning was begun in July 1945, for a national conference on the rural church, which Martin would lead in 1947, and while in Chicago for those meetings he went to see Dr. Priest again. After a careful examination the doctor found no problems except for his weight which, he said, needed to be reduced. The tremor he was now experiencing in his hands was deemed by the doctor to be hereditary and unlikely to respond to treatment. He did, however, prescribe some medication.

Early in August the atomic bomb was dropped and it was obvious that the war in Japan was about over. President Truman made it official with his announcement on August 14. With Sally and Catherine, Martin drove into town where they witnessed "a riotous but non-violent celebration." The next day gasoline rationing was discontinued and they went for a long drive to celebrate. His good intentions about dieting were shattered in Mullen where he preached on August 26—"two dinners and an extra dessert."

Once again it was time for the Nebraska Conference, during which Martin was troubled, as he often was, with a toothache. He endured the pain until he could get back to Topeka where his dentist extracted the offending tooth. He preached the next day. He had a cold during the Central Kansas Conference sessions and went to bed when it was over, but he met every session. He did better at the Kansas Conference.

Donald came home on November 10. John was stricken with appendicitis and had to have surgery, but he was discharged when he had acquired the necessary points.

When the Board of Lay Activities met in Chicago, Dr. Priest arranged for a consultation with a neurologist about the tremor Martin had developed. The neurologist examined Martin in the presence of four interns and all agreed the shaking in his hands probably would not get worse, but they told him there was nothing to be done. That evening he went to the opera where he said the great singing "deeply moved me." When he got home he discovered that Donald, Ernestine, and Billy were waiting for him at the station. They stayed four weeks.

Donald was well, and looking for a job. Although his former employment with the Missouri Pacific Railroad in Little Rock was available to him, he wanted to be sure. Donald loved to fly so much he seriously considered remaining in the service, but when he was told that it was likely he would be sent to Europe if he re-enlisted and his family would not be able to accompany him there, he said he had been away from them too long already and accepted his discharge. The holiday was truly a day of thanksgiving in which they all knew they had much for which to be thankful.

After Thanksgiving the program committee for the upcoming National Rural Life Conference in Cincinnati elected Martin its chair, and the trip to attend the Board of Mission's annual meeting afforded him the opportunity to talk again to Dr. Jay about books—always a pleasant experience.

Donald and his family left on December 17 for Little Rock and the first Christmas tree in the new house was lighted the next night. The grandchildren today remember the Martin Christmas trees. The Joe Lees were their guests for Christmas dinner, and after a quiet celebration Martin went to Chicago for the Committee on Missionary Training and the passing of the old year. Among the phrases he determined to remember was one from Bishop Homer Stuntz who, probably after attending the same kind of meeting Martin frequently endured, observed of the speaker, "He was cursed with the fatal facility of speech."

Once again the bishop had managed to read widely during the year—all or parts of thirty-two titles. Among the titles he had read were some standards like Sheldon's *In His Steps*, in which a Kansas newspaper editor resolves to govern all of his actions by seeking the answer to the question, "What would Jesus do?" He read British preacher Leslie Weatherhead's book *The Will of God*, and Quaker Elton Trueblood's *The Predicament of Mankind*. His friend Godbold's dissertation, published under the title *The Church College of the Old South*, was there as was Rockwell C. Smith's sociological study, *The Church in Our Town*. There were fewer classics on the list, but a couple of how-to volumes on reading and thinking also got his attention.

When he got home just after the first of the year, he talked with Governor Landon "about national and international problems" for an hour. Donald, who was still looking for a job, came for an interview with the Goodyear Tire and Rubber Company, but a few days later accepted his old job with the Missouri Pacific Railroad in their right of way division.

The Division of Foreign Missions meeting in February was thrilled to hear Bishop Ralph Ward, who had been a prisoner of the Japanese in China for more than a thousand days. Martin described him appropriately as "a Christian hero." The meeting of the Council of Bishops followed. He read the best-seller *The Egg and I* on his way to the Board of Missions meetings at Buck Hill Falls. When he

reached home after this round of meetings, he preached in Emporia and had to admit, "I was too tired to think vigorously."

John had been shipped to Lyons, France, and then reassigned to
the 1008 Engineers to work in the infirmary. This gave him an
opportunity to visit the French Alps and the Riviera. He sailed for
home near the end of February and after a brief stopover at Camp
Kilmer in New Jersey, and a short visit home on March 15, was
sent to San Antonio where he was honorably discharged on May
14, 1946. His father gratefully noted he "looks well and it was a
happy night in our house. Thanks be to God." John said that on
May 14 he took off his uniform and never put it on again. He spent
the summer with the family in Topeka, working at the Winter General Hospital, where Sally volunteered as a "Gray Lady," and
resumed his education at SMU when school began again in the fall.

In the lengthening days of spring and during the summer, Martin made the rounds of churches in his conferences, burning mortgages, preaching, conducting schools of evangelism, meeting with
the cabinets at various times, and serving as a member of the
search committee established to find a new president for Kansas
Wesleyan College. With World War II now ended and the atomic
age begun, he went with a group to hear scientists talk of the
peaceful uses of atomic energy. "All young men and eager to present use of atomic energy for constructive purposes," he noted.
He, like most Americans, was uncertain about the future. He
wrote to Godbold on August 21: "The atomic bomb leaves us
dazed and blinded and groping into an uncertain future. It seems
that God has said to the race, 'If you are bent on destroying your-
selves there is no need to do it by a slow, toilsome process. Here
is a way by which you can do it quickly and effectively.' " He went
on to tell his friend that he had written to the senators and con-
gressmen from Kansas and Nebraska to voice his opposition to
continuing the draft during peacetime.

Martin gave the Perkins Lectures in Wichita Falls, Texas to large
crowds and visited with old friends there including the Joe Z. Towers family, parents of John Tower, who was later the senator from
Texas. By March he was trying to get a yardman. In June he celebrated the twenty-fifth anniversary of the SMU class of 1921.

That summer the Martins did not make their usual trip to Boulder for a vacation. Martin told Godbold that their home "is so new to us and the weather was so delightful that we did not miss Boulder nearly as much as I thought we would." He took two Sundays off—a major concession—and he and Sally spent a week with Mary Catherine and John Lee in Excelsior Springs, Missouri, and another just driving around eastern Kansas. When they were at home, his mornings were spent in the office reading and keeping up with correspondence, and his afternoons were spent working in the yard and garden. When their "mini vacation" was over Martin had lost ten pounds and declared himself to be "quite refreshed for the work of the fall."

The peace and tranquility of their life at home was disrupted by Mary Catherine's romantic involvement with a man she met at work whom the Martins considered to be an unsatisfactory choice. He was divorced and the father of two children. Despite many entreaties and discussions to dissuade Catherine from maintaining the relationship, Catherine announced she was determined to continue it. When the suitor took another job and was leaving town, Martin went to see him to ask him to discontinue all communication with her, but he refused. Afterward Martin flew to Baltimore to meet and talk with his family for two and one-half hours. Earlier he had written to an attorney in Roanoke, Virginia, to inquire about him when he lived there. Sally gave the information he had gained in Maryland to Catherine, but she was adamant. He and Sally had disagreements about the situation, too. In his diary the bishop is forthright enough to admit that Sally was more willing to accept the situation than he. "S. is fine about it," he wrote. He later said that Sally did not really understand what Catherine was planning. The romance was ended, but shortly after Catherine moved back to California.

After his own annual conferences were completed, Martin went to Lynchburg, Virginia, to be with Bishop William Peele, who had been elected with Martin in 1938 in Birmingham, in the Virginia Conference and then to Columbia, South Carolina, to be with Bishop Clare Purcell in the Upper South Carolina Conference. He had never been in either conference before. While on the trip he also managed to spend three hours in the Library of Congress to read about Lincoln, a sure sign that he had weakened in his resolve to give up his interest in the study of America's Civil War president.

The Virginia Conference was so large Martin said it looked like a General Conference. It is still Methodism's largest annual conference. The trip to Columbia was made more memorable by a visit to the people with whom Donald and Ernestine had lived while stationed there and a visit to the air base out of which he had flown. He also met and heard for the first time theologian Albert Outler, a young member of the faculty at Duke, give "an exceptionally good address" to a group of young people at the First Presbyterian Church. They became friends and colleagues after Outler moved to Dallas to join the faculty of the Perkins School of Theology at SMU.

Martin concluded his visit in the Southeastern Jurisdiction by taking a plane back to Chicago. On the flight he saw the sun rise between Knoxville and Cincinnati and declared it to be "the most gorgeous spectacle I have ever witnessed." From there he went on to the Veteran's Conference in Des Moines and then home. The conference was a first attempt by The Methodist Church to address the needs of returning veterans. He and Sally did their part by purchasing a new Ford for Donald and his family and delivering it to them in Little Rock. Although it was never asked nor expected, Will and Sally were quickly repaid with money Donald and Ernestine had saved while Donald was overseas.

For a great part of her life Sally was troubled with what she and her husband usually described as exhaustion. For a time the doctors thought that she was anemic, but often she simply had to go to bed and was unable to function. She was always a person with a low level of energy, but from time to time her problem became acute. On those occasions she usually suffered from depression, too. In early December 1946 Martin canceled his trip to the meetings of the Board of Missions at Buck Hill Falls in order to take her to Kansas City to consult with a doctor who recommended that she go through a clinic for a complete physical examination. After almost a week of examinations and rest, she was feeling better and ready to be picked up just before Christmas. She was able to go with Will to a debt liquidation service at a church in Kansas City and able to host Donald and his family when they came for Christmas on December 23. Santa brought Bill a new wagon, which he and the bishop delighted in using on long walks together.

❦

Sally and William C. celebrated New Year's Day 1947 by going to see *The Razor's Edge,* which the bishop judged to have "good acting" but "inadequate motivation." Whether he thought the failure was Somerset Maugham's or the movie's he does not disclose. Later that month they added *It's a Wonderful Life, Gallant Bess,* and *The Best Years of Our Lives* plus one other of so little merit it was not even named in the diary. The first week in January he and Sally returned the visit to Donald and Ernestine in Little Rock and Martin preached to his old congregation at First Methodist. He had now begun work on the Willson Lectures, which he delivered March 11-14 at McMurry College in Abilene, Texas. They were later published by Cokesbury Press under the title *To Fulfill This Ministry.* It proved to be a popular and widely read volume, which at one time was on the list of required reading for all persons seeking to be ordained in The Methodist Church. He shared the stage in Abilene with Grace Sloan Overton. In March he paid a visit to Berea College and preached to a full house at Transylvania College—he also worked in a visit to the famous race horse Man o' War on his thirtieth birthday, and went sight-seeing in the Lincoln country. There he saw Mary Todd Lincoln's home and the Lincoln's marriage cabin. He also met the governor and senator from the state.

Mary Catherine made her decision to return to California when it was announced that the Council of Bishops would be meeting in Riverside during the first week in May. Just after Easter, Sally, Mary Catherine, and William C. retraced their route of nine years before and drove to Los Angeles. In Blythe they even stayed in the same tourist court. Once there Mary Catherine quickly found employment as a salesperson at Bullock's Wilshire and a good place to live. They had dinner at the Brown Derby, visited friends in Glendale, made a sentimental trip to see the ocean, toured Will Rogers' home, and took in two movies, *The Late George Apley* and *The Yearling*.

Martin reported to his colleagues on the upcoming Rural Life Conference. It was at this session of the Council of Bishops that Martin was chosen by his colleagues to represent them at the organizational meeting of the World Council of Churches in Amsterdam. In a symbolic way this represented a new direction in his career in which he was to be heavily involved with the "ecumenical movement," and which would lead him to prominence through the presidency of the National Council of Churches.

May 1, 1947, the Missouri Pacific transferred Donald to Coffeyville, Kansas. Because Ernestine was so near the time her second child was due to be born, she and Bill stayed with her parents in Little Rock while Donald made the move. Anne Elizabeth was born on June 24, and the entire family was reunited in Coffeyville in early August. As usual, Martin was on the train en route to a meeting when she was born and he did not actually see and meet her until August 4.

Central Methodist College in Fayette, Missouri, honored the bishop with an honorary degree at their commencement in early June.

The Nebraska Annual Conference had now changed the time of its meeting from the fall of the year to June. In time, all of the annual conferences in The Methodist Church would make the shift. Moving when schools were not in session was less disruptive to its parsonage families, and congregations had reached the place where the economy was good enough that they did not have to depend on the fall harvest to pay out their apportionments. Gerald Kennedy, Pastor of St. Paul's Church in Lincoln, and soon to be elected to the episcopacy at the jurisdictional conference in 1948, was the preacher. Martin's devotionals were on "Neglected Doctrines." He counted among them conversion, Christian perfection, and the Second Coming. The appointments proved to be hard to make because there were few openings at the upper levels. It was Martin's tenth time to preside over that conference. Before the two Kansas Conferences, which continued the older practice of meeting in the fall, Sally, John, and William C. drove for some vacation through the Black Hills to Yellowstone Park. On their way home Martin noted that Kansas and eastern Colorado "were noticeably flat after what we had seen."

One important item of conference business was electing delegates to the General and jurisdictional conferences scheduled to meet in 1948. Martin was fully aware that he probably would be moved to another area and said as much to Godbold in a letter written in November. Godbold had written that he thought it unlikely that anyone from the northern part of the jurisdiction would become a bishop, but Martin disagreed. "A different opinion prevails in this Area." The person in question was Gerald Kennedy and Godbold's prediction proved to be correct. A deadlock developed between Kennedy and Paul Quillian and after many ballots a compromise candidate, Dana Dawson from Louisiana, was elected.

So far as moving was concerned, after protesting "there is no other Area in the Jurisdiction or in the entire Church in which I would be happier than where I now am," Martin expressed his firm conviction that "if we are to maintain the principle of the itinerancy in the episcopacy, eight years is as long as a man ought to stay in one area." That has, in fact, become the rule in The United Methodist Church. "I recently told a man who was talking with me about it," he continued, "that I have a good deal of responsibility for making appointments but that once in four years I turn the business over to others without any effort on my part to influence the decision" (WCM to Godbold, November 19, 1947). Whether the jurisdictional delegates agreed with the principle, he and Sally were in less than nine months to return to Dallas.

8

Ecumenical Leader

—◄▫▥▮▯▰▱▥▮◄—

One of the more prominent features of the religious landscape of the twentieth century was the ecumenical movement. The roots of the movement are firmly planted in the World Missionary Conference, which was held in Edinburgh, Scotland, in 1910. Though by no means the first world conference ever held, it was a watershed for the rest of the century. Under the remarkable leadership of American Methodist layman John R. Mott, then in his forties, and the Scot J. H. Oldham, the conference brought together distinguished church and missionary leaders from across the world. Mott, who eventually received the Nobel Peace Prize, was a central figure in at least four world movements: he was the president of the World Alliance of the Y.M.C.A. and Y.W.C.A., the general secretary and later chairman of the World Student Christian Federation, chairman of the International Missionary Committee, and honorary president of the World Council of Churches when it was formed in 1948. He was eighty-three then. President Woodrow Wilson once described him as "the world's most useful man."

The Edinburgh conference was composed of representatives chosen by the missionary societies of the various churches. David S. Cairns, Martin's teacher at Aberdeen, was a delegate from the Free Church of Scotland. William Temple, who became Archbishop of Canterbury and John Baillie, later one of the presidents of the World Council of Churches, were both ushers at Edinburgh. The assembly, focused as it was on the task of missions, was not in the strictest sense a representative conference of churches. But it was so impressive in the program it presented and the audience it attracted that it was unique. Moreover, the Edinburgh conference was perhaps even more remarkable because of what happened after it was concluded. A continuation committee was formed and began its work to promote conversations between the churches around the world by means of a new quarterly journal, the *International Review of Missions*. It quickly became a premier scholarly journal of the time. The committee also organized a group called the International Missionary Council, which would also serve to bring the various missionary efforts into contact and discussion. J. H. Oldham served as its secretary for many years.

Although the International Missionary Council had in one sense brought the churches together indirectly around their common commitment to missions, it was quickly apparent that the disunity of the church could not be addressed without another group designed to discuss the questions of faith and the doctrinal differences that kept the church apart. Moreover, there were also questions of practice, focused in great measure on the nature of ministry and sacraments, which were also divisive. A new body was conceived and formed to open these issues for consideration. It was called Faith and Order, and the question of the unity of the church was its focus. Although its first world conference was not held until seventeen years after Edinburgh, this gathering in Lausanne, Switzerland, in 1927 showed the potential that it held for Christians everywhere. The invitation to Lausanne was issued to "all Christian Communions." It included Orthodox, Protestants, and Roman Catholics. Bishop Charles Brent of the Episcopal Church in the United States was one of its great leaders. Martin's older colleague, Francis J. McConnell, was involved in the work of Faith and Order from the beginning.

Faith and Order, which was able to hold only one other conference before World War II interrupted its work, became one of the streams that eventually flowed into the World Council of

Churches. The second stream was known as Life and Work, and the name reveals the focus of its concern—the implications of the gospel of the church for the daily life of humanity. Its first conference was held in Stockholm in 1925, and like its sister movement, Faith and Order, it was able to convene only one conference before the world fell into war. It is significant, however, that both the Orthodox Patriarchs of Alexandria and Jerusalem were among the delegates in Stockholm. Life and Work was led in its early, formative years by Nathan Söderblom, the Lutheran Primate of Sweden.

Both Faith and Order and Life and Work held their second meetings in proximity of time and place. The decision to do so was deliberate and both passed a resolution favoring the creation of a council of churches that would take over their work. It was envisioned that the joining of these two movements would fulfill the dream of one, worldwide organization of Christians. The initial planning for what became the World Council of Churches was done by a Provisional Committee before World War II, but nothing further was possible until it was concluded. The letter of invitation to the great organizational meeting in Amsterdam in 1948 was actually written by Archbishop William Temple a decade earlier. In part it said:

> The very nature of the Church demands that it shall make manifest to the world the unity in Christ of all who believe in Him. The full unity of the Church is something for which we must still work and pray. But there exists a unity in allegiance to our Lord for the manifestation of which we are responsible. We may not pretend that the existing unity among Christians is greater than in fact it is; but we should act upon it so far as it is already a reality.

The great organizational meeting of the World Council of Churches was held in the Concertgebouw August 22 through September 4, 1948, in Amsterdam. Membership in the organization was open only to churches and 147 of them became founding members of the WCC in Amsterdam. William C. Martin represented the Council of Bishops of The Methodist Church, and his colleague and friend G. Bromley Oxnam was elected one of the first presidents. He joined Dr. T. C. Chao of China, Geoffrey Fisher, Archbishop of Canterbury, Erline Eidem, Archbishop of Uppsala (Sweden), the Orthodox Archbishop of Thyateira (Western and Central Europe), Strenopoulos Germanos, and Marc Boegner, the president of the Protestant Federation of France, in the office.

The year 1948 began, however, with a much more personal and joyful occasion for the Martins when John Lee was married January 29 to Kathryn Davis in the chapel of the First Methodist Church in Fort Worth. The army chaplain whom John had met first in France, Wilson Canafax, assisted Bishop Martin in the ceremony. Kathryn had briefly visited the Martins in Topeka when Anne Elizabeth was born in June. Martin noted in his diary that "she is a lovely girl and we are glad to have her in our family."

The General Conference in 1948 met in Boston, providing a convenient opportunity for some vacation and sight-seeing in New England. Concord was of special interest since Emerson's writings had long been a favorite of Martin's. "Emerson's philosophy has meant worlds to me," he said after the visit to the town and Emerson's home. Another new experience, which was also immediately a success, was dinner at Durgan Park, the old seafood restaurant in the Quincy Market area. The portions were huge and the dining experience unique. Whenever he was in Boston, if any opportunity could be found, he returned to eat again in Durgan Park. A brief drive across the line into Maine and to Vermont completed Martin's ambition to visit all forty-eight states. Martin presided in a morning session of the General Conference on May 7 and did well despite a heated discussion on whether African Americans were to be represented on the chaplain's commission. At a reception hosted by the Commission on World Service and Finance, he stood in a receiving line and shook hands for an hour and a half. "Too much talking," he complained.

The bishops felt compelled in their Episcopal Address to clarify their position, and that of the denomination, on communism.

"We reject communism, its materialism, its method of class war, its use of dictatorship, its fallacious economics and its false theory of social development; but we know that the only way to defeat it permanently is to use the freedom of our own democracy to establish economic justice and racial brotherhood," they affirmed. The Cold War had begun.

Between the sessions of the General and jurisdictional conferences Martin held his eleventh and last session of the Nebraska Annual Conference. His devotionals that year were on "The Secret of Methodist Vitality"—"Discipline and Freedom," "Mind and Heart," "Personal and Social." Catherine came home for some vacation, and while she was there Donald, Ernestine, and their family drove over from Coffeyville to see her.

Will and Sally took the train on June 21 to El Paso for the jurisdictional conference. It proved to be a tempestuous affair with high drama provided by the episcopal election. Martin's good friend Paul Quillian and his younger Nebraska colleague Gerald Kennedy deadlocked, and neither could gain enough votes to be elected. After many ballots, Dana Dawson of Louisiana emerged as a compromise candidate and was elected. Kennedy was subsequently elected in the Western Jurisdiction, a first in the history of The Methodist Church. In part it was not a dispute about persons but frustration over the relative power of the northern and southern sections of the jurisdiction. The five Texas conferences together had almost enough delegates to elect any candidate. The delegates from Oklahoma, Kansas, and Nebraska, most of whom were formerly part of the northern branch of the denomination, resented this power and influence and joined as a bloc to resist it. Godbold was present at the conference, and when it was over Martin wrote that he "would be glad to have your opinion as to whether the spirit of jurisdictional solidarity was strengthened or weakened by the events of the Conference." He knew the answer.

The boundaries of the episcopal areas of the South Central Jurisdiction were re-aligned, as they are every four years, and Martin was assigned to the new Dallas–Fort Worth Area, which included three conferences, North Texas, Central Texas, and Northwest Texas. His old friend Lynn Landrum wrote an editorial about it on June 30 in the *Dallas Morning News*. "Will Martin Comes Back to Dallas" was the headline. After recounting Martin's earlier work as a pastor in the city for any readers who might not know of him, Landrum concluded, "The return of this outstanding religious leader to the city is gratifying not only to the friends and constituents of Bishop Martin, but also to the city generally. He is a welcome addition to the company of great spirits which make Dallas more than a market place for material gain." Landrum, a staunch conservative who wrote a regular column in the paper, became considerably less enthusiastic and more critical of the churches and Martin in the days ahead. But he had not overstated the genuine pleasure friends and Methodists had in receiving Will and Sally Martin back into their town. They were soon meeting again with the supper club, although Martin had to admit "we all looked a lot older," and he resumed his membership in the Chi Alpha discussion group as well.

The Martins celebrated their thirtieth wedding anniversary on July 1, put their house on the market the next day, and sold it to Dr. Henry Blake on the third. Suitable housing was scarce in the years immediately following the close of World War II. Martin made a special trip to Dallas on July 11 to preach at First Methodist and it took half an hour for all who wanted to greet him to get through the line and shake his hand. John and Kathryn were with him. On July 21 a telegram came from Paul Kern saying that the committee planning the next four years of the Crusade for Christ had elected Martin as its director. "I was greatly troubled by the message," Martin wrote in the diary, "and if there had been any honorable way of escape I would have taken it. Messages from others have arrived during the week. May God help me to do it well."

At the same time he was packing his Topeka office to move, Martin was making final revisions on the manuscript for *To Fulfill This Ministry*. He sent it off to Cokesbury the day he and Sally moved out of their house, and took in a movie to celebrate. The two of them took the train on July 29 for New York to attend committee meetings of the new "Advance for Christ and His Church," and to board the *Queen Elizabeth*, which would take them to Europe for the opening sessions of the World Council of Churches.

Bishop John M. Moore died on July 30. Will and Sally arrived in New York in time to hear Dr. McCracken preach at Riverside Church and to visit the United Nations meeting at Lake Success. They also saw Basil Rathbone in *The Heiress* and paid a visit to Radio City. The *Queen* was opened for boarding the morning of August 6 and she sailed in the early afternoon. By evening the bishop had lost his dinner and "was feeling unsteady." He went to bed early and slept "fitfully," but Sally was fine. The next day he was better and fell into conversation with Dr. Ischlongski, a "brain physiologist" from New York. They spent many interesting hours together during the voyage. He was a "humanist, but not a materialist," Martin said. He and Sally were seated at a table for six with Henry P. Van Deusen, president of Union Seminary in New York, theologian Reinhold Niebuhr who was a member of the Union faculty, Georgia Smith, and Mary Addison. "The conversation," Martin reported, "went slowly." Bishop Ivan Lee Holt was in first class, but came down often to talk. Other members of the various delegations were on the ship, too. On Sunday the captain, despite having available the services of a boatload of church dignitaries and luminaries, read the service of morning prayer according to the rite of the Church of England. Throughout the pleasant voyage Martin admitted he was eating too much but "getting lots of sleep."

They arrived in Southampton on August 11 and took the train to London. It was Sally's first experience out of the country. A British Methodist preacher John (Jack) Waterhouse met them at Waterloo Station and took them to his home for lunch. Later he showed them Wesley's Chapel and St. Paul's Cathedral. He was to serve as their host in London and later to visit them in the United States and allow them to return the favor. They did the usual sights in the next few days including a trip to Oxford and Stratford on Avon. In Cambridge they paid a visit to the home of their friend Gipsy Smith. Although in the few days available to them they managed to get as far north as York, they did not have time for a visit to Aberdeen. After ten days in England, they took the train for Harwich and the boat to the Hook of Holland. Once there they rode the train to Amsterdam arriving on August 22. The delegation from The Methodist Church in the United States was assigned to the Hotel Polen, which Martin found to be with "small and limited conveniences but restful." Brothers Donald and John Baillie from the Church of Scotland, the Archbishop of the Orthodox Church in India, and Quaker leader Elton Trueblood were there, too.

The opening session was in the Nieuwe Kerk at three in the afternoon. John R. Mott and D. T. Niles, Methodist leader in Ceylon, spoke to the 351 delegates. The overall theme of the gathering was "Man's Disorder and God's Design." The next morning Swiss theologian Karl Barth and Cambridge New Testament professor C. H. Dodd spoke. Princess Juliana and Prince Bernard of Holland were present for the session. The next evening the delegates were treated to a ride through the canals of Amsterdam, which were lighted for the first time since the beginning of World War II. The meeting of the World Council of Churches coincided with the Jubilee Celebration and the coronation of Juliana as queen, so the city was full of distinguished visitors in addition to the 1,500 persons who had come for the church gathering. On August 27 delegates and their spouses were guests at the royal palace for a reception where, Martin said, "the spiked punch flowed freely," of which it can be assumed most of the delegates, save perhaps the Methodists, partook liberally. The Jubilee Pageant was held on August 31 in the Olympic Stadium. In attendance were 30,000 people, including the royal family, "a great spectacle."

Martin was assigned to Section II, "The Witness of the Church in God's Design," and Committee II on policy. John A. Mackay, the president of Princeton Seminary, presided over the section and the famous German pastor Martin Niemoeller and Scottish theologian John Baillie were among its members. The sections met in the morning and the committees in the evening. George K. A. Bell, Bishop of Chichester in England, presided in the committee. After the World Council was organized, Bishop Bell was elected chairman of its Central Committee and W. A. Visser 't Hooft was named its general secretary.

The sessions filled every day but sometimes for all the delegates took second place to sight-seeing in Amsterdam and its environs. The Martins visited the museums in town and made a daylong trip to Vollendam and the Isle of Marken. They were delayed getting back and Martin missed an evening session. The meeting closed September 4, with the Archbishop of Canterbury preaching at the final worship service.

The Martins left for Paris on the 5:12 P.M. train. After checking in at the Claridge Hotel, they went to see Notre Dame and the Louvre in the morning and went out to Versailles in the afternoon. The next day they were present for the relighting of the fire at the tomb of the unknown soldier. Their last day there was spent shopping, taking a carriage ride, and attending the opera, *La Boheme* in the evening with Bishop Jim Baker. Sally always loved the opera. The boat train took them to Cherbourg where they went aboard the *Queen Mary* at six o'clock in the evening, September 9. As usual, Martin was unsteady after they sailed and sick by morning. He managed, however, to make the meeting of delegates. He was feeling better on September 12, and enjoyed talking with Roswell Barnes of the National Council of Churches and Clarence Tucker Craig, professor of New Testament at Yale, who would later become Dean of Drew Theological Seminary. They docked in New York in the early afternoon the next day and went directly to a hotel for the night. After two more days of follow-up meetings, with time in the evening to see *Annie Get Your Gun* ("wholesome amusement except for risque lines in song"), Will and Sally caught the night train to Dallas on September 15. They each had a roomette "and plenty of time to read."

John and Kathryn were at the station with Paul and Elizabeth Stephenson to meet them. Martin went directly to his office in the Cokesbury building at 1910 Main Street, where he met Ruth Greer, his new secretary. That evening Will and Sally moved into an apartment in the Stonleigh Hotel in the part of the city known as Oak Lawn, not too far from the Rawlings Street parsonage in which they had lived for so many years, and began the next phase of their lives in Dallas.

Martin's new duties as director of the continuation of the Crusade for Christ, now known as the Advance for Christ and His Church, entailed more meetings and travel, and he now began to fly rather than ride the train to many of them. He and Sally decided a new automobile was in order and purchased a maroon Chrysler "at a price higher than we ever thought we could pay." It took him and them on a round of church, parsonage, organ, and electronic chimes dedications, groundbreakings and cornerstone laying as the phenomenon of America's postwar church growth washed like a flood over the Dallas–Fort Worth Area. Fortunately, the Council of Bishops at their last meeting in December 1948 raised the allowance for automobile travel from 5 to 7 cents a mile. At the same meeting they also authorized reimbursement for air travel for the first time.

Martin's new work in the Northwest Texas Conference, which stretched from the Oklahoma border south to Abilene and to Midland in the west, carried him into parts of the state he had not known before. But as he always had, he was soon making his rounds of the churches and getting acquainted with pastors and congregations. He liked the conference and the people he met, but by Thanksgiving he had to admit he was "very tired." The holiday was spent with Donald and his family, who were still living in Coffeyville, Kansas. Just after Thanksgiving, the Council of Bishops met and Martin spoke to the newly elected bishops during their orientation program about making appointments. It was something he was called on regularly to do.

By now he was active in the work of the National Council of Churches and meeting with them when he was in New York. This was soon to be a significant part of his ecumenical experience.

He and Sally purchased a duplex on University Avenue, about a mile and one-half due west of SMU, in mid-December. They were both pleased with the arrangement. Because the bishop was gone so much of the time, Sally, who was afraid, chose to live in the upstairs of the house. The rent they received from the lower portion helped with expenses. The residence at 4223 University Boulevard still stands in a fashionable part of University Park although it is now a different color than it was when the Martins owned it. It was a spacious, comfortable house that served them well through the years and is remembered fondly by the Martin children and grandchildren. The Christmas tree always stood in the front window. The purchase price was $42,500 and they were able to make a $17,000 down payment on it with money from the sale of the house in Topeka. Sally continued to manage the family finances and years later said she doubted they would ever have been able to afford a house if she had not saved for it. It was always highest on the list of things that she wanted them to have. The same day they closed on the house, Will and Sally went to take the driving test for a Texas driver's license. He failed the first time, but passed two days later. They spent their first night in the new house on February 25, 1949.

Always one to look for new ways to do things more efficiently, such as learning to type, Martin purchased a "soundscriber" recording machine to help with his correspondence. It was, however, shortly out of order.

Paul Quillian had been ill with heart trouble for some time and after the jurisdictional conference had suffered a mild heart attack. When Martin saw him shortly after the first of the year he did not believe that Quillian looked well and concluded he was making a slow recovery. On March 28 he died. Martin noted the day in his diary by saying, "My dearest friend in the ministry had gone from the earth. . . . What a lonely feeling to be bereft of a brother whom I have loved for these twenty-six years." He and Sally immediately got in touch with Eula and hurried to be with Quillian's daughter, Thelma, the wife of Robert Goodrich, the pastor of First Methodist in Dallas. The funeral was held two days later in Houston. Martin did the prayer and the committal at the cemetery.

The session of the Northwest Texas Conference was the first over which he presided after being assigned to the new area. It met at the Polk Street Methodist Church in Amarillo. He repeated the devotional series he had used in his last conference in Nebraska. John graduated from SMU the last day of May and the North Texas Conference opened at First Church, Dallas, June 1; it was followed immediately by the Central Texas Conference, which met in Fort Worth. On the way to Fort Worth Martin was, he said, "unjustly arrested on charge of running a red light." The good news was that when the conference was over Donald and Ernestine came for a visit bringing Billy and Anne with them. They paid a visit to the zoo and went to a baseball game.

Dr. David Carter, an old friend from First Methodist, gave Martin his annual physical during the summer and pronounced him, as usual, overweight but in good health. Sally was not feeling well, troubled again with anemia and lack of energy. She was hospitalized for tests and remained there two weeks, most of which time he was away. Nothing definitive was discovered so they continued with more tests, including a colonoscopy and a bronchoscopy. Again, nothing was discovered and it was determined that her anemia would have to be treated with diet and liver injections. They never completely solved the problem.

⊸⊸⊸⊸⊸

Summer vacation was spent appropriately on a guest ranch at Fort Davis in far west Texas. Pauline and Dave Lacy went with them. It was a restful time, during which they attended part of the revival at the historic Bloys Camp Meeting. They ate good "ranch" food, rode horses, walked in the moonlight, read, and rested. All too soon, however, it was back into the fall schedule of meetings and speeches.

Martin's role in the mass meetings related to the Advance carried him to Wisconsin, which he greatly enjoyed, and increased the number of appearances and speeches, some of which were broadcast. Two meetings were held in every annual conference in the church in September and October 1949. When in Chicago he still managed to get to the planetarium and also to the movies. He saw *Home of the Brave* twice and parts of *Gone with the Wind* twice. It was a favorite of his and Sally's, and during their lifetime together they saw it a dozen times or more.

A portion of his duties with the Advance required the creation of a series of volumes designed for daily study and meditation to be used in conjunction with the mass meetings led by the bishops. He and Bishop Oxnam shared joint responsibility for them and the copyright is in their names. The title of the series is Our Faith and each pocket-size volume is separately titled and authored. The individual authors are not, however, identified, but each manuscript was reviewed by the Council of Bishops. Among the volumes are essays on the Bible, Christ, God, Holy Spirit, Immortality, the Kingdom of God, Prayer, and Love. Each is bound in a hardback format about fifty pages in length. The introduction says that for fifteen minutes each day the volumes are to be studied by the entire church.

Other features of the Advance were projects adopted by individuals, congregations, and conferences for support. These Advance Specials were, as Martin told the Council of Bishops in his report to them at the end of the first year, a way to "specialize" and "personalize" the missionary program of the church. These could be building projects, churches, schools, hospitals, missionaries, scholarships, and relief work at home or overseas. An Advance committee was established in every annual conference and the general administration and oversight of projects were given to a special committee in the Division of Home and Foreign Missions. Every congregation in The Methodist Church was expected to accept the support of an Advance Special equal to its benevolence budget. A great offering taken during the Week of Dedication was divided between Foreign Missions, Domestic Missions, and Overseas Relief. Since this money was given over and above the usual contributions, it was estimated that an additional $2 million had been received for missions in one year. It was a milestone in the life of The Methodist Church.

The bishops held a timely and informative special meeting in New York City at the end of 1949 on the subject of "Contemporary Ideologies." The growing hysteria surrounding the communist threat and the Cold War had already begun to involve the churches. A year earlier, at their December 1948 meeting, they had passed a resolution to protest a report issued by the House Committee on Un-American Activities titled "100 Things You Ought to Know About Communism and Religion." The impression created by the report was that America's churches had been infiltrated by communists. Groups like the Y.M.C.A., Epworth League, which since unification in 1939 had not existed, the Federal Council of Churches, and the World Council of Churches were identified as having been targeted for infiltration. Number eighty-two in the list of things to know asked, "Do Communist propagandists ever actually get before church groups as speakers?" The answer was: ". . . the head of the Communist Party, on one occasion at least, spoke at Union Theological Seminary in New York City." McCarthyism was about to take its place in the battle to win the Cold War.

To prepare and inform themselves about communism, its relation to the church, and its threat to the democratic way of life, the Council of Bishops held a special meeting in which they set aside four days to hear experts on the subject. They heard Arnold O. Wolfers, Master of Pierson College at Yale; Sidney Hook, professor of Philosophy at New York University; Sherwood Eddy, Y.M.C.A. leader; Louis Fischer, writer and author; John C. Bennett, professor of Theology at Union Seminary in New York; theologian Reinhold Niebuhr, Bennett's colleague at Union; Paul Anderson, the senior secretary for the Y.M.C.A. in Europe; Matthew Spinka, professor of Church History at Hartford Seminary; Norman Thomas, editor of the *Saturday Review* and sometime-candidate of the Socialist Party for mayor of New York City, governor of New York and president of the United States; Pitirim A. Sorokin, Russian-born professor of Sociology at Harvard; Max Lerner, also Russian, a professor at Brandeis and columnist for the *New York Post*. It would be hard to imagine a more dazzling array of talent and learning than Oxnam assembled to speak to his episcopal colleagues. They spoke on topics such as "The Communist Challenge and Christian Strategy" (Bennett), "Communism as a Christian Heresy" (Niebuhr), "Marxism, Socialism and Communism" (Thomas), and "The Roots and Ways of Resolution of the Russian-American Conflict" (Sorokin).

There was good reason to be prepared. In 1950 John T. Flynn's book *The Road Ahead*, appeared. It contained the chapter "The Kingdom of God," which singled out for special criticism the Federal Council of Churches, the World Council of Churches, theologian John Bennett, Bishop G. Bromley Oxnam, and missionary leader E. Stanley Jones. The work was so full of errors that the Council of Bishops felt compelled at their April 1950 meeting to condemn it and support their colleagues. Later they attempted to clarify the status of the controversial "Methodist Federation for Social Action" to The Methodist Church and eventually requested it to drop the name "Methodist" entirely since it was not an authorized agency of the church. A copy of these resolutions was sent to every minister in The Methodist Church.

On a more positive note, Donald called to announce the arrival of Margaret Catherine on December 18, 1949. After the Christmas party in Waco at the Methodist Home for orphaned children as guests of the J. J. Perkins, which became an annual event for the Martins and the Lacys, and Christmas Day in Dallas with John and Kathryn, they headed for Coffeyville to meet the new arrival. The second week in January 1950 they took the train to California to see Catherine. They always enjoyed California and took time on this trip for an extended visit to San Francisco. He preached at Glide Memorial Church on Sunday morning "to a handful."

At their April meeting, the bishops had to deal with yet another problem related to the Methodist Federation for Social Action. Stanley High, one of the editors, had published an article in the February 1950 issue of the *Reader's Digest* titled "Methodism's Pink Fringe." The *Digest* also published a condensed version of Flynn's *The Road Ahead* as the lead article in the same issue. To make matters worse, summaries of High's article were circulated to newspapers before its publication, and Oxnam wired the bishops late in January that the Council of Bishops or its executive committee needed to be authorized to make a statement in response. The General Conference is the only organization in the church that has the power to speak "officially" on its behalf.

Martin, now a member of the executive committee, was in California at the time. High, a Methodist and graduate of Boston University's School of Theology, begins the article by quoting from the masthead of the Methodist Federation's *Social Questions Bulletin*:

"The Federation rejects the method of the struggle for profit as the economic base for society and seeks to replace it with social-economic planning to develop a society without class or group discriminations and privileges" (*RD*, February, 1950, 134). He went on quoting Jack McMichael, executive secretary of the Federation, that its goal is not to "patch up" but "fundamentally to transform an economic system which has only been able to 'solve' the acute moral and social problem of mass unemployment by an economy for war." High briefly reviewed persons who had spoken at Federation sponsored events and quoted statements like the one by Harold J. Laski, "Russia is not the greatest threat to peace, it is the United States." The author said he assumed such views held by only 5,800 members of the Federation to be counter to those of most Methodists, but noted that the current president of the Federation is a bishop, "as were his two predecessors." Five of six vice presidents were also bishops; other prominent church leaders filled its offices and rolls. Sixteen bishops were members. Its offices were in the Methodist Building at 150 Fifth Avenue in New York. High's article, which created a sensation, dealt with the Methodist Federation in relation to some of its political statements and noted the disproportionate number of church leaders who had been members through the years despite the lack of its "official status" as a Methodist agency.

High was not the only one who was concerned. Some bishops, like Frederick Leete and Charles Wesley Flint, were quick to point out that of the thirteen new bishops elected in 1948, nine had been members of the Methodist Federation when they were elected. Three of seven elected four years earlier were also members. Leete asked Martin the obvious question in his letter of February 19, 1950:

> You have seen the check-up of active bishops as to membership, of course. Quite a majority is on the outside, but a good deal is being made of the fact that 2/3 of the bishops elected last time were Fed. members *before* election. It is remarked that it is strange that less than 9000 members of an "unofficial" body furnished more than twice as many new bishops as did the rest of well-toward 9 million Methodists.

He went on, "When we say that the Federation is not Methodist or official do we remember that not only are all kinds of Methodist officials in its groups, that its secretary is a Methodist preacher under episcopal appointment to the 'unofficial' organization he serves and that many of the Conferences recognize and endorse actions of the body as a whole, as well as its own groups? Quite too official to please masses of our membership in all parts of the country."

Leete was correct. Laypersons and clergy alike, especially in the South and Southwest, were upset by the article, and almost every bishop in the church, including Martin, felt compelled to issue a statement on the subject. Oxnam, with the assistance of New York Methodist lawyer Charles Parlin, prepared a response which the *Reader's Digest* refused to publish. It was later circulated in pamphlet form. The bishops as a whole, however, were so divided in their opinions about the Methodist Federation, it seemed unlikely to Martin that the council would be able to agree on a statement. Some of them, in fact, thought that since the council earlier had taken pains to distance itself from the Federation, declaring it not to be an "official" agency of the church, it would be best to make no statement at all. But they did, and Martin was greatly relieved when they were able to reach a consensus, although the trouble caused by High's article was far from over; nor was it the last publication to appear on the subject of the church and its relation to Communism.

Lynn Landrum, Martin's local nemesis, expressed himself fully in the *Dallas Morning News,* and Martin eventually went to talk to him and his editor at his office about his harsh criticism of the church. Although he came away thinking they had a satisfactory conversation and "good will come of it," Landrum did not change his mind and he did not stop writing on the subject. One acquaintance of Martin's wrote to tell him that Landrum was "foolish" when he was in Austin and "an even bigger fool" since he had returned to Dallas. After the appearance of "Methodism's Pink Fringe," Landrum on February 8, 1950, editorialized about the Methodist Federation. He began by speculating that in a group so large as the Methodist Church, it would be unlikely that the Communists would overlook them. "As a matter of fact," he wrote, "Communists have been very active within The Methodist Church." Quoting a report on "Un-American Activities in California" (1949), Landrum cited Harry F. Ward and Francis J. McConnell as having admitted "co-operation with the Socialists and the Communists." He then cited the organizations, designated as "Communist front" by the House Un-American Activities Committee, to which Bishop McConnell had belonged. His list filled three column inches of space. In his characteristic style Landrum said he did not "charge" McConnell with being a Communist, he was just amazed that "a bishop of any church should have so much spare time on his hands." He closed the editorial with a quotation from *Classmate*, a Methodist Sunday school publication, in which Joseph Stalin was praised, and with a scriptural reminder that "the children of darkness are wiser in their generation than the children of light." Many more Landrum blasts were to follow.

In the midst of all the turmoil, Martin's life and work somehow went on uninterrupted. All three of Martin's annual conferences were now meeting in the summer. The Northwest Texas Conference met first, opening on May 24 in Big Spring; the North Texas Conference followed in short order. By June 11 all three had been completed and he expressed his relief and gratitude for having had the strength to get through them. Appointments were hard to make in Northwest Texas and North Texas, and a preacher in the North Texas Conference attempted to force him to rule on a question that he had previously raised with the bishop in private, but such is the stuff out of which annual conferences are normally made. A more serious matter arose when four persons came from Waco to discuss an incident of alleged cruelty to children at the Methodist Home. Martin agreed that inquiry should be made.

He was in Amarillo to speak to young adults when news came that the armies of North Korea had invaded South Korea. There is no mention of the event that day in his diary. The summer afforded more time for movies, along with a trip to enjoy the baths in Mineral Wells, a town not far from Fort Worth. The Martin's friends Pauline and Dave Lacy went with them. There were also trips to New York for meetings on the Advance, the usual lectures at Mt. Sequoyah and, once again, a month in Colorado. John and Kathryn were there, too. The usual schedule while on vacation was for Martin to get up early and read until Sally got up for breakfast, and then to go to the university library until noon. In the afternoons he walked, and in the evening he and Sally often took in a movie. Sally was not feeling well, suffering again from low energy, depression, and what Martin now described as "crowd-phobia." Some tense moments between them were recorded, and the vacation failed to restore her to complete health. Mary Catherine came for a week, and all of them went to Central City to the Opera House to see Maurice Evans in *The Devil's Disciple*. It was, the bishop said, "rare entertainment." They were home by August 26.

Sally came down with an infected jaw just before Thanksgiving; it was only the first of a series of disasters that came with the holiday. On November 22 they started in their car for Coffeyville to spend Thanksgiving with Donald, Ernestine, and the grandchildren. Just outside of Wagoner, Oklahoma, a truck entered the highway from a side road and struck them broadside. The car following was unable to stop in time and hit them from the rear. Sally's ankle was injured and the car was disabled. Since they were unable to continue, they had to wait until the next day when Ernestine came to take them to Coffeyville where, in spite of the wreck, they had a good day. On November 25 they rode the train back to Wagoner, picked up the car, and drove to Muskogee for the night. When they got home, Sally's tooth had gotten worse and it was necessary for the dentist to scrape her jawbone to remove the infection. She was quite ill. It was also necessary to get a loan from the bank and purchase a new car. This time they decided on a DeSoto, which was delivered on December 1.

The SMU School of Theology Committee used the meeting of the Council of Bishops just after Thanksgiving as a convenient place to meet. Umphrey Lee, SMU's president, and Mr. Rule, the only members who were not bishops, joined them in New York. The Smith brothers, Angie and Frank, Dana Dawson, and the two Bishops Martin composed its membership. The subject of the meeting was the appointment of a new dean, and all indications were that Merrimon Cuninggim, son of William C.'s old professor of Christian education, would be named. Cuninggim, a Rhodes scholar and Yale graduate, would replace Eugene Hawk and begin a new era in the school thanks in part to the generosity of the Perkins family and J. S. Bridwell. After the SMU meeting, Martin heard Norman Vincent Peale do some "thin" preaching, saw *King Solomon's Mines, The Lady's Not for Burning, Kind Hearts and Coronets,* and *Cyrano de Bergerac* before moving on to Buck Hill Falls for the annual meeting of the Board of Missions. His children remember how often they would be surprised to discover he had already seen a movie or play when one was mentioned. On the way home he stopped again in New York and saw the Christmas show at Radio City Music Hall.

On December 19, dean candidate Cuninggim came to Dallas for interviews. He made a favorable impression and his appointment was recommended to the Board of Trustees. "I am convinced a good choice has been made," Martin said. Much of Martin's time was now occupied in trying to help his church address the issues around the relation of the sacraments to ordination. His concern was perhaps heightened by his experience in the dialogue of the ecumenical movement. As was often the case with Methodists, the theological issues were relegated to the background in their need to solve a practical problem. The question was whether persons who had not been ordained, but were serving local congregations under appointment from a bishop, might, under special circumstances, be allowed to administer the sacraments to their parishioners. The concession had, in fact, been granted for years in The Methodist Episcopal Church, South, and for a period of nine years after The Methodist Church was organized the southern practice was followed there, too. In 1948 the church voted to return to a more orthodox practice. Now there was a movement to urge the next General Conference, in 1952, to change the rule and allow the exception once again. Martin was opposed. He thought it diminished both the significance and need for ordination. "If merely by vote of an Annual Conference an unordained man can be authorized to administer the sacraments within his parish, why not, by the same process, authorize him to administer the sacraments everywhere?" He wanted to know if congregations would remain satisfied never to have an ordained person as their pastor.

In a paper he drafted on the subject he made some suggestions about what might be done to encourage and speed up the process leading to ordination: (1) shorten the probationary period; (2) create an *ad interim* group that would elect persons to orders and ordain them between sessions of the annual conferences; (3) help "supply" pastors complete their studies and become ordained; (4) continue the rule allowing baptism to be administered by unordained persons for another four years; (5) extend the present methods so that the sacrament of the Lord's Supper can be administered in every congregation by ordained persons who may be retired or in special appointments, such as district superintendents or chaplains. He had "a refreshing discussion" of the issue with Albert Outler, now a member of the faculty of the Perkins School of Theology, and was "pleased to find him on the right side." The bishop was slightly mistaken in his judgment, for when dealing with Professor Outler one always joined him on the "right side." The Committee to Study the Ministry, created to make a recommendation to the General Conference, determined at its meeting after Thanksgiving that the sacrament should only be given by ordained persons.

———

In January 1951, Martin met for the first time the new librarian of the Bridwell Library of the Perkins School of Theology. Decherd Turner was young, bright, and unorthodox, and for more than three decades he provided the genius and vision to create a unique collection of rare books and incunabula. He also became a good friend of William C. Martin. When in 1960 Martin was assigned the task of drafting the Episcopal Address, Turner went back to read every previous address and offered good advice on subjects and resources.

The new buildings composing the quadrangle of the Perkins School of Theology, except for Selecman Hall, which was built later, were dedicated on February 8 during Minister's Week. It was truly, as Martin said, "a great day." Eight bishops were on hand for the dedication of the Bishop's Room in the library and the formal opening of the chapel. At the end of the month he and Sally took Eula Quillian, Paul's widow who was now in Dallas serving as supervisor of Martin Hall on the Perkins campus, to see some property she owned and to tour the Rio Grande Valley. Business was combined with pleasure, which included having breakfast with Ty Cobb and his mother in McAllen.

Ruth Greer resigned her position as Martin's secretary in order to get married, and Mildred Craghead (Allen) took the job in her place. Almost every Sunday featured another dedication of a church building or parsonage. The Council of Bishops held its spring meeting at the Grand Canyon, and Sally went on to Los Angeles from there to spend some time with Mary Catherine. She always loved being in California. While there she would shop and enjoy the restaurants, as well as Catherine's company. It was good for them both.

When the round of annual conferences was finished, complicated by tooth trouble again, Will and Sally drove out to nearby Lake Dallas "and spent the day on a bluff overlooking the lake . . . plenty of sunshine." He read and slept. The most unusual feature of the day, however, was that he missed church to do it.

In September John began taking courses at the medical school of the University of Arkansas in Little Rock, which he needed to enter a Ph.D. degree program in biochemistry. Shortly afterward, Bishop Dana Dawson became ill and asked Martin to hold the Central Kansas Conference in Salina. Bishop Oxnam was one of the speakers. Martin noted that it was good to see Oxnam and be back in Kansas. He acknowledged, "My affection for them is deep." On Christmas Day he "treated" himself to a long walk with oldest grandson Bill after getting up early to watch the children open their presents. It was also their first Christmas with Margaret. Beginning the new year, he resolved to stop reading second-class mail entirely and to commit himself to "life without worry, work without hurry," and to "face the future without fear." It was a bold idea.

During 1951 Harold Mohn, the Director of the Advance for Christ and His Church, had met regularly with Martin and Johnnie Marie Grimes in Dallas to plan and eventually produce a drama scheduled to be presented to the General Conference in 1952. It was a massive undertaking, and as the conference drew closer more attention had to be devoted to it. Mrs. Grimes, the wife of Howard Grimes who taught Christian education at Perkins, was formerly on the staff of the First Methodist Church in Houston and assistant to President Willis Tate at SMU. Martin was to have a brief speaking part in the drama.

Martin's work with the ecumenical movement continued as he took the lead in establishing the Texas Council of Churches in 1952. Thirteen denominations joined to form the council and Martin was elected its first president. SMU named him a Distinguished Alumnus in March 1952. A month later he was elected vice president of the Council of Bishops.

The 1952 General Conference met in San Francisco. Martin presented the report of the committee on the Advance, presided successfully over a stormy session of the conference and admitted afterward that he was tired. The drama, *A Faith Is Born,* was presented at the Opera House on April 30 and May 1 to a full house each night. Martin, whose brief part came near the first, thought he "got through [his] part very well," both nights. Earl Moreland, former SMU classmate and longtime president of Randolph Macon Men's College in Virginia, said he thought Martin's leadership in the Advance was the high point of Martin's labors in The Methodist Church. Martin was not so pleased, however, with the action taken by the General Conference with respect to the report on ordination and the sacraments. A compromise was reached that, once again, allowed unordained persons to administer the sacrament under certain circumstances. Martin said frankly it "represented a backward step." He was even more disappointed when he left a watch that had been given to him by the Floral Heights Church in Wichita Falls on the Pullman car and was never able to find it.

When the conferences were over in 1952, he and Sally had planned to go with a group on a cruise to Alaska and to tour the Northwest. Everything was arranged and they were ready to leave when word came that the ship on which they were to sail had collided with another vessel and the trip was canceled. They decided to go ahead, however, with the land portion that included the Northwest. Martin was not feeling well when they left, and had experienced dental problems for a good part of the year. While attending the meetings of the Board of Evangelism in Chicago, he was stricken with a digestive upset. Fortunately, Sally was with him in Chicago and together they made the decision to go ahead with the tour and took the train to Billings. He was sick all the way and when they arrived in Yellowstone Park he was put to bed by the doctor. After reaching Helena, Montana, he felt worse and they decided to drop out of the party to allow him time to get some rest. They planned to rejoin the group in Seattle. He was in bed for two days in Helena and felt considerably better afterward. By the time they arrived in Seattle on August 10, Martin had improved enough to enjoy a tour of the city and go on to Victoria and Vancouver. They came home through Glacier National Park, enjoyed the lovely mountain scenery and the Many Glacier Hotel, and stopped for a night to see Donald and his family in Kansas.

August 6, 1952, John and Kathryn's first child, William Dale, was born. The next month Martin was elected to chair the newly organized Commission on Promotion and Cultivation of The Methodist Church, thereby adding another large responsibility to his already expanded portfolio. It was only the beginning.

The Council of Bishops met again in Atlantic City just before Thanksgiving, and on November 20 its secretary, Bromley Oxnam, began the morning session by announcing that Martin would be offered the presidency of the National Council of Churches. Although there is no indication in Martin's diary that he had advance word of his nomination, other evidence exists to indicate he was well aware it was coming. Bromley Oxnam was the logical choice for the position, but he was already one of the presidents of the World Council of Churches and was, as Gerald Knoff later wrote to Walter Vernon, "politically ineligible." Samuel

McCrea Cavert, who was serving as general secretary at the time, said his recollections of the background of Martin's nomination "were quite clear." He remembered his conviction that "Bishop Sherrill should be succeeded in the presidency of the NCC by someone of a *reconciling* spirit who would command confidence in all quarters at a time when the NCC was far from having won strong support from various groups, and when within the circle of the Council family, there was still much to be done in welding the various interest into an effective working unity" (Cavert to Walter Vernon, January 23, 1974). Martin had never been active in the Federal Council, which preceded the National Council, nor had he been involved in the planning that led to its organization. He was not widely acquainted with individuals in the other member denominations, but Cavert said "he was well recognized as a leader of ecumenical outlook, especially in the Southwest, who was wise in judgment, who gave steady guidance, and who had a gift for enlisting cooperation among people of differing views at many points" (Cavert to Vernon, January 23, 1974).

The nominating committee that proposed Martin's name was chaired by Earl Moreland, who recounted what happened in the committee in a letter to Walter Vernon, August 5, 1974. Cavert informed Moreland that "the Methodist Year is upon us," and told him "that my Committee should select a Bishop from our church to be President." What that unleashed, Moreland said, he would rather forget and declared, "I would never write the full details of what took place! The jockeying for place and position was something I prefer to forget!!" From this one could infer there was no shortage of candidates among members of the Council of Bishops. After consulting with others and thinking about the matter carefully, Moreland said he decided that Martin was the man to be nominated and recommended him to the committee. "Will had not been consulted or even notified about the fact that his name was before the committee." After a lengthy discussion in the committee, during which Moreland answered many questions about his friend, Martin's nomination was approved and, according to Moreland's recollection, Cavert called him in Atlantic City to ask him if he would accept the position. It was on condition of his acceptance that he was invited to New York to talk with the leaders of the council. Like Moreland, Cavert claims the credit for suggesting Martin's name to the committee after consulting with Bromley Oxnam—a tribute to his successful tenure as president. One would certainly suspect that Oxnam played a major role in the selection, and Martin acknowledged later that he did.

At the end of the council session on November 20, Martin took the train to New York to meet with the officers of the National Council. He went uptown to Union Theological Seminary to spend the morning of November 21, heard Van Dusen speak in chapel, sat in on Paul Tillich's lecture class at nine o'clock to hear him speak on the nature of sin, talked to New Testament Professor Frederick Grant about the Revised Standard Version of the Bible, done under the sponsorship of the Federal Council, and heard Old Testament Professor James Millenburg lecture on Genesis. After lunch he was in Methodist Bishop Frederick B. Newell's office to meet Bishop Henry Knox Sherrill, presiding bishop of the Protestant Episcopal Church, Dr. Cavert, Dr. Ross, and Mrs. Norman Vincent Peale. They offered him the presidency at that time and he accepted. "I had already decided to say 'Yes' with God's help," he wrote in the diary. He was formally elected at the General Assembly in Denver on December 12, 1952. He had been scheduled to preach at its opening worship service, but mechanical trouble delayed his flight and Arthur J. Moore filled in for him.

Martin took office at a crucial time in the life of the National Council. Samuel McCrea Cavert said, "Bishop Martin came to the presidency of the Council at a critical time in both its internal life and its public standing." Roswell P. Barnes identified three major problems facing the council when Martin became its president: "McCarthyism, the control of the Council by the National Lay Committee, and the restructuring of the Council" (Barnes to Walter Vernon, February 4, 1974). Senator McCarthy made his infamous Lincoln Day speech in Wheeling, West Virginia, in which he announced he had a list of 200 Communists in government service in 1952. He, in fact, had none. Cavert remembered the situation in the National Council well. The council was only two years old and the agencies that had been merged to form it were not yet working well together. In addition, any action taken or policy adopted was subject to criticism by a group of conservative business and industrial leaders led by millionaire J. Howard Pew. From the earliest days in 1950, there had been conflict between them and the leadership of the council. The issue was control.

The National Council was created in 1950 by uniting twelve agencies into one. Among the original ones were the Federal Council of Churches, the Home Missions Council of North America, the International Council of Religious Education, the Missionary Education Movement of the U.S. and Canada, the National Protestant Council on Higher Education, the United Council of Church Women, and the United Stewardship Council. Denominations that belonged to the Federal Council of Churches were represented by delegates and voted to approve the constitution of the National Council. The Methodist Church was a founding denomination. Samuel McCrea Cavert, the general secretary of the Federal Council, was elected the first general secretary of the National Council and served in that office until January 31, 1954. His successor was Roy G. Ross; Roswell P. Barnes was associate general secretary. Bishop Henry Knox Sherrill was the first president.

Ross remembered that after Martin presided for the first time over the General Assembly in December 1952, he decided "this fellow has a lot to learn." He was quickly reassured for, as he said, "What I was not aware of was his capacity for rapid growth, and shortly he was a very knowledgeable person indeed." There can be little doubt that in addition to Martin's being a southerner and a Methodist, it was his style of leadership that suited him to both the time and the presidency of the National Council. Barnes accurately described him as "even-tempered, good-natured, kind, thoughtful, with a genius for personalizing relationships, and not to be pushed around." He went on to say, "He was quiet, almost diffident and timid in manner, but strong and not easily distracted from his purposes, nor scared by threats of opposition. He fought when necessary, but with reluctance." Barnes, like everyone who knew Martin, recognized that Martin's physical presence was a significant factor in his leadership.

He was impressively big in physical stature, like a solid football guard. An analogy occurs to me: some good preaching may create an atmosphere and general impression without leaving specific ideas that can be remembered and repeated; so Bishop Martin created an atmosphere and general impression. He is more to be remembered for what he was than for what he did in any particular achievement or as a champion of any clearly defined causes. He was a real churchman.

The president of the United Church Women, Mossie Wyker, sensed the same qualities when she watched Martin preside for the first time. She told him in a letter written February 5, 1953, "You are so unhurried, so fair, and one has the feeling that your concern is for ALL and that all will get a fair hearing." She expressed her hope, "Surely we will be led on to even greater achievement under your spiritual leadership."

Cavert shared their impressions. "People remember his steady hand and wisdom rather than anything unusual." There were plenty of reasons for the new organization to require a steady hand at its helm. Cavert identified the issues in which Martin was involved that were crucial to the future of the National Council. He appointed a committee on the Maintenance of American Freedom, which was instructed "to watch developments which threaten the freedom of any of our people or their institutions, whether through denying the basic right of freedom of thought, through Communist infiltration, or wrong methods of meeting that infiltration." It was clearly a response to the onslaught of Senator McCarthy and the House Committee on Un-American Activities. Bishop Henry Knox Sherrill was named to head the committee, and a distinguished group of clergy and laypersons agreed to serve.

Perfecting the structure of the council so that it could work harmoniously as a simple and effective organization was the second challenge. A decision of lasting significance was the one to consolidate the offices in New York of the various agencies, which eventually led to the creation of the Inter-Church Center at 475 Riverside Drive. A room in that building is named in Martin's honor. Dave Lacy, his friend in Dallas, took the lead in raising money for it. The last big hurdle was the necessity to find a way to work with the Layman's Advisory Committee.

In the minds of many persons, the president of the National Council of Churches was America's leading Protestant. The organization over which Martin presided for two years represented thirty Protestant, Anglican, and Eastern Orthodox communions, which together had more than 35 million members. Godbold wrote to say, "In my opinion this is the most signal honor which has come to you in your long and distinguished career in the church." Godbold had been active in the Federal Council and had, in fact, been elected a delegate from The Methodist Church at the General Conference in San Francisco. A mix-up had, however, kept his name from being submitted on the list of delegates, and he missed the Denver Assembly where he could have voted to elect Martin and seen him for the first time in his new role. Martin reminded his friend that his words of support and confidence, similar to the ones just offered, following his election to the episcopacy in Birmingham "gave to my doubting spirits a needed boost which meant more to me than you could understand."

Stories appeared in every part of the church press and in the religion section of *Time, Newsweek,* and other national magazines and newspapers. His picture graced the January 1, 1953, cover of the *Christian Advocate*. The *Dallas Times Herald* ran an editorial of congratulations, and even Lynn Landrum, who had offered unrelenting criticism of the National Council in many columns, was impressed, but wary. "The National Council in its Denver session of its general assembly elevated to its presidency one of the ablest, sincerest and most spiritual churchmen that the Columntator has ever known—a wonderful friend of man and of God. From such a man none of us has anything to doubt or fear. But under him there is a secretariat. And the column is wondering about that secretariat." Landrum alleged that the Federal Council changed its name "because its secretariat brought suspicion upon that council and its work, conducted an 'Information Service' which got pinker and pinker as the years rolled by." Landrum was not the only critic. The mail began to flow in almost immediately and much of it was critical. In a letter dated January 17, 1953, Martin commented good-naturedly to his friend the episcopal bishop of Kansas, Goodrich R. Fenner, that "the tide of mail relative to the office has already mounted until I begin to wonder how so many people find time to write so much about so little. Fortunately, a good many of the letters are unsigned which means they call for neither a reading nor a reply." Senator Tom Connally and Governor Allan Shivers of Texas were among the hundreds who wrote letters to congratulate him. His former teacher and colleague Bishop Paul Kern wrote early in January to say, "I am now getting to the place where I shine in the reflected brilliance of my former pupils." His old army buddies saw the announcement and Leo Belig wrote for all of them. He extended their congratulations and reminded the sergeant that he had not paid his dues for the EH-13 Association. Martin sent $5 by return mail along with his thanks for their good wishes.

Cavert was the man behind the scenes. After Martin was formally elected in Denver, he requested "a brief history of the Federal Council with such information as the names and dates of those who served as its presidents." Cavert sent him a copy of Macfarland's *Christian Unity in the Making,* the history of the Federal Council to 1930. In a postscript, he said he thought the council "was too busy *making* history" during the two previous decades "to have time for *writing* it." The question of naming an official emissary to the Vatican came up almost immediately and Martin was alerted to stand by for a meeting with President Dwight Eisenhower. A telegram sent on December 15, however, informed him that Roswell Barnes had been "assured confidentially by highly placed contact that no nomination now contemplated. The proposed Friday appointment with the General therefore not required." The source of Barnes's information was John Foster Dulles. Martin was relieved. His schedule was packed and plane reservations were hard to obtain at Christmastime.

Cavert also knew that Catherine had announced her intention to marry on Christmas Eve in California and the Martins needed to attend her wedding. A few days later Cavert wrote to encourage Martin to ask Mrs. Walter Fondren of Houston for a gift of

$10,000 to support a service project and help balance the NCC budget. She had previously given $1,000 but had not renewed her pledge in 1952. Martin quickly responded that although he was "not tender-footed" about asking people for money, he thought it was premature to approach her so soon after his affiliation with the organization. In the same letter he included a copy of Landrum's editorial and asked for some assistance in making a response to him. Cavert promptly wrote to say that "Mr. Landrum is seriously in error" about the reasons why the Federal Council of Churches changed its name and described what actually had happened. Mr. Landrum, however, was not dissuaded from any of his opinions by facts.

With the calendar cleared, the Martins took the train to Los Angeles on December 20, 1952, to officiate at Mary Catherine's wedding to Rudolph Joseph Makoul. She had known him for the better part of two years and had been going steady for two or three months. "Rudy" was a dialogue director at Paramount and Columbia Studios. At the time of their wedding he was working on a picture starring Dean Martin and Jerry Lewis, and he took his prospective father-in-law to meet them and their director on the set. The new combination of "Martin and Lewis" were photographed together. About forty guests attended the wedding ceremony on Christmas Eve at which the father of the bride forgot "an unessential part of the service." He commented "C was beautiful." He and Sally rode the train home on Christmas Day.

In early January 1953, Cavert arranged for Martin to meet J. Howard Pew, chairman of the National Lay Committee. He and Pew flew to Dallas in Pew's plane for the introduction. Cavert explained to Martin in a letter written before the meeting (January 2, 1953) that the lay committee had been formed at the suggestion of Dean Luther Weigle of Yale in order to create more interest in the new organization and to "strengthen the prospects of financial support for the National Council." After attempting unsuccessfully to recruit John D. Rockefeller, Jr., Thomas J. Watson (the founder of IBM), and Cleveland E. Dodge to head it, they turned to Mr. Pew. They were uneasy about him since he "was known to have given some support to the leader of the dissident fundamentalists headed by Carl McIntire, who had formed the American Council of Christian Churches as a group opposed both to the National Council and the World Council." Pew had attended the Constituting Convention at which the NCC came into being, but gave a brief address that "created the unfortunate impression that his chief interest was in preventing the National Council from taking any liberal position with regard to economic matters." His speech had caused serious questions to be raised by the leadership about the wisdom of creating a lay committee at all. Since that time, Cavert told Martin, he thought Pew "has come really to believe strongly in the National Council." That notwithstanding, they were aware that he had been unhappy with the results of a series of studies on the Church and Economics that had been funded by the Rockefeller Foundation and carried out by the National Council, and for a time threatened to withdraw from any role in the council.

Pew had been a member of the Nominating Committee that selected Martin and was enthusiastic about Martin's election after learning from his Texas associates in the oil business, one of whom was Harry Hines, an independent operator from Dallas, that Martin was held in high esteem. Pew wanted a chance to meet Martin before the meeting of the general board at the end of the month. This was the reason for the trip. Cavert reminded his new president that Pew had given $50,000 to the organization in 1952. The meeting took place the morning of January 7 in Martin's office and lasted until noon. He does not comment in the diary about the subjects they discussed, but characterized it as "a good visit." Cavert also arranged a reception to allow Martin to meet the NCC staff on March 9.

With his election, the number of Martin's speaking invitations increased as did the number of ceremonial occasions at which he was expected to represent the National Council. One of these was a black tie dinner at the Plaza Hotel in New York City honoring Anna Rosenberg. He appeared on the program with Cardinal Spellman and Norman Vincent Peale. Rosenberg autographed his program, and he enjoyed their conversation over dinner. Later he was the guest of John D. Rockefeller, Jr., at a dinner honoring the

Japanese Crown Prince, who was visiting the United States for the first time.

His most interesting opportunity also came early in his presidency. Shortly after his election it was proposed that he make a trip to visit American soldiers fighting in Korea. It was first proposed as an Easter visit, March 26 through April 11, but after considerable negotiation it was decided there was not time enough to make the necessary arrangements and it was eventually rescheduled as a Christmas visit. Through the courtesy of the National Broadcasting Company Martin extended thirty-second Easter Sunday greetings to the troops along with those from Cardinal Spellman and President Eisenhower.

The year 1953 saw an increase in the number of committees created by the government to investigate Communists and Communism. The infamous purge and blacklisting of entertainers took place. People were frightened and it was a rare American town that did not have its superpatriot, a local version of Senator McCarthy. Television brought the hearings even closer to home. Entertainers like Pete Seeger were called to appear before congressional committees. He and Woody Guthrie were blacklisted, and writers and musicians were forced to write under assumed names.

The anti-Communist crusade, led by Senator McCarthy and the House Un-American Activities Committee, chaired by Representative Harold H. Veld, a Methodist, began to focus more and more on the churches during 1953. When Veld declared that his committee would be investigating individual clergy the announcement was repudiated by President Eisenhower, but it did not deter the congressman from his intentions. The movement was strong enough that in July Bishop Oxnam, who had been an outspoken critic of the committee and its tactics for years, requested to appear before Veld's committee to refute its claims about him. Preparing for the hearing proved difficult since the committee would not reveal any questions he would be asked. The televised hearing took place on July 21, 1953, and has been fully recorded in Oxnam's appropriately titled book, *I Protest,* and in a published transcript that appeared in *U.S. News & World Report* in its August 7, 1953, issue. Oxnam was accompanied by his friend and lawyer, Charles Parlin; Samuel McCrea Cavert was one of the more than 500 spectators. The hearing went through the entire day and until almost midnight. The next morning, July 22, Cavert wrote Martin, "I think it is even possible that yesterday's hearing may mark a turning point and that hereafter the prestige of this committee will be considerably reduced." Martin agreed with that assessment and wondered aloud to Bishop Selecman why "some people in our city . . . appear to regard McCarthy as a second Messiah. I think he is the most dangerous demagogue that has been in Congress since Huey Long." He confided to Selecman that he was going to talk to Editor Withers of the *Dallas Morning News* about it (WCM to Selecman, July 23, 1953).

There was, nevertheless, humor to be found even in the madness of the time. Cavert told Martin a story, which Martin passed along to "Brother Charlie" Selecman. It seems that a rabbit was running at top speed through the woods. A squirrel said, "What's your rush?" The rabbit replied, "Haven't you heard that Senator McCarthy is after the kangaroos?" "But you are not a kangaroo," the squirrel said. "Yes, I know," said the rabbit, "but I can't prove it" (WCM to Selecman, July 23, 1953). But Cavert had also warned Martin that testimony during the Oxnam hearing revealed the committee had a file on the National Council and urged him to insist on having a copy for the Council. Martin wrote the same day to Veld to request it. Oxnam had, among other things, questioned the procedures of the committee and the abuses to which they were subject. In October the committee's counsel, Mr. Kunzig, at Martin's request, met with Martin, Charles Parlin, and Sam Cavert to discuss possible changes in those procedures. They talked for an hour and a half and Martin was hopeful that "we made progress." Martin had met with President Eisenhower the day before on another matter.

July 1953 saw yet another crisis for the churches. J. B. Matthews, a former Methodist minister and missionary who had during the 1930s been a convert to Marxist socialism but was now the executive director of Senator McCarthy's Permanent Subcommittee on Investigations, published an article in the *American Mercury* titled "Reds and Our Churches." The opening paragraph in the article said, "The largest single group supporting the Communist apparatus in the United States today is composed of Protestant clergymen" (*AM*, "Reds and Our Churches," July, 1953, 3). "Clergymen outnumber professors two to one in supporting the Communist-front apparatus of the Kremlin conspiracy," he continued. In the article he claimed "at least" 7,000 clergy had been recruited to support Communism as "party members, fellow-travelers, espionage agents, party-line adherents, and unwitting dupes." He listed the names of a number of persons, mostly bishops, who were named in a report issued by the House Un-American Activities Committee on April 1, 1951, as participants in a "phony" Communist peace offensive. Included among those named were Methodists Paul Kern, Henry Hitt Crane, pastor of Central Methodist Church, Detroit, and Walter Muelder, Dean of the School of Theology at Boston University. Matthews singled out five persons who, "outside the known leadership of the Communist Party of the United States," were the "top pro-Soviet propagandists in the country." Among them were Methodists Harry F. Ward and Jack McMichael, executive secretary of the Methodist Federation for Social Action. The article was reprinted and widely circulated by conservative groups. Matthews's astonishing allegations were immediately challenged, and when he was unable to offer evidence to support any of them, he was dismissed from his job on the McCarthy Committee. More damage had been done in the meantime.

To add to his already bulging portfolio of responsibilities, Martin had in April 1953 become president of the Council of Bishops, and it fell to him to lead the group in making a response to Matthews's charges. The climate in the church, however, did not provide either Martin or his colleagues much support for the effort. John Q. Schisler, head of the Division of the Local Church of the General Board of Education, wrote the council in March to say that there were two primary sources of the anti-Methodist material: Verne Kaub and the American Council of Christian

Laymen. They had published a document titled "How Red Is the Federal [National] Council of Churches?" The second was the Houston office of a group who called themselves the Committee for the Preservation of Methodism. Schisler suggested that the National Council should prepare material to refute Kaub, and the Council of Bishops should make a study of the Houston group. Others whom Schisler did not mention, but who were prominent in the Christian anti-Communist movement were Carl McIntire, president of the International Council of Christian Churches, Edgar Bundy, chair of the Church League of America, who had questioned the loyalty of John Foster Dulles and President Eisenhower, and M. G. Lowman, executive secretary of Circuit Riders, a group organized by thirty-three Methodist laypersons in 1951.

A committee was appointed from the Council of Bishops to consider the larger question of attacks on the Protestant church as well as specifically to refute those made against the Methodists. It reported in December and its statement was issued to the church. It declared in part:

> We resent unproved assertions that the Protestant ministry is honeycombed with disloyalty. We are unalterably opposed to communism, but we know that the alternative to communism is not an American brand of fascism. Our time-honored and self-authenticated procedures for determining guilt and disloyalty can so easily be discarded in fanatical investigations that we must oppose those who in the name of Americanism employ the methods of repression, who speak with the voice of democracy but whose hands are the hands of tyranny.
>
> (COB Minutes, Friday, December 11, 1953, 208)

Martin left on his official visit to the troops in Korea immediately after the meeting. J. Howard Pew provided his transportation to California. Catherine and Sally saw him off in Los Angeles in front of newsreel cameras and reporters. The military provided transportation from there to the Pacific. Ralph Stoody of Methodist Information went with him. After brief stops in Honolulu and Wake Island they arrived in Tokyo, where they were greeted by a delegation of chaplains. Afterward they were given identification papers and inoculations and issued clothing suitable for travel in Korea during the winter. Martin met the famous Japanese Christian, Kagawa, at a reception and saw Sam Hilburn, a missionary from one of his conferences, too.

On December 21 they boarded General Hall's private plane, along with the general, a general from the British army, and a navy admiral, for the trip to Korea. After a stop in Pusan during which General Hall spoke briefly with President Syngman Rhee, they flew on to Seoul. That evening they enjoyed dinner as guests of General Maxwell Taylor; General Hall, the American ambassador and Mrs. Briggs were also present. Martin spoke briefly and informally in response to General Taylor's expression of thanks for their coming. The next morning they were briefed by General Taylor's staff and moved on to the headquarters of X Corps where they were greeted by General Clark and then flown to the 45th Division Headquarters. There they met General Paul D. Harkins, who took them to dedicate a chapel. Afterward, they spent the night in the VIP billet. "Sarge" Martin had come up a long way in the world.

In every place they went Martin was greeted by the commanding general, and when the trip was over he had met and spoken with virtually every American commander in Korea. Cardinal Spellman was a day behind him on almost the same itinerary. Utilizing every kind of transportation available, including helicopters the party visited chapels, hospitals, orphanages, and troops. On one of their trips the pilot allowed Martin to fly the plane most of the way. He loved it.

Christmas Day was spent with I Corps. He spoke in a service, attended a Christmas party with several hundred Korean children, and had dinner in the mess hall. The afternoon turned out to be free when a snowstorm made it impossible to fly to their scheduled appointments.

Martin spent December 26 with the Marines on the front lines and conducted an outdoor service. Afterward he had dinner with General Pate and his officers and returned to Seoul where he preached again.

General Taylor, whom Martin liked very much and described as "a gentleman of unusual distinction," was in the service.

During the remainder of his stay in Seoul there were conversations with American and Korean military chaplains, Korean Protestants, missionaries and their families, Methodists of all sorts, sometimes in the company of Bishop Lew or his staff, and between visits to schools, hospitals, orphanages, and other institutions he even managed in a few spare moments to do some sight-seeing in villages and the countryside. There were receptions, teas, luncheons—including one at the residence of the American ambassador—and dinners of all kinds. At one luncheon the vice president, Ham Tai Young, told Martin, "We have nothing left but empty hands and a devastated land." Martin commented in his diary that the vice president might have added, "and a courageous spirit."

Near the end of the visit he was received by the President of Korea, Syngman Rhee, for what Martin described as "an interesting" conversation. He was in Pusan just after the start of the New Year preaching two and sometimes three times a day. While there he was taken off shore eleven miles to an island that the Methodists were using for a "Boys Town." There were 360 boys living on the island. It was, as he described it, a "thrilling adventure." Back in Pusan he saw a picture of Bromley Oxnam on his Christmas greeting to the troops and Martin admitted he would have liked it better "without Roman collar." They flew on a Globemaster transport back to Tokyo, "the biggest thing I ever saw flying," and once again, Martin rode most of the way as co-pilot.

In Japan there were visits with the air force and with General McNaughton and the general staff for briefing. A broadcast was arranged and for seven minutes Martin spoke to the Japanese people on the topic "Our Christian Hope." There was also a visit to the naval base in Yokohama, where he toured the underground ship-building facilities created by the Japanese during World War II. While there he also attended a dedication of the Ark of the Covenant in a Jewish congregation and was greatly impressed by the role played by the cantor. He finished up with the comment in his diary, "What a day!"

What a trip! After a brief stopover in Hawaii—they were two hours late arriving and he had to be hurried to his speaking engagement before the Honolulu Council of Churches with a police escort—there was time for a much-needed night's rest. And then there were more speaking engagements, receptions, a dinner in his honor, and trips to see the island. Martin took a photograph of the grave of Ernie Pyle—a popular war correspondent killed during World War II. He was back in San Francisco on January 12 where he spoke to a group of church leaders and television reporters. The next day he arrived in Dallas where he was greeted at the airport by Sally, many friends, and the now usual group of reporters who detained him for half an hour. He opened his Christmas presents that evening and the next day made the first of what would be numerous speeches about the trip at the Woman's Club to about forty guests invited by Dave and Pauline Lacy. Asked to contribute to a symposium in the *Christian Century*, "What Can Christians Contribute to Peace in Korea?" Martin wrote in sober reflection on his trip. "This we know," he said, "peace in Korea will be an empty word if the people who live there are allowed to starve, or to become so embittered by suffering that their souls will be irreparably warped, or to feel that their land and their lives are pawns in the hands of mighty world powers that happened to choose their fields and cities as a battleground."

January 18 he was back in New York for a meeting of the National Council, and went on from there to Buck Hill Falls for the annual meetings of the Board of Missions and the Advance Committee. Appropriately, he was assigned to the East Asia Area Committee.

A great dinner was held in New York on January 22 to mark the 300th anniversary of the founding of the first Protestant Church on Long Island. President Eisenhower and Queen Juliana of the Netherlands sent greetings to the 1,600 guests. Roland Hays sang and Charles Taft spoke. Martin followed, but it was almost eleven o'clock when he finally rose to speak. "It was a big night," he recorded.

The Fourth General Assembly of the National Council was

called to order by William C. Martin on November 29, 1954. In his presidential address he thanked the persons who had led the council during its early years and then laid out his understanding of an agenda for the future. He said that he predicted the "usefulness" of the Council would be determined by its ability to hold together certain "drives." Among these was the tension between "the individual witness on the one hand and the corporate expression of conviction on the other. We need both. Can we hold them together?" Another was the ability to hold together "an informed, positive, denominational loyalty, on the one hand and an enthusiastic commitment to the Universal Church on the other." He rejected any idea that the way to ecumenical cooperation was "by scaling down of denominational loyalty." The church is called to work "out of the conviction that God has called the Church to a task so great that it can be completely fulfilled only when we stand in close ranks, marching together."

But he went on to affirm that "denominational duplication and overlapping of effort" can be eliminated. A second possibility is to work together to "serve the needs of those who need shepherding; migrants; city dwellers with no churches; rural people from whom the church has retreated . . . ; twenty million unchurched youth." And yet another, Martin told the delegates, is to unite in the areas where there is no overlap or overcrowding such as the question how to avert another war. Martin was frank to tell the delegates that he did not see the National Council as "the ultimate plan." He used the analogy of a choir he had heard that was composed of many choirs. Each was given the music to learn separately and when they all came together under a great director their voices blended and they became a mighty chorus. This, he continued, was their parable. "I dare to believe that when we come to join in that great Hallelujah chorus, each one of us will recognize certain familiar and intimate strains, and down in our hearts we will say, 'Thank God, that part of the Lord's song was brought up by the communion to which my fathers had the honor of belonging.'"

In the midst of all his travel and official duties life went on in other ways, too. John Lee Martin, Jr., called like his great-grandfather, "Jack," the second son of John Lee and Kathryn Martin, was born on March 11. John was now living in College Station, Texas, enrolled in a Ph.D. program in biochemistry at Texas A & M University. Sally and William C. took the train that very day to see him and they pronounced him "a fine 6 lb. boy." Mother and son were both doing well. They called him Jackie.

SMU got a new president, too. Willis Tate was elected by the trustees on May 6, 1954, and began a long term of service.

The great Second Assembly of the World Council of Churches was held in Evanston on the campus of Northwestern University in 1954. It opened on August 15 with Bromley Oxnam preaching to the delegates at First Church, Evanston. That evening there was a great "Festival of Faith" at Soldier's Field in Chicago, which 125,000 people attended. During the plenary session the next day Martin presented the new Bible translation that had been sponsored by the National Council of Churches, the Revised Standard Version, to the delegates. In his role as president of the National Council, Martin assisted with the opening Communion service, served as a member of the Steering Committee, and was elected to membership on the Central Committee of the World Council of Churches. His service with the National Council had brought him to national prominence, and his role as an ecumenical leader had brought him recognition that he had clearly earned.

9

Dallas–Fort Worth Area

Martin undoubtedly reached the height of his episcopal ministry during the 1950s. Early in the decade he was chosen to head the National Council, and during his term in that office he had been elected president of the Council of Bishops. The Second Assembly of the World Council of Churches held in Evanston in 1954 elected him to its Central Committee, thereby placing him in contact with virtually all of the leaders of Protestant and Orthodox Christendom in the world.

The Central Committee was chaired by the American Lutheran leader Franklin Clark Fry. Among its members were Archbishop Athenagoras, one of the original presidents of the World Council of Churches; his colleagues the Patriarchs of Alexandria and Athens; the president of the British Methodists, Eric Baker, Presbyterian Eugene Carson Blake, who would later head the National Council; the Archbishop of Canterbury; theologians Georges Florovsky and J. L. Hromadka; Dean Liston Pope of Yale; Bishop Lesslie Newbigin of India; Martin Niemoeller of Germany; and the Bishop of Harrar, Theophilos, of the Ethiopian Orthodox Church. They were together at annual meetings of the Central Committee and had the opportunity to become well acquainted. The first of these after Evanston was held in Davos-Platz, Switzerland, in late July 1955. At the end of the decade

Martin was elected by his colleagues to write and deliver the Episcopal Address at the General Conference of 1960.

The duties at home in relation to his area were greater than ever. In addition to a large geographic area and a major metropolitan center, he had more churches and preachers under his supervision than ever before. Furthermore there were institutions of all types related to the church that required his participation. He remained active on the Executive Committee of the Board of Trustees at SMU, and with its committee related specifically to the Perkins School of Theology. He regularly taught courses in preaching or church administration, too. Joseph D. Quillian, Jr., who would follow Merrimon Cuninggim as dean, encouraged it.

The Perkins School of Theology became the first educational institution in the Southwest to integrate when it admitted five African American students at the beginning of the fall semester 1952. This was two years prior to the landmark decision of the Supreme Court in *Brown v. Board of Education of Topeka,* striking down the "separate but equal" doctrine, which led to the desegregation of the public schools. Cecil Williams, recognized for his service as pastor of Glide Memorial Methodist Church in San Francisco, was one of them. It was a bold act for the time, and one which was not without its tense moments and difficult decisions. Cuninggim literally put his deanship on the line more than once and his bishop, William C. Martin, backed him. One volatile question was whether the black students would be allowed to live in campus housing. School policy dictated that all students would be treated the same, but this was challenged by influential backers. After much discussion it was reaffirmed in 1955. In the meantime, they lived on campus. Martin was a member of the committee that supported it. He also took a leadership role on a committee that enlisted the signature of more than 300 clergy in Dallas to support peaceful integration of the public schools.

As the resident bishop in Dallas, Martin might have played a more central role in the life of Southern Methodist University than he did, had he not deferred to his colleague Bishop A. Frank Smith of Houston, who served as chair of SMU's board of trustees until he retired from the episcopacy in 1960. While Martin was pastor of First Methodist in Dallas, Bishop John M. Moore filled that leadership role. Bishop Paul Martin had a close personal relation with Joe and Lois Perkins, having been their pastor in Wichita Falls and the inspiration for their large gift to the school. They naturally turned to him for advice and counsel.

There were, however, plenty of other arenas for service in the Dallas–Fort Worth Area, including large hospitals in Dallas, Fort Worth and, eventually, in Lubbock, plus a home for children in Waco and a number of church-related colleges. William C. was active in the affairs of McMurry College in the Northwest Texas Annual Conference, Houston-Tillotson College, a Black college in Austin, Texas Wesleyan College in Fort Worth, and Southwestern University in Georgetown.

The 1950s clearly was the decade of the church in twentieth-century America. It enjoyed phenomenal growth and prosperity, and that is clearly evident in the conferences for which Martin had responsibility. New congregations were begun, significant numbers of new members were added, and new clergy were recruited to serve them. During the 1950s Martin ordained 941 deacons and elders for service in his three conferences. Their numbers were almost equally divided among them—328 in North Texas, 298 in Central Texas, and 315 in Northwest Texas. He ordained almost fifty persons in the Central Texas Conference in both 1952 and 1956. The contrast with the current size of "classes" of deacons and elders is dramatic, and the increasing shortage of clergy in Methodism is due, in part, to the retirement of those who served after World War II.

In addition to his service to the Methodists, as immediate past president of the National Council of Churches Martin was automatically a delegate to its General Assembly. He was comfortable and enjoyed that responsibility. He played a significant role in the planning that eventually provided a building for the council at 475 Riverside Drive in New York City. Combining the various elements of the National Council into one building made clear sense. In addition to maintaining offices in Washington, D.C., Chicago, Atlanta, and Fort Worth, the council rented space in eight different buildings in New York City. While Martin was president of the National Council, John D. Rockefeller, Jr., had committed himself in a letter (JDR to WCM, March 16, 1954) to support the project with a gift of up to $1 million, provided the headquarters would be located in New York City. Rockefeller was clear that he would not make a firm pledge until the location was settled. He told Martin:

> Since it is not known how much such a center in New York would cost to construct and how much special assistance, if any, would be required to finance it over and above the resources of the National Council and those bodies which would be its logical occupants, there is no basis for making any definite commitment on my part. I am prepared to say, however, that I would be willing to consider participating in an amount up to $1,000,000 in connection with the acquisition of land and the possible need for equity financing of the structure.

Indianapolis, led by Methodist Bishop Richard Raines, also made a bid to place the facility in America's heartland. The final decision, however, was to build it in Morningside Heights at 475 Riverside Drive in New York. It was Rockefeller, in fact, who proposed the location, since it was in proximity to Columbia University, Barnard College, Teachers College, Union Theological Seminary, and Jewish Theological Seminary, and up the street from the Riverside Church, which his father had built for Harry Emerson Fosdick. The Board of Missions of The Methodist Church, of which Martin was also a member, was invited to move their offices into the new building if it was built. After considerable discussion at their meeting in September 1957, at which Martin was present, the Executive Committee voted to rent three floors in the new building and move from their traditional home at 150 Fifth Avenue to the "God box." Martin was in New York for this crucial meeting when Orvil Faubus, the governor of Martin's home state of Arkansas, ordered the National Guard to bar African Americans from the high schools in Little Rock, thereby creating a crisis in which Eisenhower intervened.

Martin was also involved in accepting a controversial gift from the Philip Murray Memorial Foundation of the C.I.O. The labor organization made a gift of $200,000 to support the National Council's program to apply religious principles to the world of work. Of the money, $100,000 was to be used to build a Philip Murray memorial library and research service and $100,000 spent directly to support the study (see Walter Reuther's letter to WCM, July 9, 1954, and Martin's response, July 22, 1954). Ultra-conservatives quickly saw this as a "sell out" to organized labor, if not to Communism, and an implicit confirmation of the council's leaning toward socialism. Martin and others in the council had to go to great lengths, often with little success, to explain that the foundation was separate from the C.I.O. At no place was this more difficult than at home where Lynn Landrum and the *Dallas Morning News* editorialized about it frequently. Years after the gift, in fact, Landrum still had Walter Reuther high on his list of dangerous people. In a piece titled "Kennedy on Reuther," written in March 1960, Landrum said, "Walter Reuther is a dangerous public influence, in the column's opinion. It would be a bad day for the country, if, through the National Council, or through one or both political parties, Walter Reuther should ever get America completely within his power. . . . Walter Reuther would like nothing better than just that" (*DMN*, March 7, 1960). When the gift from the foundation was made, Martin had not met the C.I.O. president, but they later arranged to have lunch together.

Martin's time was more limited by the fact that he was in greater demand as a speaker and a preacher. Since he was now appearing on television in addition to regular speaking engagements, it is little short of amazing that he managed to keep it all together. And, once again, his schedule offers eloquent testimony to the fact of his good health, energy, and physical stamina.

There was overseas travel, too. In the summer of 1955, Sally decided to go with him to the meeting of the Central Committee of the World Council of Churches in Davos-Platz, Switzerland, and while there to take some vacation in Europe. It was never easy for him actually to get away. After they arrived in New York to board the ship for Europe, Martin left Sally alone so he could make a brief trip to the Pentagon in Washington to meet with a committee on prisoners of war. General Hull had suggested Martin's name. They were charged with drawing up a code of conduct for armed forces personnel in response to the number of American prisoners in the hands of the Koreans who had betrayed their comrades or turned under the pressure of interrogation. It was an interesting session, which Martin enjoyed. He said in the diary that he suggested "two changes" but does not say what they were. When it was over he went to a luncheon sponsored by International Christian Leadership over which his friend Congressman Brooks Hays of Arkansas presided and then returned to rejoin Sally in New York. The next day was hectic. Martin's passport had been sent from Dallas to Washington and he failed to connect with it. The Martin temper was barely in check and he confessed that "my patience was not as Christian as it should have been." He was, in fact, thoroughly exasperated, but with the help of a colonel at the Pentagon it was finally worked out. The frustrating day was partially redeemed by a good dinner at New York's Town and Country Restaurant and a pleasant visit with the host, Roy Ross, general secretary of the National Council of Churches.

Passport finally in hand, he and Sally, once again, boarded the *Queen Elizabeth* for Europe on July 13, 1955. Their table mates were a couple from Rochester, New York, and two women from Vassar. For enjoyment en route Martin read Pearl Buck's new book, *My Several Worlds*. He managed somehow on this voyage to avoid being seasick and became so content and relaxed after two days that he was forced to ask himself, as only he could, "How lazy can I safely allow myself to become?" It was a question that would never occur to most people on a cruise. With his table mate, Mr. Willey, he toured the engine room and heard the captain read prayers, which Martin said he did "very well."

They docked in Cherbourg on July 18 and immediately took the boat train to Paris where, as seven years before, they were booked at the Claridge Hotel. Martin remembered well that thirty-seven years earlier he had ridden across some of the same country in one of the famous French boxcars marked *Quarante Hommes—Huit Chevaux,* the famous "Forty and Eight." He told the *Dallas Morning News* in writing about it, "I don't know how it was for the eight horses but for forty men of my size it was a trifle crowded" (*DMN,* July 31, 1955). Once settled in the hotel, he walked to the Arc de Triomphe and made a few pictures with his new camera. He found Paris still to be a city of beauty and charm. During the next few days, in addition to bus tours, shopping, and sight-seeing, he visited Pastor Marc Boegner, president of the Protestant Federation of France and whom Martin had first met in Amsterdam, at his office in the Rue de Clinchy, and sat in for twenty minutes—all that was allowed—on a session of the Chamber of Deputies. As he had when he saw it first thirty-five years earlier, Martin found St. Chappell "too beautiful for words." The cathedral at Chartes he thought "more impressive . . . than any I have seen." He was not, however, impressed with the flea market—"a jumble of junk . . . if I ever saw one," but he and Sally bought two small paintings anyway. There proved to be, however, no escaping a busman's holiday. On Sunday morning, the pastor of the American Church called to say that Kenneth Shamblin, a Methodist pastor in Little Rock who was scheduled to preach, had become ill and asked Martin to substitute. He agreed and "did very well."

After a very pleasant week in Paris, he and Sally took the train to Geneva. The headline in the report printed in the *Dallas Morning News* proclaimed "Geneva Is Talk Capital of World" (*DMN,* August 7, 1955). They made the usual tour of the city on a bus, and afterward he went alone to the headquarters of the World Council of Churches. Geneva was also home to nearly sixty nongovernmental organizations, and elaborate preparations were underway to host an international conference, "Atoms for Peace." Although he waited two hours at the WCC for the staff to return from lunch, Martin judged the long lunch "a good custom." At the Department of International Church Relief and Aid to Refugees, he learned that the number of displaced persons in the world, ten years after the end of World War II, was still in excess of 14 million. The World Council agency alone had found homes for more than 100,000. After touring the building he moved on to visit the Chateau de Bossey about twelve miles away. Purchased with two gifts from John D. Rockefeller, Jr., the chateau was the site of the Center for Ecumenical Studies, which had from its beginning been under the direction of Dr. Hendrick Kraemer.

From Geneva the Martins took the boat to Montreux, where the Palace Hotel proved to be the most palatial and splendid either had ever seen; from there they went on to Interlocken by train. When they visited Kleine Scheidegg to see the Jungfrau the altitude made them both dizzy, but he went to the top of the mountain on the lift anyway. Afterward, it was on to Zurich to see the city and visit in the home of their friend and Methodist colleague Bishop Ferdinand Sigg.

The meeting of the Central Committee at Davos-Platz in eastern Switzerland began on August 2. Franklin Clark Fry presided. Martin, Charles Parlin, and Mrs. Frank Brooks of New York represented The Methodist Church. Bromley Oxnam was expected to attend, but a plane delay forced him to cancel his trip at the last minute. The meetings, which were conducted in three languages, ran through the day and into the evening but most were interesting. The chief concerns of the committee in Davos were evangelism, the resettlement of refugees, and identifying ways to strengthen the ties between member churches of the World Council. One entire day was spent on the role of the WCC in interchurch aid and refugee relief; at the next session W. A. Visser 't Hooft read a position paper outlining the understanding of unity that the council should sponsor. Dr. Reinhold von Thadden, a layman and leader of the German *Kirchentag,* which Martin described as a "kind of German camp-meeting," spoke, too. On another trip to Europe Martin attended one of its meetings. The committee members spent one entire morning drafting a letter to the Patriarchate of Russia. Its concluding statement declared, "We pray that the way may be opened for the fuller exchange of spiritual gifts and we pray for God's guidance and direction of the ministry of the Holy Orthodox Church of Russia." Sunday worship was conducted by Bishop Henry Knox Sherrill of the Episcopal Church in the United States, and Bishop Otto Dibelius of Germany preached. "An impressive service," Martin noted. The meeting concluded on August 8 when Dr. Ernest A. Payne, a British Baptist, gave them the final benediction—"Be off with you."

Leaving Davos, Will and Sally crossed the mountains to Milan, where the news awaited them at the hotel that Uncle Martin Nelson, Aunt Stell's husband, had died. They were sad to be so far away at such a time, but they went ahead with the usual tourist things and, of course, saw da Vinci's *Last Supper*. Martin made a special effort to visit the Church of St. Ambrose thinking it to be the place where St. Augustine of Hippo was converted, but that turned out not to be true and nobody seemed to know where the actual site might be. The next day, however, with some help from an inspector at the bus company, he made his way to the place proported to be Augustine's tomb in Pavia. The friendly inspector rode out and back with him and explained on the way how the country and the bus company were run.

That afternoon the Martins went to Venice by train. The city proved to be as "exciting as we had ever dreamed," and they took full advantage of it. After dinner in an open air café in the Plaza de San Marco, they walked the streets until eleven o'clock. The next day they made the obligatory visit to a glass factory, courtesy of their hotel, and got a glimpse of a funeral gondola on the way. Their final evening they were serenaded as they rode in a gondola on the Grand Canal and walked to St. Mark's Square for one farewell look in the moonlight.

A very long boat ride in the morning caused them to miss lunch and almost the train to Florence. When they arrived, Sally was tired and the hotel produced a doctor who gave her a vitamin injection. The next morning they slept late and then took a bus tour of the city. Martin was especially interested in the slab where the heretic Savonarola was hanged. The next day they rode the bus on to Rome, passed Assisi on the way, and arrived in the early evening. "A long hoped for pilgrimage is accomplished. Thanks be to God!" Martin wrote. They toured and he walked through the city alone. They went twice to the opera, once to see *Aida* in the outdoor opera—"a magnificent spectacle that could have been done so fittingly no where else," and saw their second at the

Baths of Caraculla. By now Sally was thoroughly worn out but her husband never paused. He visited churches and preachers, and found a guide, who turned out also to be the head of the anti-clerical party of Italy, to take them on a private tour of ancient Rome. Martin decided after his first look that it would take at least a week even to make a "superficial inspection of the wonders" of St. Peter's, but in addition he also tried to see all the churches in the city, too.

Naples was the next stop, and after finding their hotel unsatisfactory they moved into the Excelsior, which gave them better accommodations and a lovely view of the sea. The primary reason for including Naples in their itinerary was to visit the Casa Materna, a children's home that had been supported by funds from the Methodist Advance. In order to reach it, they had to pass through crowded sections of the city where there was abject poverty and squalor. They found the home to be like an oasis in a desert, "a place of hallowed peace in the midst of turmoil and want." Living in the facility were 280 children, and another 200 came every day for school and play. The classroom building had been built with money raised in the Week of Dedication that Martin had led in 1952. He and Sally spent a full day at the facility, and after the children's choir sang for them in farewell they were taken back to their hotel. "What sharp contrast between the luxury on one side of the city and the squalor on the other," Martin commented. In one day, it had became a favorite place for them both.

Like all travelers who visit Naples, they went to the Isle of Capri, but Sally was so exhausted and ill she could not enjoy it. In retrospect, it is clear they had overestimated what they could do, and needed immediately to start the journey home. Their itinerary, however, called for them to continue on to North Africa, and to visit Algiers.

Sally took the next day off to rest at the hotel while Martin continued his usual pace. When he got back to the hotel, however, he discovered Sally had become ill and collapsed at lunch. A doctor was called, and he prescribed at least four days of rest, preferably in a hospital. The next day she was admitted to the International Hospital in Naples; Martin canceled the remaining portion of the trip. The staff at the Casa Materna came to the aid of the Martins and was most helpful and supportive in the situation. They provided people to stay with Sally while Martin, never one to lose any time, alternated visits to museums and other attractions with trips to the hospital to see Sally. She was released on August 26, "quite rested," and they left on the train for Rome the next morning.

They spent half a day in Rome, dividing their time between resting in the hotel and revisiting a few favorite nearby sites. They then said farewell to the Eternal City and took the overnight train to Frankfurt. Sally slept most of the way. In Frankfurt, Methodist Bishop Friedrich Wunderlich, their host, cared for all their needs and for Sally while Martin made a brief trip to Berlin. A Methodist pastor met him at the airport and showed him a refugee reception center where 3,000 people had been processed for resettlement in the past month. The pastor then drove Martin into the Soviet zone to see the Russian Victor's Monument. Martin was deeply moved by what he described as "the sad plight of a great city." The next day after more walking and talking, his host took him to Tempelhof Air Port to catch the 2:30 plane back to Frankfurt. While Sally rested, Bishop Wunderlich's assistant took Martin to Worms to see the church where Martin Luther took his stand before the Imperial Diet in 1521 and paid a brief visit on the way to another refugee camp. When she was able to get out for some shopping, Sally bought him a light meter to go with his new camera.

The morning of September 5 they were up early to take the train to Mainz to board the Rhine steamer for Cologne. From there they went back to Paris for another day of sight-seeing and then took the boat train to meet the *Queen Elizabeth* in Cherbourg the evening of September 8. The ship sailed at midnight. The ocean was rough and Martin's feeling of "uncertainty" returned immediately; he was sick by mid-afternoon. "I know of nothing more completely debilitating than sea sickness," he confessed.

The ocean calmed, and by Sunday he was feeling better but weak. Ralph Diffendorfer, general secretary of the Board of Missions of The Methodist Church and his wife were aboard, and there were pleasant times with them. They arrived in New York on September 13 to find the dock workers on strike, which complicated handling baggage. There was, however, plenty of time to make their train in the evening and they were home before bedtime the next night.

The first order of business after arrival was to introduce themselves to John and Kathryn's new baby, a girl named Sally Beth (Elizabeth), who was born on September 15. John had by now finished all the course work for his degree and was working on a research project to complete the final requirements for his Ph.D. at Texas A & M. He had taken a job teaching chemistry to begin in the winter quarter at what was then Colorado A & M University, now Colorado State, in Fort Collins.

The year 1956 was, like preceding years, filled from its first day to the last. January began with meetings of the Board of Education in Sea Island, Georgia, with a quick trip courtesy of the U.S. Navy to preach to the cadets at the Naval Air Station, Pensacola, Florida. Martin caught a ride on a navy plane to Scranton, Pennsylvania, and went on from there to Buck Hill Falls for the annual meeting of the Board of Missions; as usual it was followed immediately by the Executive Committee of the Commission on Promotion and Cultivation and the Council of Bishops. He was gone fourteen days on the trip, home four nights, and away again for the weekend.

Martin's class on pastoral administration at Perkins School of Theology had twenty-eight persons enrolled for the spring semester 1956. It met at 2:00 P.M. on Tuesdays. Despite his crowded schedule, Martin was faithful to his teaching commitment even though his class often had to be shoehorned between other things. Students had limited access to him outside of class, however. Following the first class session of the semester, he flew to New York for a meeting of the General Board of the National Council. He thought Eugene Carson Blake, the new president, "presided well."

Whether he was at home or on the road, every day was entirely filled. There were few days when he was in his office downtown; Ruth Greer Hamlett, his secretary for most of those years, described him in one word, "gone." When he was in Dallas his schedule was crowded with appointments and catching up on correspondence. One has only to read a few pages in Martin's diary to see what a busy man he was and realize how fortunate he was to have had the strength and energy to meet it. He was rarely sick, though he was troubled with bursitis, had perennial trouble with his teeth, and caught an occasional cold. The heart problems he had experienced in 1940 had apparently disappeared, but the tremor in his hands had not.

When he and Sally bought a new car friends at the University Park Methodist Church in Dallas provided an air conditioner for it, their first. General Conference met in Minneapolis in 1956 with the meetings of the Council of Bishop beginning on April 17. A great deal of time in the council was spent on the Episcopal Address, which had been written by Bishop Fred P. Corson of Philadelphia. When it was finally approved, Martin, who had now sat through five of them, said "it was better than I thought it would be." Many members of the General Conference probably regarded it as too much of a good thing since it took Corson an hour and forty minutes to read it.

The Martin's Frankfurt hosts, the Wunderlichs, joined them to celebrate Sally's birthday on April 20. Martin was elected president of the Methodist Historical Society and president of the South Central Jurisdiction College of Bishops at the General Conference session. The most significant issues before the conference, as before the nation itself, were related to race. The Montgomery bus boycott had begun on December 1, 1955, and with it a new black leader was emerging, Martin Luther King, Jr. The Methodist Church needed seriously to put its own house in order before it could have anything to say to the situation. All African American Methodists were still members of the Central Jurisdiction, the only one of six in the church that was not geographic in nature. It was created to maintain segregation among Methodists, and would now have to be eliminated. General Conference approved a plan that provided for the absorption of the Central Jurisdiction's congregations and conferences into the geographic jurisdictions, the first step in its elimination. This was also the General Conference that finally granted full clergy rights to women, something that had been proposed first in the late nineteenth century.

The South Central Jurisdictional Conference met that summer in New Orleans. Eugene Frank was elected to the episcopacy. During the session, the Dallas–Fort Worth Area honored the Martins on July 1, their anniversary. Martin had forgotten the day entirely and Sally made the most of his oversight at the dinner "to the great amusement of the group."

One of the district superintendents in the Central Texas Conference, Hayden Edwards, owned a house on Lake Whitney about 100 miles from Dallas. "The Pink House" became a favorite refuge for the Martins, and they went there often either to join the Edwardses or simply to be alone and enjoy the lake, and on a few occasions they used it for family reunions. Martin liked nothing better than sitting out at night to watch the stars, and sometimes with the grandchildren he would sleep out, too. When he was in Dallas and had time, he often enjoyed lunch with Perkins School of Theology professor Albert Outler.

Martin represented the Council of Bishops at the session of the Western Jurisdictional Conference at its meeting in Denver. Sally went with him and spent her time in Fort Collins with John and his family in their new home. After the conference, they took a few days of vacation before Will left alone to fulfill yet another overseas appointment.

The Central Committee of the World Council of Churches met in Galyatetö, Hungary, about sixty miles from Budapest, July 28–August 5, 1956. There were twenty-one delegates from the United States. Arriving in Budapest for his first glimpse at eastern Europe, he thought the people looked "sad and sullen." The 200 delegates and staff members were housed in a vacation home owned by a trade union near the Matra Mountains. Their stay was subsidized by the Hungarian church and Martin's bill for the entire meeting, including transportation, came only to $50.

He was well acquainted by now with many of those in attendance and the meeting afforded new opportunities for conversations, some during long walks, with them. There he met for the first time John Deschner, a Texan who had just completed his doctorate with Karl Barth in Switzerland and was joining the faculty of the Perkins School of Theology faculty in the fall, and heard K. H. Ting, the Anglican bishop of China. Deschner remained active in the work of the ecumenical movement and eventually became moderator of the section on Faith and Order. Martin especially enjoyed his conversations with President John Mackay of Princeton about his course on ecumenics. He found Mackay "so full of wisdom and experience that he always over-fills the measure." Martin's natural curiosity, openness, and lack of pretense or guile allowed him to relate easily to these persons and to learn from them without any fear of embarrassment. He was a man of insatiable curiosity, one of his most appealing qualities.

When the meeting was over he assisted Bishop Sigg in ordaining three new pastors at the Methodist annual conference. The final dinner, during which, to Martin's distress, the beer flowed freely and five kinds of wine were served, was given in Budapest by the government in honor of the Central Committee. It was held in a magnificent building. Martin sat across from the Minister of Church Affairs. On the way home, accompanied by Dr. Fry, and Jesse Bader, the general secretary of the International Convention of the Disciples of Christ, he stayed in the Frankfurterhof, which felt "like coming home" since he and Sally had so recently been there. While there he attended a concert given by the Salvation Army orchestra, where he saw General Mark Clark and his family. Martin had first met them in Korea. "The General seemed glad to see me and invited me to Stuttgart where he is stationed." Unfortunately there was not time to go.

Martin was in Frankfurt to attend the great church gathering called the *Kirchentág*, which he enjoyed. It was estimated that 300,000 people attended one of the sessions that featured a chorus of 3,000 and a band of 2,000. Virtually all of the prominent ecumenical and German church leaders spoke—Visser 't Hooft, D. T. Niles, Bishop Otto Dibelius, Martin Niemoeller, R. von

Thadden, and J. Lilje all addressed the delegates at various times. Martin also managed to spend half a day in Heidelberg, which he wanted especially to see because Bishop John M. Moore had been a student there. He spent his last evening in Germany at a performance of Handel's *Messiah,* and left for home on August 13. The plane encountered strong headwinds on the way home and had to make an unscheduled stop to refuel in Iceland. Martin enjoyed having the opportunity to have a brief look at the island.

He arrived in Dallas in time to watch part of the Democratic Convention with Sally, and to spend some time with John, who had just finished his Ph.D. degree in biochemistry, and his family. The problems with low energy and exhaustion that troubled Sally after their trip to Europe surfaced again, and she was admitted to the Methodist Hospital in Dallas in late August for what turned out to be a three-day stay. When she was well enough, they left for a brief vacation in Fort Collins, Colorado, to help celebrate Sally Beth's first birthday on September 15. When they returned, Sally was again not feeling well and was very tired. She had made little progress by the end of September.

Because of her health, Sally was unable to accompany her husband on his scheduled episcopal visit to the Philippine Central Conference on November 5, 1956. Despite the fact that Methodist bishops normally make an overseas visit every four years, it was his first in eighteen years of episcopal service. The flight over turned out to be memorable since about halfway from Guam to Manila an engine failed and the plane had to turn back. While waiting for repairs to be made in Guam, Martin hired a cab and made the most of "an unexpected chance to see the island." He slept most of the way to Manila.

J. B. Holt, a Texan and pastor of Knox Memorial Church in Manila, was his host during the visit. Holt and his wife, Margaret Ann, were shortly to return to the United States in order for him to become associate dean and director of admissions at Perkins School of Theology. He also served several terms as secretary of the General Conference.

Holt took Martin on a tour of the city and to see the U.S. military cemetery where there are 17,000 graves. There were also the mandatory visits to homes for children, schools, hospitals, the seminary, and congregations before the sessions of the annual conference began. Martin preached in Knox Memorial Church on Sunday and heard an anthem composed in his honor. Conference opened, with Martin presiding, and the resident bishop, Jose Valencia, was re-elected to his position on the first ballot. Methodist Central Conference bishops, unlike their counterparts in the United States, serve in the office for a term of years rather than for life, but may be re-elected.

Martin visited Manila at a crucial time. A series of resolutions had been drafted to be brought before the conference, all of which served to give it more autonomy and control over its institutions. A rising spirit of nationalism was present, which Martin judged to be healthy, and he was willing to support the resolutions that were offered to enhance it. Among them were provisions to have all funds coming to the conference administered from a central fund overseen by a national rather than by the Board of Missions in the United States; to place the administration of institutions under the control and management of the conference, and to transfer title for all property to it. Missionary supervision was to be reduced everywhere.

The Methodist Board of Missions in New York was fully aware of the content of the resolutions since Juan Nabong, the legal adviser to the conference, had written Tracey Jones, the administrative secretary of the board, to alert him that "our Central Conference is coming in the middle of November and we expect some nationalistic policies to be aired and pressed for action." Nabong also provided Jones a copy of the text of the resolutions that were proposed (Juan Nabong to Tracey Jones, Oct. 31, 1956). He had advised Jones that the best way to deal with the situation "is not to resist their nationalistic aspirations but to guide them and be sympathetic to them." It would be hard to have found a better person to do that than William C. Martin.

Jones had, of course, briefed Martin on the situation he would be facing, and was anxious for a report as soon as Martin returned home. Accordingly, the day after arriving back in Dallas, Martin wrote the board executive about the mood of the conference. "The spirit of nationalism was not as assertive as I thought it might be although it was quite apparent that the sense of maturity is on the increase" (WCM to Jones, November 21, 1956). He strongly recommended to Jones that funds allocated for the Mary Johnston Hospital in Manila under the War Claims Act being held by the Woman's Division should be released immediately in order for the hospital administration to purchase much-needed X-ray and refrigeration equipment. The bishop urged Jones to use his influence to do it, and quickly used his own by talking to the newly elected president of the Woman's Division, Mrs. J. Fount Tillman, and writing to Clara French, the responsible person at the Woman's Division of the board. Mrs. Tillman was receptive to releasing the money. Mary Johnston was the only hospital in the Tondo section of Manila that had a population of just over 350,000. Although begun as a hospital for women and children in the early 1900s, it was used during the war for the care of wounded soldiers from Bataan.

Martin was necessarily in Manila most of the time he was in the Philippines, but Holt did arrange a trip for him to Tagaytay in the south and one north to San Fernando. A special visit was also arranged in order for Martin to see the Children's Garden on the east side of the city. The children there were from destitute homes, orphaned, or abandoned. At the time Martin saw the home there were 162 children in its care. Although he had only ten days in the Philippines, much of which was taken up by the conference sessions, it was a rich and full experience after which Martin said in his diary, "I think I have learned more in these 10 days than in any similar period of time." He wrote Bishop Valencia in a letter of thanks,

> There can be no doubt, it seems to me, that one of the most strategic of all the fields in which our church is at work is the one where your ministry is being invested. This is true not only for the opportunities which it offers in itself but also for the vital relationship which it holds to the entire Asiatic world.
>
> (WCM to Valencia, November 28, 1956)

The trip home was uneventful. He slept well on the plane and arrived in Los Angeles on November 19. Mary Catherine and

Rudy were waiting for him at the airport. After a brief visit with them, he flew to Dallas in time to join Sally on November 21 at an appreciation dinner given in their honor by the North Texas Conference. Six hundred people attended. It was, as Martin said, "a big evening in our lives."

The next morning Sally and William C. drove to see Donald and Ernestine in their new home in the Heights district of Little Rock. They had been pleased to help them with a loan of $2,200 for the down payment. On the way they stopped to pick up Aunt Stell, who joined them for the trip. Everyone was pleased with the house where Ernestine continues to live.

The December meeting of the Council of Bishops in Pasadena, California, offered a convenient way to spend time just before the holidays with Mary Catherine and Rudy, and the Martins took extra days to enjoy it. One of the days there they went with their daughter to the school where she was teaching in order to meet the children. The council meeting was historic in one way: for the first time since its organization in 1939, Bromley Oxnam was not its secretary. Bishop Roy Short was elected to the office in his place. One evening the bishops heard Cecil B. DeMille's speech "Why I Made *The Ten Commandments*," and were given a special preview of the movie at the studio. Martin declared it "a great spectacle," but admitted that "most of it left me cold and wondering if its literalism would not do more harm than good."

Despite the sophistication that Martin had developed through the years, and the social prominence of acquaintances from all walks of life with whom he was routinely associated, there were vestiges of his traditional Methodist past and strict morality which, from time to time, surfaced with a vengeance. He had lost most, if not all, of his reservations about going to the movies years earlier, and movies had, in fact, become a favorite form of recreation. He loved the theater, musical comedy, and the opera, but he was never hesitant to judge certain material that he saw as "unsuitable." He was never comfortable with social dancing even though he served on college boards of trustees, including SMU, which finally approved it for their campuses. Alcohol was always taboo, and he was not comfortable whenever alcoholic beverages were being served, especially at functions of the World Council of Churches or the National Council, and he was disappointed when his colleagues partook. His children remember that when they traveled as a family, he would eat in restaurants with a bar only if no other choice was available. He was, however, very fond of the fruitcake that the Bill Nicholses, friends in Dallas and members of First Church, always featured on their Christmas menu and sent as a present to the bishop. Their daughter, Virginia, attests to the fact that one of its "secret" ingredients was a liberal portion of fine brandy. Although he was not as rigid on the subject of playing cards or other games that could be associated with gambling as he was on drinking, Martin had at least ambivalent feelings about it. Mary Catherine and Ernestine remember that while they were living with the Martins in Topeka, they would have friends over to play bridge. Sally approved of the socializing but did not play. Since he was gone most of the time, her husband was seldom present when they were playing, but when he was at home, he made no comment to them about it. They sensed he thought it was all right for them to play. He liked board games and his competitive nature was clearly in evidence whenever he played. He felt less enjoyment playing dominoes and never came to really enjoy the great southwestern version of the game called Forty-two. He would play, however.

He never relaxed his views about smoking, especially when it involved Methodist clergy. With the organization of The Methodist Church in 1940, the first step leading to ordination required the District Committee, or the quarterly conference if no District Committee existed, to obtain a pledge from applicants to abstain entirely from the use of tobacco before they could be granted a license to preach. No person could preach in The Methodist Church without such authorization and it was the gateway to ordination and full annual conference membership. In certain conferences the pledge related to the use of tobacco was also attached to the application for admission to the annual conference, and persons who refused to sign for any reason were regarded simply as having never applied. For obvious reasons the

Methodist Episcopal Church, South, had been more lenient in its stand on tobacco than its northern counterpart. As a result, a good many persons promised to abstain after being asked the question by an individual who was a known user of tobacco. The strict northern view, however, was the one that prevailed at the time of reunion.

The year 1957 began with Martin involved in a smoking controversy that did not involve membership in an annual conference but an appointment to the faculty of the Perkins School of Theology. It was precipitated by the nomination of H. Grady Hardin to become the LeVan Professor of Preaching. Hardin, the pastor of Chapelwood Methodist Church in Houston, did not have a Ph.D. degree and was seldom separated from his pipe. Martin was not pleased by the nomination and took the trouble before Hardin's candidacy actually came to a vote in the trustee committee on the school of theology to meet with Willis Tate, SMU's president, and theology school Dean Merrimon Cuninggim to tell them, "I could not approve addition to Perkins faculty if Meth minister uses tobacco." The discussion must have been tense, for Martin makes it a point in his diary to say "we kept our voices calm." The meeting of the committee that had the power to extend the invitation was held on February 6 during Minister's Week. It met through the morning, adjourned long enough for its members to attend the dedication of the Leete Collection in the Bridwell Library at 2:00 P.M., and resumed again immediately afterward. This encounter, like the one with Tate and Cuninggim, was tense but when the vote was taken Hardin was approved despite two dissenting votes, and two others who voiced their reservations but did not actually vote no. Martin voted "no." He declared it "a sad day." The irony of the situation is obvious because a number of faculty members were smokers, including both Cuninggim and Outler, favorites of Martin, and Joseph D. Quillian, a professor of preaching who had recruited Martin to teach a class and would succeed Cuninggim in the dean's office.

It is hard to imagine that fact was entirely unknown to him, especially in the case of Quillian, who was seldom without a pipe. After his election, however, Grady Hardin served with distinction as a member of the faculty until his retirement in 1980.

Many of the changes that Cuninggim implemented at the school of theology and several appointments that he made to the faculty were controversial both within and outside the school, and many persons were dissatisfied with his leadership. He raised the requirements for admission and for the first time Perkins declined to admit everyone who applied. Under Cuninggim's leadership the institution shifted from being a school for preachers to becoming a "graduate, professional" program. Some of his appointments to the faculty were more controversial even than that of Hardin, and older members of the faculty, who felt left out entirely or viewed the changes with skepticism, sometimes complained to the bishop. Director of Field Education, A. W. Martin, a Hendrix classmate, Earl Marlatt, a theology professor, and James Seahorn Seneker, Professor of Christian Education, were among those who seemed to make regular trips downtown to protest the direction Cuninggim was taking the school. All of them retired at commencement in 1957. At the same ceremony Martin was awarded an honorary LL.D. degree from Southern Methodist University. Although it is clear that Martin himself did not approve of some of the things that were being done at Perkins, there is no evidence that he ever failed to support Cuninggim and his administration.

The year 1957 was also the year that the "killer" tornado struck the southern part of the city of Dallas known as Oak Cliff. Ten people were killed and another 200 were injured in the April storm. Many stood and watched the deadly storm, including Will and Sally, as it made its way across town.

During this period, the Martins enjoyed the friendship of Andrew and Kate Cecil. A Polish immigrant, Andrew Cecil Rockover joined the faculty of McMurry College in Abilene as a professor of economics in the early 1950s. On one of his visits to the college Martin met Professor Rockover. A lawyer by training, Rockover was an unusual and extraordinary man who had held important offices in the Polish government before the country was taken over by the Communists and he had to flee. He had a quick and dazzling intellect and Martin found him a stimulating companion. Later Rockover moved to Dallas, dropped his last name, and as Andrew Cecil headed the Southwest Legal Foundation. Cecil's presence in Dallas enabled he and Martin to spend even more time together, and the Cecils and Martins became fast friends. Cecil often invited Martin to participate in conferences sponsored by the Southwest Legal Foundation and invited him on many occasions to give an invocation before a luncheon or dinner at which there was a prominent speaker or timely topic. But their favorite pastime as couples was to drive north to Lake Texhoma and spend the weekend at the lodge located there. They never found themselves at a loss for topics to discuss, and the Martins thoroughly enjoyed Andrew and Kate's company. A lecture series at the University of Dallas is named in Cecil's honor.

At the end of June 1957, Martin began writing the text for a Lenten booklet, which was published as *Christ and Our Resources*. It was designed to be read by youth and adults as part of the 1956–60 quadrennial program for the local church. The twenty-three-page paperback pamphlet was printed in large numbers and circulated throughout the church. In it Martin outlined the pressing need to make provisions to care for those we today know as baby boomers. The high birth rate, Martin knew, would make it necessary for the church to establish additional congregations and build new buildings to minister to them. It would require a great deal of money. As he always had in his ministry, Martin advocated the practice of tithing—giving a tenth of everything to the service of God and the work of God's church, as the "minimum standard" for Methodists. The pamphlet closed with a series of prayers on each of the topics. He began work on it while attending meetings in Lake Junaluska.

Sally was not happy that he was gone on their anniversary, and told him so during a telephone call. In fact, she spent a good portion of the summer in a rented house in Fort Collins near John and his family. Martin joined her there for most of August, and Mary Catherine and Rudy spent a week with them. Just before his trip to Colorado, however, Martin attended the annual meeting of the Central Committee of the World Council of Churches at the Yale Divinity School in New Haven. On the way home he stopped in New York to hear Billy Graham, America's new revival preacher, speak in Madison Square Garden. There were 18,000 people present, and Martin was favorably impressed with what he saw and heard. Earlier the same day he had lunch at the United Nations and heard Secretary General Dag Hammarskjøld and A. Frederick Nolde, a member of the World Council staff. The Bishop of Chichester, G. K. A. Bell, responded. It was, Martin said, "a really big day." He finished the manuscript for the Lenten booklet while he was in Colorado and, in what had become almost a regular event, had two more teeth extracted. This time he also had to have a partial plate.

He flew directly from Colorado to Oberlin College in Ohio for a week-long meeting of the World Council of Churches North American Study Conference. The theme for this session was "The Nature of the Unity We Seek." Claude Nelson, a member of the WCC staff, and Yale professor Robert L. Calhoun spoke the first day; Visser 't Hooft led the Bible study during the sessions. Martin's judgment was that "theologians dominated." His friend Outler spoke on September 4 and Clarence Tucker Craig led the division sessions. It was at Oberlin that Martin first met the colorful and creative Baptist preacher from North Carolina, Carlyle Marney. He does not say what he thought of Marney, but there is no doubt they were individuals who were not cut from the same piece of cloth.

The regular meeting of the General Board of Missions was followed by the General Board of the National Council of Churches. This time Martin had to confess, "If I were not basically committed to this cause much of the work would be intolerable." Although Martin on the whole greatly enjoyed his episcopal service and was entirely committed to it, from time to time, he, like almost all of his predecessors in the office, had passing thoughts of resigning. It should be noted, however, that although it has crossed nearly all of their minds at one time or another, since 1784 only two persons have actually done it—Leonidas L. Hamline and James Armstrong. In a small notebook titled "Thoughts," Martin made an undated entry in which he reflected on the reasons why he had not resigned from the episcopacy. Because it is written in the clear, firm hand of his middle life, these thoughts were likely recorded when Martin was in his prime and, perhaps, in such a moment as this. He began by asking, "What right have I to seek release from this difficult task," and acknowledged the reality that "someone must fill this place if our form of government is continued." And in the spirit of Emerson's understanding of "Compensation," though he does not credit him with it, he concluded, "After all, life reaches its highest level only through sacrifice. This office will give me ample opportunity for entering into that element of life."

A study of the jurisdictional structure had been ordered by the General Conference and twelve bishops, including Martin, were appointed to the committee. On October 9, he and the others, chaired by lawyer Charles Parlin, held hearings in which twelve people made "as good a case as can be made for the abolition of the Jd system." The panel held another hearing in St. Louis with the same results, but St. Louis was more fun for Martin since being there enabled him to have breakfast with Albea Godbold and to see *Cinerama*. Despite the overwhelming testimony in favor of eliminating it, the jurisdictional system still exists. The Council of Bishops held its final meeting in 1957 in Gatlinburg, Tennessee, at the entrance to the Great Smoky Mountains National Park.

Conversations were now being held in Martin's three cabinets to see what churches might do to help prepare their communities for the integration of the public schools. Bill Elliott, pastor of the Highland Park Presbyterian Church in Dallas, called a meeting of denominational executives to discuss "interracial problems." Martin was there for the meeting and to hear his friend Brooks Hays, the liberal congressman from Arkansas, speak at lunch. There was another meeting a month later. The Civil Rights movement was now in every daily paper and on television. President Eisenhower's stroke on November 26 alarmed the nation. The General Assembly of the National Council of Churches

began in St. Louis on December 1. Martin preached at the opening session, and on December 4 another prominent Martin, Martin Luther King, Jr., also addressed them.

The beginning of 1958 was auspicious for the Martins, with the
birth of Nancy on January 2. She was adopted two weeks later by
Catherine and Rudy from the Methodist home in Waco. As he had
most of his other grandchildren, Martin had the pleasure of baptizing her six months later in Dallas. She was a joy to them all.

America's race problem clearly was not going away, and the
most pressing issue now was the court-ordered desegregation of
the public schools. Dallas was in the throes of it. An informal
body simply known as The Minister's Group began meeting just
before Thanksgiving in November 1957 and organized itself in
January 1958. It was somehow appropriate that Martin, a member of this group, had been named the Protestant representative
to a committee of three who were to direct the observances of
Brotherhood Week, sponsored by the National Conference of
Christians and Jews. The other members were John LaFarge,
associate editor of *America* magazine, and Rabbi Louis Finkel-
stein of the Jewish Theological Seminary in New York. Dwight
Eisenhower was the honorary national chairman of the national
observance. Episcopal Bishop Avery Mason was elected to chair
the Minister's Group and Dean Merrimon Cuninggim of the
Perkins School of Theology served as its secretary. Confidential
minutes of their meetings were kept. Statements issued in other
cities were collected, and Arthur Swartz and Edward Tate prepared a tentative draft for consideration by the committee. John
Anderson, Paul Frank, and Paul Sims were eventually added to
form an editorial committee. One of the model statements they
obtained was issued in Houston in October 1957. Bishop Frank
Smith was one of those who signed.

A delegation was appointed to visit with Mayor Thornton and
to report the sense of their discussion with him; by March it was
decided that a statement should be issued as soon as it was ready.
It was clear to all of them that their undertaking should be kept
in strictest confidence. They met twice during March in a room at
the Umphrey Lee Student Center on the SMU campus with about

twenty people present each time. The final form of the statement was ready for release in April, and a group of 300 clergy from churches in the Dallas area signed it. The statement declared enforced segregation to be "morally and spiritually wrong," and advocated the following principles: (1) to seek God's help in solving the problems; (2) to maintain law in order—"We urge that all citizens encourage and support the declared intention of city officials and law enforcement agencies to see that law and order are maintained in Dallas"; (3) to call on churches, community organizations, and the media "to aid in the solution of this problem"; (4) to call on all citizens to "assist the School Boards as they attempt to lead the community"; (5) to urge Christian parents "to create proper attitudes towards race" and to set an example for their children; and (6) to encourage understanding through the free interchange of ideas and opinions. Martin was joined at a press conference on April 26 by Bishop C. Avery Mason, Presbyterian Dr. John F. Anderson, Jr., and Dr. Foy Valentine, director of the Christian Life Commission of the Baptist General Convention of Texas, to read the statement. Thirteen denominations were represented by the clergy who signed.

The *Dallas Times Herald* praised the "manifesto" in an editorial, and said, "In substance, the ministers say to the public and the school board, 'Let's face it. Nothing is to be gained by delay.' And the ministers, in effect, are offering to take the lead in removing all racial barriers." The *Dallas Morning News* was also affirming, but pointed out in its editorial that "regrettably, they did not include the equally true converse: Enforced integration is also morally and spiritually wrong." Its editor, Harry C. Withers, had behind the scenes ensured that the group would be assisted in releasing the statement and receiving favorable publicity. Martin wrote Withers to express his appreciation (WCM to Harry C. Withers, April 28, 1958). Dallas's Jewish Rabbis immediately joined their fellow clergy in supporting the statement.

It was a progressive step to take and Martin was prominent and public in the undertaking. He at once began to get letters about it, and not all were favorable. "I have known you a long time," one short one said, "I am glad to *find you out* you are a no good '*Rat.*' " Lynn Landrum immediately involved himself in the discussion and wrote in his column that "the brethren of the pronouncement although believing and professing that they speak the will of God, know perfectly well that they do not represent the rank and file of the churches to which they severally give guidance." Landrum's final word: "The column says it is best to take force out of the race problem, and let blacks and whites associate or segregate as each individual prefers for himself and his children. Why not?" (Lynn Landrum, "Thinking Out Loud," *Dallas Morning News,* April 30, 1958). There were rumors that African Americans were being organized to present themselves for membership in the congregations of several ministers who had signed, but nothing actually materialized. Reports coming in from ministers across the city were generally favorable to the stand they had taken. In a few weeks, however, the Rev. Carey Daniel, president of the White Citizen's Council of America and pastor of the First Baptist Church of West Dallas "one upped" the statement when he demanded equal time and released his own signed by 330 ministers who opposed integration. They all affirmed their belief "that enforced integration is wrong, and I am opposed to the mixing of white and Negro children in our public schools" (*DMN,* May 18, 1958, I, 9). Martin told Oxnam in a letter they were "mostly of the super-fundamentalist groups" but noted, "We are in for a real struggle" (WCM to GBO, June 18, 1958).

There were also many letters of appreciation from both clergy and laypersons, and they came from all over the country. Martin's colleague Bishop Donald Tippett wrote from San Francisco: "I'm proud to be a colleague of yours. I always have been—but more now than ever. Your leadership in the Dallas minister's statement of *Desegregation* increases your already mountain-high stature" (Tippett to WCM, May 20, 1958). Edmund Heinsohn, pastor of the University Methodist Church in Austin, told him, "I see in the language and in the contents the workings of your heart and mind," and he told of his congregation's decision to integrate in October 1957. A flood of letters, pro and con, went to the *Dallas Morning News* and William B. Ruggles, editor of the editorial page, took a minute to write Martin, "It seems to me that all of them miss the point." It was that kind of issue.

April was also the time for the regular meeting of the Council of Bishops, which was held in Miami. There Martin was elected to write and deliver the Episcopal Address to the General Conference of 1960 in Denver. This was added to the invitation he had already received and accepted to give the 1959 Peyton Lectures at Minister's Week at SMU. The council elected him on the second ballot and Bishop Frank Smith, who also received votes, moved to make it unanimous. The election was not a complete surprise to Martin since it was the turn of the South Central Jurisdiction to provide an author. He did not, however, seek the responsibility and, he said, "There would have been no disappointment in my heart if I had not been chosen." Smith wrote to him later that day to say, "Your election today to write the Epis. message gives me great delight. You are the one man in the church to write this message which will come at one of the most crucial periods in the life of the Church" (Frank Smith to WCM, April 8, 1958). Robert G. Mayfield, general secretary of the Board of Lay Activities, became slightly confused by the announcement and wrote the other Martin, Paul, to congratulate him on being selected. Paul Martin sent it on to William C. with a note attached—"Honor to whom honor is due!" Martin said it was the greatest honor that had been bestowed on him by his colleagues in the Council of Bishops.

As he was wont to do, Martin reflected at some length in his diary about the task and assessed his gifts for completing it. "I suppose it is correct to say that I am better prepared to undertake this assignment than I have ever been before," he wrote, and remembered with some reassurance the passage in Paul's second letter to the Corinthians that "my power is made perfect in weakness." It was an honest and accurate assessment of his status. He also realized that "it is a staggering responsibility to be called upon to be the spokesman for Methodism in an hour like this," but he knew he needed to resist being overcome by that thought. The task, he realized, "is largely a matter of massive toil. A vast amount of research must be made, both by me and by others who will be asked to help." He also recognized that parts of the address should be delayed as long as possible in order to be up-to-date and pertinent. Other sections that dealt "with the more permanent elements of the life of the church should be written as soon as possible." Martin was excited by the assignment. He had, he said, always wanted to write something "permanent" and this was his opportunity. He was also glad to undertake the necessary research. "It would not be presumptuous I believe, for me to regard my whole life as being, in a sense, a preparation for the discharge of this my most difficult and most challenging assignment. The realization of this fact is not to be a burden to me but a source of strength and inspiration. . . . Methodism needs a marching song. I wish I could write it."

He began by reviewing the last five addresses, which had been written by Bishops Corson, Kern, Oxnam, Moore, and McConnell, and made a tabulation in chart form of the subjects they covered. There were fifty-five topics ranging from apostolic succession to war. He wrote each of the bishops in the council to ask how long the address should be and whether a few fields should be treated in depth rather than attempt to cover the full range of topics. He also asked the bishops to name three or four "major issues that trouble the church today." Virtually all of the active bishops responded as well as more than half of those who were retired. Some sent papers or articles for him to consider. The majority included a plea for brevity, probably because Corson's address in 1956 had lasted so long. Martin's research revealed that the addresses had averaged a little more than twenty-thousand words in length—that translates into about eighty typed pages! He wrote specifically to ask advice from the bishops who had delivered the most recent addresses, and asked Bishops Richard Raines, Gerald Kennedy, Willis J. King, resident bishop of the New Orleans Area of the Central Jurisdiction, Nolan Harmon, and Lloyd Wicke to represent their respective jurisdictions as a Committee of Six to review his early drafts before they were circulated to the entire council. Oxnam urged him to include a section on planned parenthood and birth control.

From their replies and his own reflection, Martin decided

immediately that major issues such as race, and the related topic of the Central Jurisdiction, ecumenism, higher education, the family, and delinquency all had to be considered. He created a list of topics and set up a file folder for every subject. There were folders on health and human welfare, young people, doctrine, worship and sacraments, Pope John XXIII, theology, missionary recruitment training, quadrennial programs, jurisdictional structures, higher education, the family, evangelism, ecumenical relations, stewardship, alcohol, tobacco, church and state, economic relations, Negro higher education, world missions, and public schools. He asked Decherd Turner, the librarian of the Bridwell Library at the Perkins School of Theology, to recommend a student to brief the previous addresses for him. Turner said he would do it himself.

The first Episcopal Address was given in 1812 by Bishop William McKendree. America's first native-born son to be elected was very much a "junior" bishop to the venerable Francis Asbury with whom he served. After conferring with several of his colleagues, but not with Asbury, McKendree stood in the conference of 1812 and read his address to the members of conference on Tuesday afternoon, May 5. Asbury, who was surprised and not altogether pleased, rose and confronted McKendree: "I never did business in this way, and why is this new thing introduced?" Facing Asbury, McKendree replied, "You are our *father*, we are your sons; you never have had need of it. I am only a *brother*, and have need of it." Asbury sat down with a smile on his face, and the Episcopal Address became a permanent part of every conference thereafter. McKendree designed his remarks to provide an agenda to direct the business of the conference, but it no longer serves that purpose in the General Conference. When done well the Episcopal Address is a statement for and about the church, and as such must cover a wide variety of subjects. It is a mandate to the church, a clarion call to commitment and action, marching orders for the future.

From his summary, Turner created for Martin a list of topics that had been covered in previous versions of the address. It included such subjects as doctrine and the times, Negroes, holiness, numbers, perfection, periodicals, relations, slavery, revivals, sanctification, science and religion, temperance, and theological schools. Turner also excerpted from them a variety of general quotations that might prove useful. Martin was introspective about the nature of any Episcopal Address and his relation to it as author. "In a sense," he wrote,

> it must be an expression of myself. It will be unrealistic and there-fore ineffective if it speaks in terms that are not in keeping with my own nature and personality. It must be more than I am, far more, but it must not contradict what I am. All that I know and believe and feel and dare must be infused into this message. It will be the voice of all that Methodism has been, is now and all that it might be speaking through me.

The first week of February 1959, while preparing to write the Episcopal Address, Martin fulfilled his earlier commitment to deliver the Peyton Lectures at SMU's Minister's Week. He confided to his audience at the first lecture that a few weeks earlier a man had told him "when you are preparing these lectures, I will be praying for you on one knee and then when you start with that Episcopal Address, I will be praying for you on both knees." All four lectures were given without a manuscript, and in many ways they demonstrated the skill Martin had acquired from a lifetime of preaching from notes out of the fullness of his experience and reading. In many ways they reveal the mature thought of Will Martin, ecumenical spokesperson and pastor at his best. They showcased a gifted preacher describing the practice of his craft; and reading the transcriptions made from recordings, it is easy to agree with his own assessment that they were "as good as I am capable of doing just now." They are worth reviewing, especially in the light of his assignment to speak to the church on behalf of his colleagues in the episcopacy.

The lectures were directed to preachers who made up the large majority of his audience and he declared to them his intention just to "talk to his brethren out of his heart." He promised everything he would say would have direct bearing on the parish ministry and be verified out of his own experience and that of ministers he had known through the years. The central theme of all four lectures was preaching.

The opening lecture was given the title "Sent Out to Preach." Every preacher, Martin said, ought to begin by asking a simple question, "Am I preaching the gospel?" And in order to be the gospel, preaching had to acknowledge two important realities, which he described in the language of the theme of the first Assembly of the World Council of Churches, "Man's Disorder and God's Design." Out of that, Martin said, came the possibility of reconciliation and forgiveness, the two great hinges on which the true gospel hangs. It doesn't matter on which side you begin, man or God, so long as they are held together.

Once this is clearly identified, the preacher must use knowledge and experience to express the gospel to hearers. There is nothing that has been learned that is not relevant, no experience that is unrelated. The best formal preparation for preaching, the bishop said, comes from extensive reading in a variety of fields. "The nearest I ever came to losing my religion since I became a preacher was when I wasn't reading anything but religious books." He urged them to read more than one book at a time, to purchase the books they wanted to read, and to spend mornings five days a week in the study reading. And finally, he said, once you have something to say, learn to say it well. He urged them to avoid distracting mannerisms, effecting emotions they did not feel and using words the congregation could not understand. Whether they knew it or not, the first lecture contained a thumbnail sketch of his own pilgrimage to becoming a great preacher.

That evening he spoke on the subject "Preaching in a Day of Turmoil." Since modern preaching had to be done in a time of unrest, preachers had no choice but to address controversial subjects. He gave them four suggestions on how it could be done: (1) be sure of your motivation and approach it as a preacher, not as an expert or even as a moral reformer; (2) get the facts before you speak; (3) "Never discount the transforming power of the

Christian Gospel"; and (4) "trust your laymen." He illustrated two areas of disagreement in society that he believed demanded bold preaching and knowing the facts—the relation of the church to industry and the "liquor business." He illustrated the latter by a long list of statistical data related to the number of alcoholics and problem drinkers and the cost of their illness to society. These data were a by-product of his work on the Episcopal Address. "The old sermon won't do, get a new one," he said.

Martin urged them to acknowledge the progress made in race relations as an illustration of the "transforming power of the Christian Gospel." "We have a long way to go, but let's give thanks to God for the progress that has been made." He reminded his audience that slavery had been gone for ninety-five years and it was no wonder that black people were impatient and asking, "Oh Lord, how long?" That could only be expected. And, finally, he urged them to take the risk of preaching on such subjects. Their laypersons were more ready and able to hear than they might think. He admonished younger preachers by saying, "You'll be surprised again and again to find how many laymen there are in your church that aren't lagging back behind but are out in front of you." He got a standing ovation when he finished.

The third lecture carried the title "The Preacher as Interpreter." Martin spoke of clergy as interpreters of the Bible, the Sacraments, and suffering. The second topic gave him an opportunity to decry again the ruling of the General Conference allowing unordained persons to administer the sacrament of the Lord's Supper. Not only was it against the principles of early Methodist practice, it had created an obstacle for the denomination in the ecumenical dialogue. "You Methodists just pulled yourself out of the main stream of orthodox Christianity as interpreted by the Church." He urged them to get back to their roots and admonished them to take care in reading the scriptures to their congregations. In fact, he urged on them his practice of memorizing the scripture. He had not, he said, for the past nine years of his ministry in the local church ever read the scripture. It was not difficult to learn it, he said. Read it over five or six times each day during the week and by Sunday you will have it memorized. "I found that when I had read the Scripture lesson often enough to read it properly, it didn't take much more time to be able to read it without looking at the Book." Suffering was a basic part of life and it came to everyone. A preacher had to have a word from the gospel to say about it.

In the last lecture, for which we do not have a title, he told the story of how George Frideric Handel composed the *Messiah*. Locked in his apartment for twenty-four days, hardly eating or sleeping, Handel illustrated for him the essentials of great preaching. He had a great theme; was able to get to the heart of it; and he paid the "toilsome price of preparation." Martin remembered his Old Testament professor at SMU, John A. Rice, had told the students, "The effectiveness of any sermon you preach will be determined by the margin of difference between what you say in that sermon and the total area of your knowledge in that particular field." He went on to say that the composer put everything into the piece that he had—"all that he had learned, all that he had composed," went into it. Martin ended the lecture with a reference to the "Hallelujah Chorus": "Brethren, every real sermon must have in it a Hallelujah Chorus. . . . Search for it, plead for it, pray for it, look for it."

The Episcopal Address was written in Fort Collins, Colorado. John helped his parents obtain the house of a professor who was away during the summer, and Martin moved there on July 4, 1959, and was there through August. Donald and his family came for a week and Bill stayed with them for a month and a half. Martin said he and Bill became "better acquainted," during that time but allowed, "Some things about his outlook are encouraging; others in need of radical change." Surely every grandfather has expressed similar conclusions about a teenager.

The writing was slow and, as he said, "Every word came at a price." At times he described himself as plodding. Most of the time he was troubled with sciatica and in almost constant pain; he even considered for a time going back to Dallas. His original idea to consider one topic at a time quickly proved unworkable, and he shifted to consider the address as a whole. Following the advice he had given in his Peyton Lectures, he read and wrote in the morning and spent afternoons and evenings doing other things.

When he got back to Dallas, he began having regular conversations with Albert Outler. He mentions in October that he had lunch with Outler who "had worked over three sections to their great advantage." A week later they met until three o'clock in the afternoon on the text. In the meantime, the usual routine of a bishop continued. In September, he took his first trip on a jet-propelled aircraft. He was amazed to discover that it took him as long to get his bag and go from the airport to the LeSalle Hotel as it did to get from Dallas to Chicago. Armistice Day 1959, he wrote the final words of the first draft. It contained about 13,000 words. He took this draft to the meeting of the Council of Bishops, which met in the luxurious Camelback Inn in Phoenix. They discussed it all day on September 19, and Martin found their criticism "mostly constructive and helpful." A copy of the draft was sent to all bishops who were not in attendance, and he quickly heard from a number of them with their suggestions. Retired bishop Charles Flint told him in a shaky handwritten letter, "It is too long— much," and encouraged him to "cut out all elaborations and preachments" (C. W. Flint to WCM, December 10, 1959). Paul Martin wrote, "I do not think we have ever had a finer message than the one you have written" (PM to WCM, November 27, 1959). Bishop Newell said that the fact that none of the comments at the council were critical "is a miracle" (Frederick B. Newell to WCM, November 23, 1959). Most, however, made suggestions. A comparison of the draft reviewed by bishops in Phoenix with the text that Martin actually read to the conference in Denver reveals that they accepted the substance of his message without change. The name of the section "The Church and World Mission" was changed to "Into All the World," and it was relocated in the text to the place first occupied by the section "Church and the Industrial Order." The draft Martin took to Phoenix did not contain the unfinished sections "Church and Higher Education," "Methodism and the Public Schools," "Institutions of Care and Healing," "Methodist Laymen," "The Art of Communication," "City, Town and Country," and "Family," but they clearly were intended from the beginning. After all the revisions were made, the final form of the address was a manuscript sixty-nine pages long containing 19,462 words, only slightly less than the last five, which were all judged to be too long. This is the text that was published. The copy that Martin read to the conference on April 27, 1960, however, was typed in capital letters and is much shorter.

After returning to Dallas from Phoenix, he met with Outler and went over the suggested changes with him. Outler urged him to "tighten up the introduction and step up the pace." He also warned him "too much repetition about our theological heritage & responsibility will arouse allergic reactions at least in some quarters." Outler continued, "By the same token, there will be many there listening for specific and negotiable clues to the controversial problems in the areas of race relations and economic & industrial relations—& will be disappointed if these sections are not at least a little more specific." Outler's overall impressions: "splendid conception of the relevant issues, in the right order & proportion & with a fine balance between general principles & practical implications, between the complementary emphases of doctrine and action." He was critical, however, of the pace and of the places where generalities "turned up," where "one might hope for more specific or more concrete, negotiable questions." Outler thought something needed to be included about the issues of war and peace, disarmament and the possibilities and dangers of co-existence (Martin Archives: undated notes in Outler's handwriting).

Martin and Outler worked together on the final draft until almost literally the time to leave for Denver. Martin also sent it to Mary Catherine, who made editorial suggestions. The final conclusion was written on Easter Sunday while he and Sally were riding the train to Colorado. The bishops looked it over once again in Denver and a number of changes were suggested, only one of which was major. That effort was skillfully finessed and final approval was given on April 23. The next day he chose the sections that would be read and prepared his reading copy for typing. His secretary's life would have been made considerably easier had the computer been available, for each version required a complete retyping.

Donald called February 12, 1960, while Martin was in the final stages of preparation, to say that his third daughter had been born. She was a week early. The Martins now had eight grandchildren. Three days later Martin broke away long enough to fly to Little Rock to greet Alice "through the window" of the nursery of St. Vincent's Hospital. A preaching engagement at Hendrix College made it convenient to see her. His old friend Marshall Steel was now president of Hendrix. First grandson, Bill, spent the night with him at the hotel and accompanied him to Conway. After chapel, lunch with the Steels, and another quick look at Alice, he was on the night train for Dallas and back to work on the Episcopal Address. He finished the section on higher education on February 17 and began the section on laymen and stewardship. His life during this time was hectic almost beyond belief: in addition to spending every spare moment on the address, he kept his usual daunting schedule. For example, on March 11, he flew to Austin to address the Committee on Texas Methodist History, attended a luncheon in honor of Bishop Frank Smith, and returned to Dallas in time to conduct the funeral of Pauline Hubbard's husband, Jim. After the funeral he returned to Austin for a dinner in the evening. The next morning the area cabinet met until noon; he flew home and then to Wichita Falls in time for J. S. Bridwell's dinner at 6:30 P.M. to honor the Perkins Lecturer, Ralph Sockman. He rode back to Dallas (175 miles) the next day with Decherd Turner, worked in the office, spent a night at home, and the next morning took a train to Abilene to attend the McMurry College Board of Trustees meeting, attend the Willson Lectures, and meet the Northwest Texas Conference cabinet. He was home before noon the next day, spent the afternoon in the office, and took friends to Nieman Marcus to dinner in the evening. Almost every week was similar.

10

The Last Years of Active Service: Teaching at Perkins

⸺⬥⸺

The General Conference opened in the Denver Civic Auditorium at 11:30, April 27, 1960. John had come from Fort Collins to hear the address and be with his father. Martin's colleague from Nebraska, Bishop Gerald Kennedy, presided in the session. The address was called as the "order of the day" and Martin took an hour and fifteen minutes to read it. It went well. A long journey was finally over. In a retrospect done on the twenty-fifth anniversary of his election to the episcopacy in 1963, he told a reporter from the *Dallas Morning News* that writing the address was the most difficult assignment he had ever been given by the church. "This responsibility required a vast amount of research in an effort to bring within the compass of fewer than 20,000 words the major emphasis in the realm of doctrine and service of the Methodist Church and to point the way toward future endeavors," Martin remembered (*DMN*, May 2, 1963).

Martin was selected to preside the next day in the evening session, but he declined. Perhaps it might have been easier to go ahead, for he was finally to preside at the last session prior to adjournment when ninety-two reports were on the agenda and had to be considered before the delegates could leave for home. This assignment was both a tribute to his skill as a presiding officer and a testimony to the confidence that the committee and his colleagues in the episcopacy had in him. He had been given a daunting task, but he moved the conference carefully and swiftly through its agenda with his usual gracious and firm leadership. His task was made somewhat easier by a decision made by the delegates to give the presiding officer the right to close debate when he thought it appropriate. It is very unlikely they would have given that power to some of their presiding officers. Denver was a watershed in the history of The Methodist Church. The giants of the past were swiftly passing from the scene at a time great leadership was sorely needed. Bromley Oxnam, Frank Smith, and Arthur Moore all reached the mandatory age of retirement in 1960 and were formally retired by their jurisdictional conferences in the summer. Frank Smith lived only two years afterward, and Oxnam lived three.

Bishop A. Frank Smith was certainly correct in defining the time as "one of the most crucial in the life of the church," and Martin's Peyton Lecture on "Preaching in a Day of Turmoil" could hardly have been more relevant to the situation facing the church and society. The World Order Conference of the National Council of Churches meeting in Cleveland in November 1958 had urged the admission of Red China to the United Nations. This sparked a protest within Martin's beloved First Methodist Church in Dallas, and in a host of other places, too. Martin was present at the meeting. Cold War politics were escalating to a crisis over Berlin and the placing of missiles in Cuba. The student-led counter sit-ins began in Greensboro, North Carolina, on February 1, 1960. James Lawson, a Methodist student in the divinity school at Vanderbilt had been expelled in March for his role in a sit-in. He was later to work with Dr. King in the Southern Christian Leadership Conference. One of the resolutions coming before the last session of the General Conference was in support of the sit-ins. The Freedom Rides were shortly to follow. Martin's diary observes, "Here & elsewhere difficult decisions had to be made." Martin Luther King, Jr., joined the sit-ins and was sent to jail in Georgia. The Student Nonviolent Coordinating Committee (SNCC) was formed; Eisenhower was near the end of his term, and a young Democratic senator from Massachusetts named John

F. Kennedy was running against his Vice President, Richard Nixon, for president. Martin had given the opening prayer in the Senate on April 15, 1959, and talked with Kennedy for the first time the same day. "He seemed quite frank," Martin said. On behalf of the Senate, Martin prayed:

> We give Thee grateful thanks for the abundance of Thy mercies by which our Nation was brought to birth and by which it has been guided and guarded and sustained, even unto this day. Grant, we beseech Thee, to Thy servants, the President and the Members of the Senate, such a full measure of Thy wisdom that they may be able to interpret wisely and faithfully, Thy will for the people whom they represent and for this Nation and the nations of their world. And may the decisions which they make this day and every day be so fully in accord with the principles of justice and freedom that the people will be guided aright and the peace and welfare of the world advanced.
>
> (*Congressional Record*, April 15, vol. 105, #56, 5253)

The anti-Communist crusade continued to grip the country and involve the churches. The January issue of the *American Mercury* kicked off 1960 with an article written by Harold Lord Varney titled "S.M.U. Pampers Leftism" (*American Mercury*, January 1960, 16-22). Varney revealed to his readers that this "leftism" was masquerading as "internationalism" in the Dallas Council on World Affairs, whose leader was H. Neil Mallon, head of Dresser Industries. "Its principal base of operations is the Southern Methodist University," headed by "The Rev. Dr. Willis Tate," Varney said. Somehow the fact that Tate was a layman had escaped his attention. SMU and Tate had allowed John Gates, former editor of the *Daily Worker*, to speak on campus in 1958. Since, as the article said, "Nothing in his [Tate's] previous record indicated that he would turn out to be so pliable to the Left," people were questioning the source of the change and the "most probable key to his attitudes, it is generally agreed, is Bishop William C. Martin." Martin, the article claimed, "has virtually ruled Texas Methodism," and "his voice in the conduct of SMU is paramount" (p. 20). Martin, associated in the National Council with persons like Oxnam, Eugene Carson Blake, and John Mackay, all of whom were characterized as "leftists and ecumenical churchmen," had taken steps while its president to squelch the report of the National Lay Committee, and had "whitewashed" Oxnam when he was under investigation by Congress. Martin had also attended both the World Council of Churches in Evanston and the controversial Fifth World Order Conference in Cleveland, which advocated the recognition of Communist China in 1958. "The unhappy drift of Southern Methodist University toward Left interests would not have been possible without Bishop Martin's guarded acquiescence" (p. 22).

On February 11, 1960, the United States Air Force began distribution of Air Force Reserve Training Manual NR 45-0050 INCR. V, Vol. 7, containing the section "Security Education and Discipline," which discredited the loyalty of the clergy and charged the National Council of Churches with being a "Communist front" organization. Officials of the National Council of Churches lodged a formal protest with the Department of Defense the same day. Written by the Air Training Command at Lackland Air Force Base, San Antonio, Texas, the course, designed for reserve noncommissioned officers, began by saying, "From a variety of authoritative sources [unnamed], there appears to be overwhelming evidence of Communist anti-religious activity in the United States through the infiltration of fellow-travelers into churches and educational institutions." Under the heading "Communism in Religion" it went on to charge, without citing evidence to support the allegation, that thirty of the ninety-five persons who worked on the Revised Standard Version of the Bible, sponsored by the National Council of Churches and issued earlier, "have been affiliated with pro-Communist fronts, projects, and publications." It specifically named Walter Russell Bowie of Grace Church in New York, Henry J. Cadbury of Harvard, George Dahl of Yale, Frederick C. Grant of Seabury-Western, and Leroy Waterman of the University of Michigan, since all had been affiliated with the National Federation for Constitutional Liberties, which had been named by the House Un-American Activities

Committee, without evidence, as "one of the viciously subversive organizations of the Communist Party." Methodist missionary E. Stanley Jones was named because "he has consistently urged a collectivist form of government for America and praised the Soviet slave state as superior to the American system" (pp. 15-16). Jones had the previous year been chosen by the *World Outlook,* a publication of the Methodist Board of Missions, as "The Outstanding Methodist." The overall argument in the text was sealed with a quotation from Herbert A. Philbrick, author of *I Led Three Lives,* who had said in a speech before the Daughters of the American Revolution, "There are more names of ministers than any other profession on the list of Communist supporters in this country" (pp. 15-16).

A firestorm of protest erupted from denominations, congregations, the National Council of Churches, and even the national press. The *Christian Science Monitor* printed an editorial by Roscoe Drummond, "Manuals—Aims, Rights, Duties," on February 27, 1960; the *New York Herald Tribune*'s editorial on February 18, 1960, carried the title "How Silly Can Things Get?" It demanded that the Air Force "make known which of its bird-brains is writing its manuals these days." The Air Force writer, Homer H. Hyde, a longtime civilian employee, had, in fact, drawn heavily from a tract produced by the lay organization in The Methodist Church called the Circuit Riders, "30 of the 95 Men Who Gave Us the Revised Standard Version." Two other sources were pamphlets written by Billy James Hargis, whose organization, "The Christian Crusade," in Tulsa had routinely attacked the theology and political views of the National Council of Churches. Hyde told the New York *Daily News* in an interview that his pastor had told him about the Christian Crusade, and admitted he had taken his material from the pamphlets "The National Council for Churches Indicts Itself on 50 Counts of Treason Against God and Country," and "Is the National Council of Churches Subversive?" Representative Edith Green of Oregon read a study of the material in the training manual into the Congressional Record in a speech delivered on April 19, 1960. Of the material in the Air Force publication she discovered that 77 of the 143 lines of text were taken verbatim from the pamphlet "The National Council of Churches Indicts Itself" (*Congressional Record,* April 19, 1960, 7673). Ralph Stoody, the general secretary of Methodist Information, circulated a reprint of the Congressional Record to every district superintendent in The Methodist Church. Hargis immediately volunteered to testify before the House Un-American Activities and affirmed in his letter to its chairman, Francis E. Walter, "After twelve years of research and study on this subject, I am convinced that there is evidence to prove that Communists have infiltrated the National Council of Churches, its affiliated denominations and the Unitarian denomination." He published a copy of his letter in the March 1960 issue of *Christian Crusade* magazine. Rep. Walter was quoted in the national press as saying the Communist charges "are true" (NY *Daily News,* February 19, 1960).

The *New York Times* weighed in with an editorial at the same time (February 19, 1960) titled "Out of Thin Air," and published another a month later, "An Attack on Religion" (March 29, 1960). The *Washington Post* came in on February 26 with "Guilt by Extrapolation." The *Dallas Morning News* was on the opposite side. Most of its articles, which appeared during February, March, and April 1960, carried the familiar name of Lynn Landrum. In a column titled "Are Churches Infiltrated?" Landrum refused to say outright what he knew, but hinted that he had files in his office to document the fact that "the church leadership of the United States has been infiltrated by Communism" (*DMN,* February 19, 1960). On February 29 he took on the translators of the Revised Standard Version of the Bible, claiming that "10 of the 22 active translators also wound up backing all sorts of petitions, pronouncements, funds and organizations which were leftist, radical or actually subversive" (*DMN,* "Why Do They Sign Up?" February 29, 1960). Landrum began his column on March 3, 1960, saying, "Bishop William C. Martin is one of the most dedicated Christian gentlemen the Columntator has ever known," but Landrum criticized Martin for having said that persons who "seek to destroy the council" are, in fact, "seeking to destroy the churches which are affiliated with it." Landrum then reopened the case of a favorite target, Harry F. Ward, a professor at Union Seminary and an influential member of the Methodist Federation for Social Action. Bishop Bromley Oxnam's name frequently appeared in Landrum's column, too. He rose to the subject again in his next issue and responded to criticism from clergy who, he said, "cannot be brought to realize that there is such a conspiracy and that they are looking right down the muzzle of it right now" (*DMN*, "The Church Is of God," March 5, 1960). At other times Landrum openly declared himself to be "everlastingly against the National Council of Churches." Although he continued to describe Martin as "my good friend, that wonderful Christian man," he nevertheless faulted him because he "can't see that it [the NCC] is a left wing circus." Although in time the *News* conceded in an editorial that the Air Force manual was not the appropriate place for an accusation against the churches, it declared that "the Air Force . . . was correct . . . [and] right." Landrum never changed his mind.

In a storm of protests, the manual was quickly withdrawn, and a formal apology extended to the President of the National Council of Churches by the Secretary of Defense. Martin expressed his thanks for that apology in the Episcopal Address in Denver. None of this, however, seemed to have significant impact on concerned laypersons in the church on both sides. Martin's mail was filled with letters demanding explanations or complete withdrawal of the denomination from the National Council of Churches. He faithfully and patiently answered them all. A number of telegrams, obviously the result of an organized effort, were sent to him from Muleshoe in Northwest Texas while he was in Denver at General Conference. One from "Mr. and Mrs. Kenneth Precure and Family" said, "SIR, REGARDING THE BISHOPS DEFENSE OF THE N.C.C. I SAY ITS HOOEY." Carroll Pouncey wired all seventy-four bishops in care of Martin and said, "I PROTEST THE BLIND ACCEPTANCE OF NATIONAL COUNCIL PRONOUNCEMENTS BY LEADERS IN THE METHODIST CHURCH."

All of his annual conferences and the jurisdictional conference followed the adjournment of the General Conference on May 7.

Eugene Slater, Kenneth Pope, Aubrey Walton, Kenneth Copeland, and Martin's old Arkansas friend Paul Galloway were elected to the episcopacy at the jurisdictional gathering in San Antonio. Martin was presiding in the session in which Bishop Slater was chosen. He had a difficult time during the annual conferences because of a severe throat infection which required treatment and reduced his energy. He observed in the diary after they were over, "It humiliates and almost frightens me when I discover as in this period of sub-normal physical vitality how dependent my spiritual morale is upon the state of my health." The jurisdictional conference reduced the scope of his duties by re-aligning the boundaries of the Dallas–Fort Worth Area, removing the Northwest Texas Conference from Martin's oversight. It was combined with the New Mexico Annual Conference to form a new episcopal area. Just prior to the meeting, in anticipation that it would be Martin's last time to preside, the Northwest Texas Conference hosted an appreciation dinner, which 1,100 people attended, and presented him with a new automobile. He and Sally drove home in it. His final devotional addresses were titled "Some Deepened Convictions from These Twelve Years," "It Isn't the Same Old World," and "The Church Is One."

In the midst of this, his doctor and old friend, David Carter, Jr., wrote him a brief letter that clearly contained medical as well as personal advice. Carter told Martin that while reading the biography of Howard A. Kelly, he had come across a quotation from the surgeon's diary that he, without actually saying it, obviously thought relevant to his harried patient. "Leisure and work are both necessary; each lends zest to the other. Leisure is not a luxury of living; it is a necessity" (David W. Carter, Jr., to WCM, June 17, 1960). Although Martin probably needed to hear it, the habits of his life were far too well established for him to take it to heart.

He represented the Council of Bishops at the sessions of the Central Jurisdiction, where he spoke twice and participated in the consecration service of its three bishops. Plans were beginning to be made to absorb it into the geographic areas. More petitions, requesting consideration by the General Conference, had pertained to that subject than any other in 1960. After a brief vacation he and Sally drove to Los Angeles for a visit with Mary Catherine and daughter Nancy. As always Martin enjoyed walking on the beaches. They received word while they were there that Martin's Uncle Ed Ballard had died, the last of his mother's brothers and sisters.

These were difficult days for Martin. He was tired and physically depleted; he had just come through a stressful and difficult time preparing the Episcopal Address; and he was constantly under criticism because of his association with the National and World Councils of Churches. His reading reflects the state of his mind and soul. "Was helped by Georgia Harkness' article on 'The Dark Night of the Soul,'" he wrote in a diary entry in September 7, 1960. The article to which he makes reference was published in 1944 when Harkness was professor of Applied Theology at Garrett Biblical Institute in Evanston. Its title was taken from a work written in the sixteenth century by St. John of the Cross which deals with "the sense of spiritual desolation, loneliness, frustration and despair which grips the soul of one who, having seen the vision of God and been lifted by it, finds the vision fade and the presence of God recede" (Georgia Harkness, "The Dark Night of the Soul," *Religion in Life*, Summer, 1944, 333). Martin had described himself in the same terms years earlier when he discovered again David Cairns's book. Later the same month he wrote, "I am determined by the grace of God to love the good in every person I am associated with without regard for his attitude toward me." In November he admitted, "Awoke in a depressed mood," and asked himself the question, "Is Christianity dependent upon Western prestige?" But during his devotional period he said a sense of reassurance came over him and he affirmed, among other things, that "Christianity has faced greater odds." He and Sally enjoyed Christmas in Fort Collins.

The usual schedule filled Martin's time in 1961, including a series of services in Temple and another set of Willson Lectures at the Methodist children's home in Waco. Paul Martin became president of the Council of Bishops at its spring meeting in Boston.

In the meantime the Civil Rights movement had gained significant momentum to attract national and international attention and was entering a new phase that came to be focused on the freedom rides. Organized by the Congress of Racial Equality (CORE) they began in the summer of 1961 when James Farmer recruited twelve persons of both races for training to test and break down the segregated accommodations in bus stations across the country. By September a large number of persons had become involved. The first two groups set out on May 4, one traveling on Greyhound and the other on Trailways. John Glenn made his historic flight into orbit on May 5. Martin mentioned Glenn's flight in his diary, but did not acknowledge the freedom riders. Each group was composed of blacks and whites. Bound for New Orleans, they planned to stop in bus stations to challenge segregated facilities all across the South. Blacks sat in the front of the bus, whites in the back. The first attack on them took place in Rock Hill, South Carolina; the bus was burned by a mob outside of Anniston, Alabama, and the rest is history. The troubles soon engulfed the newly inaugurated John Kennedy and the federal government set out to enforce the law. The FBI was heavily involved, along with the Justice Department under the new Attorney General, Robert Kennedy. Just prior to the start of the freedom rides, Martin, Catholic Bishop Thomas Gorman, and Rabbi Levi Olan were given awards by the Dallas chapter of the National Conference of Christians and Jews for "furthering the ideas of the Brotherhood of Man under the Fatherhood of God." Martin's old Arkansas friend Brooks Hays, now Assistant Secretary of State, spoke at the dinner.

Martin's devotionals in the annual conferences that historic year, 1961, were titled "Enduring Realities in a Changing World." They included "Human Nature," "History," and "Hope." In September Tom Shipp, pastor of Lover's Lane Church in Dallas, called to say that he had received an African American woman into membership. Martin marked it "the opening of a new chapter that will have its repercussions. We should welcome the day."

Controversy arose around Perkins School of Theology when Schubert Ogden, a new professor of systematic theology, published a book on the theology of Rudolph Bultmann titled *Christ Without Myth*. The title alone was sufficient to spark a variety of discussions, many of them in local churches, on the "too liberal" stance of the seminary. Martin discussed "demythologizing" with Outler over lunch, and although he was not sympathetic with Ogden or his scholarship, he continued to inform himself about it. Delegations continued to wait on him in his office to discuss the Communist presence in the World and National Councils of Churches. In a way untypical of Martin, but no doubt revealing of his harassed state of mind, he described one of the persons who called on him as a "most unreasonable man." As a rule these discussions were seldom productive and they were always time-consuming.

Lynn Landrum, his unrelenting critic at the *Dallas Morning News,* had a heart attack on August 30 and died on September 1, 1961. Martin went immediately to the hospital when he heard of Landrum's illness and later held his funeral. "No unhappy memory can be allowed to mar a friendship like ours," he wrote in the diary that day, but it must have been difficult. The Interstate Commerce Commission ruled in November that racial segregation in interstate bus terminals was illegal.

He and Sally agreed that their Colorado vacation that summer was "one of our most enjoyable and rewarding vacations." It was renewing and invigorating. In addition, he managed to lose six pounds while they were gone. They spent time with John and his family, got better acquainted with their grandchildren, forcing him truthfully to admit "they test my patience more than I should feel." Visits were paid to the familiar sites around Fort Collins, Boulder, Estes Park, and Glenwood Springs. He managed to get a speeding ticket for driving 55 in a 40-mile zone, and discovered in Glenwood Springs that a suspicious banker would not take his check without a verification of necessary funds from the bank in Dallas, necessitating a long distance call at his expense. John's oldest child, Bill, remembers that while they were there they went out to eat in a Chinese restaurant. Seeing a large Chinese character on the wall, he asked his grandfather if he knew what it meant.

The reply was, "Yes, it means children should eat all their vegetables."

In November 1961 Will and Sally made their last trip to attend the World Council of Churches, this time in New Delhi. Fifty people came to the airport to see them off. Martin and Perkins professor Albert Outler were the only official delegates from Texas representing The Methodist Church. When they arrived in Madrid, instead of going to bed Martin went off to get information while Sally slept. That night, however, he went to bed at nine-thirty, woke at two in the morning, went back to sleep, and did not wake up again until noon. He said it was the longest he ever slept at one time in his entire life—the bishop was getting older and was tired.

From Madrid they went on to Rome where they met Bishop and Mrs. Henry Knox Sherrill, who were on their way to a meeting of the Executive Committee of the World Council. They traveled together until Istanbul. Albert Outler met them there, and Martin and Outler kept an arranged appointment with Athenagoras, the Patriarch of the Orthodox Church. He already knew Martin since both had been members of the Central Committee. They discussed the application of the Russian Orthodox Church to join the WCC. After some sight-seeing with Outler and attending a dinner given by Athenagoras at the Patriarchate in honor of the Metropolitan of Finland, which ran so long they had to leave before it was over to make their plane, they arrived in New Delhi on November 17. Lance Webb, former pastor of University Park Methodist Church in Dallas, was on the plane. The Martins were assigned to the Imperial Hotel, an old but luxurious place that was a considerable improvement over the one in Amsterdam in 1948.

The Third Assembly opened on November 19 in perfect weather with all the color and pageantry such a gathering can provide. U. Ba Hmyin of Burma preached "a good sermon." In the afternoon Bishop Lesslie Newbigin of India and W. A. Visser 't Hooft spoke of the work of the International Missionary Council and the World Council of Churches. The Methodist delegates held a caucus afterward and agreed unanimously to vote for the admission of the Russian Orthodox Church, a crucial issue about to come before the body. All together about 200 Methodists were in New Delhi in various capacities. Lawyer Charles Parlin hosted a dinner in their honor on November 25. Many were friends and acquaintances of the Martins.

Martin got off to a poor start by taking a cold and having to miss a session to stay in bed. It is interesting that Sally, who usually became ill on their trips, loved India and went through the entire experience there without incident. Later when Martin was feeling better he tried to walk to or from the Imperial Hotel to the meeting place twice a day—a total of two miles. He was assigned to the section on Unity, and the committee "World Mission and Evangelism."

There were many social occasions, too. They celebrated Thanksgiving with Lance Webb and the Finis Crutchfields in the home of a visiting University of Ohio professor and his family who were members of Webb's congregation in Columbus. "A delightful American Thanksgiving dinner" with them and their three children, Martin noted. Another evening Bishop Shot K. Mondol invited the Martins to join fellow Methodist Bishops Raines, Amstutz, Ensley, Short, Corson, and their spouses for "a delicious dinner and good fellowship" at his home. Bishop Corson and Bishop Wunderlich were guests in the home of the Mondols during the meeting. Early in the session, Martin used his influence successfully to get Ensley a seat on the Central Committee. Martin also met the vice president of India later in the week at Mondol's and enjoyed a reception with Sally at the home of United States Ambassador John Kenneth Galbraith.

There were schools of the church to visit in the Delhi area and other institutions that wanted to honor the Martins. Everywhere they went there were always flowers and gifts, but the poverty of the nation was impossible to ignore. Will and Sally were deeply moved by the throngs of hungry children they saw on the streets. On Sunday, December 3, Martin preached through an interpreter in the largest Protestant church in the city. The next day Prime Minister Nehru brought greetings to the assembly in a brief address. It was closed on December 5 by the American Lutheran Franklin Clark Fry. "His ability to use the fitting word is phenomenal," Martin said. Martin Niemoeller preached at the final worship service.

When the assembly was over the Martins joined Bishop John Wesley and Margaret Lord on a trip to Agra to see the Taj Mahal. "It was all we had dreamed of and more. There are no words that can properly describe its symmetry and beauty." He summed it up by saying, "This was an outstanding day in a lifetime." As a kind of final act, so typical of him, Martin spent a few minutes in the Indian Parliament. The American Embassy had told him it would be impossible to gain admittance, but he managed to talk himself into both houses. While Martin continued an active round of visits to churches and sight-seeing, including a trip to Isabella Thoburn College and the church at which E. Stanley Jones began his ministry, Sally stayed mostly at the hotel to get some rest. He preached once again at Centenary Church in New Delhi on December 10 and they said good-bye to India the next day.

From Delhi they took British Overseas Air to Hong Kong with a brief stop in Bangkok on the way. Missionaries Dick Bush and his wife, Mary, met them when they arrived in the Crown Colony late in the afternoon and took them to the stately Peninsula Hotel—"Luxury such as we have not seen before," Martin said. There were more visits to churches and missions, the usual tourist sights, and a mandatory stop at John Yew's, the "Methodist tailor," to purchase clothes for Sally and two suits for the bishop. A hired car and driver Eddy Chang took them to the New Territories and to see the border with "Red" China, and the first "American" dinner since Thanksgiving was provided by Mary Bush at her home. The Chinese fare was often served in as many as fourteen courses and necessitated a siesta after it was finished, but even that was not enough protection and the bishop became ill with an upset stomach before leaving for Tokyo on December 16.

The first real day of leisure since leaving home was in Tokyo, and he and Sally made the most of it by sleeping, walking at leisure, and window-shopping. Once again he was staying in the Imperial Hotel, but clearly the country had changed since his first visit eight years earlier. The morning of December 18 was spent sight-seeing, but the afternoon once again started the round of "official" visits. At Aoyama Gakuin College the president prepared a traditional Japanese lunch for the Martins. "I ate with some reluctance," Martin confessed, "but S. ate with apparent relish." One of the dormitories on campus had been built with money donated by churches in the Northwest Texas Annual Conference.

They left Tokyo at midnight for the almost seven hour flight to Honolulu and experienced that disconcerting phenomena known to every traveler from the Far East—they lived through the same day twice. Having exceeded their $200 allowance they had to pay almost $50 in duty on their purchases, and getting through customs took more time than usual. Once at the hotel they were ready for some rest.

The next day there were more churches to see and a tour around the island. The plane for Los Angeles was delayed half a day on December 23, giving one last chance for a look around. Martin spent the time walking by the sea. Catherine met them when they arrived, and they spent Christmas with her family. "A quiet Christmas Day with more to be grateful for than can be remembered." Amy, the maid who moved with the Martins from Dallas twenty-four years earlier, came to help Catherine with dinner and to see the Martins. "We enjoyed the visit with her." On December 28 they touched down again at Love Field in Dallas to be greeted by a body of friends. "Safely home after so long a journey. Thanks be to God!!! We unpacked, called a few people and went to bed. . . . This record is closed."

The record was drawing to a close on Martin's active ministerial career, too. Many of his contemporaries and associates had already taken the retired relationship. Bishop Boaz died on January 2, 1962. As always the year began with a trip to Buck Hill Falls for the Board of Missions, but it got off to a bad beginning when he left and lost his bag on the subway going into New York. His major business in his annual conferences was the promotion of the United College Fund, a statewide effort to raise money for the Methodist colleges in Texas. R. E. "Bob" Smith of Houston made a lead gift of $600,000, and chaired the effort. Martin was honored for his efforts on behalf of Methodist higher education when his portrait, done in oils by the well-known artist Warner Sallman, was presented to Texas Wesleyan College in Fort Worth. It hangs in the administration building. The original idea for having it painted was Hayden Edwards's, and the money for it was donated by the Johnnie Johnsons.

⸻

The first meeting of the Council of Bishops in 1962 was held in Mexico City. While there Martin experienced an irregular heartbeat and resolved to give up coffee. The altitude was likely a factor, too. He noted in the diary that he was also experiencing a "heaviness" in his chest when he walked in the morning at home, and his blood pressure had reached 170/100 by the middle of December 1962—too high to suit his doctors. In early May tragedy struck Sally's family when her nephew, Brice's only child, William Martin Beene, was killed in a motorcycle accident. It was a great shock. He was in his early thirties when he died and left a wife and small child.

The Martins spent their summer vacation in 1962 in California. Mary Catherine found them an apartment in Newport Beach. She and daughter Nancy spent a great deal of time going places with them including a trip to Yosemite National Park and the Hearst Castle. Martin described it as "a refreshing vacation." When they got home he went to see *The Bird Man of Alcatraz*. Reading Harvard sociologist Harvey Cox's new book *The Noise of Solemn Assemblies* was a "disturbing" experience.

He and Sally continued to enjoy time in the company of the Cecils, but a great friendship was ended when Dave Lacy died in September. Martin said that at the funeral, "I spoke about a beloved friend." Pauline Lacy gave him a new suit for doing it. Frank Smith died a month later just before the Cuban missile crisis. Martin, like most Americans, heard Kennedy on October 22—"a fateful hour" when the crisis was at its height and the Russian ships were nearing the blockade. About the same time he noted that "the situation in Mississippi becomes more tense." The Supreme Court ordered the admission of James Meredith to the University of Mississippi in October, unleashing violent campus riots.

He began the Willson Lectures at Hendrix College on October 23. Donald drove him over and attended the first, "The Summons to a Higher Conformity." Bill, a Hendrix student, joined them, and much to his grandfather's satisfaction was discovered to be "doing better in school." The second lecture, "On the Edge of a New World," was delivered in the evening. Afterward he drove with Donald to Petit Jean State Park to see the development there. In addition to the Willson Lectures, during 1962 Martin held protracted services in Grand Prairie, Beaumont, Graham, Okmulgee, Oklahoma, and Beatrice, Nebraska. He preached at the Pastor's School in Georgetown as well.

Honors continued to be heaped on Martin as he neared the end of his service. The North Texas Annual Conference named a training center at their camp on Lake Bridgeport for him and another building for Sally. A new dormitory at McMurry College was named William C. Martin Hall and a new church in the Fort Worth suburb of Bedford was given his name, too.

Martin's last full year of active service in the episcopacy was 1963. Despite a troubled and increasingly divided society, it went along pretty much as usual until November 22. He taught a class at Perkins beginning in late January, attended the regular meetings of the various committees and boards to which he belonged, and carried on the business of his conferences. He continued to be gone from home much of the time. This had through the years been a source of tension between Will and Sally, and it did not change as he neared retirement. He was still gone far too much of the time to suit her, too focused on the church and its work, and she sometimes became exasperated enough about it to write him sharp letters. Although she said when interviewed years after his retirement that she never asked him to stay at home, Sally spent a lot of her time alone. On one occasion she was ill when he began preparing to leave in order to fulfill a speaking engagement. She asked him not to go, but he said he needed to make the trip. Frustrated and angry she asked him if he would come home for her funeral if she died. He said he would and got on the train. The matter-of-fact phrase in one diary entry says more than it should—"Dave Lacy took me to the station and S to the hospital."

Although Sally was genuinely supportive of her husband and his work, she did not feel the obligation to be at his side on all occasions. She was independent and had an identity separate from that of the "bishop's wife." As her gentle and deeply devoted friend Mildred Martin (Mrs. Paul Martin) told me once in an interview, "Sally did what she durn pleased." There is a story that Sally was walking with Eula Quillian past the section of seats reserved for the spouses of the bishops at one of the General Conferences. When they passed the section, one of the women seated in the front row said to Sally, "She can't sit in here." Sally's quick and pointed reply was, "I know that, and she doesn't want to anyway." The honor of being the bishop's wife never paid great dividends to Sally Martin. She once told her daughter-in-law Ernestine, "All I ever wanted in life was a small house with a white picket fence." She was always able to "set him straight" when she thought it was in order and did so. Once a reporter from the newspaper called to ask about a large and impressive wedding ceremony Martin had conducted. Sally, who answered the telephone, told the reporter she knew nothing about it but could hardly wait for the bishop to return home since he normally gave her the fee he received from the groom. When she asked him about it, he hung his head and confessed he had not mentioned it because he was "a little short of cash." She loved it.

The wide discrepancy in their energy levels was always part of Will and Sally's problem as a couple; she was sick a good deal of the time despite the fact that she lived to the age of ninety-seven. He was seldom even tired until the very end of his life. He was reserved. She was emotional, outspoken, and seldom hesitant to speak her mind. He worked almost entirely out of his head, she out of her emotions. He was intentional to a fault. She needed to be with people, made friends easily, and enjoyed the company of close friends. He was seldom alone but had few close relationships. When she flared and criticized him, invariably it put him in a somber and depressed mood, and they sometimes had long talks together about their differences. Driving together so they could talk in privacy was one of the ways they used to get through such times. There were occasions when she left for extended visits with one or another of the children. On one of those trips she asked Mary Catherine to help her find an apartment, but about the time this happened Will called and Sally announced she was going home.

Sally was a wonderful grandmother. "Gram" was tolerant of her grandchildren and their wants to a fault. Once when Bill and the preacher's son in Fort Collins joined forces to try their hand at making home brew, Sally was amused and understanding when they got caught while the bishop could see nothing humorous in the entire episode. She was a wonderful cook, a gracious hostess, and she kept a lovely home. She had good things to eat, and when the grandchildren were around she always allowed them to sample whatever she had. Even before fancy parties she gave them a taste. All in all, however, Will and Sally had a good and long life together. "Miss Sally" was a favorite of most of the people who knew her, and few of them ever knew of the difficulties the Martins had in their marriage or of her bouts with depression. The difficulties got worse in their years of retirement, however.

Martin Luther King, Jr., went to jail in Birmingham on April 12, 1963. The famous "Letter from the Birmingham Jail," addressed to white clergy in the city, followed shortly afterward. The resistance movement was nearing its climax and the famous "children's miracle" in which thousands of schoolchildren, some of whom went to jail, protested segregation. Race was the topic of the day and both church and country were caught up in its sounds and images. Martin, too, was giving his attention to the issue.

In the summer of 1963, Dean Joseph D. Quillian, Jr., broached the subject of Martin's coming to Perkins School of Theology after retirement from active service to be the first Bishop in Residence in the history of the school. While that title was not used until Paul Martin assumed the position in 1968, the position was designed for William C. Martin and modified to fit others who came after him. The Bishop in Residence would be a member of the faculty, teaching regular classes with responsibilities to serve on committees' membership and the privileges of faculty status. Martin reported directly to Dean Quillian and often provided him with advice and counsel. He would also be expected to be available as a resource to students, especially those serving as pastors of churches while in school, and to discuss with all students their concerns about ministry and encourage them in their dealings with the church. Martin would be given a four-year term, and for many years the bishops serving in the position changed every quadrennium. It was an innovative idea that has continued at Perkins and has been copied by other United Methodist schools of theology.

Martin liked Quillian's idea and agreed to think about the job even though about the same time he found himself facing active opposition from Quillian and the Perkins faculty to a tithing campaign, which he strongly supported, being planned for the North Texas Conference. He met with them but dismissed their protest as having "no sure foundation on which to stand." The disagreement did not sour his relation to them or to Perkins.

There seems little doubt that at this time he and Sally expected to spend their retirement years in Dallas. They had lived there longer than in any other place during their married life and were well settled with secure roots and many friends. They owned a comfortable home and had even purchased cemetery lots in Restland on the northern edge of the city. Jack Folsom, lay leader of the North Texas Conference, told him of a plan to purchase and give the Martins a house in recognition of their service. Martin promptly vetoed any consideration of the idea as inappropriate, but was willing to accept an honorary citizenship and the keys to the city of Fort Worth.

Led by Martin Luther King, Jr., a vast crowd of civil rights advocates converged on Washington August 28, 1963, for a great march on the nation's capital for freedom and jobs. They stepped from their buses and trains singing, "Woke up this morning with my mind set on freedom. Hallelu, hallelu, hallelujah!" King inspired them with his now-famous "I Have A Dream" speech. Four Sunday school children were killed in the bombing of the Sixteenth Street Baptist Church in Birmingham two weeks later.

The Council of Bishops met in Detroit the second week in November 1963. Sally was not feeling well and decided not to make the trip. The council business was filled with discussions of the race issue and the message that would come from the bishops at the upcoming General Conference. The urgency of the topic was highlighted by the presence of seventy young clergy who threatened to picket if the bishops failed to take a clear stand. The impending merger with the Evangelical United Brethren Church was also hotly discussed. While in Detroit, Martin had lunch with Bishops Holt and Purcell, a group Martin described as "the remnant of the class of '38."

On November 19 Martin spoke at Dillard University in New Orleans and the next day at Wiley College, both black institutions. The morning of November 22 he went to the fifth floor of his office building on Main Street to watch the parade honoring President John F. Kennedy and his wife, Jackie, who were visiting the city. Sally was at the Trade Mart waiting for the luncheon to begin following the parade. A banner headline in the *Dallas Morning News* that morning had announced "Storm of Political Controversy Swirls Around Kennedy on Visit." The article announced that the "divided Texas Democratic party continued its feud," and reported that Senator Ralph Yarborough, angry because he and his wife had not been invited to a reception at the Governor's Mansion, "let go a blast" at Governor John B. Connally as the plane carrying the president sped toward Texas. Despite the warm reception that was given to the Kennedys when they arrived, five minutes after Martin saw him ride past the Cokesbury Building waving to the crowd, the president was dead. The tragedy of Dallas and the nation began.

Upon hearing the news, Martin hurried home where he and Sally spent the rest of the day together watching television reports. About mid-afternoon the *Dallas Morning News* called and asked for a statement. Like many Americans, the Martins were awake much of the night, "stunned by the events of the day." Martin kept his regular schedule on Sunday which took him to Sulphur Springs in the morning and then later to Picton for a dedication service. He heard the news of Oswald's murder at noon that day. Although he was unaware of it at the time, a sermon had been preached in Northhaven Methodist Church in Dallas by its thirty-two-year-old pastor, William A. Holmes, which would bring even more attention to Martin and to Dallas.

Holmes, who later became the pastor of the Metropolitan Methodist Church in Washington, D.C., had reported in his sermon that some Dallas schoolchildren had cheered when Kennedy's death was announced. His sermon was titled "One Thing Worse Than This," and was based on the text from Matthew's Gospel that tells the story of Pontius Pilate washing his hands in the case of Jesus and declaring, "I take no responsibility for the death of this man." The "one thing worse," Holmes declared, would be for the citizens of Dallas to refuse to accept their responsibility. Dallas was the city, he told his congregation, where Vice President and Mrs. Johnson were cursed by a crowd in a hotel lobby; where Ambassador Adlai Stevenson was heckled while making a speech and was struck with a sign; where many leaders had been fearful of what might happen if the president visited the city, and where "4th grade children in a north Dallas public school, clapped and cheered when their teacher told them of the assassination of the President last Friday afternoon." It was his contention that the children had learned such hate in their homes. "In the name of God," Holmes asked, "what kind of city have we become?" When the sermon was finished, an usher handed Holmes a note saying that Oswald had been killed during the sermon and he informed the congregation of that news.

The sermon was immediately picked up on the news wires. The Wednesday evening before Thanksgiving Holmes made a television appearance that was carried across the nation, and within five minutes the switchboard at the station received a number of threats against the minister's life and that of his family. They were removed immediately from their home and placed in seclusion under twenty-four-hour police guard (see *New York Times*, Thursday, Nov. 28, 1963, C-26). Dallas Independent School District Superintendent, W. T. White, quickly denied Holmes's allegation, but one or more teachers confirmed the truth of his remarks. Eleven clergypersons stepped forward to say they could support his claim and invited the newspapers to examine their evidence. Martin went to see Holmes where he was in seclusion, and the distracted state of Martin's mind is clearly illustrated by the fact that on the way he ran a red light and hit a car. Fortunately, no one was injured. He had also called earlier at Parkland

Hospital to inquire about Governor Connally and left messages for Nellie Connally and Lady Bird Johnson.

The day after Thanksgiving, a group of seventy pastors met for lunch to discuss the situation and Bill Holmes's statement. The discussion lasted more than two and a half hours, but Martin reported there was almost entire unanimity in the decisions. Their resolution expressed "wholeheartedly our defense of our brother William A. Holmes and every other minister's right in freedom of the pulpit, to declare the mind and spirit of Christ in every area of human life." Afterward Martin was interviewed on television and made a statement. He also wrote a pastoral letter to the congregations and clergy of Dallas on November 30. In part the statement, intended to be read in every Methodist congregation on Sunday morning, said:

> The tragic events of the past week have compelled all of us, preachers and lay people alike to re-examine our own lives and the social order in which we live under the insistent probing of the questions, "How could these heinous crimes have been committed here?" The crowds of people who thronged our churches last Sunday and Monday gave evidence that there is a deep desire in their hearts for a renewal of confident faith in realities that cannot be shaken by the forces of evil. This is no time for hysterical self-condemnation but the demands of a righteous God will be satisfied with nothing less than the firm resolve that by His help the insane bitterness and hatred which inspire such crimes shall be purged from our lives as individuals and as a people.

Martin's response brought both praise for his support of Holmes and harsh letters of criticism. One signed "A Dallasite" said, "Catholics attend mass for relief from their shock and grief, but your members attended church for the same reason and were accused of creating a 'climate' that encouraged a *maniac* to murder the President." The writer prayed, "May God help you to correct your thinking before you *ruin* your own church." On December 3, Martin prepared a form letter to be sent in reply to those who wrote. In part it said,

I have complete confidence in Bill's integrity, and in the soundness of his purposes. It was, in my opinion, unfortunate that he should have used as an illustration an incident that he did not feel free to document. There have certainly been enough instances in Dallas during the last ten days, and during preceding months, to fully illustrate the tragic results that bitterness and hatred can bring to the lives of individuals and groups.

He concluded by expressing his hope that in the future Holmes would resolve "to secure the opinion of at least a few trusted friends before making a decision that involves such far-reaching consequences as this one has done."

Newspapers all across the nation carried articles and editorials about Dallas and its role in the assassination. The city to this day carries the stigma of being the place where Kennedy was shot. One of the pieces written to counter the trend was done at New Year's by merchant prince and now elder salesperson of the city, Stanley Marcus. Marcus outlined a number of things that were "right" with Dallas, but moved in the bulk of his editorial to speak of the things that still needed its attention. He agreed with Erik Jonsson, a distinguished citizen, "that a city, like individuals or business institutions, must take an honest look at its inventory and be willing to consider its faults as well as its assets." He listed three: First was a slum problem that had not been addressed. Second was a spirit of "absolutism." Quoting an editorial written by Tom Yarbrough, a staff correspondent of the St. Louis *Post Dispatch* who said, "Democracy is a method of reaching a consensus. Those who reject the consensus reject democracy," Marcus urged "the acceptance and insistence by all citizens on toleration of differing points of view." The final point was to shift the attention formerly given to growth "to the quality of our endeavors." He concluded by saying, "Dallas should forget about its 'civic image' as such. The best public relations comes from doing good things and by not doing bad things. Let's have more 'fair play' for legitimate differences of opinion, less coverup for our obvious deficiencies, less boasting about our attainments, more moral indignation by all of us when we see human rights imposed upon."

Martin wrote his thanks to Marcus, who was an acquaintance of Sally's, and said, "Your analysis of our situation is, in my opinion, one of the most factual and sympathetically understanding that I have seen. I am personally grateful for the courage and insight which it reveals" (WCM to Stanley Marcus, January 8, 1964).

—⟨⟨⟨⟩⟩⟩—

Martin expressed in his diary on New Year's Eve thanks "to God for a year of rich and trying experiences." One of the interesting curiosities in the Martin archives is a subpoena issued to William C. Martin, Thomas Tschoepe, vicar general of the Catholic Diocese of Dallas, W. A. Welsh, national president of the Christian Disciples of Christ and pastor of the East Grand Christian Church in Dallas, and Thomas Fry, pastor of the First Presbyterian Church to appear in Criminal District Court #3, February 10, 1964, as witnesses for the defendant, Jack Ruby, in his trial for murder. There is no indication on the form that it was ever served "officially"; we know that Martin never appeared in court, but the subpoena certainly does exist.

Shortly after the assassination and subsequent murder of Lee Harvey Oswald, Martin began to get a few letters from persons who wished to contribute to the support of Oswald's widow and family. A fund was established through the Fort Worth Council of Churches to receive and disburse contributions, and Martin advised interested persons of its existence. A memorial book fund was quickly established by the Democratic Women of Dallas. Martin, along with Willis Tate, president of SMU, Rabbi Levi Olan of Temple Emanuel, Catholic Bishop Thomas Gorman, and others agreed to endorse the effort. Its first project was to place copies of Kennedy's Pulitzer Prize–winning book, *Profiles in Courage,* in all the libraries of the city and county.

By the time emotions and feelings were beginning to adjust to the tragic events in Dallas, the Martins were caught up in the final days of Will's active service. Sally went with him to New York and on to Buck Hill Falls for his final meeting with the Board of Missions. They saw *The Chinese Prime Minister,* which Sally liked, *Oliver*, and Robert Preston in *Nobody Loves an Albatross*. The World Division of the Board, which Martin had chaired for so many years, expressed appreciation for his service and gave him a standing ovation and a reception. In addition to Dean Quillian's offer to come to Perkins, Bill Dickinson offered Martin office space and a place on the staff of Highland Park Church. What he thought was a routine meeting of the Executive Committee of the Commission on Promotion and Cultivation in late-January turned out to be in his honor. They gave him a slide projector. The second week in February he gave the Willson Lectures at Texas Wesleyan College in Fort Worth. They were appropriately titled "Enduring Realities in a Changing World." The lectures were titled, "The Price and Challenge of Change," "On the Edge of a New World," "Marching to a Distant Drum Beat," and "This Is Life." He and Sally were given an elegant suite at the Fort Worth Club to use while they were there. The conference laymen gave a banquet in Martin's honor on the last day of the lectures, attended by 400 people, and gave him a gift certificate.

The South Central Jurisdictional College of Bishops held its regular meeting in Lincoln and all eight of the active bishops were made "Admirals in the Nebraska Navy" by Governor Morrison. The World Division meeting in New York presented him a piece of Stuben glass. The Texas Methodist Planning Commission honored him with a banquet at the Lakeview Assembly near Palestine, Texas, on February 25. Martin commented that he had recently discovered that "retiring a bishop is apparently a favorite indoor sport." His longtime Arkansas friend Bishop Paul V. Galloway, now serving the San Antonio Area, described Martin as having all the necessary qualifications of a bishop—"a strong sitter," "a firm stander," "a strong walker," and "an enduring runner" (*The Texas Methodist*, March 13, 1964).

In between celebrations and the regular meetings, he taught his regular class in pastoral administration at Perkins and managed to find time to preach in a weeklong series of services in Waxahachie. He and Sally took Pauline Lacy to see *It's a Mad, Mad, Mad, Mad World*, which he thought was "very funny." He saw it many times in coming years. By contrast, he thought the *Fall of the Roman Empire* "an almost meaningless spectacle. An enormous waste of money and of our time." He and Sally had planned to join Andrew and Kate Cecil for a brief vacation in Biloxi, Mississippi, in March, but car trouble forced them to cancel their plans. When the necessary repairs were completed, they went instead for a few days to Natchez and toured the houses. Afterward the Board of Trustees of Southwestern University gave a dinner in his honor and presented a gift of a silver coffee service.

The Council of Bishops met in Pittsburgh just prior to the opening of General Conference. Almost all the bishops and most of their wives were present. Sally was there, too. The meetings for him were interspersed with trips to a dentist to repair a broken front tooth.

The General Conference opened on April 26, 1964. Martin presided for what he described as "another last time" at the evening session on April 30. He helped Gerald Ensley preside the next morning and heard Albert Outler preach. Race was the principal issue before the conference and "in most of the voting the south was out-voted on racial matters." Martin was successful, however, in leading the effort to bring the next General Conference session (1968) to Dallas. It would be the first in that city since 1930 when the Methodist Episcopal Church, South, held its quadrennial conference there, and would become the site of the merger of The Methodist Church and the Evangelical United Brethren, which formed The United Methodist Church. Although the delegates failed to finish their business by the stated time of adjournment, when it was finally over on May 8 the Martins took the train for home in the company of their friends Paul and Mildred Martin.

Once home he attended his last meeting of the SMU Board of Trustees and attended the groundbreaking ceremonies for the Sally Martin Recreation Hall at the North Texas Conference camp in Bridgeport. By this time Sally was completely exhausted and had retreated to rest. When he preached in Olney the members of the church presented him a rod and reel plus a tackle box on the somewhat misguided assumption that after retirement he expected to spend time by a lake.

The North Texas Conference, which met first in the 1964 round of conferences, hosted a great retirement dinner at the Sheraton Hotel in downtown Dallas on May 25. Tickets were $5.50 each. Highland Park senior pastor Bill Dickinson presided, Bill Mann sang several of Martin's favorite hymns, Bishop Everett Palmer from the Pacific-Northwest Area spoke for the Council of Bishops, and J. V. Folsom, lay leader, spoke for the conference. Mrs. Fitzhugh Talbot, president of the Minister's Wives Club, spoke words of appreciation to Sally, describing her as having endeared herself by her qualities of "love for people, her gracious spirit, her humility, her warmth and strength." Bishop Palmer described Martin as "like a tree" standing tall, "Texas at its best," a "landmark" for younger bishops coming into the council. Along with the speeches Folsom presented a gift of almost $7,000 to cover the cost of a trip to the Holy Land (see North Texas Conference Edition, All Church Press, June 5, 1964). Martin declared it "one of the great evenings of our lives." Perhaps he should have said, "another of the great evenings." His devotions the last year were titled "Time Is Always on God's Side," "This Is a Living Universe," and "Liberty Comes with Christ's New Law." At the ordination service he asked all the persons he had ordained during the past sixteen years to come forward—"an impressive sight."

The Central Texas Conference followed with yet another dinner at the Texas Hotel in Fort Worth with more than 500 present. Their gift was a "shiny new Olds" which was brought into the ballroom and presented to the Martins. Again everyone he had ordained came forward at the ordination service. Sally stood with him when the concluding doxology was sung.

Martin's retirement became official after the meeting of the jurisdictional conference in July, but by mid-June he was packing boxes of books and preparing to move out of the office he had occupied for sixteen years at the Cokesbury Building on 1910 Main Street in downtown Dallas. Martin wrote a farewell column in the *Texas Methodist* to the preachers and Methodists of the Dallas–Fort Worth Area just prior to the opening of the jurisdictional conference. Thanking them for their generous gifts, he concluded, "The trip will be over in a few months and the car will wear out, but the friendships which we have formed through these years will never wear out and the deep running sense of gratitude for fellowship that is rich and inspiring will never be over."

He preached his last sermon as an active bishop June 28, 1964, on the occasion of the formal opening of the Walnut Hill Methodist Church in Dallas. Donald, John, and their families were present. The next day he presided at the opening session of the jurisdictional conference, which conveniently was meeting in Dallas. W. McFerrin Stowe of Oklahoma City was elected to fill the place held by Martin in the Jurisdictional College of Bishops. Bishop Kenneth Pope was assigned to the Dallas–Fort Worth Area.

Approximately 600 people came to the retirement dinner on the day when forty-six years earlier Will and Sally had been married. Bishop Kenneth Copeland presided; granddaughter Nancy serenaded them with a violin recital. Paul Martin spoke and remembered 1938 in Birmingham when he had laid his hands on Martin's head in his consecration as a bishop of the Methodist Episcopal Church, South. He praised him for four things: "the ability to demonstrate, hard, straight, fearless thinking"; possessing the "heart of a pastor"; a compelling sense of "divine mission"; and the "inner certainty of his own soul." Martin concluded his remarks by quoting the poet and philosopher Tagore. "When you took your leave, I found God's footprints on my floor." The *Dallas Times Herald* article about his retirement headlined it as "The Passing of an Era," and indeed it was. For all of those who said with good reason that "he looked like a bishop," the writer described him as wearing a 44-long coat, six feet tall, weighing 188 and agreed he was "solid as the rock of Gibraltar . . . majestic in appearance, his motion and talk slow, deliberate" (*DTH,* June 21, 1964).

Martin's farewell remarks were printed in a small pamphlet published by the First Methodist Church in Dallas and titled "If This Were the Beginning." He began by expressing the feelings that all persons coming to retirement have felt. He noted that he had for forty years listened to similar speeches at annual conferences, and now it was his time. He expressed his appreciation to his family and to Sally. "Those of you who know her can testify that she has never been too greatly impressed by the exalted position of the episcopal office. If I had ever been tempted to delusions of grandeur, she would quickly have deflated that erroneous notion." He told the audience about his plans to join the faculty at Perkins "for a period of teaching and counseling." He said he hoped to do some "evangelistic preaching" but warned them he was already booked until the summer of 1965. While he admitted he would be glad to lay down the problems, he told the audience, "I wish that instead of retiring, I were beginning all over again." He knew the days ahead were going to be difficult but, he said, "I would like to have a greater share of participation than will now be possible."

Martin predicted that the world was ready to "rebel against the tyranny of materialism and . . . assert its instinctive faith in the ultimate and all-embracing reality of the spirit." It will, he continued, "be a great time for preaching." In the days ahead the church will not have the option not to play a role. He cited examples of those who had "lifted up their voices in calling the Church to a courageous championing of the rights of the rejected and the oppressed." Among those he mentioned were Bishop Atticus G. Haygood, who championed the cause of the freed slaves in his book *Our Brother in Black,* and the conference preacher, Harold Bosley. He closed by expressing his hope that the church "will move, more confidently and more vigorously, into its appointed ministry of reconciliation."

> There is, in my opinion, no place in any Church for prejudice, bitterness, and intolerance. But the Church excludes no one who, in a spirit of penitence, earnestly desires to walk with Christ. It is in the business of taking people as they are and, through the transforming grace of Christ, of setting their lives on a different course. I am not suggesting the lowering of standards or the compromising of convictions but the Church dare not, in pharisaical self-righteousness, detach itself from any area of human need.

Sally came to stand with him when he finished. The *Daily Christian Advocate* reported that "the audience, swept by the dignified emotion of the closing moments of a great career, sang 'Blest Be the Tie That Binds,' in a gesture of farewell and benediction to Bishop Will and Mrs. Sally Martin" (*DCA*, July 2, 1964).

When the conference adjourned the Martins went home with their children and grandchildren, had lunch, and then headed to the Edwards's "Pink House" on Lake Whitney to spend their first days in retirement. While there they ate fried chicken and catfish, looked at slides, sang, and slept under the stars. Martin preached on July 5 in the little church at Morgan, and in commemoration of the occasion used the text John 12:32, from which he had preached his first sermon fifty years earlier. They were back in Dallas on July 7 in time for him to take and pass the mandatory physical at SMU and to see *The Pink Panther*, which he, predictably, said "was no good by my standards." Decherd Turner sent help from the Bridwell Library to finish moving his books from the downtown office, and then it was back to the Pink House for some leisure time with the Edwards. They celebrated with an elk filet dinner. While there he read Warren Leslie's *Dallas: Public and Private*. He found it "a disturbing account but, on the whole, sound."

When he returned home he began unpacking in his new office at Perkins and finished moving out of his Cokesbury Building office on July 16. Bishop Kenneth Pope was already moving in. He also said good-bye to secretarial support which by now he had come to take for granted and found himself having to get "reacquainted with the typewriter." Writing two letters took two hours. Pauline Lacy helped to ease the pain of the transition by taking him and Sally to Nieman Marcus for dinner. Catherine and her daughter, Nancy, were still with them as was Donald's Margaret. Taking Catherine and Nancy to the airport, Martin had a wreck in the new car, "which caused me much anxiety." Repairs cost $75. Margaret stayed with them until the first week in August. He and Sally ate out more than ever, made some long-overdue trips to the movies, and went to see Donald and his family in Little Rock. While there he and Donald made a short trip to Randolph to see the Tennessee relatives.

Planning the trip they had been given to the Holy Land and getting settled at Perkins all took time, but in August he and Sally were off for some real vacation in Colorado. Sally was troubled with vertigo on the way and had chest pains while they were in Fort Collins causing her to miss many of the excursions, but it was a fine time for all of them. They were home on September 1 and six weeks later left on the long anticipated trip to the Holy Land.

Just before they left, Martin received a long letter from Albea Godbold. He had wanted to be present for the festivities but had been unable to attend the jurisdictional conference. Godbold was in a philosophical mood as he reflected perceptively on his old friend's transition from active to retired status.

> I have often thought that while there is no entirely smooth and satisfactory way for a person with ambition, drive, and love for his work to retire, it is probably exceptionally difficult for a bishop in The Methodist Church to take off the harness and adjust to retirement. There is no way to taper off in the work of the episcopacy. Up to the very day of retirement a bishop has full responsibility and full work. The day after retirement, he has no responsibility and nothing whatever to do unless he himself has arranged for it in advance. . . . I know it was hard on Ivan Lee Holt, and I have heard it was not easy for A. Frank Smith.

Reflecting on his own outlook at this point in life Godbold asked if he and Martin were as "hopeful, confident, and enthusiastic" as they were "two score years ago." He wrote,

> True, when we marched away to the first World War, it was morning and we believed that we were going to help the world to take a great leap toward perfection. There was heroism in our souls and we were willing to follow the great leaders of the time over the rim of the world if need be for the sake of the idea. Soberly we have since learned that the world is not going to be remade in a day, but even so we have never lost confidence in the ideal, and we still follow the gleam.
>
> (Godbold to WCM, October 2, 1964)

Godbold had, without knowing it, echoed the sentiments Martin expressed in his statement to the jurisdictional recognition dinner, and just before leaving on the Holy Land trip he replied— in longhand. He told Godbold he had been preaching in Little Rock and Memphis and had kept busy. "How it will be later on, I cannot tell but, thus far, retirement has had no unhappy elements." He said he was thinking about writing two small books, one for clergy and the other for laypersons, but was not sure "when the pressure is off" whether he would actually get it done. His work at Perkins would begin in the second semester. He closed by telling Godbold, "I am deeply and enduringly grateful for your friendship."

Will and Sally flew to New York on October 12 and boarded the *Constitution* the next day. Their stateroom, due to the generous gift from the conferences, was the most comfortable they had ever had. They discovered the Folsom's had sent fruit and the Bill Nichols family had sent flowers for their cabin. The ship, with a passenger capacity of 1,088, was only about half full. Martin learned the captain was both a Methodist and the son of a Methodist preacher and concluded they had "been in safe hands." He read Harry Emerson Fosdick's *Pilgrimage to Palestine* (1927) while Sally had a "long sleep."

The voyage was smooth, Martin managed to avoid seasickness by eating a light dinner, "mostly tomato juice and yogurt" and preached, at the invitation of the night chef who was a Methodist local preacher and director of the Christian Fellowship on the vessel, to a well-filled room, including the captain, in the Steward's Mess on Sunday. They made a stop in the Madeira Islands and went ashore to visit Funchal, its capital, and take the tour up the mountainside. He told the readers of the *Texas Methodist* that the quality of the fine wines for which the Islands were famous, "does not come within the range of our Methodist acquaintance" ("Bishop and Mrs. Martin Write About Tour," *Texas Methodist*, November 6, 1964).

On October 21 they arrived in Gibraltar and toured the "rock." Its fortifications caused him to reflect on "the completeness with which nuclear weapons have pushed into a rapidly receding past" such fortresses once considered impregnable. Two days later, at nine o'clock in the morning, they reached their destination, Naples, and debarked. Some of the same staff members were at the Excelsior Hotel when they checked in. Sally shopped, but the weather was bad and curtailed their sight-seeing. They did pay a return visit to the Casa Materna and eventually to Pompeii and the Blue Grotto. Martin rode the chairlift to the top of Anacapri. They went on to Rome from there.

Albert Outler was in Rome attending the third session of Vatican II and had gotten Martin a pass to sit with the Protestant observers in one of the sessions. The topic being discussed was "The Relation of the Church to the Modern World," and the focus of the discussion was birth control. Cardinal Leger of Canada, Cardinal Suenens of Belgium, and Patriarch Maximus of Antioch in Syria urged a reconsideration of the traditional prohibition of the church. Since all the speeches, save the one by Patriarch Maximus who spoke in French, were in Latin, a priest from Birmingham, England translated for them. It was, he said, "one of the real great experiences of my life." After the session, he had lunch with Outler who later joined the Martins for dinner at their hotel.

From Rome it was on to Cairo by air. After taking four tours, Martin discovered that his camera had been improperly loaded and he had failed to get any pictures. He talked to the dean at the American University about a possible position on the faculty for John but failed to report what he learned. By making a great effort, he learned on November 4 that Lyndon Johnson had been elected president by a large majority. He and Sally had voted absentee while in Naples. At the pyramids they watched the sound and light presentation and wrote the folks at home that if they could have selected any place to be with them, this should have been the one.

Late in the afternoon of November 4 they flew to Luxor to visit the Valley of the Kings. They were there four thoroughly engrossing days. These exciting days were somewhat marred by an event when they were leaving, however. Martin attempted to take a picture of the airport, forbidden at the time by national security laws, and was apprehended by a soldier who demanded his camera. When Martin refused, he called his captain. The matter was being resolved in an agreeable manner when a two star general suddenly appeared with soldiers who confiscated the offending roll of film. He promised Martin he would send it back if there were no pictures of the airport. In the meantime, the plane waited for them to board. Fearful that it would leave without them, Martin gave up his pictures of Luxor. It was not a pleasant experience. After a stop in Cairo, they flew directly to Beirut. They learned of the death of G. Ray Jordan, Martin's old friend, while they were there.

In Beirut they visited the American University and the Near East School of Theology, and toured the usual sights. In the School of Theology library he learned from the *New York Times* that Earl Cabbell, former mayor of Dallas, had been elected to Congress. They took trips to Baalbeck, Damascus, and Biblos, and there witnessed for the first time what Martin described as "a congestion of human wretchedness and despair—the refugee camp." From Lebanon they planned to fly directly into Jerusalem but their plane was, without any notice, diverted to Amman, Jordan. The Martins did not actually know, in fact, where they had landed until they had left the airport and were on the way to the Intercontinental Hotel. They happened to share a taxi with an American living in Lebanon who explained to their surprise they were not in Jerusalem. Arriving at the hotel, they left their bags in the cab and without delay made arrangements to be driven into Jerusalem. Although their arrival was delayed about three hours by the detour through Amman, they were able to get a glimpse of the capital of Jordan and enjoyed the ride through the countryside to Jerusalem. They were finally in the Jerusalem Intercontinental Hotel on the south end of the Mount of Olives by midafternoon and Martin entered "a doxology of praise that at least we have reached the City of David, the place where our Lord walked among men." In a letter to the children he described their feelings as those of "pilgrims who have been moving toward a city for a long time—in this case, for many years—and have at last arrived" (WCM to Donald Martin, November 16, 1964).

Nothing escaped their attention in Jerusalem. A chance encounter with eighty-six-year-old Bertha Spafford Vester, author of *Our Jerusalem, an American Family in the Holy City, 1898-1949*, alerted the Martins to the name of the director of the Palestinian Archaeological Museum, Dr. Yusef Saad, who showed them through the museum and the Dead Sea Scrolls. They began their sight-seeing in Bethlehem, where they were surprised to meet the Lacy Crains and the Clayton Halls from Dallas in the Church of the Nativity. They went to Jericho and the Dead Sea; later Will and Sally walked together through the Garden of Gethsemane in the moonlight—"My most moving experience so far on this trip. *He* [Jesus] *could have walked away.*" Before leaving the city they went back for a final visit with Mrs. Vester and had tea.

The morning of November 21 they took a cab to the Mandelbaum Gate and walked into Israel. In those days tension was very high between Israel and the Arab world and the gate was one of the few places where it was possible to cross into Israel. They spent the day looking at the sites on that side of the line, spent the night, and went on to Nazareth and Tiberius on the Sea of Galilee the next day. Sally had taken a cold and was running a temperature when they left Jerusalem in the morning and by night it had reached 100 degrees and she began taking medicine. The next morning, however, she was better and they walked by the Sea of Galilee and put their hands into the water. They were in Tel Aviv by two o'clock in the afternoon. The day after Thanksgiving they flew to Athens and took a room with a magnificent view in the Grand Bretagne. In each place letters from home were waiting for them at the American Express Office, but Martin was disappointed not to have heard from more of his children.

The first evening they were in the city a friend of Andrew Cecil's, Harry Georgiapalus, who had been at the Southwest Legal Foundation in Dallas, contacted them at their hotel. Cecil had written to him about the Martins' visit. Sally continued to be sick from a cold, so the first few days she stayed in the room while the bishop toured the museums which, he said, "she is not enamored of" anyway. He climbed to the top of Mars Hill and was inspired by the Acropolis—"one of the greatest architectural marvels in the world." It was clearly visible from their room. Their guide for most of the stay was the wife of the librarian of the school for priests operated by the Greek Orthodox church. In addition to drives through the countryside, they made a one-day trip to Crete, which proved to be something of a disappointment—"it would have been a great one for an archaeologist," Martin commented. As always, his interest in government prompted Martin to seek and gain permission to attend the Greek Parliament, which was in session. The debate he witnessed became so unruly that the opponents had to be separated by soldiers and the meeting adjourned. The city of Corinth proved to be one of the most interesting things he saw. Their last night in the city he and Sally climbed to the top of the hill of the Acropolis and enjoyed one last look over Athens.

Italy was the last stop. In Rome on December 6 they attended a service at the Methodist church, talked with its pastor, Allen Keighley, and then walked to the Vatican in time to hear the Pope bless the great crowd assembled in St. Peter's square. The visit was short, but there was time for Sally to do some shopping and for them to look again at favorite sights and enjoy the Excelsior Hotel.

On December 10 they rode the train to Florence. Will and Sally especially enjoyed seeing the Browning home there. As was his preference and custom, Martin walked miles through all of the places he visited. After Florence, they backtracked to Rome and flew home from there on December 15 via Paris, Shannon, Ireland, Gander, Newfoundland, and Nova Scotia.

It was a long trip and when they finally reached Dallas they had been awake for twenty-three hours. Alsie and Artha Blair Carleton were at the airport to meet them. "How grateful I am," Martin commented the next day, "not to be thrown into heavy responsibilities until there is time to rest." Sally was so completely exhausted that the doctor had to be called. Martin notified the boys, who were planning to come with their families for Christmas, that their mother was ill and would be unlikely to be able to have them. She, however, recovered enough to insist that they go ahead with their plans and come. Ernestine and Kathryn prepared the Christmas dinner, and Sally went back to bed after they left.

It was soon discovered that Sally had contracted hepatitis on the trip and her subsequent slow recovery was discouraging to both her and her husband. She soon fell into a serious period of depression, which is characteristic of persons suffering from the disease. It was a difficult time. Eventually a practical nurse had to be hired to stay with her. As in the past, their friends brought food and helped as they could. By the middle of February 1965, it was necessary to check her into the Scott and White Clinic in Temple for a thorough examination and rest. Tests revealed that although her liver had cleared they could expect both the exhaustion and depression to continue for some time. Raleigh White, one of the clinic's founding doctors, was a good friend of the Martins and he saw to it that Sally received special care. She came home on February 27 and the next day Martin drove alone to Bedford, near Fort Worth, to preach for the first time in the new building of the William C. Martin Methodist Church. Just over a week later, he gave his second series of Willson Lectures at McMurry and attended the dedication of the Martin dormitory on March 10.

11

Retirement

By the end of January 1965, Martin had been in his new role at Perkins for a month and had established a routine. One of the first things he did was to interview all of the Methodist students seeking ordination about their conference relations. He also continued many of the same duties of his former routine, such as preaching in various places on Sundays, almost without interruption. During March he taught his class, kept regular office hours, interviewed students, and participated in faculty committees and meetings. The flood of invitations to preach, and now to lecture and show his slides of the Holy Land, continued unabated, and Martin accepted most of them. He fulfilled his long-standing commitment to preach for five days in the church at Pleasant Mound and judged it "a good revival." In April he held a similar series of services in Beaumont and went directly from there to attend the meeting of the Council of Bishops in Houston.

The council meeting provided a convenient opportunity to visit with many old friends, including Dave Bentliff, Bob Smith, and others. As he nearly always did when the bishop came to town, Bentliff bought Martin a new suit. The primary business of the council was the racial situation and the upcoming merger with the Evangelical United Brethren. On that subject, Martin said, there "was not much enthusiasm and some dragging of feet." Newly elected Bishops Lance Webb and Jim Thomas took time to pick his brain about making appointments. When the council adjourned, he and Sally joined the Hayden Edwardses at the Pink House in Morgan. Martin finally got to try his new fishing rod on the lake.

When in Dallas he often had lunch, as he had for years, with Jack Folsom and Alsie Carleton, and he and Sally spent more time with old friends. Andrew Cecil often invited him to attend, and sometimes to have a part in activities sponsored by the Southwest Legal Foundation, and there were frequent weekends with him and Kate at the Lodge on Lake Texhoma. In June the inevitable finally happened and the rest of his teeth were removed so he could be fitted with a new plate. "A major step which I had known was coming for 8 months," but not as much of an ordeal as he had feared, he said. Shortly afterward he and Sally drove out to see the finished Sally Martin Hall at Lake Bridgeport. "She was pleased," Martin noted.

One significant change in their lives was that sometimes Will and Sally would watch the Sunday service on television rather than actually attend. Usually they selected the one broadcast from the Highland Park Presbyterian Church. As changes came he reflected in the diary, "Life is a mixture of joy and sorrow but it is not the will of God that we should be depressed." From the time when he first read Emerson's "Essay on Compensation," Martin believed and steered his life by the essay's principles. "A great man," Emerson wrote, "is always willing to be little. Whilst he sits on the cushions of advantages, he goes to sleep. When he is pushed, tormented, defeated, he has a chance to learn something; he has been put on his wits, on his manhood; he has gained fact; learns his ignorance; is cured of the insanity of conceit; has got moderation and real skill." For every "yes" in life, there is a "no." "Compensation" is a fact of life, not something that is delayed until the afterlife. Martin's experience had convinced him that Emerson had spoken truly when he said, "But for every benefit you receive, a tax is levied."

The Martins' stamina and patience were tested during the summer when they kept both of the John Martin houses in Fort

Collins while John and Kathryn attended a special course at the University of North Carolina. While it was always pleasant to be in Colorado, there were lawns to be watered and mowed at two houses, groceries to be bought, unanticipated challenges such as those presented by a stopped up sewer line that flooded the basement, and a high wind that blew the top out of a tree. But there were still many pleasant leisure-time activities like reading and sight-seeing. Sore muscles showed him "how soft I have grown," and he finally had to confess he was "very tired from too much activity." John and the family returned on July 27. They finished seven weeks in Colorado hearing John teach his Sunday school class and "were inordinately proud."

Leaving Colorado they drove on to California by way of Kingman, Arizona, and Barstow, California, to see Catherine and her family. She had gotten them an apartment that Martin described as "very nice." The long drive had left him with a sore back, but it did not keep him from walking on the beach and a full schedule of sightseeing in Carmel and the Monterey Peninsula. "Not much reading, but in this wonderland it seems a pity to stay with a book." They were in Los Angeles when the riots began in Watts on August 12, 1965. There were good days getting better acquainted with granddaughter Nancy and renewing old acquaintances. They said good-bye to Catherine and her family on August 30 and started home. Martin said that despite the bloody riots in the city, the time "was profitable to me physiologically and spiritually." He and Sally were both glad to be back in Texas after ten weeks away.

Granddaughter Anne enrolled in SMU during the fall semester. Donald and the entire family brought Anne to school and the Martins helped to get her established in Boaz Hall. She quickly developed a fairly regular pattern of coming to spend the night at her grandparents' or dropping by, sometimes with friends, for meals. A large shopping center named North Park opened just north of the campus that year. It was of interest, too.

Martin's usual routine of class, meetings, and events at SMU and Perkins established itself once again. The God Is Dead movement, which Albert Outler once described as the theological equivalent of Chicken Little's announcement, was in full swing and had a depressing effect on Martin. "Grateful am I for a deepened insight into the truth that the Creator is superior to the creature in love as well as in power." A few untied loose ends, such as the completion of the Wesley Foundation Building at North Texas University in Denton, occupied his time, too. Dave Bentliff eventually made a $35,000 gift to construct the chapel. With the exception of a few trips to nearby places, and one long one with Sally to Seattle to attend the Council of Bishops meeting, he was mostly in and around Dallas. They did manage a brief visit to renew their acquaintance with Galveston in late November and it became a favorite mini-vacation spot.

Shortly after they returned from Seattle, Sally slipped in the shower and suffered what was first thought to be a sprain. She was later discovered to have a fracture in her back. She was hospitalized for a week, not out of the house again until just before Christmas, and wore a brace until the middle of March the next year. During that time friends, as always, rallied with food and concern. "Mae Fee always comes to our rescue," Martin wrote. She was both a friend and their next-door neighbor. The year ended with Dr. Bill's marriage to Jacquelyn Crouch in Lexa, Arkansas. He was the first grandchild to marry, but Will and Sally were not able to attend.

Martin's daily routine in retirement was to rise around six o'clock in the morning and walk half an hour or forty minutes. When he returned from his walk, he prepared breakfast for himself and Sally and was usually in his office at Perkins by eight o'clock. He normally taught a morning class, came home for lunch and took a brief siesta afterward. After resting, he returned to the campus to attend meetings or keep scheduled appointments until four or five o'clock. Immediately after work, or in the early evening, he would take another walk. He and Sally usually watched television, read, or played dominoes at night. He never missed the news. Saturdays were devoted to chores and necessary errands. There was more time for reading and he did a lot of it on a variety of subjects. His Perkins colleagues kept him constantly aware of what was current.

Sally continued to lapse into episodes of serious depression and little could be done to help her. They were unpleasant and difficult times for them both. In early 1966 after Sally suffered a particularly troubling bout with it, Martin wrote in his diary: "With the courage and comfort of the Holy Spirit I can endure whatever comes." He lived out of that conviction. He described Sally's condition variously in the diary as "despondent," "in a bad mood," "exhausted and depressed," "unusually tired," "unhappy." Her red blood count was discovered to be far below normal. During some of these times she would refuse to eat. About the same time Sally was suffering through her depression, Anne came back to school with mononucleosis. In addition to his work, Martin now did the chores, shopping, and laundry, stayed with Sally, and helped Anne as he was able. "When confronted by the question at the end of the day, Was anything worth while accomplished today? we can always answer with truth: I am one day nearer home than when the day began." He wrote on February 21, "I now have more frequent cause to call to remembrance Emerson's Law of Compensation." He might have been thinking of the section that said, "So do we put our life into every act," or another, which said, "There is no penalty to virtue; no penalty to wisdom; they are proper additions of being. In a virtuous action I properly *am*; in a virtuous act I add to the world."

On March 18 Martin finished interviewing 114 Perkins students who planned to seek ordination in a Methodist annual conference. Sally, who was now much stronger, left the next day to fly alone to Los Angeles to see Catherine and Nancy. During the time she was gone, Martin preached in protracted meetings in Ada, Oklahoma, and in Wichita, Kansas, where the College Hill and University congregations joined to hear him. While he was there he heard from Donald that he was to become a great-grandfather in the fall. After a brief time at home, he held a third revival in Sweetwater, in West Texas, where a former member of his cabinet in the Northwest Texas Conference, Dallas Dennison, was pastor. Always a pastor at heart, Martin was renewed by the association with preachers and laypersons and loved having the opportunity to preach. Moreover, Sally was greatly helped by her trip to California. When she returned home, "she was much improved," Martin wrote.

Martin obviously was thinking about his own mortality. There are many references to old age in the diary and notations about individuals who died or were stricken by disease. Floyd Poe, his longtime friend and member of Chi Alpha, was now "a pitiable example of what old age plus paralysis can be." He called on a woman whose demented son, whom Martin had received into the church, had beat her husband to death with a chair, and asked himself, "What currents of thought and behavior have been given right of way in my life." His blood pressure was still too high, and Dr. Lester Keyser at the SMU Health Clinic gave him some medication for it which helped.

All five annual conferences in Texas met together in Dallas in 1966. Martin gave the memorial address in Moody Colosseum on the SMU campus to the combined delegates and presided over several of the sessions of the Northwest Texas Annual Conference for Bishop Eugene Slater. Two thousand appointments were read when it closed. Afterward he and Sally drove to Fort Collins and then with John and his family to Yellowstone Park. All eight of them slept in the same room, but they had a good time.

Later in the summer Donald accompanied his father when he preached in Randolph; half the church, Martin said, was filled with Ballards. A tablet marking the day stands in front of the church. In August he and Sally rode the train to California to see Catherine and Nancy and, once again, took an apartment in Newport Beach. It provided direct access to the beach and Martin seldom missed a day without taking a long walk. John and his family joined them there for part of the time. Disneyland was included on the agenda. It was Martin's third visit and he vowed it likely to be his last. They returned to Dallas on August 19. It had been a busy summer.

One of the early members of the SMU School of Theology Faculty, Robert Goodloe, died just about the time school began in September and Martin spoke at the funeral. The Council of Bishops met in Chicago at its regular time before Thanksgiving, and, once again, the main topic of discussion was the proposed merger with the Evangelical United Brethren. Forty votes were cast in the council against it. He and Sally met their great-granddaughter, Angela, on Thanksgiving Day in Little Rock. On December 3 they went along with three Perkins students to attend the Assembly of the World Council of Churches in Miami. Many old friends were present for the six-day event, and they enjoyed being near the sea again. While there, Bishop Lloyd Wicke asked William C. to do some ministerial recruitment for the Methodist Board of Education, and he agreed to so do during the fall semester of 1967. They spent New Year's Eve at the Lodge on Lake Texhoma with the Cecils.

The Oldsmobile given to them by the Central Texas Conference had seemed cursed from the beginning, and was damaged again in a fender bender on the SMU campus early in 1967, so Martin traded it in. Sally was pleased with the new car. By February, however, it had been hit twice, although he does not say how it happened. As he grew older Martin seemed to have particular difficulty backing up and parking!

Sally's doctors advised her to play golf to help her back, but her energy level was still low when the year began. A bout with food poisoning in March and an irregular heartbeat did not did help. She, in fact, had to cancel a trip to California in the spring because of it. She had for many years been troubled with skin cancers and had them removed from time to time; she also experienced episodes of vertigo and fainting. In May she went again to see Dr. Anderson at Scott and White in Temple. He gave her advice on how to deal with the heart problem and prescribed medication. Martin went to the library to read about fibrillation. A part of his reading was a book titled *How to Avoid a Heart Attack*.

They discovered they liked mini-vacations in the Baker Hotel in Mineral Wells, about sixty-five miles from home, and Sally enjoyed stopping for lunch and shopping on the way over or back in Nieman Marcus in Fort Worth. Movies continued to provide a constant source of entertainment and always drew a comment in the diary. On one occasion he remarked that "if we had not had a pass, we would have felt cheated." Movies never went uncritiqued.

Anne continued to be with them often and they enjoyed taking her to places she liked to eat. One of their favorites was a popular spot atop the Southland Center in downtown Dallas called Port's O'Call. Another was the Zeider Zee. She sometimes went as her grandfather's escort because Sally had become uneasy in crowds. Martin continued to walk but now did much of it in the new North Park Mall. It was air-conditioned and not too far from their house on University Boulevard. Sometimes Sally went with him and shopped while he walked. Now an even larger North Park remains a favorite spot for walkers and shoppers.

In February he went to Nashville to begin his consulting assignment with the Board of Education about ministerial recruitment. He worked with Mark Rouch and Gerald McCulloh on the plans for Ministry Sunday and spoke to a conference on the issue "The Campus Ministry and Recruitment." He met them again in Columbus in March and April to speak to various groups about it. He worked with the board until September.

The regular pattern of interviewing students about their conference relations and teaching a class continued at Perkins. By April 21 he had conducted 170 of them. He became less reluctant to miss the regular meetings of the faculty but almost always attended lectures and discussions by members of the faculty and guests. He was regular in his attendance at chapel even though the variety of services there sometimes did not suit his taste.

The Council of Bishops held its March meeting in Buffalo, and Martin enjoyed seeing the Falls again. He reported to the Council on his work with the Board of Education on recruitment. Once home he and Sally decided to visit the "First Monday" event at nearby Canton—the largest flea market in the world. Martin predictably reported what they saw was "mostly junk." He fared better on their trip to New York. They managed to get tickets to see Mary Martin and Robert Preston in *I Do, I Do,* and he thought it was "excellent." The next night they saw *Marjorie.* He reminded himself, "Never complain about old age. It is a privilege many people are not allowed to enjoy." The Colorado mountains provided their usual lift to Martin's spirits during July and August.

At the end of August he and Sally were thinking of selling their home. Martin had eighteen months earlier spoken with banker Eugene McElvaney about investments which might be made with money from the sale. Sally had been looking at houses and had seen several she liked. He had gone with her to look at a few of them. The reason is not clear why at this time they were considering making the change, but there are some obvious aspects related to their situation that might have prompted it. For one, he was coming to the end of his work at the seminary; they were living upstairs, and as they grew older getting up and down could become a problem. However, at no time had they complained about it. Sally had been afraid to live downstairs when he was gone so much of the time and had chosen the upstairs half of the house when they moved in. Moreover, they had a lease with an individual whom they were both reluctant to ask to move. They did not make any change, however, until 1971, and then it was sudden and the decision seemed to have been made on the spur of the moment.

Martin and three others read papers on the episcopacy at the Council of Bishops meeting in November, but the real excitement was a resolution on the escalating conflict in Vietnam and the upcoming merger with the Evangelical United Brethren. Martin had discussed the proposed merger at various times with Albert Outler, who was opposed, but does not say what he thought about it. Christmas was spent with Catherine in California. Their good friend Hayden Edwards died on New Year's Day, 1968.

The Council of Bishops and the General Conference met in Dallas in April, 1968. On Sally's birthday ten bishops and their wives joined the Martins for lunch at the Chaparral Club in honor of the occasion. With an experienced eye Martin noted that the episcopal address, delivered by Bishop Lloyd C. Wicke, took 110 minutes to read and received no applause—"a solid meaningful statement but not much fire." Outler preached at the opening session.

William C. and Sally moved downtown into the hotel for convenience, but she returned home before the conference was over. It was a significant gathering. Churchwide support for theological education was adopted in the form of an apportioned Ministerial Education Fund, and the merger creating The United Methodist Church was approved. The long-standing rule on tobacco and alcohol as related to clergy was modified, too. For one of the few times in Martin's memory the presiding bishop had to be replaced because the business became so snarled he could not continue. Martin gave the closing benediction.

When Donald came to pick up Anne in May, he lured his father to the driving range where for the first time in seventy-four years Martin drove a bucket of balls. Robert Kennedy was shot on June 5 and died the next day. Martin was attending the Texas Annual Conference when "the gloom of this tragedy fell on all of us." He and Sally celebrated their fiftieth wedding anniversary in Hot Springs. The Don Martins gave them silver candlesticks "and paid for lunch." The next day, however, the faculty and staff of Perkins gave them a surprise party. Nearly everyone was present, including representatives from both newspapers.

Perkins professor and former district superintendent in Martin's North Texas Conference cabinet, Alsie Carleton, was elected to the episcopacy at the jurisdictional conference. Martin escorted him to the platform. Paul Martin was named to replace William C. as Bishop in Residence at Perkins. During the summer Martin moved out of the office he had occupied to make room for Paul Martin, and into a less desirable one in the library provided for him by Decherd Turner. In the interim he used one vacated by Alsie Carleton, and eventually was given the use of an office assigned to a faculty member on leave. He was now, for the first time, entirely without responsibility. When the faculty gathered on its annual retreat in September he said that it "gave me the feeling of being an 'ex.'" He also noted that he was "experiencing for the first time in many years what it is to live by a schedule of my own making." The end of his term at the seminary marked the actual beginning of retirement. Although he remained active, Martin was frequently troubled now with fatigue and had, once again, experienced trouble with his back and was in pain much of the time.

The idea of a move was on both Will and Sally's minds as the years at Perkins were drawing to a close. They consulted with a real estate agent about establishing the value of their house and once, when in Little Rock, took time to look for an apartment to rent. "All were filled with no expectation of vacancies in places we would like." A final decision was postponed and the subject pushed into the "maybe" category.

⫘⫘⫘

Once finally relieved of his duties at Perkins, Martin nevertheless continued pretty much the same routine as before. He walked every day. "My morning walk," he said, "is a golf game, a nature hike, a turn at the guns and a period of meditation all wrapped into one." He functioned more than ever as a pastor to friends in the community and at SMU. Calling on the sick or bereaved was an ordinary task many days for him. As friends grew older there were more calls for him to make to hospitals and funerals to hold. There were now also casualties from the escalating conflict in Vietnam. The Glen Johnsons lost a son. Once in a while there were even a few weddings of children of former parishioners. SMU events were always of interest and he attended many of them, sometimes alone. He continued to help Sally with chores around the house, kept the yard, did the grocery shopping, took care of the cars, and prepared or brought in meals when Sally was ill. In the evenings they usually watched television or read. He managed to plow through Hans Küng's massive work *The Church* and the work of his Perkins colleague, Schubert Ogden, but gave up on Moltmann's *Theology of Hope* as "too abstruse for me." They enjoyed eating at Nieman Marcus though Martin confessed, "I always eat too much there." He had continually to watch his weight, as he had most of his life. But at no time did his curiosity wane nor did he cease to look for ways to expand the horizons of his knowledge and experience.

One of those opportunities came in January 1969, when Dale Smith, the senior minister, invited him to join the staff of the Paradise Valley United Methodist Church in Phoenix. He and Sally had enjoyed Phoenix and their previous experiences with the Paradise Valley congregation and Martin was tempted to accept the offer, but he finally decided the "hurdle appeared to be too great to S and me." It was not just the idea of making a radical change that put them off. The "irregularities" of Smith's proposal, Martin said, "are too great to overcome." Smith persisted, but Martin was unable to see his way clear to make the move. He did, however, agree to come for a month during the fall.

There were revival meetings in Waco and in Hot Springs, Arkansas. While there he experienced chest pain during lunch and began an irregular heart rhythm that continued until about 8:30 P.M. A local doctor gave him a prescription for quinidine and he continued with his schedule. On April 1, however, it caught up with him. He had been experiencing arrhythmia during the day but preached at noon. Toward the end of the service he "felt discomfort," and by the time he reached his room his "heart was skipping wildly." It continued the next day and the services were canceled. Donald came to see about him in the morning and put him on the plane for home at noon. Despite rest he experienced an increase in the irregularity. By April 5, however, he had converted to a normal sinus rhythm and walked forty-five minutes before going to the office. He did not tell Sally about the problem and was one of fourteen retired bishops present for the Council of Bishops meeting when it began in Charleston, West Virginia, on April 8. Following the custom in the council to honor members and spouses who had died during the year, Martin gave the memorial address honoring Jackie Selecman. Martin was to be troubled with fibrillation in varying degrees for the rest of his life.

Anne graduated from SMU in May and moved to the Martins' before going on to her job. Shortly afterward (May 28) there was an unpleasant encounter with her grandmother that caused her to leave their home abruptly. Martin ran to stop her as she left their house, and then drove hurriedly to try and overtake her. A severe heart fibrillation resulted and he was sent to Baylor Hospital by ambulance and placed in the intensive care unit. Anne, in the meantime, had gone to the home of a friend and called her father, who came immediately to get her and to see about Martin. He stabilized and was released from the hospital on June 2. While there he had, as often he did, devised a plan for the future. He summarized it and his feelings by saying, "My present plan of procedure is to live as simply and sanely as I can & if my heart elects to skip some beats, not to worry about it." He had decided to let things take their course and not to worry about the consequences. He was fully prepared for either death or life. Three days after he was dismissed from the hospital, he walked forty minutes.

The astronauts walked on the moon on July 20, and Martin celebrated his seventy-sixth birthday a week later. Anne married Don Crary on August 9 in Pulaski Heights United Methodist Church in Little Rock. Will and Sally Martin gave the flowers as part of their wedding gift to their granddaughter, and Martin assisted the pastor, Jim Argue, in the ceremony. Reconciliation had been accomplished.

William C. and Sally felt well enough in late August to keep John's younger children, David and Sally Beth, while John, Kathryn, and the older boys went to Prague to attend an international conference on nutrition. Keeping the children proved to be a rigorous undertaking. They were just at the age when it was hard to keep them at home and Sally Beth did not want to go to bed. When school began, it was even harder to get them up and on the bus. Kathryn's parents, who lived in Denver, provided relief on the weekends. It was, Martin said, "very quiet with children away." The younger Martins returned on September 10 and the elder Martins returned to Dallas and a quieter life the next day. John Bookhout, the son of Sally's dear friend Pauline, died on September 15.

The Martins returned to Arizona to fulfill their obligation at the Pleasant Valley United Methodist Church on October 1. Martin was reading Outler's *Psychotherapy and the Christian Message* and *Theology of Evangelism* at the time. He preached for Dale Smith, who was away part of the time, taught courses and Sunday school classes, and called on prospective members. Catherine and Nancy came to see them there. They had to move twice in order to get suitably housed, and the busy schedule made them both glad they had not accepted the offer to join the staff. In addition, Smith and his wife separated causing additional strain in the parish.

The Martins enjoyed Thanksgiving in Galveston with the

Cecils and Christmas with Donald and his family in Little Rock. William C. baptized Angela on December 28. The last entry for the decade of the 1960s is a quotation from Acts 20:24 taken from the New English Version of the Bible: "For myself, I set no store by life; I only want to finish the race, and complete the task which the Lord Jesus assigned to me, of bearing my testimony to the gospel of God's grace."

For most of the remainder of his life, Martin was blessed by reasonably good health and for all of it with a sound mind. Although there were some difficult times for him, a tape he made for the Council of Bishops meeting in Little Rock shortly before he died reveals the inner strength of his persona. His voice is strong and his mind clear. Once free of his responsibilities at the seminary, he began immediately to begin putting his files in order and to select the books he planned to donate to the Bridwell Library. He always had a project.

After his siesta, Martin now usually spent afternoons at home rather than returning to the office. The nightly news at five o'clock was mandatory, and he did not expect to be interrupted by anyone while it was on. It was, of course, often filled with the sights and sounds of the escalating war in Vietnam. The troubled climate caused by the war caused Lyndon Johnson not to see another term, and in November 1968, Richard M. Nixon defeated Hubert Humphrey and George Wallace to become president of the United States.

As friends, colleagues, and former parishioners grew older, there were more funerals to conduct or attend. Martin never said "no" when asked to participate in those final tributes, but some were an emotional drain. When the husband of Mae Fee died, their longtime friend and neighbor, Martin admitted it was "a difficult funeral for me." On his morning walk February 10 he noted a deep sense of "gratitude and re-commitment." "I do not want to presume on God's mercy," he wrote, "but I want to use his blessings for the fullest possible contribution to the service of his church and people." In order to make preparation for the eventuality of their own deaths, he and Sally, who owned cemetery lots in the Restland Cemetery in far north Dallas, decided to sell them and to purchase new ones in the Hillcrest Cemetery nearer SMU. They also established an endowed scholarship fund at Perkins in their names with an initial contribution of $500. Others, like the Luther Kirks and Dallas Dennisons from Northwest Texas, made donations to it, too.

On Sunday mornings, they usually attended the services at First Methodist to hear Bob Goodrich, but they sometimes stayed home to "worship on television." He continued to attend the meetings of the Council of Bishops but Sally seldom went with him unless the city in which they were meeting was especially attractive to her. At its April 1970 meeting, there was a "first" when a group of blacks protested and blocked the entrances to the room in which the bishops were meeting. Later on, a church service at which Martin was present was disrupted, too. These events took place in St. Louis prior to the first General Conference of The United Methodist Church.

Though retired, Martin's advice and experience continued to be respected in the council and he sometimes served as a consultant to the committee responsible for planning the orientation program for newly elected bishops. In October 1968 he wrote a letter to the new class of bishops about their relation to the Council of Bishops. "You will discover," he told them, "that the Council is not primarily an administrative agency but is in reality, at a much deeper level, a fellowship." Speaking of its procedures, he also observed with quiet humor that "cloture on debate and discussion is never invoked, although you will be strongly tempted in that direction." He urged them to get acquainted with at least some of the 378 bishops who had been elected and consecrated to the episcopal office before them. "Each man in this succession has something of value to say to you if you can find time to listen." He counseled them that it was not essential or desirable for the bishop to speak on every subject and urged them to find more adequate ways to determine when and how a bishop should speak. There is a quotation in the "Thoughts" notebook that describes the basic humility that often enabled him to keep silence. "The greater the sphere of our knowledge, the larger is the surface of our contact with the infinity of our ignorance." In response to a subsequent request from the council he also drafted portions of a manual to be given to newly elected bishops. The manual covered relevant topics such as making appointments, and presiding.

The uncertain times of the late 60s and 70s were enough to distract anyone, but in his usual fashion he remained focused, optimistic, and remarkably nondefensive about most things that happened. "The Christian Church is in a period of reformation & renewal for a united advance. Such times are always fraught with turmoil and upheaval," he wrote in the diary on January 17, 1970. Later he said in his diary, "In the interest of the growth of the Kingdom I would not be unwilling for the Methodist Church to die but I would be pleased to see it reborn into a new and more inclusive Christian fellowship." He was supportive when his daughter, Catherine, went on strike with teachers in California. He had a part in the service held at First Church, Dallas, in which black congregations of the former Central Jurisdiction were incorporated into the North Texas Conference. He counseled his friend Eugene Slater as he was confronted with a protest by homosexual members of the clergy advocating gay rights which disrupted sessions of the Southwest Texas Conference. He attended the dedication of the Kennedy Memorial in Dallas, and was horrified, as were most Americans, by the shooting of students protesting the Vietnam War on the Kent State University campus in Ohio. "These are deeply troubled times," he said afterward.

The long family vacations in Colorado effectively stopped after August 1970, when Martin had to be hospitalized for four days in Denver because of severe heart fibrillation. Doctors warned him the altitude might have been a factor in bringing it on. Catherine and Nancy were with him and Sally at the time. Afterward he decided that the digitalis which he was given to regulate his heart caused him to be depressed, and discontinued it without telling his doctor. He also decided on his own to quit drinking cola drinks and iced tea because of the caffeine. But he and Sally continued to make short trips to see John and his family in Fort Collins despite the risk.

In October 1970, Martin and Sally spent a week in Little Rock with Alice while Donald and Ernestine were away on a trip. While there they took the opportunity to go through an apartment in the Quapaw Towers, but again they made no decision to move. It is clear, however, they were considering it again. On the way back to Dallas they stopped in Prescott, Arkansas, to visit Aunt Stell, who had sold her home in Blevins and was now living in a nursing home there. She was unhappy with the arrangement and glad for a visit with them.

Although he no longer had any official relation to Perkins School of Theology nor regular duties there, Martin continued to maintain an office in the library and to read as widely as ever and regularly to attend lectures and other functions at the school. He almost never missed hearing a visiting scholar.

Movies continued to be the Martins' favorite form of relaxation and he and Sally rarely missed a new one. Although Martin's tolerance for the more realistic products of Hollywood had increased dramatically from the days when he led the family out of the theater in protest, he would still walk out when he found their content too offensive. Most simply bored him, however. Perhaps in response to the quality of new releases, they went to see many of their old favorites again—*Gone with the Wind, The Sound of Music,* and *It's a Mad, Mad, Mad, Mad World* remained favorites.

Martin selected reading material much the same way. In addition to new books, he re-read parts or all of his favorites from years past. Archbishop William Temple's book, *Nature, Man, and God* came again to his attention and he commented while reading it, "I came to a fuller realization that every moment of my existence is a gift of God. This conviction given partly out of Wm Temple's affirmation that the Christian spirit does not lay claim to immortality but to the hope of resurrection" (Diary October 24, 1970). He re-read David S. Cairns's *The Faith That Rebels* and, once again, expressed appreciation for the way in which it had enabled him years earlier in a "dark night of the soul" "to break through the bars of a 'closed universe' and enter into the freedom of a 'faithful' Christian." But he remained curious about new ideas and often took the advice of his Perkins colleagues about what to read. In addition, he tried to read most of the books that they wrote, including controversial ones such as Schubert Ogden's *Christ Without Myth*. He rarely agreed with Ogden but read his books, nevertheless. He almost never selected fiction for his leisure reading despite Sally's earlier admonition, holding Marshall Steel up to him as an example, that it would broaden the scope of his experience to do it. In that regard he never changed.

———

Despite the fact that William C. had entered the army during World War I in hopes that his descendants might never have to fight, Bill became the third generation of Martins to serve his country in a war. In early 1971 Bill's second daughter, Jennifer Ellen, was born. The most significant change in the Martins' retirement years also came in 1971—they moved from Dallas back to Little Rock. It is easier to understand their reasons for making the change than it is to know what precipitated it. The diaries make it clear they had considered moving to Little Rock for a number of years, coming close enough to a decision at one time to have a real estate agent price their house for possible sale, but it was never more than a possibility. The best explanation for leaving Dallas is obviously Martin's own—for reasons related to health they needed and wanted to be nearer family, he said. In his Letter of Farewell dated August 15, 1971, he wrote, "We have considered this move for many months but a recent touch of physical infirmity gave added warning we should be near one of our children." The reference is probably to the heart irregularity that had troubled him in Denver during the previous summer. Little Rock seems to have been the only location they considered seriously. Catherine was firmly ensconced in Los Angeles, which was too far away from friends and most family. John was in Denver, but both Will and Sally were uneasy about living there, and Donald was in Little Rock. "Our older son and his family are there and a pastorate of three years resulted in many enduring friendships." Their immediate family was in Arkansas. Donald and Ernestine were permanently settled and Bill was completing a medical residency there; Anne and her family were in Little Rock, too. John, although it was not anticipated at the time, was soon to accept a new position on the faculty at Texas Tech and move to Lubbock and then in a few years to Russellville, Arkansas. Martin concluded his farewell letter by saying, "We try to console ourselves with the thought that, with us, moving has been a part of life's routine and after this one, we have only one more." They, in fact, had two more.

Simply understanding the reasons he gave for moving, however, fails to provide a satisfactory explanation of what led them to put their house on the market on June 25, 1971. It has all the appearances of a sudden decision. Will and Sally, in fact, told two very different versions of the story. He said that Sally had always wanted to move back to Little Rock when they retired, and since she had willingly followed him across the country to his various appointments, it was now her turn to select a place and he would accede to her wishes. She claimed that although they had discussed it from time to time, no decision had been made until one day he came in and announced "We're moving to Little Rock," and said he was going to put the University Boulevard house on the market. Later Sally told the children he had overheard someone at Perkins remark that "there were too many bishops around," came home, and announced they were leaving. She said his desire to move, once again, forced her to give up the home she loved and her friends of more than thirty years. Good friends of Sally's report that she was lonely in Little Rock, and despite the fact that she lived there for more than twenty years before she died, she never managed to make new friends to replace the ones she had left behind in Dallas. Daughter-in-law Ernestine thought Sally expected to move to Little Rock at some time, but she was not ready to leave Dallas at the time they moved. It does have all the appearances of a spur-of-the-moment decision.

Martin's diary reveals that after making the decision to sell the house, they first approached their downstairs tenant, Mrs. Collier, but she was unwilling or unable to pay the $65,000 asking price. When she declined, it was listed with a real estate agent and purchased the same day at the asking price by the first couple who saw it. The Martins had a contract by 5:00 P.M., and both were shocked by the speed with which it happened. The evidence points to the conclusion that neither had seriously entertained the possibility of having to move so soon. In fact, they had no place to live in Little Rock and had to call Ernestine and Donald to find an apartment for them. Martin accepted the situation in characteristic fashion. "The happenings of this day were astonishing. Just as I confidently believed that the guidance of the Spirit was in the purchase of the apartment 22 years ago, so I believe sincerely that the same guidance was manifested in the sale of it." Sally, who may have been less sure of the leading of the Spirit and who certainly was more attached to and emotional about the house, awoke during the night deeply troubled about leaving the place they had lived for more than twenty-five years and questioning whether they had done the right thing. She was a person who needed friends, and she was facing the reality of leaving them to begin a new life at age seventy-six in a city they had left four decades earlier. William C. reconsidered with her all the reasons for making the change and determined, at least to his own satisfaction, there were no grounds for thinking they were making a mistake. Sally, he said, seemed to feel better the next day, too.

Since they had only five weeks to give possession of the house, preparations for moving took almost all their time. He had to go through all of his books and papers in the office to determine what would be left in the Bridwell Library. Both the office and house had to be packed. This work was interspersed with rounds of parties, tributes, and farewells to friends of forty years. In the meantime, Donald and Ernestine found an apartment for them in Little Rock. They chose one that was acceptable and the best alternative available on short notice. It was located in the Quapaw Tower Apartments on the ninth floor, across the street from historic McArthur Park. The Martins did not actually see what had been rented for them until the day they moved in.

The packers came on Monday, August 9, 1971, and the Martins said their final good-byes to Dallas and left for Little Rock the next day. Catherine and Nancy came to drive one of the cars and to be with them during the move. Sally rode with her daughter who reported that her mother cried most of the way. The movers arrived in Little Rock on August 11 and settled them into their apartment. Sally was not pleased with it. Although it had large and pleasant living areas, the bedrooms seemed dark and cramped to her. In fact, she never liked it although she lived there for nine years.

Arrangements had been made for Martin to have space for an office at First United Methodist Church, and he quickly started to work getting it ready. They put their membership there, too, although Sally later said she would rather have joined Pulaski Heights United Methodist Church. There were all the usual chores brought on by a move—opening a bank account for Sally, car registration and inspection in order to get new license plates, obtaining an Arkansas driver's license. In between unpacking and errands there were visits from old friends who warmly welcomed them back to the city and lots of time spent with Donald and his family. Sally was fighting depression, but she and Catherine began to hang pictures while William C. was away at the office unpacking his books and papers.

Being in Little Rock did not change Martin's routine. He continued going to the office in the morning, sometimes ate lunch in a restaurant, and then returned home for his siesta. As he grew older, he ate lunch at home most of the time and doubled the number of siestas. Catherine and Nancy left for California on August 29. The city of Little Rock gave Martin its "official" welcome ten days later when he ran a red light, was stopped, and fined $20. The price of violations had gone up since the old days in Houston when similar breaches of the law cost him a dollar, and the experience was depressing. Even watching "Hee Haw," now one of his favorite television shows, didn't help him to feel better.

Pauline Hubbard came in the middle of October to see about the Martins and to look over their new surroundings. Mae Fee came shortly after Pauline left to stay with Sally while Martin attended the Council of Bishops meeting. Their presence provided a real boost to her morale. The day after Pauline left, however, Sally fell in the elevator and re-injured her back. Although X rays at first revealed no broken bones, she was in a great deal of pain and was sore for days.

In early December more X rays were made and showed she had an impacted vertebra. Once again, she had to wear a brace. Many days Martin described her in the diary as "despondent."

The ground floor of the apartment building had a game room, which proved useful for walking when the weather was bad, and Martin used it regularly during the winter months. Alice, Donald's youngest daughter, came often to spend the night and to swim in the pool during warm weather. He often walked around the pool when the weather was pleasant. Sometimes Alice would bring a friend when she came. They usually had Sunday lunch with Ernestine and Donald, went with them on a Sunday afternoon drive, and often took ice cream and went for an evening visit during the week. Mary Catherine and Rudy separated in February 1972, and were later divorced.

Martin occupied his time with reading, making pastoral calls, or telephoning friends who were sick. He kept a record of his calls. There were new projects, too. He researched the record of Grandfather Beene, who had been a member of the state legislature from Hempstead County in 1881, and read Arkansas history. He arranged the diaries in his office and began reading the ones for 1928–31, the years they were first in Little Rock. He put together all the devotional addresses he had given to the annual conferences through the years. He went through the current roll of the First United Methodist Church and discovered he still knew one hundred people whose names were listed. By examining his own records he discovered, among other things, that he had known 172 bishops in his lifetime and had held 97 revivals in 90 churches. He later revised that figure upward to 120 and added "in fifteen states." What Martin appears to have been doing is a reprise of his life. At one time he thought about writing his autobiography, and others wanted to get someone to do the writing for him, but by now he had given up that idea. At one time a committee was formed to oversee the task and raise the necessary funds to publish it.

He continued to be troubled by atrial fibrillation and was on quinidine most of the time. Among the Martins' acquaintances, the Marshall Steels, who now lived in Conway, and the Paul Galloways were always careful to check on them and to include them in events.

Donald and Ernestine stayed in constant touch and were their first line of defense and assistance. Donald had by now become chief of the Right of Way Division of the Arkansas Highway and Transportation Department. He and Ernestine were still living in the house on Oak Street that the Martins had helped them to buy. Anne and her husband presented them with a third great-granddaughter, Cora, in March 1972. Margaret had surgery for a benign ovarian cyst the first week of June. She died of cancer in 1994.

Sally stayed in bed all day on their fifty-fourth wedding anniversary. She had earlier agreed to go for a drive, but changed her mind and stayed at home. The next day he did manage to get her out for lunch at the Big Apple, a favorite restaurant in Heber Springs, a town about seventy miles away, and to spend the night at the Lakeview Motel.

The diaries kept so faithfully through the years are changed in 1973 to include fewer details, and are kept in bound date books rather than in diaries. He resolved to record only significant events, but he often wrote comments on those he thought special. It was a deliberate decision on his part, just as it was to begin keeping a diary in 1914, for the entry for May 25 reads: "On this day I begin a new policy with respect to the record I am to keep here during my remaining [years]. Only events of some significance will be recorded which means that on some days the page will be substantially blank." Early in January 1973 he also noted that "since my days of preaching are almost over I must find new initiative for a continuing interest in the search for truth. Writing is the evident answer. This could be an exciting experience." Another new project. His first effort was a series of Sunday school lessons that were published in the Arkansas *Methodist*. The necessary trips to their editorial offices provided a ready excuse to stop by an "ice cream place" for dessert. All of his life he enjoyed melons, fresh berries, and ice cream, and he had now given up fretting about his weight. He finished the last of the series of lessons on April 30. Immediately after, he began doing research for a biography on "Brother Forney" Hutchinson, and served on a committee that was responsible for the publication of a history of Methodism in Arkansas.

Sister Sally also received a welcome from the Little Rock Police. In July she was stopped for driving in the middle of two lanes. She lost her temper and used "abusive language" on the arresting officer. He did not take kindly to her attitude and threatened to take her to jail. When he learned what had happened, Martin immediately began work on a plan to keep her from having to appear in court and sought the help of a lawyer, who spoke to the judge of the Police Court on Sally's behalf. He ordered her to take a driving test. When she took the test, she failed its written portion the first time and had to take it again. Successful results in hand, Martin and the lawyer returned to see Judge Butler, who dismissed the charge of "abusive language" and fined her ten dollars for driving in the middle of the road. Two days later Martin had a wreck at the grocery store. Such events always depressed him.

Significant writing and other projects were delayed when on September 11, 1973, William C. and Sally were seriously injured in an automobile crash. On this occasion they were not at fault. They were on their way to Hot Springs when a car driven by nineteen-year-old Robert Lee Pemberton, who, the police report stated, "had been drinking," attempted to pass a car, lost control, crossed the center median, and struck the Martins' car on the left front fender. All three persons were injured in the crash. Will and Sally were taken by ambulance to the nearest town, Benton, where they were examined at the Saline Memorial Hospital and sent back to Little Rock for treatment. Because there were no rooms available at either St. Vincent's or the Baptist Hospital when they arrived, the Martins spent the night at home. Their physician grandson, Dr. William C. Martin, Jr., spent the night with them in their apartment and the next day got them admitted to the Baptist Hospital in what was listed as "serious" condition. Martin was sent directly into the intensive care unit suffering from five broken ribs, a concussion, cuts to the head, and internal injuries. Remembering the episode later, he said nobody should have to endure such pain. Sally had two broken ribs and injuries to her face. Eventually five of her teeth would have to be removed because of the trauma. Martin spent the next twenty-two days in Baptist Hospital and sixteen more in the Medical Center in rehab before being released on

October 19. He was able to dress himself and leave the house for the first time on November 2. Two weeks later, while dressing, he blacked out and fell into his closet. Although not seriously injured in the fall, he was shaken by the experience and his recovery was prolonged. His doctors attributed this experience to poor circulation caused by hardening of the arteries. The doctors warned Martin to be careful about exercising.

Once recovered, Martin continued to drive the car around town and resumed his practice of spending two hours each day at his office. Sally relied on him to take her on errands and to her regular Friday appointments at the hairdresser, but television came more and more to take the place of trips to the movies.

Their good friend Paul Martin died in Dallas on February 13, 1975. The Martins went immediately to be with Mildred and to have a part in the funeral. They were feeling well enough in the spring to make a trip to Honolulu for a church meeting, but it was their last time out of the continental United States. They continued to enjoy regular excursions with family members to William C.'s beloved Arkansas mountains, the Petit Jean State Park, and Mt. Sequoyah. Martin preached once at the Little Rock Annual Conference and presided in some of its sessions, but he had to take extra medication in order to do it. He and Sally also made a trip for him to speak to the fiftieth anniversary celebration of the Men's Bible Class in Dallas, and they enjoyed four days there with dear friends. When they returned to Little Rock Sally was despondent for days and "pined for Dallas." She went to New Orleans with William C. in November for the meeting of the Council of Bishops, and to Los Angeles where they spent Christmas with Catherine and Nancy.

⚯

With his usual determination, Martin resolved to remain "hopeful, cheerful, busy." When he was eighty-five, he reminded himself, "When I am tempted to be unhappy because the depletion of energy makes it impossible for me to do some things which I once could do, I should remind myself that I ought to be joyfully grateful that after

85 years of living I am not afflicted with any ailment that could keep me in constant pain or could put an end to this earthly journey."

Martin preached the sermon at SMU's Minister's Week in February 1976. His title, "Freedom in Christ," acknowledged the beginning of the bicentennial year of America's history, and outlined the privilege of Christian freedom to learn, pray, and witness. In the sermon he recounted the story of an Alpine climber who was caught in an avalanche and was killed. The inscription on his tombstone proclaimed, "He died climbing." Martin told his audience he wanted it to be said of him that "he died learning." Just before his death he began again to study the stars.

He did not feel well enough to attend the 1976 General Conference in Portland, and Sally was ill during the July sessions of the jurisdictional conference. She experienced severe breathing problems and was hospitalized six days; he knew she needed him to stay with her rather than attend. It was a concession not only to Sally but to age and retirement for throughout his active service, she was often ill when he left to preach or attend a meeting, and he nearly always went anyway. She was discovered to have a scar on one lung, a vestige of an earlier bout with flu, and some emphysema. Following the illness, she suffered yet another prolonged period of depression. They drove back to Hot Springs for the first time since their almost-fatal accident to see Mae Fee who was there, and in hopes the outing would improve Sally's mood. Catherine came for a visit and was with them in Little Rock when sad news came that Jack, Brice's wife, had died the morning of August 20. She had been ill for some time but her death was a shock to all of them. She was "a remarkable and loveable lady," Martin said. Sally was deeply depressed once again, but Brice took his loss well. Donald drove his father to see Brice regularly through the balance of the year.

Martin, who usually got up about seven, would begin the day by reading a portion of the Bible and spending time alone in prayer. For a long time he read the modern translation of J. B. Phillips and the popular commentaries by William Barclay. He and Sally read the short daily devotionals from the Methodist *Upper Room* and would nearly always say the Lord's Prayer together at the table. He would prepare their breakfast, and on days when Sally was either in one of her moods of depression or not feeling well, he would serve her in bed. When the meal was over, he would then go to his office at the church for about two or two and a half hours. There were always people there to whom he liked to talk, including the bishop, Ken Hicks, whose office was nearby. His old friend Paul Galloway came often to visit and would sometimes take him to lunch. Galloway was especially good to remember birthdays and special occasions. Martin read and wrote letters to friends who were sick or had lost loved ones, and he wrote his own letters of congratulations for special occasions. People remembered them, too. At Christmas 1978 they received 144 cards from friends, relatives, acquaintances, and 52 from bishops. He acknowledged them all. They celebrated their sixtieth wedding anniversary that year, too.

In Martin's mind, 1978 was a kind of turning point for Sally and him. He complained of "low energy" and Sally continued to have periods of depression. The problems affected his ability to function. He backed the car into a tree in the middle of May and on June 1, his careless driving caused a minor accident that brought serious emotional distress to Sally, who was with him when it happened. She refused to eat for two days and he described the time as "unpleasant." She was, however, well enough to make a trip to California to see Catherine and Nancy for a week at the end of July. Shortly after they returned from the West Coast, he planned to attend a meeting in Lincoln, but Sally was not well enough for him to leave her alone. He wrote Walter Vernon to explain why he was not present. Admitting how much he had looked forward to being there, "as a kind of home-coming since we had enjoyed nine delightful and rewarding years with the Methodists of Nebraska," he told Vernon, "Oh well, there comes a time when our life-style has to change. Maybe this is the time" (WCM to Walter Vernon, August 6, 1978).

When Sally was well she would prepare their lunch, and in afternoons devoted to errands they shopped for groceries together. Sally kept a regular appointment to get her hair fixed and William C. would sometimes read in the mall while she shopped; if he felt up to it he would walk, but as he grew older he walked less and less. At least once every week Donald and Ernestine would come to take them for a drive or to their house for family meals and visits. Most evenings they read or watched television together. "The Waltons" was a favorite. They maintained their keen interest in politics and faithfully watched any press conference or address by the president. Among the presidents, they especially liked Jimmy Carter. Sally remained a dedicated, lifelong Democrat.

Martin's problems with the car grew more serious and he reached the place when he should not have been driving at all. Ernestine once agreed to take him somewhere only if he agreed in advance she would drive. She was dismayed when she found him behind the wheel when they started home. They bought a new Ford LTD from Cliff Peck in June 1978, which was delivered to them the next month. In the interval the bishop had another accident that necessitated repairs even before the old car could be traded. He had trouble parking and backing and hit a number of cars in the parking lot of their apartment building; in December he ran a red light in the new car and collided with another vehicle. He now told the injured parties to fix the car and send him the bill without going through his insurance company. Sally was a better driver, but she was uneasy when driving and avoided doing it. Gradually their favorite trips to the Red Apple Inn or to the Arlington Hotel in Hot Springs were possible only when Donald or others could take them.

They continued to go together at least once a year to California to see Catherine and Nancy, and Sally, when she was able, would sometimes go alone. They made regular trips to Lubbock where John was now a member of the faculty at Texas Tech. Trips anywhere, however, were difficult. Martin had shoulder and back pain, which was finally diagnosed as phlebitis, and Sally continued to have heart and breathing irregularities. She was hospitalized in June 1979 and again in April 1980 because of it. Her internist, Dr. Morse, recommended a consultation with a psychiatrist about her continuing moods of depression but his suggestion was greeted with a firm no from both Sally and Will. Dr. Morse, a contemporary of Sally's grandson Bill, usually managed to offend her on any office visit by calling her by her first name, and she was not about to take his advice concerning anything so intimate as her emotional condition. Besides, the time for dealing with that had long since passed.

During the summer of 1980 they moved from the Quapaw Apartments to the Forest Place Apartments. The move was necessitated by a decision of the owners to convert the Quapaw into condominiums that would be sold. They did not wish to buy. Sally liked the Forest Place apartment much better. It had a patio with a view of a nearby wooded area, which both Martins enjoyed. About the time they moved Martin recorded "two aspirations" in his diary. The first was "to avoid being a burden to others," and the second was "to help as many persons as I can in as many ways as I can."

For some time he had been suffering from an enlarged prostate and his urologist recommended surgery to give him some relief. Martin entered St. Vincent's Hospital for the procedure, which was performed on Tuesday, September 16, 1980. He seemed to stand the operation well and his recovery was progressing normally when between 4:00 and 4:30 P.M. without warning he went into cardiac arrest. He was moved into the coronary care unit in critical condition and the family was warned that he might not live through the night. During the night he had stabilized somewhat, but was discovered to be bleeding internally. Although he was only slightly improved by Friday, he made rapid progress over the weekend and by the following Monday was able to sit up for meals and was moved to a private room. LPNs or sitters, however, stayed with him around the clock. He was not able to come home until October 1. Catherine came to help her mother.

Martin suffered from heart problems the rest of his life. By now he and Sally had to have help in order to continue to live on their own, and they were fortunate to have had the love and care of Betty McHatton during their final years. She was first assigned to them by the nurse's association and then went into their employment full time on June 17, 1981. She continued to work for them until September 29, 1992, when Sally died shortly after entering a nursing home. She prepared their meals, kept the apartment, ran errands, and helped them with their medication. After Bishop Martin's death, she was Sally's companion, taking her to lunch and on shopping trips. Mrs. McHatton remembered that after breakfast each morning "Bishop" would go into the corner of a room that he used for his "study" and begin his day reading scripture, singing a hymn, and praying. He kept a cheerful countenance, maintained the semblance of his old routine, and always watched the nightly news. He loved to talk about his work, but neither he nor Sally ever talked to McHatton about their families and Martin never mentioned his father. Daughter, Catherine, has said that he deliberately destroyed the letters from his father when he went through his papers after moving to Little Rock. There are none in the archives today and Donald had only one or two in his papers. One item that ironically does exist is a copy of the receipt for court costs Jack Martin paid after he was tried for murder. It also contains the names of persons who donated money to help him pay them. Sally did once tell McHatton that Will's father was "a hard man."

After W. C.'s death, Sally never liked to be alone and was usually depressed on cloudy or rainy days. Betty McHatton always tried to plan something special to cheer her up during those times. Her presence made life much easier for Donald and Ernestine because she was able to do many of the things for the Martins they had previously relied on Donald to do. Sally lived until 1992. John Lee was with her when she died after an illness of three weeks. Although she managed to take the death of her husband in stride, Donald's death from cancer in 1991 was devastating to her.

In 1983, the Council of Bishops met in Little Rock. In a recorded greeting that was played at their opening session, Martin welcomed them to the city and told them how much he and Sally wanted to attend but admitted their doctors would not allow them the privilege because of their "heart problems." His voice is strong and clear, betraying little of his real physical condition. He could not resist reminding them in the greeting that he had been elected a bishop in the Methodist Church, South, forty-five years before and had twenty-six years of active service. He was a month away from his ninetieth birthday. In closing his remarks, he admonished them that at no time in the past had the world needed to hear the gospel that the church had been created to proclaim more than in the present. It was his text for a lifetime of service.

William C. Martin, the last surviving bishop of the Methodist Episcopal Church, South, the last ever to be elected to that office by a General Conference, and the senior bishop of The United Methodist Church died peacefully on August 30, 1984, after a short illness. He was not feeling well when he woke up on Saturday morning and went back to bed. When McHatton went in to give him his morning medication at nine o'clock, she discovered he had suffered a heart attack. He died three days later. The afternoon he died he told Kathryn, who had come for a visit, to tell their children that he loved them very much. The pastor of First Church, Clint Burleson, had come to see him and was present when he died.

Sixteen bishops of The United Methodist Church attended his memorial service in the First United Methodist Church of Little Rock. Bishop Eugene Slater gave the eulogy. Bishop Roy Short, Martin's colleague in the council for thirty-six years, said in his brief remarks that he thought there was a verse of scripture for every person and the one that best fit Bishop Martin was Psalm 37:23. In the King James version which he quoted it reads, "The steps of a good man are ordered by the LORD: and he delighteth in his way."

Everybody who knew Martin knew how much he loved to walk. The representative of the Council of Bishops, Bishop James S. Thomas, one of the first two African American bishops to be assigned to a white area, captured the essence of Martin's good life in his well-chosen words. Bishop Thomas remembered that he had joined the council in 1964, the year Martin retired. When he, with some trepidation, entered the room to attend his first meeting, Martin came over to greet him, put an arm around his shoulders, and said, "Let's take a walk, Jim. It will be good for us both." As they walked twenty blocks or more on New York City streets, Thomas remembered that Martin gave him no advice on how to be a bishop, knowing he was too new in the role and inexperienced to appreciate it. They, as he had done for so many years in so many roles and with so many people, just "walked together."

Martin's Writings

I t should not be surprising that William C. Martin was almost as busy with his pen as with his speaking, administration, and preaching. When one sees the volume of material that flowed from him onto the printed page in a variety of places and on a large number of topics, it is interesting to be reminded that Martin found writing difficult when he first began in January 1923, to write a weekly "editorial" on some phase of the activity at Grace Church, Houston. But he continued to believe it was important, stuck with the task, and soon became both proficient and even prolific.

His first published writing appeared in his hometown newspaper in Blevins, Arkansas, where he reported in two letters of his experiences in the army in World War I. Following his graduation from seminary most of his writing was done to inform or edify the members of his congregations and appeared in the church bulletins. While at Port Arthur, he wrote to the newspaper on a variety of subjects that were of concern to him; in one (January 10, 1927) he urged the school board to prohibit dancing between the sexes in school buildings, and in another he opposed the election of Alfred E. Smith. He regularly summarized one of his Sunday sermons for inclusion in the Monday issue of the Port Arthur *Daily News*. Since his practice was to preach from brief notes, this required actually writing the sermon for the first time and usually took most of Monday morning. While in Port Arthur, September 1926, he also published an article in the Texas *Christian Advocate* on the "relation of the preacher to social righteousness."

As the scope of his responsibility increased along with his prominence, he began to be invited to write for Methodist publications. He contributed to the Texas *Christian Advocate* and wrote a piece for the *Christian Education Magazine. The Upper Room,* a small, popular quarterly booklet that he and Sally, like thousands of other Methodists, read for morning devotions, used his devotional on July 8, 1936. Over the years he published fifteen. By far the largest volume of his writing appeared in periodicals of the church, and their number increased dramatically after he was elected to the episcopacy in 1938. In each of the areas in which he served, there was a publication to which he contributed on a regular basis. These included "The Bishop's Column" in the *Southern California Messenger,* and the Central edition of the *Christian Advocate* contained "A Bishop's Letter" during his service in the Omaha Area. After moving to Texas he wrote for the Texas *Christian Advocate,* which became the *Texas Methodist* in 1960. Beginning in 1961 there was a special North Texas Annual Conference edition of the *Texas Methodist* in which he wrote a regular column titled "Our Bishop Speaks." He wrote extensively in the *Christian Advocate* beginning in 1940 when he joined the South Central Jurisdiction. The topics covered in these regular contributions reflect the concerns of the time in which they were written as well as Martin's own issues. His contributions to the *Southern California Messenger* clearly reflect concerns related to the unification of the Methodist Episcopal Church; the Methodist Episcopal Church, South; and the Methodist Protestant Church; and the organization of the Methodist Church it produced. But he also took time to discuss the importance of the Sunday evening service, and he urged his readers to oppose racetrack gambling. Throughout his ministry the familiar concerns of missions, evangelism, temperance, and stewardship found support in his columns. For more than thirty years, including many years he was in retirement, he contributed to the Arkansas *Methodist*. Its editor invited him to write a series of Sunday school lessons on the work of Christ, which appeared for thirteen weeks beginning in February, 1973.

Over the years he was to contribute comments and articles to *Church School Magazine; Classmate; The Methodist Layman*, for which he wrote the introductory article to its first issue in December 15, 1940; *Methodist Story; Tidings; Together Magazine* (published from 1957–1962); in addition to a number of state papers, like the Arkansas *Methodist*, which was published under the general heading of the *Christian Advocate*. While in the Dallas–Fort Worth Area, he wrote regularly for the publications of Texas Alcohol and Narcotic Education, which was generally known under its acronym TANE; and during his time as president of the National Council of Churches of Christ in America (1952–1954), his writing appeared in publications like the *National Council Outlook*.

Martin's first monograph was the small piece designed for circulation among army recruits in the induction centers of World War II under the title *When Temptation Comes*. Thousands of copies of the eighteen-page booklet were printed and circulated by the Y.M.C.A. and The Methodist Church. In 1948 Martin's name appears as editor of the volume edited from papers given at the National Methodist Rural Life Conference, held in Lincoln, Nebraska, in the summer of 1947. Although he chaired the conference and was actively engaged in its planning, he had little to do with the volume other than to write a two-page introduction. In 1949 he published his first book, *To Fulfill This Ministry* (Abingdon-Cokesbury). The manuscript was prepared for and delivered as the Willson Lectures at McMurry College in Abilene, Texas. Martin assigned the royalties from the book to the college to assist it in providing financial aid to students. The book was later chosen for inclusion on the list of readings required for all persons seeking ordination in The Methodist Church. It went through fourteen printings, sold more than 25,000 copies, and was translated into Korean. The year 1949 also marked the publication of the eight-volume *Our Faith* series published for The Methodist

Church by the Division of Education and Cultivation of the Board of Missions and Church Extension. The books all carry Martin's name and that of Bishop G. Bromley Oxnam as authors. Martin chaired the Advance for Christ and His Church, which commissioned the work for study in all Methodist congregations. Although Martin reports that each volume of *Our Faith in—God, the Bible, Christ, the Holy Spirit, Immortality, the Kingdom of God, Love,* and *Prayer*—was carefully reviewed by the entire Council of Bishops and approved by them, he does not make reference either to having written any of them or to discussions with Oxnam about them. He is the author of *Proclaiming the Good News,* which was published by Tidings in 1954, and of the piece on stewardship titled *Christ and Our Resources,* which was produced by the Methodist Publishing House.

Martin often wrote introductions for volumes written by others, usually for his friends. He wrote briefly for Paul Quillian's book of sermons, *Not a Sparrow Falls,* and did an introduction to a book of poetry, *I Thank Thee Lord,* written and privately published by Glenn Flinn and Dan Ferguson in 1953. A year later he wrote for Roy L. Smith's *Stewardship Studies,* and for Robert E. Goodrich's *What's It All About* in 1955. In the early sixties he wrote for seminary classmate J. O. Haymes' *History of the Northwest Texas Conference.* In 1960 he wrote and published the *Episcopal Address.*

When Martin's writings are assembled, the sheer number is impressive. They are but another witness to the busy life he led and to the fertile and creative mind of the man.